Governance and Politics of the Netherlands

COMPARATIVE GOVERNMENT AND POLITICS SERIES

Published

Maura Adshead and Jonathan Tonge
Politics in Ireland

Rudy Andeweg and Galen A. Irwin
Governance and Politics of the Netherlands (4th edition)

Tim Bale
European Politics: A Comparative Introduction (3rd edition)

Nigel Bowles and Robert McMahon
Government and Politics of the United States (3rd edition)

Paul Brooker
Non-Democratic Regimes (3rd edition)

Kris Deschouwer
The Politics of Belgium: Governing a Divided Society (2nd edition)

Robert Elgie
Political Leadership in Liberal Democracies

Rod Hague and Martin Harrop
*Comparative Government and Politics: An Introduction (9th edition)

Paul Heywood
The Government and Politics of Spain

Xiaoming Huang
Politics in Pacific Asia

B. Guy Peters
Comparative Politics: Theories and Methods
[Rights: World excluding North America]

Tony Saich
Governance and Politics of China (3rd edition)

Eric Shiraev
Russian Government and Politics (2nd edition)

Anne Stevens
Government and Politics of France (3rd edition)

Ramesh Thakur
The Government and Politics of India

Forthcoming

Tim Haughton
Government and Politics of Central and Eastern Europe

*Published in North America as **Political Science: A Comparative Introduction (7th edition)**

Comparative Government and Politics
Series Standing Order ISBN 978–0–333–71693–9 hardback
Series Standing Order ISBN 978–0–333–69335–3 paperback
(outside North America only)

You can receive future titles in this series as they are published by placing a standing order. Please contact your bookseller or, in the case of difficulty, write to us at the address below with your name and address, the title of the series and one of the ISBNs quoted above. Customer Services Department, Macmillan Distribution Ltd, Houndmills, Basingstoke, Hampshire, RG21 6XS, UK

Governance and Politics of the Netherlands

Fourth Edition

Rudy B. Andeweg
and
Galen A. Irwin

First edition 2002
Second edition 2005
Third edition 2009
Fourth edition 2014

Published by
PALGRAVE MACMILLAN

Palgrave Macmillan in the UK is an imprint of Macmillan Publishers Limited,
registered in England, company number 785998, of Houndmills,
Basingstoke, Hampshire RG21 6XS.

Palgrave Macmillan in the US is a division of St Martin's Press LLC,
175 Fifth Avenue, New York, NY 10010.

Palgrave Macmillan is the global academic imprint of the above companies
and has companies and representatives throughout the world.

Palgrave® and Macmillan® are registered trademarks in the United States,
the United Kingdom, Europe and other countries.

ISBN 978–1–137–28994–0 hardback
ISBN 978–1–137–28993–3 paperback

This book is printed on paper suifor recycling and made from fully managed
and sustained forest sources. Logging, pulping and manufacturing processes
are expected to conform to the environmental regulations of the country of
origin.

A catalogue record for this book is available from the British Library.

A catalog record for this book is available from the Library of Congress.

Typeset by Aardvark Editorial Limited, Metfield, Suffolk, England, UK.

*Without the work of numerous scholars
who have studied the Netherlands,
this book could never have been written.
We dedicate this book to them,
especially two whom we lost far too young:*

*Hanne Marthe Narud
and
Peter Mair*

Contents

List of Illustrative Material

Map

Boxes

Figures

Tables

Preface to the Fourth Edition

The first edition of this volume appeared shortly after the parliamentary election of 2002, which is still seen as a turning point in the politics of the Netherlands. Although the shocks of the first political murder in the country in 330 years and 'the long year of 2002' have now receded, the aftermath of these events is still felt in the country. Geert Wilders and the Freedom Party, as the ideological successors to Pim Fortuyn and his LPF, have placed immigration and European integration high on the political agenda. The Freedom Party's success in the election of 2010 led to a new coalition construction, in which the Freedom Party supported the Cabinet but did not provide ministers. When this experiment failed, however, a new election was necessary in 2012. After that election, the Cabinet formation process was altered, to eliminate the role of the monarch. The Cabinet formed after the 2012 election did not control the majority of seats in the First Chamber, which led to the greater importance of this chamber, as the Cabinet was forced to seek support from opposition parties.

The world financial and economic crisis of 2008 reached the Netherlands, and turned budget surpluses into deficits and raised unemployment. Internal economic problems, as well as the challenges to the euro, demanded the attention of the government. Controversies about sending Dutch troops to Afghanistan showed that foreign policy was no longer insulated from party politics. In 2013, for the first time in more than 122 years, the King, as the monarch is described in the Constitution, was actually a male, after a female Regent and three Queens. Discussion of these and other changes have necessitated the publication of a new edition of this book. As with previous editions, we shall provide updated information, when necessary, to cover major new developments, and in particular elections results and coverage of cabinet formation, on the book's website: http://www.palgrave.com/politics/andeweg.

Recent changes have not affected the reasons that the Netherlands has long been a welcome object of study by scholars of democratic politics, both Dutch and from other countries. The country was placed on the map, so to speak, of comparative politics by the work of Hans Daalder and Arend Lijphart. They studied Dutch politics in an attempt to understand how a country that was deeply divided socially could still achieve political stability. Yet 'consociational politics' has not been the only characteristic of Dutch politics to generate attention among political scientists. The country has one of the most proportional electoral systems in the world. Students of coalition theories have been puzzled by government coalitions that stubbornly defy the rules of theories. Those concerned with interest groups have been intrigued by the Dutch version of neo-corporatism. How the 'polder model' has contributed both to the 'Dutch disease' and the 'Dutch miracle', and whether this model could be exported, has attracted considerable scholarly interest. The Netherlands has also been both admired and criticized for its progressive positions on such social issues as drugs, prostitution, gay marriage, and euthanasia.

The study of such topics requires in-depth analysis by specialists on each subject, which of necessity leads to a degree of fragmentation. The aim of this volume is to draw on this literature to present a comprehensive overview that assumes no previous knowledge of the topic on the part of the reader. We hope thereby to make governance and politics of the Netherlands more accessible to both a Dutch and non-Dutch readership. We are pleased that the book is both used as an introductory textbook for students in the Netherlands and often cited as a source by the very authors on whom we have relied when compiling the volume.

Perhaps the fact that the volume is relied on by students and scholars both within and outside the Netherlands is related to the combination of authors. One (Andeweg) is Dutch by birth, but has studied and worked extensively in the United States and United Kingdom. The other (Irwin) was born and raised in the United States, but has lived and worked in the Netherlands for more than 40 years. Both have often been called upon to explain the basics and quirks of the Dutch system to foreign visitors, students, and observers. To a degree it has been their pertinent questions that have led to this book being written, as they encouraged the attempt to provide explanations of Dutch governance.

One cannot complete yet another edition of a book without being indebted to a number of people. An earlier volume preceded these four and was included in the Comparative Government and Politics Series, under the editorship of Vincent Wright. His untimely death prevented him from playing a role in the later volumes, but without his friendship and support, the original book, and thus the following editions, would never have existed.

Our indebtedness also extends to those many authors, both Dutch and non-Dutch, who have provided the scholarly work without which this book could not have been written. To acknowledge this debt, we have dedicated the book to them, and in particular to two who were also dear friends whom we lost far too soon. It is always risky to single out those who have been especially helpful in the production of this volume, as we will surely overlook someone deserving of such recognition. Ruud Koole, Hans Vollaard, Markus Haverland, and Joop Van Holsteyn have provided constructive criticism and insightful suggestions that have led to various revisions in the text. Annemarie Walter, Tom Louwerse, Philip Van Praag, Simon Otjes, Josje Den Ridder, Jean Tillie and Harmen Van Der Veer have supplied invaluable data and information, often prior to their own publication of the information, to allow this volume to be as up to date as possible. As always, we are indebted to our colleagues in the Department of Political Science at Leiden University, who have challenged and stimulated us through our discussions, often at the lunch table. And finally, we acknowledge our indebtedness to those students who have used the book and provided valuable feedback.

Producing a new edition requires a considerable amount of tedious work in searching for the most recent data and ensuring that everything is ready for publication. To assist us in this work, we have been fortunate to have the help of several dedicated student assistants. For the first two volumes, Alma Caubo demonstrated an uncanny ability to find the information we needed in libraries and archives and on websites. For the third edition, Rosalie Belder proved she was capable of continuing the work at the same high standard, and for this volume, Arthur Belle has followed in their footsteps, and Martijn van Nijnanten provided invaluable service in the preparation of the bibliography. We are most grateful to all of them for their assistance.

Finally, a driving force behind all editions has been our publisher, Steven Kennedy. For this edition, many of his tasks were taken over by Stephen Wenham. Together they again managed to convince us to take on the work of producing a new volume. Once again we did so reluctantly, but once again, now that it is finished, we are grateful for their insistence. We hope that they, and all those who have assisted us, are pleased with the result. Nevertheless, despite all their best efforts, mistakes, errors, and omissions will still be found; we absolve them of all responsibility and gladly accept any blame .

RUDY B. ANDEWEG
GALEN A. IRWIN

The authors and publishers would like to thank the following for providing permission for the use of copyright materal: University of California Press for Figure 2.3, from A. Lijphart (1975) *The Politics of Accommodation: Pluralism and Democracy in The Netherlands*, 2nd rev. edn.

1

The Country, the Nation and the State

A 'Small' Country

The Netherlands is a country with a surface area of some 42,000 square kilometres located on the North Sea around the Rhine–Meuse estuary. By some standards, the country is not particularly large, and the Netherlands is often referred to even by the self-deprecating Dutch as a 'small' country. Granted, the area is about twice the size of Wales or half of Scotland, and equal to the size of the states of Massachusetts, Connecticut and Rhode Island combined. Yet a definition of size that relies only on landmass is far too limited. Even though just over 4,000 square kilometres of this area is uninhabitable, as it is covered by the water of rivers, canals and lakes, the remaining space is used with great efficiency to provide homes for 16.8 million people. With an average of 493 people per square kilometre, it is one of the most densely populated countries in the world. In terms of inhabitants, it has 1.5 times the populations of Belgium or Portugal, more than twice the populations of Austria or Switzerland, and more than Norway, Denmark and Finland combined. In the past, the Dutch controlled a colonial empire smaller only than those of France or Britain, and today the gross national product (GNP) of the Netherlands is among the highest (17th or 18th) in the world. 'Small' is thus quite relative and in some respects it is one of the 'largest' countries of the world.

Whether one chooses to call the country 'large' or 'small', the amount of land would have been smaller without the efforts of its population. Virtually no discussion of the Netherlands is complete without reference to the well-known adage, 'God made the world but the Dutch made Holland.' By draining lakes and marshes to create new land, the Dutch may have had more impact on the shape of their country than other peoples, but whoever may be said to have made it, we have the problem of what to call it. The official name is The Kingdom of the Netherlands, but legally this also includes municipalities and independent countries in the Caribbean. In colloquial speech it is often called Holland, but this is actually the name of its once most famous province. The French call the country 'Les Pays-Bas', but this translates into 'the Low Countries' in English, and is then usually meant to apply also to Belgium.

1

In this book we shall refer to the polity as 'the Netherlands'. Its twelve modern provinces are shown in capitals in Map 1.1. Thus, while there are many themes that could be used to begin a discussion of the political system of the Netherlands, the interplay of geography and people may serve as well as any other. There is little doubt that, in their little corner of the world, the land contributed to shaping the people and the people have helped to shape the land. Understanding this relationship will help the reader to understand the society and politics of the country.

Map 1.1   *The Netherlands: Provinces and Major Cities*

The Struggle Against the Water

Of course, the land area of the world began to take shape before people could have much influence on it. In many areas of the world this shape has changed little since the prehistoric days that determined its form. In others, the interplay of factors such as earthquakes, volcanic eruptions and/or water have altered the land even during the period of recorded history. The area of land identified as the Netherlands falls into the latter group.

During the Ice Age, British and Scandinavian glaciers grew together, blocking the North Sea. The courses of the Rhine and Meuse rivers were altered, though as the ice melted they partially returned to their old courses. The glaciers also brought the sand that began to form what have become the higher, southern provinces of the country. As the climate warmed and the ice melted, peat bogs began to form, first in the western part of the country, and later towards the east. In places, the sea flooded areas that had once been above water (Van Valkenburg, 1943; Keuning, 1965).

When the sea broke through the connection between England and France, the force of the water in the channel brought sand from the south and created the walls of sand dunes that are still characteristic of the Dutch coastline. Behind the dunes was a large lagoon that gradually began to fill with sand and soil brought by the rivers from higher ground. Peat bogs, swamps and lakes characterized the land behind the dunes.

The earliest inhabitants of the lowlands were tribes who came to the area to hunt reindeer. Gradually, the hunters and fishermen were joined by farmers and cattle herders. Sometime after 100 BC, four waves of immigration took place: three Germanic from the north and one Celtic from the south-east. The Greeks had vague ideas of the existence of the lands of the Celts, but it was Julius Caesar's Roman expeditions that brought the first direct contact between the inhabitants of the great civilizations and those of the lowlands. With the Romans also came the first recorded history of the area in the works of Tacitus and Pliny. It was the former who wrote of the legendary Batavians. Caesar and his successors pushed northward to the banks of the Rhine, but to the Romans the area had little meaning other than the furthest extension of the Empire to the north.

The Rhine and Meuse rivers provided natural barriers to the Romans, and while the armies of Augustus crossed the rivers and included the Frisians in his Empire, the Romans later pulled back and never really made subjects of the inhabitants to the north. As Vlekke has written, 'the Romans set little store by the marshlands of the west and the north of the Low Countries which held no allure for them' (Vlekke, 1943).

Assaults by German tribes and by the sea finally drove the Romans from the area. The Franks gradually gained in power and pushed the Frisians back to the north, so that the Frankish kingdom of Charlemagne and his successors included much of the Low Countries. Frankish power brought with it the introduction of Christianity to the region. Frankish domination, however, did not greatly affect the social institutions of the people. The marshy areas of the north and west did not support the kind of large land ownership that was necessary to support feudalism, so this social system was never fully established in these areas. No nobility developed in what later became the provinces of Holland, Zeeland and Utrecht; instead, the Low Countries remained a territory of small landowners and free peasants. In remote areas of the north, free peasants were able to continue as democratic peasant republics for centuries. The area was less conducive to the development of a manorial system than to the development of cities, which sprang up at virtually every juncture of waters and at every harbour.

Three times in history, the sea broke through the natural protective dunes to alter the landscape. About 300 BC the sea broke through via the estuaries of the Scheldt, Meuse and Rhine to inundate areas in the south-west of the country. The second principal incursion of the sea occurred about AD 270, and was a key factor in driving the Romans from the area. The third period of incursion began in the tenth or eleventh century and resulted in the flooding of large areas – creating, for example, the islands in the current provinces of South Holland and Zeeland. In the north, areas of dunes were washed away; now only small islands formed by the remnants of these dunes indicate where the coast once was. Behind these islands, new seas (or bays) were created, the largest of which was the Zuiderzee, which over a few centuries expanded to cover a substantial area of the north of Holland.

This last incursion led the increased populations of the area to take protective measures that were to alter the landscape. In about the eleventh century, the first dikes were built to protect inhabited areas from flooding (Vlekke, 1943; Keuning, 1965). The threat of water came from three sources. In addition to the threat from the sea, there was the threat of periodic flooding from the great rivers. Moreover, the surplus of yearly rainfall had to be disposed of lest large areas revert, at least seasonally, to swamps. Thus the systems of dikes were extended to cover increasingly large areas, and methods, including the use of windmills, were devised to drain off surplus water. By combining the use of dikes and drainage systems, areas of land could be reclaimed from the sea and from lakes.

From the very beginning, the battle against water was not something that could be left to an overlord (or a little boy putting his finger in the breached dike), but required the combined efforts of the population. Since everyone behind the dike profited, maintenance could not justifiably be left only to those whose land bordered the water. Water control boards were organized with the responsibility of maintaining the system. It is often claimed that, dating back at least to the thirteenth century, these were the first democratic organizations in the country and one of the oldest forms of democracy in Northern Europe.

Nature has thus left those who inhabit the area with what may justly be described as the 'nether lands' or 'low lands'. No point is higher than about 30 metres above sea level. In the northern and western parts of the country, most of the area ranges between 0 and 2.5 metres below sea level. In some larger areas that have been drained the level is even lower; the region in which Amsterdam's Schiphol airport is located lies 4.2 metres below sea level, and new areas have been created that once lay under as much as 6.9 metres of the waters of the Zuiderzee (Keuning, 1965).

Today, though windmills no longer play a role in the system, dikes and drainage systems must nevertheless be maintained. More than half of the country must be protected artificially against water incursion, and more than half of the population live in areas that would be under water, at least at high tide, if protection were not maintained. In 1994 and 1995, some towns and polders behind river dikes became flooded, and the government hastily began a campaign to reinforce and heighten the dikes. There are dormant plans to drain another portion of the former Zuid-erzee, and proposals have been made to relocate Schiphol airport to an island to be built off the North Sea coast. It is the long history of the struggle against the water through the building of dikes and land reclamation through drainage that gives rise to the saying that 'the Dutch built Holland'.

Three Boundaries

Both the people and nature have interacted to shape the land. However, the mere shape of the land is not the only factor of importance in understanding the relation between geography, social structure and politics. There are no mountains or natural boundaries separating the Dutch from their neighbours, and even modern satellite photographs will not reveal the important boundaries that separate peoples and have such an important impact on them. In the area of the Rhine river delta, three bound-aries – linguistic, religious and political – divide the peoples of the lowlands. The fact that these three boundaries do not coincide influences the politics of both the Netherlands and its southern neighbour Belgium even today.

The Boundaries of Language and Religion

In his discussion of 'The Borders of the Netherlands', De Vrankrijker (1946) distin-guishes 'structural borders', which he defines as natural borders or those resulting from geographical position, and 'historical borders', which simply through their long existence gain permanence and acceptance. The Rhine and Meuse rivers pro-vided structural borders for the Romans, and though they never really subjugated the inhabitants to the north, they did leave a lasting imprint by building a highway from Cologne through Aachen and Tongeren to Bavai in northern France and on to the sea coast.

The building of this highway, and the Roman colonization along its route, was one of the most important events in the history of the Netherlands. It determined the furthest extent of Germanic influence in the north-western corner of the European continent and fixed for many centuries to come the dividing line between Romanic and Germanic peoples in this area (De Vrankrijker, 1946).

The Roman highway and the structural border of the rivers thus introduced two rough, but discernible, dividing lines between north and south. To the north, Germanic influences prevailed; and to the south, the Romans imposed their authority and customs. The highway became the boundary between Germanic and Romanic languages; to the north, Dutch is spoken, and to the south, French. The rivers were to become the border between Rome and the Reformation, between Catholicism and Protestantism. As neither the linguistic nor the religious border eventually coincided with the political boundary between two countries, both would later play a role of political significance. As the influence of the language demarcation is felt in the area of the Low Countries now known as Belgium, it will not be discussed further in this book. However, no discussion of Dutch politics is complete without a mention of religion.

The Political Boundary

At the end of the Middle Ages, the Low Countries were not excluded from the attempts to carve out larger entities that were to become the nation-states of Europe. The politics of this period is quite complicated, involving war, marriage and intrigue. As one scholar stated, 'It is obvious that the federation of the Netherlands provinces was primarily due to accidental circumstances' (Vlekke, 1943, p. 74). The beneficiaries of these accidents were the dukes of Burgundy, who were able to carve out a temporary buffer state between France and Germany. Yet, just as fate had brought Burgundy into existence, it also brought its demise when the lands passed into the Hapsburg dynasty through the marriage of Duchess Mary to Maximilian of Austria, son of the Holy Roman Emperor.

Charles V, as a descendant of the Hapsburgs, combined the rule of the Low Countries with the thrones of Spain, Naples and America, the princedom of Austria, and election as Holy Roman Emperor. He was the last of the 'natural' princes of the Low Countries, having been born in Ghent, speaking French as his mother tongue, but being well acquainted with Dutch (Vlekke, 1943). On his abdication in 1555, he passed the Low Countries and Spain to his son, Philip II. In this accidental union, Philip was far more interested in Spain, though this might never have resulted in serious problems had not other events intervened (Schöffer, 1973). Philip never gained the loyalty his father had received, and the local authorities became more inclined to establish their independence. Revolt ensued when this flexing of local political muscle was combined with the forces of the Reformation.

Though the people of the Low Countries were known for their piety and devotion, they were aware of the excesses and faults of the Church, which were exposed and discussed by Erasmus and his followers. Even before Philip ascended the throne, religious reformers, largely inspired by Huldrych Zwingli, had become popular. In 1552, Charles V crushed an Anabaptist revolt by expanding the powers of the Inquisition, but the suppression of the Anabaptists was only a short-term success. Under these new powers, heretics could be prosecuted without regard for the traditional processes of law. Thus religion and politics became enmeshed as the struggle for religious freedom was intertwined with the fight to protect traditional political freedoms. Remnants of such groups came into contact with John Calvin, and Calvinism quickly became the dominant force in the Protestantism of the Low Countries.

With the abdication of Charles V, the stage was set for the conflict between Lowlands Calvinism and Spanish Catholicism. There was considerable discontent at all levels within the Low Countries, but it was the Calvinists who provided the backbone of the revolt against Philip, opposing the new king on political as well as religious grounds. The Calvinists had the organization and the discipline necessary to lead the revolt. In 1566, the churches in western Flanders were stormed; sculptures were destroyed and all that was sacred to the Catholics was desecrated. The movement quickly spread northwards to Amsterdam, Leeuwarden and Groningen. Just as quickly, however, this first revolt was suppressed, but further from Brussels the influence of Calvinism continued. Despite this initial stabilization of the situation, Philip chose not to attempt further pacification, but instead sent the Duke of Alva to centralize control. Never before had a Spaniard been appointed as governor of the Low Countries, and the zeal with which Alva attempted to carry out his orders made him and the king even more hated. Rather than pacify, Alva, through his ruthless enforcement of centralization and heavier taxation, helped to unite the national opposition.

This opposition was led by William of Orange, a German count of Nassau by birth, who had inherited rich lands in the Low Countries as well as the principality of Orange in southern France. He was educated at the court of Brussels and was a favourite of Charles V. A decent man, rather more intellectual than most of his rank, he sympathized with those who protested against the injustices of Spanish rule. Though he felt the initial Calvinist revolt had been inopportune, he became caught up in the events. After the suppression of the revolt by Alva, only he had the will and resources to continue. His attempt, with the help of French Huguenots and German Protestant princes, to invade the Low Countries in 1568 failed dismally. Though his own resources were eventually depleted, he continued to provide inspirational leadership.

When on 1 April 1572 the 'Sea Beggars' captured the town of Brill, the revolution spread rapidly. On 19 July, representatives of the towns of Holland met in Dordrecht, where William of Orange was proclaimed 'Stadtholder' (literal meaning *locum tenens,* or substitute for the king; in practice, the governor and commander-in-chief) of Holland and Zeeland. However, without personal resources he was dependent on the States-General (which is still the official name of the Dutch Parliament). In January 1579, the rebel northern provinces met at Utrecht to form 'a closer union' in which they were to retain their sovereignty, but would act as a single body in foreign policy.

Alva regrouped quickly in the south and, when the threat from France failed to materialize, headed north. Yet, even after his replacement, the Spanish were never able to crush the revolt, and hostilities dragged on for 80 years. After William was assassinated in 1584, his son Maurice succeeded him and successfully reorganized the army to reconquer Groningen and the towns in Overijssel and Gelderland. He also moved south and occupied some Flemish towns, thus securing a buffer zone to protect Zeeland.

With the domination of Spanish forces in the south, the Counter-Reformation was able to re-establish Catholicism, so that when Maurice recaptured parts of the area the inhabitants were firmly Catholic. The peace treaty of Westphalia in 1648 established a political border to the south of the religious border: to the south, the Hapsburg reign continued, with the new and independent Republic of Seven United Provinces to the north. This situation was to continue throughout the remainder of the seventeenth and eighteenth centuries, until Napoleon conquered and eventually annexed the country. This 'French period', as the Napoleonic occupation is commonly referred to in the Netherlands, left an important imprint on the political institutions of the country, as we shall see later in this chapter.

On the defeat of Napoleon, the Congress of Vienna was convened to redraw the map of Europe. In an effort to create a buffer state between the major powers, the southern provinces were once again united with the north and the Netherlands was raised to the status of a kingdom, with William I as monarch and Grand Duke of Luxembourg. Perhaps, with patience and understanding, William might have succeeded in undoing the effects of 250 years of separate development, but this was not his manner and in his haste to establish a modern, centralized state he quickly alienated many of his new subjects in the south. Catholics feared his Protestantism and his support of state over church schools. They also opposed him in his attempts to centralize authority at the expense of local interests. Liberals, on the other hand, supported him in his centralizing and anti-clerical tendencies, but opposed his restrictions on the freedom of the press and his promotion of Dutch interests. The king favoured Dutch people over Belgians in his appointments and had decreed that Dutch was to be the official language in the Flemish areas. After 20 years of 'Frenchification' during the Napoleonic occupation, the Flemish elite resented the imposition of Dutch as the official language. Despite their own differences, Catholics and Liberals joined in a 'union of oppositions' to rid the Belgians once again of 'foreign' oppression. On 23 November 1830, the National Congress declared an independent Belgium and excluded the House of Orange from the possibility of ever ascending to the throne of their country.

Thus, after only 15 years of unification, the Netherlands and Belgium were again separate. Hostilities continued for several years, but in 1839 King William accepted the terms of separation. Through the 'forces' of history, three boundaries had thus been drawn through the territory at the mouth of the Rhine. Yet none of these – political, religious or linguistic – coincided. The political boundary that defined the two nation states left each with a boundary dividing it internally, and producing the basis for an important source of political cleavage. To the south, Belgium was relatively homogeneous religiously, but divided into French- and Dutch-speaking areas. To the north, the Netherlands was linguistically homogeneous (with the exception of the northern province of Friesland, where Frisian is also spoken), but divided into predominantly Protestant and predominantly Catholic areas.

Apart from a temporary change of the Dutch–German border after the Second World War, the political boundaries of the Dutch state within Europe have not changed since 1839. Change has taken place, however, in Dutch territories outside

Europe as a result of decolonization, especially after the Second World War. The Japanese occupation of the Dutch East Indies reinforced the independence movement there, and immediately after the war this movement declared independence unilaterally and took up arms against the Dutch. The Netherlands was not prepared to give up the colony, and when negotiations failed it waged two large-scale military campaigns (euphemistically called 'police actions'), in 1947 and 1948. Militarily, these campaigns were successful in terms of regained control over the islands and the capture of the leaders of the independence movement. Politically, however, they proved disastrous: the Netherlands became one of the first countries to be condemned by the UN Security Council, and US pressure on the Dutch government finally forced the acceptance of Indonesian independence in 1949. In the early 1960s history repeated itself when Indonesian forces infiltrated Dutch New Guinea (Irian Jaya). The Dutch defended their colony militarily, but the USA forced the Dutch to give up their last colony in Asia. By the 1970s the Dutch had learned their lesson, and they almost forced independence on their South American colony, Surinam, in 1975, and in 2010 the Dutch Antilles was disbanded. According to the new Charter, the islands of Aruba, Curaçao and Sint Maarten became components of the Kingdom of the Netherlands, whereas the even smaller islands of Bonaire, Sint Eustatius and Saba became special municipalities of the Netherlands. Box 1.1 summarizes important events of Dutch history.

National Identity and Political Culture

Calvinism and Tolerance

There are those who argue that there is no such thing as a unique 'Dutch identity' (see Box 1.2 and Van Rossem, 2012). On the other hand, there are entire books devoted to the topic (for example, Lechner, 2008). Space is too limited here to attempt to resolve the differences or settle the issue; nevertheless, it does seem useful to mention briefly a few topics and characteristics that recur frequently when discussing the Dutch. This goes beyond the usual wooden shoes, tulips, windmills, and cheese, which are so often the images that come to mind when referring to the Netherlands. They are the sorts of things that a people share – a common past, shared experiences and collective memory that produce bonds between individuals and define them as being 'Dutch'.

The important dates in the history of the Netherlands listed in Box 1.1 include some of the events that have just been discussed in discussing the "boundaries" of the country. Some of these events, as well as individuals associated with them also have been influential in shaping the national identity and political culture of the country (if in fact these actually do exist.) In a later section of this chapter, it will be noted that many of the developments in the evolution of the Dutch Constitution have come about because of foreign influences. It is therefore also rather interesting to note that two individuals who can be associated with the founding of the modern Netherlands were themselves not 'Dutch' at all: John Calvin and William the Silent.

BOX 1.1

Important Dates in Dutch History

1st century BC to 4th century AD	Romans occupy the southern portion of the Low Countries.
7th century	Conversion to Christianity carried out largely in this period.
12th and 13th centuries	Expansion of towns and granting of many city charters.
13th and 14th centuries	Foundation of the higher water control boards (*'hoogheemraadschappen'*) to coordinate the control of water.
1384–1579	Burgundian and Hapsburg rule.
1566	Revolt breaks out against Philip II of Spain.
	William (the Silent) of Orange eventually becomes leader of the revolt.
1579	Union of Utrecht; northern provinces first agree to cooperate.
1648	Peace of Westphalia ends the Eighty Years' War; Spain acknowledges the independence of the Netherlands.
17th century	The 'Golden Age'.
1795–1813	Period of French Rule; from 1795 until 1806 as the Batavian Republic.
1815	Kingdom of the Netherlands founded at the Congress of Vienna.
1830–39	Belgians revolt; Belgium leaves the Kingdom.
1848	Introduction of ministerial responsibility.
1914–18	The Netherlands remains neutral during the First World War; Kaiser Wilhelm seeks refuge following the war.
1917	'Great Pacification', resulting in universal male suffrage, proportional representation, and state financing of church schools.
1940–45	German forces occupy the Netherlands.
1949	Former Indonesian colonies gain independence; The Netherlands becomes a founding member of NATO.
1952–58	The Netherlands becomes a founding member of the European Economic Community.
2002	Assassination of populist politician Pim Fortuyn; The Netherlands exchanges the guilder for the euro.
2013	Willem-Alexander is inaugurated as King (the first male to accede to the throne since 1890).

John Calvin was born in 1509 in the Picardy region of France, but he fled France for Switzerland in 1535 where he became important in the reform of Geneva. He never visited the Netherlands, and his theology arrived there after that of Menno Simons (founder of the Mennonite church) and the Anabaptists, but he eventually became more important than Simons. One reason Calvinist theology won out was that, in contrast to Catholicism and Lutheranism, Calvin argued that it was justifiable to revolt against an ungodly government. Thus it gave justification to the resentment against the Spanish king, described above. The Calvinists provided the backbone for the revolution that was to establish the independence of the Netherlands.

Other teachings of Calvin have been crucial in the development of characteristics that are considered to be descriptive of the Dutch. Terms frequently mentioned in this regard are hard work, frugality, sobriety, reserve, conscientiousness, thrift, tenacity of opinion and so on. In 2009, at the celebration of the 500th anniversary of the birth of Calvin, observers noted that Calvinism was no longer tied exclusively to religious beliefs (it is often said that even Dutch Catholics are Calvinists!), and then Prime Minister Jan Peter Balkenende proudly stated, 'Many say we are the most Calvinist nation in the world' (Expatica, 2009).

The 'Father of the Fatherland', William the Silent, was also not Dutch, at least not by birth. Even the national anthem, which is named for him – the Wilhelmus, proudly begins: 'William of Nassau, I am of German [*Duitse*] blood'. The term 'Duits' could also refer to the Dutch at the time, but William was actually born in Germany. The anthem, however, continues 'true to the Fatherland [i.e. the Netherlands] I remain until my death'. His role in the revolt against Spain has also been discussed above. In 1544 he inherited the title Prince of Orange, a principality of that name in the south of France. This became the founding of the House of Orange, which is still referred to today (see Box 1.3) The name of the principality is also the name of a colour, so that colour has become associated with the Netherlands. It was part of the flag adopted for the Union of Utrecht in 1579 and features prominently in Dutch sports teams and national celebrations today.

The Union of Utrecht can be taken as the founding of the modern Netherlands, and two years later the fledgling country became *de facto* independent. Sovereignty was offered to the king of France and the queen of England, but both refused, and the country became the first modern Republic. The country was a union of sovereign provinces and, according to the treaty, decisions were to be taken unanimously. This proved not always to be the case, but the consultations attempting to reach decisions acceptable to all are said to be the foundation of what centuries later would be known as Consensus or Consociational Democracy (see Chapter 2).

Through what Israel has described as developments that occur 'only rarely in history and only when internal changes combine with exceptionally favourable circumstances without', the fledgling new country grew into a world power within a century. In the 1590s, the economic circumstances of the Republic improved; commerce and shipping expanded, and it became possible to increase the size of the army (Israel, 1995, p. 241). Few countries have a period in history that is so important that it is known as the Golden Age, but this is how the world and the Dutch refer to the period roughly encompassing the 17th century.

The new federal structure of the Republic made it possible to devise a new type of economic venture: a chartered, joint-stock monopoly, the United East India Company (VOC), which might be called the world's first multinational corporation (see Chapter 9). Its success led to the Netherlands becoming, alongside Spain, France, and England, one of the great colonial powers of the world. Amsterdam was a (perhaps *the*) financial centre of Europe, and the Republic was a world leader in science (Christiaan and Constantijn Huygens, Anton van Leeuwenhoek), the law (Grotius) and the arts. According to Lechner, 'Rembrandt is still a key figure in how the Dutch think about themselves… [He] may well be the quintessential Dutchman' (2008, p. 46).

However, and perhaps more important in the long run, the Golden Age established traditions of openness and tolerance in the Netherlands. In 1661, the Leiden manufacturer and political scientist Pieter de la Court wrote 'that our manufactures, fisheries, commerce and navigation, with those who live from them, cannot be preserved here without a continual immigration of foreign inhabitants – much less increased or improved' (quoted in Israel, 1995, p. 624). With the necessity for immigration, the regents who, in the absence of a monarchy and a landed aristocracy, governed the country, could not make extensive demands on the beliefs of the new arrivals. The Dutch Reformed Church was perhaps *de facto*, but never *de jure*, a state church, and other religious groups were tolerated. Though adherents of other faiths did not receive full benefits of citizenship, they were allowed to practise their religion, at least if it was not done so too openly (see Chapter 3). Thus, one can still find their 'hidden churches' in Amsterdam and The Hague. Jews were accepted at a level that was unique in Europe. Other religious groups also arrived, including the Puritans, who came to Leiden in 1609. Some of this group sailed to America on the *Mayflower* in 1620 to found the Massachusetts Bay Colony. The Puritans were not the only ones who took advantage of the relative freedom of the press in the Netherlands. Galileo published his *Discourse on Two New Sciences* there in 1638, and philosophers, such as Spinoza and Descartes, profited from the climate of tolerance of thought.

In more recent times, though the Netherlands was ranked fourth (behind Denmark, Finland, and Norway) in the 2012 United Nations World Happiness Report, this was a remarkable recovery after the traumatic events of the twentieth century. The middle of that century was marked by the Great Depression, the Second World War, and the loss of an empire, all of which had an impact on the country. The impact of the Second World War on the Netherlands cannot be underestimated. The end of the German occupation in 1945 is often seen as a 'rebirth' of the country. It is interesting to note that there are no annual celebrations of either the Union of Utrecht or the Kingdom of the Netherlands, but each year on May 4 there is an evening of remembrance for the fallen in the Second World War (and subsequent conflicts), and a day of celebration on May 5 to commemorate the country's liberation in 1945.

Daalder (1985) has argued that the war produced greater support for parliamentary democracy. Experiences with the occupation led to the rejection of authoritarian solutions that had been proposed in the 1930s (and even during the war) as a reaction to the economic difficulties of the Great Depression. It brought a greater appreciation of domestic institutions and led to the acceptance of a larger role for the state. The latter was important in producing the conditions for the establishment of the welfare state. And it produced a greater acceptance of the various groups within Dutch society, especially Catholics and socialists (see Chapter 2).

The war, and the subsequent decolonization, led to a reassessment of the place of the Netherlands in the new international order: 'Within a decade after the fiasco in New Guinea, the Dutch had shed their reputation as a short-sighted colonial power and exchanged it for the role of one of the most progressive countries in the West: The Netherlands would be a "guiding light" [*gidsland*] for the world' (Kennedy, 1995, p. 53; *our own translation*). After the traumatic experience with the Nazi invasion, the country abandoned its long-established neutrality and became a member of NATO and a supporter of European integration (see Chapter 10).

In the 1960s, the Netherlands underwent an amazing transformation, from, in the eyes of many, a boring society of petty bourgeoisie, with a strong influence of religion, to one of the most secular, progressive – even permissive – countries in the world. The country became known for its policies towards drugs, prostitution, abortion, and euthanasia. Kennedy argues that one reason that these changes were tolerated, and even stimulated, by the elite, was the desire to reshape the society that had emerged from the war (Kennedy, 1995). He concludes that 'in both the seventeenth century and in the sixties of the twentieth century, Dutch political leaders drew the same conclusion: in a pluralistic and rapidly changing society, keeping the reins loose was the best option. Good government meant above all that one should ensure that things did not get out of hand – in the Netherlands – and a strong realization of the limits of one's own ability to keep a tight reign on societal affairs (Kennedy, 1995, p. 209; *our own translation*).

While the permissiveness of the 1960s and 1970s has given way to a less open culture in recent years, especially with regard to immigrant minorities (see Chapter 2), it is interesting to note that more liberal attitudes with regard to homosexuality and the role of women have become part of the Dutch identity that is deemed worthy to defend against foreign influences, and they even found their way into the government's official 'civic integration' test for newcomers (see Box 1.2).

BOX 1.2

What Makes One Dutch?

In September 2007, the then Princess (now Queen) Maxima made a speech at the presentation of a report entitled *Identification with the Netherlands* that had been prepared by the Scientific Council for Government Policy. The Queen, who was born in Argentina and married King Willem-Alexander in 2002, described her seven-year journey to become Dutch, and her search for the Dutch identity. There is no 'Dutch' identity and no such thing as 'the' Dutchman, or 'the' Argentinian, she stated: 'The Netherlands is just one cookie with your coffee, but it is also enormous hospitality. It is large windows and throwing the curtains wide open, but it is also privacy and *gezelligheid*' [a Dutch term that cannot be properly translated, but implies cosiness, warmth, and friendliness].

The report had also reached the conclusion that a clear and unequivocal Dutch identity does not exist, but it was the speech by the princess that was the focus of criticism. From the right, Geert Wilders of the Freedom Party called it 'well-intentioned, politically correct silliness'. Rita Verdonk, former Minister of Immigration and Integration, charged that Maxima did not understand how the Dutch people felt: 'She sees herself first as a citizen of the world, then European and only then as Dutch; most Dutch see it the other way around.' Other parties granted the princess the right to her own personal observations, but were critical of the report. A Christian Democrat spokesperson stated: 'The national identity does exist. The monarchy itself is a good example. Of course, there is pluriformity, but we have a collective history and national symbols that bind the Dutch people.'

Perhaps some insight to the question of what binds the Dutch people can be gained from the 'Civic Integration' examination that certain categories of aliens must take before receiving permission to settle in the country. In addition to knowledge of the Dutch language, the examination tests knowledge of Dutch society. For that purpose, the exam contains 30 questions out of a list of 100 that are made public. Presumably, these questions provide some insight into the Dutch identity, or at least into what the Dutch government considers essential for potential immigrants to know about Dutch society in order to blend in.

In attempting to define national identity, the report *Identification with the Netherlands* distinguished various dimensions of the concept, at least four of which – a territorial, a cultural, a historical, and a political dimension – can be found in the examination questions.

The *territorial* dimension is tested by questions such as:

- Is the Netherlands larger than Turkey and Morocco?
- What does the name 'Netherlands' imply?
- What is a dike, and what would happen if the dikes were not there?
- Does small imply that only few people live in the Netherlands?

The *cultural* dimension of identity is represented by a variety of questions:

- What is typical of Dutch traffic? (Answer: bicycles)
- If someone goes for a visit, do they generally make an appointment or do they just drop in?
- At school, are there separate classes for boys and girls, or are they together in the class?

→

→

- When one meets, does one first offer one's hand or immediately sit down?
- May women in the Netherlands themselves choose whom they will marry?
- Who works in the Netherlands, just men, or both men and women?
- Is it important to learn Dutch as soon as possible?
- Why is it good to watch Dutch television with your children?

Judging by the questions, the *historical* dimension is summed up by the Revolution, the Golden Age, the Second World War and the colonial past.

- Who is in this picture? (Answer: William the Silent/William of Orange)
- How long did the war with Spain last?
- Were the ships of the United East India Company for fishing or trade?
- Who painted this painting? (Answer: Rembrandt)
- Which country occupied the Netherlands during the Second World War?
- Why is Anne Frank famous?
- Which former colony became independent soon after the Second World War?

Clearly, the monarchy is deemed to be an important part of the national identity (note that these questions are now outdated):

- Where does the Queen live?
- Who is in this picture? (Answer: Prince Willem-Alexander and Princess Maxima)
- What country does Princess Maxima come from?

The following questions test the *political* dimension of Dutch national identity:

- What is the most important law in the Netherlands?
- Who is the chair of the Council of Ministers: the Prime Minster or the Queen?
- How often are elections held – every four years or every six years?
- Is there separation of church and state in the Netherlands?
- Does the Netherlands have a state religion or are there many religions?
- Is discrimination tolerated or punishable by law?
- Do women have more rights than men, or the same rights?
- Are newspapers, radio and television free in their opinions?
- Is homosexuality allowed or punishable?
- Is female circumcision allowed or punishable?
- Is it allowed to hit women or is this punishable?

In the 2012 Dutch Parliamentary Election Study, respondents were asked several questions relating to national identity. Very small percentages indicated that that they did not feel an attachment to the Netherlands (2%) or that they were not proud to be Dutch (5%). Only 15 per cent felt themselves to be more European or cosmopolitan than Dutch. No less than 82 per cent agreed or fully agreed that Dutch customs and traditions should be preserved (only 3 per cent disagreed). And virtually all respondents felt (57 per cent agreed fully and 37 per cent agreed) that it would be a shame if the Dutch language were to disappear. However, respondents were tolerant about learning the national anthem; only 52 per cent felt that each Dutch person should know it. Finally, they showed an element of tolerance towards immigrants, with only 23 per cent agreeing that only those who were born in the Netherlands could be a real Dutch person.

A Nation of Joiners

In Box 1.2, there is some additional information in an attempt to define a 'national identity' for the Netherlands. One aspect that seems often to be overlooked in discussions such as those mentioned above, or in defining just what a 'Dutch' citizen is, relates to the civil society of the Netherlands. A study of the membership of voluntary associations in the early 1990s listed the Netherlands as one of the 'Nations of Joiners' (Curtis et al., 2001). In fact, this study of levels of voluntary association membership across 33 democratic countries, which included 16 types of voluntary organizations, found that Dutch citizens had the highest average number of memberships. Even when trade unions and religious organizations were excluded, the Dutch still had the highest average number of memberships. When only those organizations in which an individual was actively engaged in unpaid work for the organization were included, the Netherlands still ranked fourth behind Canada, the United States, and the former East Germany (ibid.). A more recent study from 2008/09 revealed that this pattern has continued. In comparison with 15 other European countries, the Netherlands forms a cluster with Norway and Denmark as being high on both frequency of social contacts and organization memberships. The Netherlands is exceptionally high on voluntary activities (Van Houwelingen et al., 2011).

Before approximately 1967, Dutch civil society consisted of three to five highly organized subcultures (see Chapter 2). The role of citizen activity in this period was ambiguous, even contradictory. On the one hand, citizens were mobilized to be active within their subculture's organizations such as churches, trade unions, political parties and so on, but on the other, the role of the citizen was generally a passive one (Daalder, 1974). The members of the subcultural organizations put their trust in their leaders, who then negotiated the necessary compromises between the subcultures. The role of the citizen was basically to provide support for the leadership without making too many demands.

Much has changed since the late 1960s, however. Subcultural organizations have weakened in general, but the impact has been most noticeable in the religious subcultures. From being one of the more religious societies in Europe, by the year 2000 the Netherlands had become the society within Europe with the lowest percentage of religious adherents (although not the lowest in church attendance) (SCP, 2000, p. 133). Regular (almost every week) church attendance dropped from 50 per cent in 1966 to 16 per cent in 2006 (De Hart, 2013). This secularization of society has had far-reaching effects on the politics of the country, as will be seen throughout this book.

At the same time, a 'silent revolution' helped to change the Netherlands in the direction of a 'post-materialist' society (Inglehart, 1977; Inglehart and Welzel, 2005). These changes have brought a shift from 'materialist' to 'post-materialist' associations. Thus, while membership of trade unions had dropped substantially and was below the average for Europe (SCP, 2000, p. 132), the Dutch had become supporters of other organizations. They had the highest percentage of citizens giving support to Greenpeace in Europe; they are second only to Switzerland in support for World Wildlife Fund, and second only to Iceland in membership of Amnesty International; and they were among the strongest supporters of the Red Cross and Médecins Sans Frontières. They ranked second only to Sweden in membership of consumer organizations, and second only to Denmark in membership of a sports club. Only Denmark and Sweden had lower percentages of people not belonging to any sort of organization. In many cases, the differences between the top and the bottom countries are quite substantial (SCP, 2000, p. 157). By 2010, the numbers donating to Greenpeace had dropped, but the slack was taken up by other organizations and 22–23 per cent were donating to environmental organizations (Van Houwelingen et al., 2011, p. 193).

However, the organization that published these comparisons with other countries has noted shifts in the organizations to which citizens belong, and an overall decline in membership and activities in voluntary associations. Between 1994 and 2003, membership of political parties declined by 17 per cent, of churches by 9 per cent, and of women's organizations by 33 per cent. Growth was seen in nature and environmental organizations (+34 per cent), consumer organizations (+22 per cent) and organizations focusing on sport and recreation (+10 per cent). Overall, there has been a decline in the number of active members in organizations. The report noted that the decline in membership and level of activity did not generally indicate a decline in interest in the purposes of these organizations, but that there were now many other ways in which citizens could express their interests and affinities (De Hart, 2005).

In the Dutch Parliamentary Election Studies of 2010 and 2012, respondents were asked to indicate whether they were a member of various types of organizations. Figure 1.1 shows the percentages that indicated their membership of the various types. The categories are not fully equivalent to those of previous studies so it is difficult to show trends, but they do support conclusions found elsewhere. For example, membership of more traditional organizations such as churches and trade unions is equalled or exceeded by membership in post-materialist organizations such as environmental organizations and organizations related to the Third World, human rights or peace. The largest percentage is membership of sports clubs, which are found in the Netherlands for almost any conceivable sport. Even excluding churches and trade unions, these data show that two-thirds of Dutch citizens are member of one or more organizations. Indeed, the country still seems to be a country of joiners.

In Chapter 3, membership of political parties is discussed more extensively. As was stated above, this is one type of organization that has declined in membership. However, Dekker (2000) has argued that focusing only on changes in membership of political parties, religious groups and trade unions is no longer sufficient to understand how Dutch citizens participate in civic life. He has grouped civic activities into five categories to help in understanding these changes: informal opinion formation, party participation, mobilization, activism, and protest potential. Studying the percentage of citizens involved in these five types of activities between

1972 and 1998, he found that two categories show a decline. 'Party participation', including membership and any activity on behalf of a party during an election, fluctuated between 25 per cent and 30 per cent until 1994, after which time the figure dropped to only 18 per cent. 'Mobilization', which includes contacting a public official about a political or societal problem and/or stimulating an organization to take action concerning such a problem, dropped from 42 per cent in 1972 to a low of 22 per cent in 1986, and fluctuating since. One category shows no trend: 'informal opinion formation', a category based on self-reported active participation in the discussion of political questions, has been fairly stable, with around half of the population reporting participation of this type. Finally, two types of activity have become more popular. 'Activism', which includes participation in so-called 'action groups' or taking part in a demonstration. Changes in question wording must be taken into account when comparing the figures for this category, but Dekker concludes that this type of activity rose between 1977 and 1998. 'Protest potential' also seemed to be on the rise. This category comprised the self-reported potential for taking action if an Act of Parliament was felt to be unfair or unjust. Whereas the percentages in the 1970s and 1980s were in the teens, those in the 1990s were close to 25 per cent.

Unfortunately, changes in question wording limits longitudinal comparison. Figure 1.2 gives more recent figures for some political activities. Though these percentages are in general lower than for membership of organizations, they require

Figure 1.1   *Membership of Organizations, 2010, 2012 (% of the adult population)*

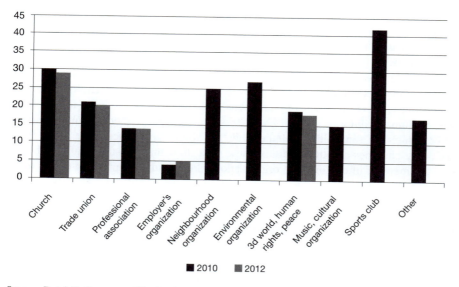

Source: Dutch Parliamentary Election Study, 2010, 2012.

a greater level of activity than merely paying membership dues or making a contribution. Of interest is the high percentage that indicated having taken part in a political discussion or action via the internet, email or Short Message Service (SMS). This indicates that new technological developments are also changing the face of political participation. In general, though this is the only percentage that exceeds 11 per cent, citizens have the choice of various forms of activity. Looking across all activities, fully 40 per cent of the respondents indicated having taken part in one of these activities. In 2010, respondents were also asked how great was the chance that they would take action if they found a bill before Parliament to be unjust. Approximately 20 per cent said the chance was good or very good, and an additional 50 per cent said there was some chance they would take action.

There is little indication in this or previous election studies that voters are less interested in political questions or that they are discussing them less. They may not be as active in party affairs, they indicate a willingness to step in if things go wrong. Dekker refers to the concept of the 'monitorial citizen' introduced by Schudson (1998): not a citizen constantly gathering political information or engaged in political debate, but someone who, while concentrated on his own affairs, keeps a watchful eye on the collective interest and is willing to step in if necessary (Dekker, 2000, p. 89).

Figure 1.2 *Percentages Reporting Having Participated in Various Political Activities, 2012*

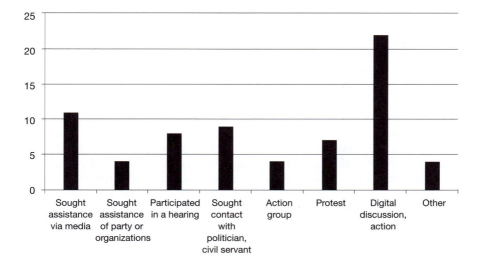

Source: Dutch Parliamentary Election Study, 2012.

Constitutional Development

The international events that helped to establish the borders of the Netherlands and influenced its national identity and political culture have also had a profound impact on the Dutch Constitution. Little is left to remind the current observer of the Republic of the Seven United Provinces, but these changes rarely resulted from purely domestic developments. The Republic was a loose confederacy with little in the form of national political institutions. As Schama put it, 'Indeed national unification in the case of the Dutch is a contradiction in terms since they had come into being as a nation expressly to avoid becoming a state' (Schama, 1987, p. 62). Power rested firmly in the hands of the individual provinces. The 'French period' lasted only from 1795 to 1813, but the Napoleonic occupation left the country highly centralized. Local customs and regulations were set aside by national legislation modelled after the French codifications; the judiciary was reformed and centralized; a national tax system was introduced; the once sovereign provinces were relegated to the status of French *départements* and, as we shall see in Chapter 8, are now the most impotent of the three layers of government. It is true that regional elites continued to play a role for some considerable time after the provinces' institutional power was broken, and it is also true that the French found support among parts of the elite who felt that the confederal Republic had outlived its use and radical reform was necessary. Yet the French influence has been crucial: between 1795 and 1798 the Dutch National Assembly was deadlocked among federalists, unitarists and moderates, despite the French presence and despite the exclusion of the Orangists. After a first draft of the Constitution was voted down in a referendum, a new Assembly was elected, reflecting the same divisions. The French then instigated, or at least supported militarily, a coup d'état by the unitarists and pushed through a draft Constitution made in France.

The French must share responsibility with the British for another radical change – the transition from a republic to a monarchy (see Box 1.3). William of Orange's role in the struggle against Spain made him the 'father of the fatherland', and ever since that time the House of Orange has played a prominent role in Dutch history. As 'Stadtholders', they provided military leadership, but even in this respect they were dependent on provincial governing bodies. Only occasionally did all provinces appoint the Prince of Orange as Stadtholder, and there have been times when the provincial elites preferred a 'Stadtholder-less period' (as they are known in Dutch history books) to curb the influence of the House of Orange. The French first maintained the Netherlands as a republic, but before annexing the country outright the Emperor Napoleon created a Kingdom of Holland with his brother Louis on the throne. This monarchical experiment had no lasting effect apart from the fact that King William I did later fall back on some of the arrangements of 1806–10. When the Prince of Orange returned to the Netherlands from exile in London after the defeat of Napoleon in 1813, he was met on the beach near The Hague by three patricians who, acting of their own accord and without any legitimate basis, offered him the sovereignty of the country. This was formalized and legitimized on 12 February 1815 when, as already mentioned, the Congress of Vienna created the Kingdom of the Netherlands. The Congress acted on a proposal by the British, who may have done so out of a geopolitical desire to have a strong buffer state north of France, or to give the Prince of Orange compensation for the fact that the English princess had broken off her engagement to the Dutch prince. Whatever motivated the British proposal, it is clear that not only the unitary state but also 'the Dutch monarchy is no home-grown product' (Cramer, 1980, p. 11). However, except for a half-hearted attempt at a socialist revolution in 1918, a return to republican government has never been seriously considered.

BOX 1.3

The Dutch Monarchy

Since the introduction of the monarchy in 1815, the office has been filled by the following individuals:

Willem I	1815–40
Willem II	1840–49
Willem III	1849–90
Emma (Regent)	1890–98
Wilhelmina	1898–1948
Juliana	1948–80
Beatrix	1980–2013
Willem-Alexander	2013–

On 30 April 2013, Willem-Alexander, the eldest son of former Queen Beatrix, was inaugurated as King of the Netherlands. In the Netherlands, the King is not crowned, since he became King the moment Beatrix signed the act of abdication. The Constitution prescribes that the inauguration is to take place in Amsterdam at a joint session of the States-General (that is, the First and Second Chambers of Parliament). The royal regalia, including the crown (symbol of the sovereignty of the Kingdom), the sceptre (symbol of the authority of the King), the orb (symbol of the territory of the King), the sword (symbol of the power of the King), and the national standard or banner, are placed on a table, together with the Constitution and a copy of the Statute of the Netherlands. The King then swears an oath to uphold the Constitution and the Statute. The King never wears the crown on his head.

Though the Constitution speaks only of a King, in the absence of male heirs in the House of Orange, for over a century the 'King' was a Queen. However, only in 1983 was the Constitution altered to designate the eldest child of the monarch as heir to the throne, irrespective of the child's sex. The only political involvement in the succession is the constitutional requirement of parliamentary permission for a marriage by a ruling monarch or heir to the throne. Without such permission, the marriage results in exclusion from the line of succession.

→

→

Only twice has the government declined to ask parliamentary permission for a royal marriage: in 1968, Irene, sister of then Crown Princess Beatrix, was engaged to marry Don Carlos Hugo, at that time a pretender to the same Spanish throne from which the Dutch had liberated themselves after an 80-year struggle. The fact that Princess Irene converted from the traditional Protestantism of the House of Orange to Catholicism also played a part in the government's decision. By 2001, religion was no longer a consideration, when Parliament gave permission for the marriage in 2002 of then Crown Prince William-Alexander to a Roman Catholic woman, Maxima Zorreguieta. If that marriage was somewhat controversial, it was because the father of the bride had been a junior minister in the Videla dictatorship in Argentina. In 2003, the government refused a request to seek parliamentary permission for the marriage of the King's brother, Prince Friso, and his fiancée, Mabel Wisse Smit, in a controversy over the latter's previous contact with a well-known criminal.

For 2013, the King received an income of €825,000 (indexed for inflation) and €4,408,000 for personnel and expenses. The Queen received €327,000 and €574,000, and Princess Beatrix (the former Queen) received €466,000 and €947,000, respectively. In addition, €26,995,000 was allocated for expenses of the monarchy, including the Cabinet of the King, service personnel, expenses for aircraft, for the royal yacht, the Netherlands Government Information Service and so on. In addition to these direct costs, indirect costs including the maintenance of palaces, transportation, security, state visits and special events, are estimated to bring the total costs to approximately €100 million. In terms of its own private fortune, the Dutch royal family is still considered to be one of the world's wealthiest families.

The Netherlands is a constitutional monarchy, and the role of the King is primarily that of a ceremonial head of state. Each year, on the third Tuesday in September (Prince's Day), the King ceremonially opens the parliamentary year by reading the 'Speech from the Throne'. The message itself is, however, prepared by the Cabinet, just as the Cabinet is ultimately responsible for everything the King and other members of the royal household say and do in public. It would be a mistake, however, to conclude that the King has no political influence. He receives the Prime Minister each Monday to discuss affairs of state, and receives visits by the other ministers several times a year. Though the contents of these meetings are not made public (the 'Secret of the Palace'), ministers have admitted that her long experience and diligent attention to public issues made Queen Beatrix an influential sparring partner. Whether King Willem-Alexander can gain such influence remains to be seen.

It is unlikely that the relationship in the past between the reigning Queens and the Cabinet have been without conflict, but few of these conflicts have become public knowledge. For example, in 1948, Queen Juliana refused to confirm the death sentences of three German war criminals, and the sentences were subsequently changed to life imprisonment. In the Lockheed Affair of 1975–6 the Cabinet dropped all thoughts of criminal proceedings against Prince Bernhard after Queen Juliana, his wife, reportedly threatened to abdicate (see Chapter 2). In 1972, the Cabinet suddenly withdrew a bill regulating membership of the royal household after it had been amended in Parliament, to restrict the number of members falling under ministerial

→

→

responsibility. It was rumoured that the Queen had threatened to withhold her constitutionally required signature to the amended bill. In 1996, the Minister of Foreign Affairs inadvertently admitted that it was primarily at the Queen's insistence that the government opened an embassy in Jordan. Finally, the government was embarrassed when news broke in 1998 that the Crown Prince would become a member of the International Olympic Committee (IOC), which was then riddled with corruption scandals. On becoming King, Willem-Alexander resigned his position with the IOC.

An incident involving Princess Margarita, a niece of the then Queen Beatrix, and Margarita's husband led to a clarification of the position of the King's Office in 2003. This office is a 'part of the central government and serves as a link between the King and his ministers' (www.kabinetvandekoning.nl). Without the permission of the governmental ministers, the director of the King's Office had ordered the national intelligence agency to investigate the Princess's husband, Edwin de Roy van Zuydewijn. As a result of this incident, the King's Office was brought under the direct ministerial responsibility of the Prime Minister.

It was always argued that the greatest influence of the Queen was seen in the Cabinet formation process, in which she appointed informateurs and formateurs. However, after decades of discussion, in 2012 Parliament removed the prerogatives of the Queen in the formation process and organized this itself (see Chapter 5). Politicians may occasionally complain about royal interference, but any criticism of the monarchy is constrained by its popularity among the general population. It is generally assumed that this popularity received an enormous boost during the Second World War, through the leadership shown by Queen Wilhelmina when the government went into exile in London. Since then, surveys have never found more than 10 per cent of the population in favour of abolishing the monarchy. Of the major political parties, only the Labour Party has at times been formally committed to a return to a republican form of government, but, ironically, three times it has been a Labour Prime Minister who has extricated the House of Orange from a potential constitutional crisis: in the 1950s, when Queen Juliana came under the influence of a faith-healer; in the 1970s, when the Prince Consort was accused of having accepted bribes from the Lockheed company; and in 2001, over the past of the then Crown Prince's prospective father-in-law.

After more than a century of Queens as head of state, it will be interesting to see how the Dutch react to a male on the throne. Though the spouse of a Queen is not given the title of King, the opposite is not true for the spouse of the King. So the Dutch retain their Queen in Maxima.

To the list of foreign influences we must add the Belgian contribution. As mentioned earlier, the enforced union of the Dutch and the Belgians in 1815 was shortlived, but it did leave its imprint on the Dutch Constitution in the form of a bicameral parliament. We saw how the conditions in the once powerful provinces of Holland and Zeeland were not conducive to the development of a landed gentry, and being a republic for two centuries had not strengthened the role of what little aristocracy there was in the northern Netherlands. Neither factor had applied to the Austrian Netherlands, and the nobility had fared better there. The southern aristocracy was not content with merely being one of the estates represented in the States-General, as was the northern tradition. Thus a First Chamber, or Senate, was created, its members to be appointed for life by the king, in which Belgian aristocrats were joined by Dutch patricians and new, hastily created, Dutch peers. The First Chamber remained after the Belgians left. The method by which it is composed is the single institutional aspect of the Constitution that has been changed most often, which testifies to its lack of domestic roots (see Chapter 6). Yet proposals to abolish the First Chamber, while made regularly, have never met with success, if only because, according to the Constitution, the First Chamber must assent to its own abolition.

A unitary state, a monarchy, bicameralism: these have been fundamental characteristics of the Dutch political system since 1815. None was endogenous, but none has ever been seriously challenged. Since 1815, the Constitution has been revised 15 times, but only two of these revisions altered basic governmental institutions: the introduction of direct elections and a parliamentary system of government in 1848; and of proportional representation and universal male suffrage in 1917 (female enfranchisement following only two years later). These two reforms were not imposed from abroad, but international events played a major role in their introduction. This is especially true with respect to the introduction of ministerial responsibility, the first, and crucial, step towards a parliamentary system. This reform of 1848 was initiated by the King himself in reaction to the February Revolution in France. After hearing of those events, he quickly set aside his rivalry with the king of Belgium and sought support from Prussia. When the revolution spread to Germany in March, King William II, left on his own, decided to steal the revolutionaries' thunder by commissioning a constitutional revision. As the King himself admitted, on 16 March 1848 he changed 'from ultra-conservative to ultra-liberal within 24 hours' (Boogman, 1978, p. 51). The reform of 1848, drafted mainly by the liberal leader Johan Thorbecke, brought direct elections and ministerial responsibility to Parliament, though it took many years for the implications of that latter change (the necessity for a government to enjoy the confidence of a parliamentary majority) to take hold.

The changes of 1917 were less influenced by foreign powers and circumstances during the First World War. The political parties at the time were bitterly divided, and the war, during which the Netherlands maintained a precarious neutrality, certainly helped to rally the parties around the common interest. The major issues to be resolved were the financial position of religious schools and the extension of suffrage. In 1913, two parliamentary commissions, in which the leaders of all major parties were represented, were charged with the task of finding a solution for the two problems. This proved no easy assignment, and only after years of negotiations was a package deal, known as 'The Great Pacification of 1917', hammered out, containing, in addition to state financing of religious schools, the introduction of universal male suffrage and an electoral system of proportional representation (see Chapter 2).

Since 1917 only one opportunity for foreign interference with Dutch political institutions has presented itself: the Second World War. As discussed above, while the German occupation had enormous consequences for Dutch culture and Dutch foreign policy, historians emphasize the constitutional continuity between the pre- and post-war periods. As Blom concludes: 'Dutch political institutions triumphantly withstood the test of the war. Though during the war most of them were temporarily suspended, they reappeared virtually unchanged at the end of the war' (Blom, 1977, p. 247). The German occupation was insufficiently subtle as to rule through institutional engineering and left little to inherit. Perhaps a partial exception should be made for the institutionalization of corporatist organizations that were to become so characteristic of Dutch socio-economic policy-making (see Chapters 7 and 9). Before the war, corporatist reforms had been proposed, especially by Catholics, but it was the Germans, not the Dutch, who made a start with the corporatist reorganization of economic life. After the war these corporatist bodies were modified (fewer powers for the chair, better representation of labour), but not dismantled, and the German legacy became the starting-point for further efforts in this direction by the Dutch government (see Chapter 7).

With the exception of the creation of corporatist bodies and their mention in the Constitution and a few other (minor) amendments, the constitutional framework of today, represented graphically in Figure 1.3, has remained unchanged since 1917. To change the Constitution a special procedure and a qualified majority is needed. Any constitutional amendment first needs an ordinary majority in both Houses of Parliament; Parliament then has to be dissolved (this is usually planned to coincide with scheduled elections), and after elections both Houses must vote on the proposal again. In this second reading a two-thirds majority is needed.

This discussion of the historical and constitutional development of the country has provided an initial introduction to the main institutions and actors in the governance and politics of the Netherlands. The next chapter introduces the developments in the cultural context within which these institutions and actors must function. There we shall discuss how religious and social minorities led to the development of a social system of '*verzuiling*' and a political style of consociationalism or consensus democracy. Having thus set the stage, the subsequent chapters look at the role of individual actors and institutions, and their contribution to the governance of the Netherlands: the parties (Chapter 3), elections (Chapter 4), the core executive (Chapter 5), Parliament (Chapter 6), the bureaucracy, organized interests and the judiciary (Chapter 7), and subnational and supranational (that is, European) governments (Chapter 8). To illustrate the outcome of the interplay between these actors and institutions, two chapters analyse two policy domains: socio-economic policy (Chapter 9) and foreign policy (Chapter 10), selected because they have attracted the most attention from foreign observers and because they represent very different styles of policy-making. These chapters also introduce the economic and international environment of Dutch politics. The final chapter seeks to integrate the main findings, and, after an evaluation of the strengths and weaknesses of the Dutch system of governance, assesses its prospects.

26

Figure 1.3   *The Constitutional Framework of Dutch Politics*

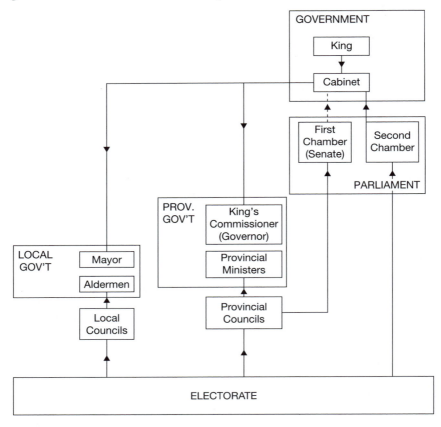

2

A Country of Minorities

Three Threats to Stable Government

In May 2002, the assassination of the populist politician Pim Fortuyn and his party's dramatic gains in the general election (see Box 2.1) briefly made Dutch politics front page news around the world. In general, however, the Netherlands does not often feature in foreign newspapers, on CNN or BBC World. This lack of attention has little to do with the country's small size: many countries that are smaller, such as Israel, are in the news almost daily. The real reason is that Dutch politics usually lacks the drama, conflict and violence from which headlines are made. The peacefulness and stability of Dutch politics actually constitute a major achievement because, historically, there have been three potential threats to stable government in the Netherlands: the structural lack of an electoral majority party, the existence of at least two distinct ideological dimensions in Dutch politics, and the segmentation of Dutch society.

Minorities

The Netherlands is a country of minorities, which is without doubt the single most important characteristic of Dutch politics. From the introduction of universal suffrage to the present, no political party has ever succeeded in winning an electoral (or even a parliamentary) majority, and it is unlikely that we shall witness such a majority in the near future. The largest percentage ever received by a single party was 35.3 per cent of the vote (the Christian Democrats in the 1989 parliamentary elections) and this left that party still 22 (out of 150) seats short of an overall majority in the Second Chamber of Parliament. With the exception of the Liberals, the political groups that make up the Dutch political landscape originated as minorities not only in a numerical but also in a social-psychological sense; they were underprivileged social groups. The term Liberals was used to denote a heterogeneous and loosely organized group of secular, or at least latitudinarian (that is, with broad and liberal standards of religious beliefs and conduct), relatively well-to-do citizens. Though a numerical minority in the population at large, the Liberals dominated Dutch politics for a long time during the nineteenth and early twentieth centuries.

Prior to the introduction of universal suffrage in 1919, they at times even enjoyed a parliamentary majority. The explanation is a simple one; the Liberals' electoral importance was enlarged artificially by restrictions of the franchise on the basis of property and income criteria. As economic growth and legislation enfranchised more and more citizens, the Liberals were gradually crowded out of political power.

BOX 2.1

'The Long Year of 2002'

The autumn of 2001 marked the beginning of what is now known in the Netherlands as 'the long year of 2002', a period of political confusion and shock that ended in the spring of 2003. The year 2002 was dominated by a single politician, Pim Fortuyn, and included his meteoric rise in the polls; his assassination only nine days before the elections of May 2002; the impressive election result for his party (List Pim Fortuyn, or LPF) and its inclusion in the new governing coalition; the party's inability to govern, leading to the resignation of the government, which in turn caused early elections in January 2003, in which the LPF lost heavily and was excluded from the new coalition.

The epithet 'maverick' certainly applied to Fortuyn, who began his career as a Marxist lecturer in sociology but later became a columnist for a conservative weekly. Openly gay and with a flamboyant life-style, he seemed the most unlikely candidate to rout a coalition that claimed responsibility for the 'Dutch miracle' (see Chapter 9). Gratitude, however, is not known to be a prominent consideration among voters. The feeling that the 'purple coalition' (see Chapter 5) had outstayed its welcome grew as discontent emerged over problems such as hospital waiting lists, teacher shortages, street crime, traffic jams and policy fiascos.

The greatest discontent waiting to be mobilized, however, was anxiety over the development of the Netherlands as a multi-cultural society. Fortuyn's campaign began when he was adopted as leading candidate for a new party, Liveable Netherlands, itself the product of a motley collection of local protest parties. However, the turning point in his campaign came in February 2002, when he declared Islam to be a 'backward' culture (the actual Dutch word used also means 'mentally retarded'). In an attack on the prevalent political correctness with regard to ethnic minorities he also advocated the abolition of the constitutional ban on discrimination if that meant that freedom of speech was restricted. The Liveable Netherlands Party immediately dropped him as its leader, and in order to participate in the election he hastily put together a list of candidates under his own name. Fortuyn later toned down some of his more extreme statements and always denied being a right-wing extremist, but opinion polls showed that his support was based on a combination of anti-establishment sentiments and fear of immigration and the unsuccessful integration of ethnic minorities. This same combination has fuelled the rise of right-wing populists in other countries. The other Dutch parties denounced Fortuyn's anti-immigrant stance and proposals such as a 25 per cent reduction in government employees, and denial of disability benefits to cancer patients, but most of their leaders proved no match for his rhetorical skills and impertinent wit. The campaign soon became vitriolic, however

→

→

(with, for example, Fortuyn comparing the Minister of Public Health to Osama bin Laden, and himself being compared with the French far-right politician Jean-Marie Le Pen).

On 6 May 2002, Fortuyn was shot at point-blank range by an animal rights activist. This first assassination of a political figure in 330 years sent a shockwave through the Netherlands and led to an unprecedented display of mourning. Accusations that by 'demonizing' Fortuyn the media and the Left had created a climate of opinion that made the assassination possible ('the bullet came from the Left') led to street riots and threats against left-wing politicians that would eventually even cause Labour leader Ad Melkert to leave the country. Though virtually all parties ceased campaigning at that point, the elections went ahead as scheduled on 15 May. Given the extraordinary circumstances, the results came as no surprise, though they were without precedent: never before had so many seats changed hands (46 out of 150); never before had a governing coalition lost so heavily (43 seats), nor had a single party (Labour) suffered such a haemorrhage (going from 45 to 23 seats). Above all, never had a new party made such an impressive début: the assassinated leader's LPF became the second-largest party in Parliament, with 26 seats. An election day poll showed that the murder had changed the voting preference of 12 per cent of the voters. Some voters used the ballot box to send a message of condolence, but others, apparently fearful that polarization would destabilize the country, produced a last-minute swing towards the Christian Democrats.

With such popular support for the LPF, the option of isolating the party was rejected by the other parties, and the LPF was invited to join a centre-right coalition with the Christian Democrats and Liberals led by the Christian Democrat leader Jan Peter Balkenende. However, without prior experience in government, without a coherent programme, and without its founder and leader, the LPF proved unable to function as a governing party. From the start, scandals and conflicts were the order of the day both within and between the party's delegation in the Cabinet, the parliamentary party and the party executive. An LPF junior minister was forced to resign within eight hours of being sworn in when it transpired that she had lied about her role in a military dictatorship in her native Surinam. LPF ministers did not heed the doctrine of collective ministerial responsibility and repeatedly launched ideas without consulting their Cabinet colleagues or even the Prime Minister. As rivals in a struggle for the party's leadership, two of its Cabinet ministers were not on speaking terms. During its first month in Parliament, the party expelled several MPs for various reasons, and changed its leadership twice. Conflicts within the party executive centred on the influence that ordinary party members were to have, but particularly on the party's finances. Together, these conflicts within the LPF paralysed the government, and after only 87 days in office, the parliamentary party leaders of the Christian Democrats and the Liberals 'pulled the plug' from the coalition.

Early elections were held in January 2003. The LPF did badly, dropping from 17 per cent to 5.7 per cent of the vote. The internal conflicts were cited by many voters who withdrew their support from the party, but some of the wind was also taken out of the LPF's sails because all the other parties, and the VVD (Liberal Party) in

→

→

particular, had moved towards LPF's position on immigration and integration. Contrary to their expectations, the Christian Democrats and the Liberals made insufficient gains to obtain a parliamentary majority between them. The big winner of the 2003 elections was the opposition Labour Party that recouped most of the losses it had suffered only the year before. After an abortive attempt to form a coalition of Christian Democrats and Labour, the Christian Democrats and the Liberals managed to persuade the small Progressive-Liberal party D66 to join them in government. It was one of the longest government formations in Dutch history, taking 123 days, but its conclusion in May 2003 did mark the end of 'the long year of 2002'. It is a year that will long be remembered in Dutch politics.

Initially, however, the other minorities felt excluded and disadvantaged because of Liberal dominance. To the extent that the Eighty Years' War of Independence can be perceived as a religious war, the Catholics were identified with the losing side. Under the Republic they could not practise their religion publicly; they were barred from holding public office, and the two predominantly Catholic provinces, Brabant and Limburg, were ruled by the central government as conquered territory. Gradually, the discriminatory legal provisions were abolished, but the Catholics remained wary of a Protestant backlash and were slow to organize themselves openly. Hence it was only in 1926 that the Catholic party was founded.

At the first national census in 1879, 35.9 per cent of the population identified itself as Roman Catholic. In part because of a higher birth rate, the proportion of Catholics rose to 40.4 per cent in the final national census of 1971. Since then, even the church's own figures show the percentage dropping to under 25 per cent in 2012 (KASKI, 2012). Protestants constitute the second religious minority. The more orthodox Protestants felt the impact of Liberal dominance not only in politics, but also within the Dutch Reformed Church, the main Protestant denomination, where latitudinarians held power in synods and parish councils. In addition, many of the orthodox Protestants felt underprivileged in economic terms, calling themselves *'de kleine luyden'*, 'the little people'. They were the first to organize themselves as an emancipation movement. While some of these orthodox Protestants remained within the Dutch Reformed Church, in 1834 and around 1880 others eventually broke away to found several *Gereformeerde* Churches (as the Dutch term *Gereformeerd* also translates into 'Reformed' in English, we use the Dutch term to avoid confusion; members of these churches are referred to as *Gereformeerden*). Later, these religious differences sustained, next to several very small parties, two major Protestant political parties: the Anti-Revolutionary Party (or ARP, supported primarily by *Gereformeerden*), and the Christian Historical Union (or CHU, backed largely by Dutch Reformed).

In the 1879 census, a majority (54.5 per cent) of the population reported identification with the Dutch Reformed Church, but ideologically many of these can be classified as Liberals. The *Gereformeerden,* who were only just beginning to organize themselves, formally comprised 3.5 per cent, but in the following census 8.2 per cent identified themselves as *Gereformeerd*. The percentage long remained at a level of between 8 per cent and 10 per cent of the population, but by the year 2000 it had dropped to 4 per cent (Becker, 2005, p. 60).

In contrast to the relatively stable percentages for Catholics and *Gereformeerden*, the position of the Dutch Reformed Church has changed rather dramatically. Even by 1889, the percentage reporting adherence to this church had dropped to less than 50 per cent. In the twentieth century, each decennial census showed a drop of between 3 per cent and 5 per cent, and by the last census in 1971 less than a quarter (23.5 per cent) reported such identification. Subsequent figures show continued declines to 12 per cent in 2000 (Becker, 2005, p. 60). In 2004, the Dutch Reformed Church and the *Gereformeerden*, together with the small Lutheran Church, merged into the Protestant Church in the Netherlands (PKN), reversing their nineteenth-century separation. Since then it has no longer been possible to determine the sizes of the individual denominations, but together they now organize about 11 per cent of the population.

The major religious groups have always been minorities and these have become smaller as time has gone on. The rise in the percentage of those claiming no religious identification is therefore substantial. Throughout the twentieth century this percentage has risen and in 1971 passed the percentage of Dutch Reformed identifiers (23.6 per cent to 23.5 per cent) for the first time. Since the early 1980s, the percentage has continued to rise rapidly. Depending on how the question is posed in current surveys, more than half of the population report no religious identification (Becker, 2005, pp. 62–3).

The Liberals had to face political competition not only from these religious minorities, but also from the working-class movement and its political representatives. The Social Democrats entered the political arena relatively late. The Netherlands was slow to industrialize, and while there is some dispute about the exact timing of industrial 'take-off', it is safe to say that industrialization did not really begin until the period between 1860 and 1880. Before the start of the twentieth century there was hardly an economic basis for a working-class movement. When industrialization rendered the ground fertile for Social Democracy, mobilization of the masses was already well under way, however slowly and cautiously, along religious lines. The appeal of the denominational parties crossed the newly developing class divide and left the Social Democrats with only the secular manual workers to organize, a category that was far from a majority. As we shall see later, some Marxist commentators do not consider this to be an historical accident, but see religious mobilization as a bourgeois strategy to weaken class consciousness: the famous 'opium of the people'. However, whether by accident or design, the Social Democrats, too, had to reconcile themselves to a minority status.

The size of social classes is more difficult to measure than for religious preference. In the decennial census, citizens were asked about their religious adherence, but not their class adherence; such information has only been available since the advent of national surveys. Only objective data are available to assess the historical development of the class composition of the population. In Chapter 9, the changes

Figure 2.1   *Divisions within Dutch Society*

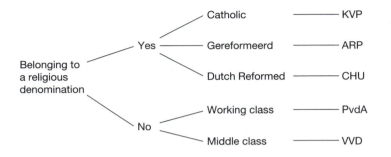

in sectors of employment are discussed, revealing a decline during the twentieth century in the percentage of the population employed in agriculture and industry, and a shift towards the service sector. The rise of the service sector has coincided with a rise in the level of education. As late as the 1960 census, 56 per cent of the population had only received a primary school education; today a mere 6 per cent of the population aged 25 to 65 has had only primary school education. In contrast, the percentage with post-secondary education has risen from about 8 per cent in 1971 to more than 32 per cent in 2011 (Statistics Netherlands).

Related to such changes are alterations in the perception of social class identification. Beginning in 1971, Dutch academic surveys began to ask to which social class people felt they belonged. In 1971, the classes were fairly evenly mixed: 40 per cent identified with the working class and 46 per cent saw themselves as middle class (down the years, about 2 per cent has considered itself to be of the upper class). In a similar survey in 2010, a considerable gap appeared: only 29 per cent of the population saw itself as working class, while 68 per cent considered itself middle class (Dutch Parliamentary Election Study, 2010).

Having completed our brief *tour d'horizon* of the most important political minorities in Dutch politics, the political situation can be summarized neatly by the tree model shown in Figure 2.1, which also lists the political parties that represent the social minorities. While some of these parties carried different names before the Second World War, and though the Liberals were rarely able to confine themselves to just one party, these minorities found political expression during the gradual extension of the suffrage, and their political parties have dominated politics at least since the introduction of universal suffrage.

Two Dimensions

Governing a country of minorities is no easy task, but the Dutch situation is further complicated by the fact that the political parties cannot be ordered along a single ideological dimension. As Figure 2.1 shows, both religion and social class played an important role, and hence political competition was ordered by two different ideological dimensions. This would be inconsequential if the ordering of the parties on the two dimensions had been the same, but it was not. As in most other countries it is possible to position the parties on a left–right socio-economic dimension. On this dimension, 'left' stands for more and 'right' for less government intervention in the economy and equality of income distribution, and so on. Some non-economic issues, such as defence, conform to the same party ordering, where we find the Labour Party to the left, the Liberals to the right, and the Christian Democratic parties somewhere in between. Depending on the issue and on the period, the ARP could sometimes be discovered to the left of the KVP, and the CHU to the right, and sometimes vice versa.

In addition to this dimension, until recently the religious dimension also structured political competition, giving rise to conflicts on numerous ethical or cultural issues such as education and abortion. In fact, this dimension overshadowed the socio-economic one during much of the first half of the twentieth century. The 'antithesis', as the secular/religious cleavage was called, was visible in Parliament, with MPs for secular parties being seated to the left of the Speaker, and MPs from religious parties to his right. Confusingly, therefore, the terms left and right applied to the religious as well as the socio-economic dimension. On the left of the religious dimension we find the Social Democrats, and the Liberals in roughly the same position. The Christian Democrats take a position clearly to the right of centre, outflanked only by the fundamentalist parties.

The salience of two ideological dimensions, each with a different ordering of the major parties, created special problems. In a country of minorities, the only alternative to minority governments is coalition government. Coalitions are usually formed by parties that are ideological neighbours; but neighbours on which ideological dimension? At the socio-economic level, coalitions of Christian Democratic parties with either Liberals or Social Democrats are obvious possibilities. However, when it comes to ethical issues, the secular party in either coalition is faced with the constant temptation to 'commit adultery' with the secular party in opposition. Based on the religious dimension, a coalition of Social Democrats and Liberals may seem most likely, but the opposition Christian Democrats are then in an ideal position to drive embarrassing wedges between both coalition parties on socio-economic and related issues. Thus the formation of coalitions is complicated (see Chapter 5), and whatever coalition comes about has in the other dimension a built-in source of conflict between the governing parties.

Pillarization

The most notorious impediment to stable government in the Netherlands has yet to be mentioned. The minorities introduced above were not merely the constituencies for five major political parties; they were tightly organized social groups or subcultures that structured not just politics, but nearly every aspect of social life in the Netherlands. For example, take the life of a hypothetical Catholic citizen during the 1950s. As conversions were extremely rare, our citizen's parents would almost certainly have been Catholics. If he or she had been born in a hospital, it would have been in the 'Saint Elisabeth Hospital', or some other appropriately named Catholic hospital. It would not have been a 'Deaconesses Hospital', which is a common name for a Protestant hospital. Nor would it have been an 'Academic Hospital', which is where 'Socialist' and 'Liberal' babies were delivered. If the birth took place at home, there would have been a midwife and maternity care from the 'White-and-Yellow Cross', the Catholic healthcare organization, not from the Protestant 'Orange-and-Green Cross' or from the secular 'Green Cross'.

The father, if involved in manual labour, would have been a member of the Catholic trade union and not of its Protestant or Socialist rivals. If he had had some other occupation he would have belonged to the Catholic Farmers' Association, the Catholic Retailers' Organization, the Catholic Teachers' Union, or whatever. The mother would probably not have been a member of any of these organizations, as no other Western country had such a low percentage of married women in the workforce (see Chapter 9). Perhaps she sang in a choir, named, for example, after 'Saint Cecilia'. She would definitely not have joined the Protestant 'Cantate Deo Choir', let alone the Socialist (and mixed!) 'Voice of the People Choir'. The family would have subscribed to a Catholic newspaper such as *De Volkskrant,* and would have avoided reading the Protestant *Trouw,* the Socialist *Het Parool* and the Liberal *Nieuwe Rotterdamsche Courant.* These were national newspapers, but a local paper for each subculture was also to be found in most regions. As far as the other media are concerned, our young Catholic would have grown up listening to, or watching, programmes aired by the Catholic Broadcasting Organization (KRO). Radio-stations and television channels are owned by the government, and broadcasting time was distributed to the KRO and its counterparts NCRV (Protestant), VARA (Socialist) and AVRO (Liberal). Each of these organizations published a radio/TV guide with special features on its own programmes, and those of its competitors hidden in small print. Originally there were only two radio stations, one shared by the religious broadcasting companies and the other by the secular organizations. This facilitated social control; when priests made house-calls they were rumoured to 'check the dial' on the radio receiver!

Our young Catholic would have attended Saint Bernadette Nursery School, Saint Joseph Primary School and Saint Agnes Comprehensive, while his or her Protestant peers would have been enrolled in a 'School with the Bible', or even a school admitting only children of one of the Protestant denominations. Socialist and Liberal children would have attended a public (that is, state-run) school. However, depending on the location in inner city or suburb, these schools would sometimes have been populated predominantly by either Liberals or Socialists. In addition, Liberal children disproportionately attended private, non-denominational schools, such as Montessori schools. On completion of secondary schooling, our Catholic would perhaps have enrolled in one of the two Catholic universities (at Nijmegen and Tilburg). Protestants could go to the Protestant Free University of Amsterdam, or to one of the theological Colleges. There was no Socialist university, unless one considers the Municipal University of Amsterdam as such, being administered by the Amsterdam municipal government, which was dominated by the left. The State Universities (Leiden, Utrecht, Groningen) attracted the remainder of the students, predominantly Liberals.

As far as leisure activities are concerned, our Catholic might have been a member of the Catholic Boy Scouts, and if he played football, he did so on Sunday, not on Saturday. To this day, Protestants play football on Saturday, and there are two separate amateur leagues. Of course, highlights from the Saturday matches were broadcast by NCRV, and whereas non-Protestant newspapers gave only short reports of the Saturday results, *Trouw* provided extensive coverage, including articles and photographs, of Protestant football.

Marriage to another Catholic would be a matter of course, as intermarriage was extremely rare. There is even a Dutch proverb which translates (rather awkwardly) into English as 'two faiths on one pillow; between them sleeps the Devil'. In 1960, for example, a mere 5.3 per cent of all married Catholics had a non-Catholic spouse. At the end of his/her life, our Catholic might die in a Catholic home for the elderly, and be buried in the Catholic graveyard by a Catholic undertaker. Literally from cradle to grave, this Catholic would have lived his or her entire life within the confines of a homogeneously Catholic subculture and its organizational infrastructure. In Dutch, these subcultures are known as *zuilen* (pillars), and the segmentation of Dutch society into these subcultures as *verzuiling* (pillarization).

This life history of an imaginary Catholic may seem impossible, except for the obvious but troubling parallel with Northern Ireland. Indeed, to some extent our story presents a caricature of pillarization. The choice of a Catholic as an illustrative example is, however, not entirely accidental, as the Catholics maintained the most extensive network of organizations. Such a network is one aspect of the degree of pillarization of a group. Lijphart (1971) has listed five such criteria to measure the degree of pillarization:

- the role of ideology or religion within the pillar;
- the size and density of the pillar's organizational network;
- the cohesiveness of that organizational network (coordination, interlocking directorates);
- the degree of social 'apartheid', or the absence of deviant, that is non-pillarized, social behaviour; and
- the extent to which pillarized behaviour and loyalty was encouraged by the subcultural elite.

On each of Lijphart's criteria, the Catholic pillar scored very highly, and the Catholic pillar was to a large extent built and maintained by the Catholic clergy. The Church played an important role within the pillar, with each and every Catholic organization from the national trade union to the local bowling club having a priest as 'spiritual adviser'. The organizational network was extremely tight, with separate Catholic organizations for nearly every form of social, economic and political activity. These organizations also enjoyed a monopoly; if rival Catholic organizations emerged, they would soon be 'persuaded' by the clergy to disband. The Catholic Church hierarchy provided guidance and coordination for this huge organizational network, and interlocking directorates were numerous. Social apartheid was probably highest among Catholics, if only because almost half of them lived in the two southern provinces where non-Catholics were rare. The other subcultures were much more dispersed, though pillarized pockets could be found in particular villages or neighbourhoods. To say that pillarization was encouraged by the Catholic elite is something of an understatement; as late as 1954 the bishops issued an episcopal letter condemning Socialism and Liberalism, and forbidding such 'sins' as membership of the Socialist trade union or listening to the Socialist broadcasting organization. The structure of the Dutch pillars is summarized in Figure 2.2.

The other pillars did not attain the same degree of pillarization on some or all of Lijphart's criteria. Protestant pillarization, for example, differed from Catholic pillarization in at least three respects. First, it is not clear whether one should speak of one or two Protestant pillars. For some activities there was only one organization catering for all Protestants – for example, trade union activity and healthcare, but for other activities there was often more than one. We have already noted the existence of two major Protestant denominations, and in addition there was a wide array of smaller churches in various shades of religious orthodoxy, and these religious

Figure 2.2   *The Structure of the Dutch Pillars*

	Catholics	Protestants		Socialists	Liberals
		Dutch Reformed	*Gereformeerd*		
Party	KVP	CHU	ARP	PvdA	VVD
Trade Union	NKV	CNV		NVV	Some whilte-collar unions
Employers' organizations	NCW			–	VNO
Broadcasting	KRO	NCRV		VARA	AVRO
Healthcare	White/yellow cross	Green/orange cross		Green cross	
Schools	Catholic schools	Schools 'with the Bible'		State schools	
Universities	Nijmegen, Tilburg	Free University, Amsterdam		State and municipal universities	
Newspapers	*Volkskrant*	*Trouw*		*(Het Parool), Vrije Volk*	*NRC, Handelsblad*

differences were reflected in some other areas of social life, most notably in politics. Second, the Protestant Churches did not provide the same leadership and coordination to their satellite organizations as did the Catholic Church. This is partly a result of rivalry among the Protestant Churches, but also because the organizational culture of the Protestant Churches conferred considerably more autonomy on local church councils, compared with the more hierarchical Catholic Church. Third, the degree of social apartheid was lower among Protestants. The *Gereformeerden* came closest to Catholic levels of pillarized loyalty. The Dutch Reformed, however, formed a 'broad church' encompassing a large group of fundamentalists as well as several more latitudinarian currents. This religious heterogeneity resulted in a much lower degree of pillarized behaviour. The CHU, for example, was never able to attract a majority of Dutch Reformed voters.

The situation within the secular minority resembled that of the Protestants. Here too there is confusion concerning the number of pillars. Some authors speak of an *'algemene zuil'* (general pillar – virtually a contradiction in terms) and point to the fact that Social Democrats and Liberals often made use of the same school system, the same healthcare organizations, and so on. Others refer to two pillars and emphasize the activities for which Social Democrats and Liberals had separate organizations, such as politics and broadcasting. Both minorities also lacked the central leadership that made the Catholic pillar such a cohesive one.

The confusion over the number of pillars is based in part on different definitions of the concept. One of the major authors on *verzuiling*, the sociologist Kruyt (1950), emphasizes the organizational infrastructure based on a particular philosophy of life. On that basis he rejects the use of the word *'zuil'* for Social Democrats and Liberals. He argues that before the Second World War, the Social Democrats could still perhaps have been classified as a 'pseudo-pillar', but after the war they lost all claims to that title because of de-ideologization and the severing of formal links between organizations such as political parties and trade unions. In Kruyt's view, the Liberals never qualified as a pillar. Many organizations commonly referred to as 'Liberal', such as the broadcasting organization AVRO, rejected that label themselves. If the Liberals organized as such, they did so reluctantly, only to offer an alternative to the other pillars' organizations, or to defend their once-dominant position.

Lijphart rejects such a narrow interpretation of pillarization and defines a *zuil* primarily as a subculture. Though he concedes that the Social Democrats scored much lower on most of his criteria of pillarization than *Gereformeerden* or Catholics, he maintains that they still formed an easily identifiable subculture within Dutch society. Finally, if we turn away from the supply-side of pillarization to behaviour patterns, the secular working class was relatively loyal to the Social Democratic pillar; less than the *Gereformeerden* but certainly more than the Dutch Reformed. The Liberals, however, form a pillar only by default, even in this respect: 'it tended to be the place where those who could not be accommodated in the Calvinist, Catholic or Socialist pillars ended up, and in that sense might even be referred to as a pile or a heap rather than as a pillar' (Wintle, 2000, p. 142).

Using our original example of an imaginary Catholic as an illustration is therefore somewhat misleading in that the Catholic minority was by far the most
pillarized one. The *Gereformeerden* were a close second, followed by the Social
Democrats. The Dutch Reformed take fourth place, with the Liberals providing
more or less the exception to the rule of pillarization.

To qualify our description of pillarization further, it should be noted that there
have always been isolated social activities that remained relatively untouched by
it, or for which pillarized organizations faced non-pillarized competition. There
were, for example, no pillarized Technical Universities. Some professions (such
as law or medicine) knew no pillarized associations, and large companies, and in
particular multinationals, were pillar-blind in their recruitment of personnel. The
national newspaper with the largest circulation, *De Telegraaf,* was never affiliated
with any pillar. The 'Amsterdam Pillarization Project', an historical analysis of
pillarized organization at the local level, found so many exceptions to pillarization
that it sparked a debate among historians about the very usefulness of the concept
(see, for example, Pennings, 1991; De Rooy, 1997; Blom, 2000). However, the
study only looked at developments until 1925 (that is before pillarization reached
its zenith), and ignored local chapters of national pillar-organization. Moreover,
as Toonen argues:

> one should expect the system to allow for the existence of non-pillarised structures when
> locally pillarised structures were either somewhat impractical, counter-productive or sim-
> ply obsolete in the case of extreme local or regional homogeneity within the population.
> (Toonen, 2000, p. 173)

Nuances and exceptions notwithstanding, the importance of *verzuiling* in structuring Dutch society up to the second half of the 1960s can hardly be understated,
and pillarization had significant political consequences. As the minorities were not
just political groupings, the political parties were not autonomous political agents,
but rather the embassies of the subcultures in The Hague (and not the subcultural
command centres they have been in other deeply divided European countries such
as Austria or Belgium; see the contributions to Luther and Deschouwer, 1999).
Political strife was exacerbated by the depth of the subcultural cleavages, and the
animosity that existed between the pillars. The minorities were introvert, isolated
and hostile towards one another, and at times emotions ran high. In 1911, unprecedentedly large Socialist demonstrations in favour of universal suffrage were considered too dangerous for the Queen to come to The Hague for the traditional opening
of the parliamentary year. In 1913, referring to the conflict about state-financing of
religious schools, the prime minister spoke of 'a wedge being driven into our population, splitting the Dutch people in two'.

In later years, such anxieties abated, but distrust between the pillars remained.
During the 1952 Cabinet formation, the Catholics claimed the portfolio of Foreign
Affairs, but the other parties feared a papist Europe as all the other Foreign Secretaries
in the budding European Community were Catholics. As a compromise, the Nether-

lands had *two* Ministers of Foreign Affairs between 1952 and 1956, a Catholic and a non-Catholic – with the latter responsible for European affairs (see also Chapter 10).

Pillarization thus posed a further threat to stable government, already jeopardized by the absence of a parliamentary majority and by the existence of more than one ideological dimension. This was the central problem confronting Dutch politicians, and the central puzzle for analysts of Dutch politics. In the words of Robert A. Dahl, reacting to a similar description of the situation by a Dutch colleague: 'Theoretically your country cannot exist' (Daalder, 1989, p. 26).

Consociational Democracy

'Theoretically', Dahl had a point. The collapse of the eminently democratic Weimar Republic has profoundly influenced democratic theory. In a renewed quest for 'stable democracy', post-war political scientists were preoccupied with finding an alchemy for stability and democracy. Stability is fostered by social homogeneity, by the absence of division. Democracy, on the other hand, presupposes at least a modicum of disagreement. The answer to the simultaneous needs for homogeneity and heterogeneity was provided by the pluralist theory of cross-pressures. Social cleavages are to be rendered harmless by cross-cutting each other; that is, social groups that are homogeneous with respect to one social cleavage are heterogeneous with respect to another. In his trade union, for example, a church member would encounter secular working-class comrades, and in his church he would encounter upper- and middle-class brethren. Thus the individual is pulled in different directions; he or she is *cross-pressured,* experiencing cross-cutting loyalties, which supposedly have a moderating effect on political views, and thus reduce the intensity of political conflicts. The puzzle of stable democracy is solved by having both centrifugal forces (social cleavages) and centripetal forces (cross-pressures) at the mass level.

Pillarization, however, prevents such cross-pressures from arising at the mass level: the cleavages are not bridged by organizational overlap. Yet 'Dutch democracy is eminently stable and effective', as Lijphart asserted (1975, p. 19), albeit not entirely without exaggeration. The Dutch solution, and Lijphart's contribution to democratic theory, is to show that social heterogeneity need not be balanced at the same (mass) level. It can also be compensated for at the elite level (see Figure 2.3). Since the masses can either be heterogeneous (segmented or pillarized) or homogeneous (or at least cross-pressured), and the elites can compete or cooperate, four situations are possible.

The two situations in which no deep cleavages exist need not interest us here. In a segmented or pillarized society, competition among the elites exacerbates the divisions and inevitably leads to instability. Lijphart cites Weimar Germany, the French Third and Fourth Republics, and Italy as examples of such centrifugal democracies. When the threat to stability by social division is offset by a 'politics of accommodation' at the elite level, we have a consociational democracy. In addition to the Netherlands, Lijphart has listed Austria, Switzerland and Belgium as European examples.

Figure 2.3   *Lijphart's Typology of Democracies*

		Mass level	
		Cross-cutting cleavages	Segmented
Elite level	Cooperation	Depoliticized Democracy	Consociational Democracy
	Competition	Centripetal Democracy	Centrifugal Democracy

The Dutch term *verzuiling* or pillarization is very appropriate in this light; the separate pillars were standing apart as in a Greek temple, only to be joined at the top, thus supporting the roof of the Dutch state.

Lijphart dates the beginning of consociational democracy in the Netherlands to the period 1913–17. As discussed in Chapter 1, this period saw the resolution of two highly divisive issues – the financial position of religious schools, and universal suffrage – in the Great Pacification of 1917.

With regard to the 'school struggle', the Liberals, and to some extent the Social Democrats, defended the state school system in which children of all creeds and classes went 'undivided' to the same school. The Protestants and, more hesitantly, Catholics advocated state funding for their own parochial schools. In the conflict over universal suffrage, the Social Democrats faced resistance from some Liberal groups and the denominational parties, the Christian Historicals in particular. In the eventual compromise, the Christian Democrats obtained state-financing of religious schools, and the Social Democrats achieved universal suffrage. The Liberal parties, which opposed both reforms, also received some satisfaction: the introduction of universal suffrage was to be accompanied by a change in the electoral system from single-member district and absolute majority to nationwide proportional representation (see Chapter 4). This allowed the Liberals to survive, as the abolition of the property and income restrictions would have rendered them a minority in virtually every district.

As Lijphart noted, the name under which this package deal is known to the Dutch, the 'Great Pacification', reminds one of international politics, as if the Dutch compromise was a peace treaty between sovereign nations. This parallel once more illustrates the precarious nature of the Dutch political system; it is seen not as a democracy based on a single society, but as *a consociational* democracy. Lijphart actually described Dutch politics in terms of international decision-making; he cites foreign policy prescriptions by Carl von Clausewitz and Woodrow Wilson in his discussion of the seven 'rules of the game', to which the Dutch elites apparently adhered to facilitate their cooperation:

- the business of politics – that is, politics is not a game, but a serious business;
- agreement to disagree;
- summit diplomacy;

- proportionality;
- depoliticization;
- secrecy; and
- the government's right to govern (without undue interference from Parliament or political parties).

Elsewhere, in more general analyses of consociational democracy, Lijphart has reduced his 'seven rules' to four basic principles: (1) executive power-sharing or grand coalition; (2) a high degree of autonomy for the segments, seen as the two most important principles, with the two secondary principles being (3) proportionality; and (4) minority veto (see, for example, Lijphart, 1977).

If we look at these seven rules of the game or at the four basic principles, they all seem to derive from the same simple precept: clear-cut, zero-sum game, yes/no decisions are to be avoided at all cost. Attempting to reach such decisions puts a system with permanent minorities under enormous stress. Even if it proves possible to reach decisions, they will result in clearly identifiable winners and losers, thus creating resentment among at least some of the minorities, and thereby mortgaging future decisions.

The first step in avoiding zero-sum decisions is the decentralization of policy-making, not to local authorities, but to the 'corporate' minorities: Lijphart's segmental autonomy. As Van Schendelen has pointed out:

> In the pillarized society the cleavages between the four main social groupings were such that 'the common government' could handle only a few issues and usually only in a procedural way, leaving as much substantial decision-making as possible to the pillars themselves. These pillars organized their own interference in socio-economic and private life. They created their own welfare organizations (for income, health, housing, education), industrial corporations, trade unions, services, banks and so on. (Van Schendelen, 1987, p. 65)

The functional decentralization of government authority to socio-economic regulatory commissions, in which pillarized interest groups were heavily represented, provided one way to reduce the risk of overloading central political decision-making. We shall return to this relationship between consociationalism and corporatism in Chapter 7.

However, the decentralization of policy-making may merely transform conflicts over the content of policies into conflicts over the distribution of the resources available to carry out those policies. In such situations, the rule of proportionality may bring relief. Lijphart argues that

> The rule of proportionality is of fundamental importance to the success of the politics of accommodation in Holland. The establishment of the accommodation pattern of politics by the peaceful settlement of 1917 was intimately related to this rule: both the suffrage and the schools questions were settled on the basis of proportionality. The rule has been faithfully adhered to ever since. (Lijphart, 1975, p. 129)

Indeed, proportionality has become so ingrained in Dutch political culture that it has become almost synonymous with fairness. The Dutch are appalled when they learn how majoritarian electoral systems in other countries, such as the UK and the USA, 'distort' election outcomes. Not only are the seats in both Houses of the Dutch Parliament, in provincial and in municipal councils, distributed to the parties in proportion to their share of the vote (see Chapter 4), portfolios in Cabinet and in provincial and municipal governing bodies are similarly distributed among the parties in the ruling coalition. Broadcasting time on the state-owned networks is handed out in rough proportion to the size of the broadcasting associations' membership. Schools are financed on a proportional basis; that is, according to the number of pupils enrolled. Mayors in all municipalities and the governors of all provinces are appointed by the central government (see Chapter 8), and all major parties receive a share of these appointments more or less in line with their electoral strength. The same can be said for government subsidies to housing associations and healthcare organizations. The parties keep a keen eye on top civil service appointments, and occasionally complain of under-representation.

Decentralization-cum-proportionality has its limits, however. Especially those issues that crossed the boundaries between policy areas, and in which several rival interest groups had a stake, remain within the government's domain. In handling such issues, political leaders generally do not seriously attempt to win outright, but rather seek to arrive at the best compromise possible. Rules or characteristics such as executive power-sharing, minority veto, agreement to disagree, summit diplomacy and secrecy are illustrative of this quest for compromise. It even led one British observer to comment on 'the invertebrate character of coalition government' (Gladdish, 1972), but the word compromise has no such pejorative connotation in the Dutch context.

However important and successful such prophylactic measures have been, there are still stubborn issues left that cannot be delegated, compromised or proportionalized. It makes no sense to 'solve' the abortion question by distributing the number of abortions proportionally to Catholic, Protestant and secular clinics. The problem of decolonization could not be solved by distributing the islands of Indonesia among the pillars. Such issues where yes/no decisions seem inescapable are most dangerous to the Dutch political system. Faced with this type of problem, non-decision-making often seems less harmful than forcing a solution. Avoidance of such decisions takes three forms: postponement of the decision; defusion of the political dispute by technical arguments (depoliticization); and removal of the responsibility from the government. The three tactics are often used in combination, hence the appointment of an expert committee (preferably composed proportionally) to study the problem is a familiar feature of Dutch politics: 'putting hot potatoes in the refrigerator', as the jargon has it.

Some successful depoliticizations have become 'classics' in the literature on the politics of accommodation in the Netherlands: the committee of constitutional experts that resolved the controversy, in 1964, over Princess Irene's conversion to Catholicism and marriage to a pretender to the Spanish throne by recommending that they should not seek parliamentary permission for the marriage; or the committee of 'wise men' that investigated suspicions that Prince Bernhard had accepted bribes from the Lockheed aircraft company in his capacity of inspector-general of the Dutch armed forces, by concluding, after the Lockheed affair had ceased to be front-page news, that the prince had merely acted imprudently; the all-party commission that 'defused' the controversial issue of nuclear energy by organizing a 'broad social discussion' on energy policy, in which every citizen was allowed to participate, and that took so long that all interest had evaporated by the time the commission presented its conclusions to the government in 1983; or the 1984 compromise on the stationing of American cruise missiles in the Netherlands, when, after long delays, that decision was effectively placed in the hands of the Kremlin (see Chapter 10); or the strategy of non-decision-making with regard to euthanasia, leaving the judiciary with the responsibility of finding a solution (see Box 7.1). Depoliticization, however, is not confined to these more-or-less famous cases: it is a routine instrument in day-to-day policy-making.

These strategies of political accommodation are greatly facilitated by the institutional framework of Dutch politics. In more recent comparative work, with the Netherlands as one of 36 cases, Lijphart developed a distinction between majoritarian democracy, defined by 10 institutional characteristics that concentrate policy-making in the hands of a majority, and consensus democracy that is characterized by an equal number of features that broaden involvement in policy-making as much as possible (Lijphart, 2012). Whereas consensus democracy looks primarily at institutions, and consociational democracy refers mainly to the behaviour of the elites, the two concepts are clearly related. The Netherlands scores highly as a consensus democracy, especially on what Lijphart calls the executives-parties dimension (a multi-party system; multi-party and often oversized coalition government; proportional representation; a legislature that is not dominated by the executive; and corporatism). The score on the federal–unitary dimension is not as high (an independent bank and a constitution that can only be changed by a qualified majority, but no power of constitutional review for the judiciary) and Lijphart's classification of the Netherlands as semi-federal (see Chapter 8) and of its Parliament as 'symmetrically bicameral' (see Chapter 6) are not beyond criticism. On the whole, however, the Dutch constitutional design offers no obstacles to elite accommodation.

Alternative Interpretations

These illustrations conclude our outline of the theory of consociational democracy. So far we have followed Lijphart's interpretation of Dutch consociational democracy, albeit in our own words, giving our own examples and placing our own emphases. Lijphart's interpretation is appealingly simple; the Dutch faced a problem, being the threat to political stability posed by social segmentation, and found a solution by replacing elite competition with elite cooperation.

However, both of these elements of Lijphart's theory have been challenged. While there has been a lively international debate on various empirical and normative aspects of consociational democracy (see Andeweg, 2000), we shall confine our discussion to criticisms of the theory as applied by Lijphart to the Dutch case.

In the first place, Lijphart's very definition of the problem has come under attack. Pillarization, it is argued, was not without its moderating cross-pressures. In a sense the class cleavage cross-cut the religious cleavage within the religious pillars; they had to accommodate both working-class and middle-class members of their pillar. These cross-pressures were not to be found within individuals, but they did moderate political conflict. Lijphart has even been accused of finding a solution for a problem that did not exist. It is argued, for example, that pillarization was not a problem to which elites had to respond, but a conscious strategy on the part of the elites to strengthen their own position. In this interpretation, pillarization was a form of social control rather than the result of emancipatory movements organizing themselves to fight Liberal domination. (Neo-)Marxist authors assert that pillarization was primarily a reaction by the ruling classes to the emergence of a working-class movement. As we saw earlier in this chapter, there can be no doubt that the mobilization of citizens along religious lines prior to industrialization took much of the wind out of the red sails. However, it hardly seems plausible to suggest a conspiracy to delay industrialization in order to pre-empt a Socialist surge. The strongest evidence in support of the Marxist interpretation of pillarization is the fact that many religious organizations, apart from church and party, sprang up not before but after industrialization took off. In the case of the trade union movement it is clear that religious organizations were often formed in direct response to attempts at Socialist unionization. The case of the trade unions, however, stands relatively isolated, and the most erudite of Lijphart's Marxist critics, Stuurman (1983), is careful not to deny emancipatory aspects to pillarization, next to aspects of social control.

The historical development of pillarization also plays a crucial role in the critique of those non-Marxist scholars who nevertheless espouse a social-control view of pillarization. They point out that many pillarized organizations were formed not only after the advent of industrialization, but also after the Pacification of 1917 itself. As we have seen, this episode plays a central role in Lijphart's interpretation, because, in his view, it first established the cooperative mode of elite behaviour. If this Pacification is to be seen as the elites' successful solution to the problems posed by pillarization, as Lijphart claims, is it not strange that the problem became aggravated only after the solution? Lijphart never denied that pillarization reached its zenith only after the Pacification, but maintains that social divisions were already deep and potentially dangerous before the elites started to cooperate in 1913–17. That pillarization increased rather than decreased after 1917 was all part of the elites' peace-making efforts: 'good fences make good neighbours'. In addition, it should be emphasized that the social control perspective and the emancipation perspective need not be mutually exclusive.

The second strand of criticism questions Lijphart's explanation of elite coalescence in the Netherlands as a 'self-denying prophecy', a conscious and courageous effort to offset the threat of the nation falling apart. In support of this 'self-denying prophecy' he emphasizes the social turbulence accompanying the struggles for state-financed parochial schools, and for universal suffrage, and argues that the unrest was deemed so pernicious as to prompt the leaders into spontaneous cooperation. Others, however, doubt that the nation's survival was ever in any real danger, in part because pillarized mobilization had not yet reached the level it would only attain after the Pacification. Indeed, with the benefit of hindsight, social unrest in the 1910s seems innocuous enough compared with what happened in the streets during the 1930s or 1960s. However, that is hardly the point. What is important is the danger, not as we perceive it now, but as the elites of the day perceived it at that time. While some evidence can be found to support Lijphart's view that the elites did fear the worst – such as the Prime Minister's speech on a 'wedge' driving the nation apart – it is difficult to ascertain exactly how dangerous they thought the situation really was.

Perhaps we do not need to know the answer, because even if we assume that the leaders did see the nation as being on the verge of a civil war, the question still remains: what made the elites so courageous and sagacious as to put the nation's survival above their own tribal interests? Suspecting that Dutch leaders are not inherently more prudent than their counterparts in deeply divided countries such as Cyprus or Afghanistan, the self-denying prophecy merely gives us a description of *what* happened, not *why* it happened. In an attempt to answer that question, Hans Daalder has drawn attention to the striking similarities between the rules of the game of consociational democracy, and the way in which politics was conducted in the much earlier days of the Dutch Republic. The pillars replaced the provinces, but the emphasis on elite bargaining and compromise, and on the autonomy of the constituent parts, can be found both before 1795 and after 1917. The very term 'consociationalism' is borrowed from Althusius, a seventeenth-century German political philosopher who was certainly aware of politics in the neighbouring Republic of the Seven United Provinces. Calling the package deal of 1917 a Pacification is an echo of 1576, when the (then 17) provinces put up a united front against the Spanish terror and agreed to respect their religious differences in the Pacification of Ghent. Elite cooperation, Daalder argues, was no self-denying prophecy, but the continuation of traditional practices.

The weakness in Daalder's explanation is the miraculous and timely re-emergence of an elite culture that belonged to a political system of days long gone. As the historian J.C.H. Blom notes:

> It is not out of the question that the tradition of compromise contributed to the later 'pillarised' compromises. But on closer examination of the historical processes in the so-called 'long nineteenth century' (1780–1914), the specific nature of the pillarisation – in contrast to the situation of the Republic – was more important. The whole train of events during the 1780–1815 period (the Patriot period, the Batavian Republic, the French period and the creation of the new Kingdom of the Netherlands) in fact resulted, in terms of political administration, in a unified nation state that differed substantially from the Republic. The development of the parliamentary system, the democratisation of state and society, and the

tremendous growth in government intervention in the nineteenth and twentieth centuries resulted in our modern mass society with its own administrative and political complex, differing even more substantially from that of the Republic. (Blom, 2000, pp. 162–3)

Even if the Republican culture of compromise had survived among the ruling classes, why would the leaders of the new emancipatory movements adopt the ways of those they were trying to replace? Only adherents to a social-control theory of pillarization have no difficulty in explaining this anomaly: the leadership was composed largely from the ranks of the traditional elites; they mobilized the pillars to secure their own position and to defend their long-set practice of consensual politics against the dangers of an extended franchise and industrialization. It is true that the old 'regent classes' did provide leadership to some of the new emancipatory organizations, particularly in the Catholic pillar, where the 'notables' had been active as Liberals before the clergy decided to end the papal–liberal alliance, and in the Dutch Reformed part of the Protestant pillar. However, there seems to be considerably less evidence of continuity in elite recruitment when we look at the *Gereformeerden* and the Social Democrats. Yet they too conformed to the rules of consociational democracy. Why?

Perhaps the answer lies in the very first characteristic of Dutch politics mentioned in this chapter: the *zuilen* were *all* minorities. It does not seem too unreasonable to suppose that history might have taken a different course had one of the blocs been able to nurse any hope for an outright victory, as is the case in some other divided societies, such as Northern Ireland. The Social Democrats, for example, have occasionally left the fold of elite accommodation when falling victim to the majoritarian illusion. This happened, for example, in 1918 when, on the eve of the first elections under universal manhood suffrage, leftist hopes for a majority were high and when the smell of revolution was in the air. The reality of minority status for all the pillars, however, meant that militant intransigence would reduce one's influence to that of a voice in the wilderness, whereas by sharing power at least something could be gained. We suggest that, rather than a noble defence of national unity or a revival of ancient elite customs, the self-denying prophecy was an act of rational behaviour on the part of political leaders with an eye towards the interests of their respective subcultural constituencies. This interpretation is supported by the experience of other certified consociational democracies, with the exception of Austria. It is also borne out by later developments, to which we now turn.

Depillarization

If consociational democracy was designed to ensure political stability, it has not been without its vulnerable moments. Leaving aside external *force majeure* in the form of the Nazi occupation, the inter-war years in particular witnessed several challenges to stable democracy, starting with the half-hearted call for revolution by a social democratic leader, and ending with widespread criticism of parliamentary democracy and the rise of an indigenous National Socialist movement in the 1930s. Immediately after the Second World War, portions of the elite planned a renewal of Dutch politics rather than a return to pre-war practices. Five years of occupation during which ancient political foes had become allies in the underground resistance, and during which visions of a more harmonious and less segmented society had developed, resulted in an attempt to break through pillarization. This 'Breakthrough' (*Doorbraak*) eventually failed, largely because religious leaders, and especially the Catholic clergy, were quick to rebuild their respective pillars. In many respects the post-war years even became the heyday of consociational democracy, and of political stability. For example, in the 1948 parliamentary elections, the net change consisted of four seats out of 100 in the Second Chamber.

This period came to an abrupt end in the second half of the 1960s. In the 1967 elections, 15 (now out of 150) seats unexpectedly changed political hands. In both the 1971 and 1972 elections this figure rose to 20, earthshaking by Dutch standards. However, these elections were merely the harbingers of the much higher volatility in later elections, such as 1994 (with 34 seats finding new occupants) and 2002 (46 seats changing hands). As Mair points out, 'Within [Europe] levels of electoral instability in the Netherlands during the 1990s were exceeded only by those in Italy, where the parties and the party system had been completely reconstructed in the wake of corruption scandals, a major electoral reform, and a host of new party formations' (Mair, 2008, p. 238). Increased electoral volatility is just one indicator of the changes; there were also large-scale demonstrations and riots in the big cities, and old organizations merging, folding or facing new competition. Depillarization is the key word to describe the changes, and it can be measured by the same criteria that Lijphart offered as measurements of pillarization.

First, the role of ideology or religion within the subcultures has declined. Not only did the size of the pillars decline because people no longer expressed a religious identification, those who continued to identify with a religion began to change the degree to which they practised their faith. This was particularly true among Catholics, who were once among the most faithful in Europe. Surveys prior to 1960 showed that approximately 90 per cent of all Catholics attended mass regularly. In the 1960s this declined to about three-quarters, and to less than a half in the 1970s. By the time the twenty-first century had begun, the figure had fallen to less than a quarter. The percentage of Dutch Reformed adherents who attend religious services regularly has varied traditionally between a quarter and a third. The percentage of believers attending services has not changed so dramatically, but since the size of the group has diminished the actual number of weekly attenders has dropped substantially. Even the most faithful, the *Gereformeerden*, have shown drops in levels of church attendance. Whereas once almost 90 per cent attended weekly, this number is now down to about two-thirds of identifiers. As we shall see in more detail in Chapter 4, religion has lost most of its predictive power with regard to voting behaviour.

Second, just as the size and density of the pillarized organizational infrastructure was a measure of pillarization, so the number and size of non-pillarized organizations indicates depillarization. In politics there has been a surge of small parties, often breakaways from the pillar parties. With a small number of exceptions, newcomers have not been very successful, as a Dutch commentary implies, in a remarkable metaphor: 'New parties came and went like mushrooms in the autumn of Dutch politics.' There was a right-wing split from the Social Democrats; both right-wing and left-wing splits from the Christian Democrats; a Farmers' Party which sprouted its own split-off groups; a Retailers' Party; at least three parties for pensioners and one for animal' rights; and several populist right-wing parties. Only a few have survived (see Chapter 3). In politics, the pillarized organizations eventually recouped some of the ground initially lost, but in other areas, such as broadcasting, they have not been so fortunate. At one point, the two largest broadcasting associations within the public broadcasting system were TROS and Veronica, both without any subcultural affiliation.

Third, the cohesiveness of the pillars has diminished, and most formal ties between organizations within one pillar have been severed. There are also fewer and fewer interlocking directorates. The parliamentary parties, for example, once recruited many of their members directly from the leadership of other organizations belonging to the same pillar (see Chapter 6), but this phenomenon has almost completely disappeared.

Fourth, social apartheid is waning. At the individual level this is evidenced by a transition from closed to open competition in elections, to be analysed more fully in Chapter 4. At the organizational level we may observe mergers of organizations formerly belonging to different subcultures. Instead of three healthcare organizations, in many municipalities there is now only one 'Inter-Cross' or healthcare organization known by some other name; the Socialist and Catholic trade unions are now combined into the FNV trade union federation; the Christian and secular employers' organizations merged into VNO-NCW; in 1973 the Dutch Reformed and *Gereformeerde* churches, together with the smaller Lutheran church, began a process that led to the merger mentioned earlier; and, last but not least, the three main Christian Democratic parties have fused into one party, the Christian Democratic Appeal (CDA).

Fifth, and finally, pillarization is no longer encouraged by the elites. Whereas the bishops still threatened 'deviant' Catholics with exclusion from the holy sacraments in 1954, in 1967 a bishop announced on television that party choice was a matter for each Catholic's individual conscience. In summary, the life story of our imaginary Catholic detailed above would be quite different had he or she been born after the mid-1960s.

Just as the degree of pillarization varied from one subculture to another, depillarization did not affect each of them equally. The religious pillars were affected most, but the *Gereformeerden* proved relatively impervious to change, and there has even been a reinforcement of pillarization around the small fundamentalist Protestant denominations, with a new broadcasting organization (EO, now the second largest in the public broadcasting system) and political party (Christian Union; see Chapter 3). Meanwhile, the Catholics experienced the fastest and most far-reaching

depillarization. The strength of the Catholic pillar in the past, the central coordinating role of the church, now proved to be its weakness. Given its central role
within the pillar, when the church swayed, so did the entire *zuil*. Again, the Liberals
provide the exception to the rule: there was little for them to depillarize, and in
many respects organizations that had been regarded as vaguely Liberal in the past
were now in the best position to benefit from the changes.

One of the most intriguing puzzles of recent Dutch political history is what trig-
gered this avalanche of change, and there is no shortage of conjectures and hypotheses. Those who saw pillarization as the by-product of the emancipatory struggle
of different minorities see depillarization as the result of successful emancipation.
Now that the goals have been reached, discipline within the pillars is relaxed, and
the minorities integrate into Dutch society at large. Those who interpreted pillarization as a form of social control suggest that depillarization is a sign of insecurity or
failure on the part of the elites. As Houska asserted:

> The organizations of the political subcultures of Western Europe grew and flourished
> because elites acted decisively to create and sustain them. They did so because they saw
> in organizations a way to achieve certain goals ... More recently, subcultural organiza-
> tions have declined and cohesion has been lost – in part because of a changed social and
> economic environment, but also in large measure because elites saw better or at least less
> costly means to achieve their goals. (Houska, 1985, pp. 149–50)

Other factors that are regularly mentioned in this context include the contention
that pillarized loyalty was undercut by the homogenizing message of television or by
increased mobility, either social or geographical. A failure of socialization is often
suggested by authors who point to student protest, a generation gap, or the numerical prominence of youth in general. Such explanations sound rather plausible, and
perhaps there is some truth in them. However, in so far as empirical evidence is
available (in the 1960s, survey research was still in its infancy in the Netherlands)
none of the hypothesized sources of change is supported (Andeweg, 1982).

Multiculturalism as a New Social Cleavage?

Even more interesting than the question of what caused depillarization is the question whether the social cleavages that structured pillarization have simply disappeared or have been replaced by new cleavages. The most likely candidate would
be ethnic diversity, as the composition of Dutch society has changed profoundly
through immigration (Entzinger, 1998). Today, the mention of 'minorities' to a
Dutch audience will evoke associations not with the 'original' minorities mentioned
at the beginning of this chapter, but with newly arrived ethnic minorities. Immigration is not a new phenomenon, and the Dutch acceptance of English Separatists
(at the beginning of the seventeenth century, including those who would become
the American Pilgrims), French Huguenots (around 1700), and of Portuguese and
Spanish Jews (in the sixteenth and seventeenth centuries) has given the Netherlands

a reputation for tolerance. Dutch commentators have pointed out that this tolerance may have been more pragmatic than principled: as long as the newly arrived did not affect the way of life of the natives they were left alone, but a melting-pot scenario never aroused much enthusiasm (Van Doorn, 1985). This tolerance was put to the test when immigration increased.

In most years since the early 1960s, the Netherlands has had an immigration surplus; immigration accounts for between a third and a half of the growth in population. The three main sources of such immigration are 'guest workers' recruited in the 1960s mostly from Turkey and Morocco who, when their stay proved to be permanent, were allowed to bring their families or prospective spouses into the country; people from the (former) Dutch colonies with immigration peaking around the time that independence was granted, with the largest groups hailing from Surinam and the former Dutch Antilles; and asylum-seekers, their numbers fluctuating, but declining from more than 50,000 per year in the 1990s to around 10,000 per year in the most recent decade, and their country of origin varying with the occurrence of political violence in the world (recently Somalia, Afghanistan, Iraq and Iran) (see Figure 2.4). There are other groups of immigrants: almost half of the 3.5 million *allochtonen* (that is, inhabitants who are born abroad or who have at least one parent who was born outside the Netherlands) came from Western countries, primarily those in the European Union (EU).

However, despite recent concerns over immigration from Poland, Bulgaria and Romania, the current debate about immigration and integration focuses primarily on the non-Western immigrant groups mentioned: on the 393,000 Turks and 363,000 Moroccans, on the 347,000 Surinamese and 144,000 Antillans, and on the

Figure 2.4   *The Impact of Immigration on the Composition of Dutch Society*

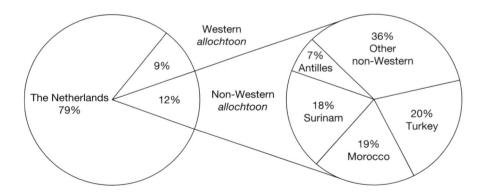

Note: allochtoon = originating from another country.
Source: Statistics Netherlands (Central Bureau of Statistics), *Jaarrapport Integratie 2012*, The Hague/Heerlen: CBS, 2012, p. 37, table 2.1.1.

non-Western asylum seekers (data for 2012; see www.cbs.nl). They are perceived as ethnic minorities and their integration in Dutch society is relatively slow, as is shown by lower levels of education – 18 percent of non-Western immigrants have only had primary education, compared with 6 per cent of indigenous Dutch people (*autochtonen* in Dutch); high unemployment – 13 per cent of non-Western immigrants and 4 per cent of the indigenous population; and high crime rates – the proportion of suspects among non-Western immigrants is three to four times higher than among *autochtonen* (CBS, 2012). Non-Western immigrants are also concentrated in the big cities, especially of the *Randstad* (a conurbation consisting of the four largest Dutch cities: Amsterdam, Rotterdam, The Hague and Utrecht plus their surrounding areas). A third of the population of Amsterdam, Rotterdam and The Hague is non-Western, with higher birth rates lifting that proportion to more than half among the young inhabitants of those cities.

Perhaps the most important reason is that non-Western immigration accounts for the growth of Islam which today, with an estimated 914,000 to 950,000 Muslims (Forum, 2012, pp. 8–9), is the third-largest religious denomination in the country. Apart from France, few countries in Europe have a higher percentage of Muslims than the Netherlands (5.5 per cent of the population).

For a long time 'political correctness' prevented a debate on the issue of the integration of Muslims and other non-Western immigrants. When the taboo was eventually broken in the 1990s by the Liberal party leader Frits Bolkestein and the Social-Democrat writer Paul Scheffer, the initial perspective was a communitarian one: how can Dutch society continue as a society when a growing part of the population does not share that society's core values? The values that were seen as being threatened by Islam were those of the Enlightenment (the right to criticize religious dogma, the separation of church and state) and relatively new postmaterialist ones such as women's emancipation and gay rights. After '9/11' in 2001, fears of Muslim terrorism reinforced these concerns, and shifted the balance to a more provocative brand of Islam-criticism. Pim Fortuyn's impact in this respect has been much greater than the short period in which he could address the issue of multi-culturalism before he was killed (see Box 2.1), but others have also attracted international attention.

Somalian-born Ayaan Hirsi Ali entered politics as a researcher for the Labour Party, campaigning for the rights of Muslim women. In 2002, she was recruited by the Liberal Party as a candidate for the 2003 elections. As an MP, she was active not only in Parliament, but at least as much outside, through publications and television programmes, quickly radicalizing in her views (Hirsi Ali, 2006, 2007). In 2004, she wrote the script for an 11-minute television film, *Submission*, about Muslim women being raped or beaten. The film was directed by Theo Van Gogh, a columnist and filmmaker notorious for his outrageous statements about Jews, Muslims and generally anything and anybody that was still respected in Dutch society. Some time after *Submission* had been shown on television, Van Gogh was murdered by Mohammed Bouyeri, an Amsterdam-born Muslim of Moroccan descent (see also Buruma, 2006). Bouyeri was part of a small group of young Muslim fundamentalists, known as the *Hofstadgroep*, of which most members were later convicted of planning a range of terrorist attacks. A knife was stuck in Van Gogh's body with a message threatening others, including Ayaan Hirsi Ali.

In 2006, a controversy arose over accusations that Ayaan Hirsi Ali had supplied incorrect information (about her name, age, and provenance) in order to gain asylum and Dutch citizenship. She resigned her seat in Parliament and left the Netherlands to work in the United States.

Her position as the most outspoken critic of Islam in the Netherlands was taken over by Geert Wilders, who left the Liberal Party over its position on Turkish membership of the EU to start his own Freedom Party (see Chapter 3). The party appealed to a similar electorate as Pim Fortuyn, but with a more radical anti-Islam position, becoming the third-largest party in 2010 and a partner in the governing coalition (see Chapter 5). Wilders has called the Quran a fascist book, advocated banning it, and called for a halt to immigration from Islamic countries. He proposed levying a 'rag tax' on wearing headscarves. He has received several threats against his life and lives under permanent protection by the security services. In 2008, the Public Prosecutor decided not to act on charges of incitement to hatred and discrimination against Wilders, but in an appeals case a court ordered his trial. Eventually, after a time-consuming trial, Wilders was acquitted in 2011 on the grounds that his comments were directed against an abstract religion, not against that religion's adherents. The verdict has been interpreted widely as giving priority to freedom of speech over the ban on discrimination.

Given this extraordinary sequence of events, immigration and integration, in particular of Muslims, are now important issues in Dutch politics and society. However, it does not seem to result in a new social cleavage or domestic 'clash of civilizations'. The number of Muslim organizations is growing, with 475 mosques (in 2007), 43 Islamic primary schools with a total of about 9,300 pupils (2007), one Islamic high school (2013), one small Islamic broadcasting organization and so on (Forum, 2010, pp. 37–9). At present, these organizations lack the coherence to form a pillar. It is symptomatic that there are not one, but two peak organizations representing Muslims to the Dutch government: the contact organization Muslims and Government (CMO) and the Contact Group Islam (CGI). The internal divisions are sometimes of a theological nature, though most Muslims in the Netherlands are Sunni, with Turkish Alevis and Surinamese (and Indian and Pakistani) Ahmadis constituting minorities, but country of origin seems more important. There are several organizations of mosques: three Turkish, one Moroccan and two Surinamese, still leaving some mosques unorganized. The social position of immigrants also varies according to their country of origin: the Surinamese have integrated the best into Dutch society; Turks tend to live their lives primarily within their own communities, with relatively low crime rates, whereas Moroccans tend to have more contact with indigenous Dutch people, but also have higher crime rates. Finally, the fact that many *allochtonen* do not have and/or do not want Dutch nationality also reduces the numerical potential of any political party that would enter elections specifically to represent them. Even without a Dutch passport, long-term immigrants are allowed to vote in local elections but, with few exceptions, they are less inclined than indigenous voters to turn out to vote. Between 2007 and 2012, a Dutch Muslim Party (NMP) tried, but failed to win any seats in local elections. In summary, the potential for a Muslim 'pillar' in Dutch society seems rather low at present.

Among indigenous Dutchmen, anxiety about the Netherlands becoming a multi-cultural society was widespread long before it was allowed on the political agenda. Before 1994, immigration and integration barely received a mention when voters were asked about the most pressing problem in the country, but in 1994 difficulties with minorities and refugees suddenly reached the top of the voters' political agenda (26 per cent of the first problems mentioned), and it has remained one of the top priorities in subsequent election years (Aarts and Thomassen, 2008, pp. 216–18). However, this does not mean that indigenous Dutch people form a homogeneous group with regard to this issue. This is illustrated in Table 2.1, with the reactions to statements about illegal immigrants, immigration of Muslims, and Turkey's potential membership of the EU. On allowing illegal immigrants to stay in the country, public opinion is fairly evenly divided; nearly two-thirds is against forbidding all immigration by Muslims; and more than a third is in favour of Turkish membership of the EU.

The pattern is very different, however, according to how people voted in the 2010 elections. In general, voters for Green Left and, to a lesser extent D66, are most permissive with regard to immigration, and Green Left is also the only party with a majority of supporters in favour of Turkey's accession to the EU. Voters for Geert Wilders' Freedom Party and for the small, orthodox Protestant SGP most clearly

Table 2.1 *Attitudes towards Illegal Immigration, Muslim Immigration, and Turkish Membership of the EU, 2010*

Voters	'Illegal immigrants should be allowed to stay' % (fully) agree	'Immigration of Muslims should stop' % (fully) agree	'Turkey may become a member of the EU' % (fully) agree
All	44	34	42
CDA	48	32	40
PvdA	56	21	49
VVD	30	28	35
SP	51	37	41
GL	71	12	62
PVV	23	67	31
CU	44	29	35
SGP	27	78	19
D66	52	14	49

Source: Dutch Parliamentary Election Study, 2010.

take the opposite view on these issues. Of the largest parties, Labour voters tend to be more permissive compared with Christian Democratic voters, and in particular compared with Liberal voters. These differences of opinion, and the policy positions of these parties, reflect the history of pillarization. The Liberal VVD, for example, argues that assimilation into the Dutch culture is preferable to the development of separate *allochtone* organizations, just as its predecessors had argued against separate Catholic and Protestant schools a century earlier. Christian Democrats and Social Democrats, based on their own experience, see more mileage in such separate organizations as contributing to the emancipation of the immigrant minorities, and are also more accepting of a greater cultural diversity in the long run (Trappenburg and Mudde, 2000; Van Thijn, 2000). Regardless of these differences, however, all major parties have elected *allochtone* MPs to Parliament. After the 2012 elections, 15 *allochtone* MPs were elected, or 10 per cent (most with a Turkish or Moroccan background). Even the Christian Democratic parliamentary caucus regularly includes Muslims. In 2006, the Balkenende IV government was the first to contain *allochtone* junior ministers.

For these reasons it is more accurate to see attitudes with regard to multi-culturalism as forming a dimension on which people take different, often strongly held, positions , rather than as a social cleavage setting *autochtonen* and *allochtonen* apart as social groups or subcultures. As such it is part of a more general cultural dimension identified by Kriesi et al. (2008). We shall return to this cultural dimension, and to the question of whether it is replacing the religious dimension, in Chapters 3 and 4.

The Consequences of Depillarization

The absence of the development of new social cleavages brings us back to depillarization and its consequences. In Lijphart's view, it was the social cleavages that prompted Dutch elites to abide by a number of 'rules of the game' to facilitate cooperation and safeguard democratic stability. The erosion of the social cleavages led naturally to a debate about the continued relevance of elite cooperation and its rules of the game. Sometimes authors discerned the development of a more adversarial style, but at other times a 'restoration' of consociational practices has been observed.

In terms of Lijphart's typology of democracies (see Figure 2.3), depillarization has transferred Dutch society into another category. Now a supposedly more homogeneous society in combination with continued elite cooperation would classify Dutch politics as a 'depoliticized democracy'. However, this is not what most authors observed during the late 1960s and early 1970s. They noted that political competition seemed to intensify, partly as the result of a change in electoral strategy by the political parties in an effort to win over depillarized voters. Some even speak of a tacit agreement by Social Democrats and Liberals to accelerate the demise of the religious pillars by mutual polarization. Partly, also, intensified competition was the result of attempts at democratization.

The elitist character of the politics of accommodation came under increasing attacks. The Netherlands was not the only country in the 1960s where calls for direct democracy in universities and factories could be heard, and where political parties faced increasing competition from single-issue citizen action groups. In the Netherlands, however, the critique was not only that representative democracy was not enough, but also that representative democracy itself was not fully opera- tive. It was the combination of depillarization and calls for democratization that led Lijphart (1975) to speak of 'the breakdown of the politics of accommodation'. In his view, the Dutch elites realized the dangers inherent in the disillusionment with the politics of accommodation. Once more, they showed their wisdom and prudence by resorting to a 'second self-denying prophecy': the conscious introduction of a measured amount of competition into the political system. This brings the Nether- lands into the more familiar category of centripetal democracy, together with such countries as the UK and the USA. The consequences of this transformation can be seen in Table 2.3, where we contrast Lijphart's seven rules of the game of conso- ciationalism, with what Daalder observed as the fashionable opinions after 1967 (Daalder, 1974).

Since 1977, however, the new political style seems to have evaporated, and Van Praag (1993) observes a restoration of most of Lijphart's old set of rules, though some of them are now used selectively. Continued depoliticization is masked by symbolic politicization, and the only real change has occurred with regard to 'the government's right to govern', but in a different direction than predicted by the fashionable opinions of the 1967–77 interlude.What we have summarized as a greater politicization of the government's composition in Table 2.2 consists of three developments mentioned separately by Van Praag: a greater involvement of the parties in the governmental majority in policy-making, and the general accept- ance that the leader of the largest party in the coalition should become the Prime Minister, and that the composition of the government cannot be changed without going to the electorate first. We shall return to this politicization of the government in Chapter 5. Lijphart now agrees that there have been few significant changes in the elite culture since 1967. He attributes the original 'myopic and exaggerated interpretation of the degrees of difference and change' (Lijphart, 1989, p. 140) that led him to suggest a second self-denying prophecy to his presence in the Nether- lands at the time. If we use the indicators of consensus democracy rather than those of consociational democracy the decline is also quite small: since 1967 there have been more minimum-winning and fewer surplus-majority coalitions. And if

> the present consensual atmosphere differs from that of the days of pillarisation ... it is rather due to converging visions on many political issues than the result of negotiations among political elites despite their initial differences in principle. To exaggerate: 'com- promises then, consensus now'. (Koole and Daalder, 2002, p. 39)

Since Koole and Daalder wrote those sentences, the 'long year of 2002' (see Box 2.1) has resulted once again in the observation of a shift away from consensus-seeking towards a more confrontational style. Pennings and Keman (2008) mention the populist exposure of the established parties' cartel, conflict and debate about immigration and integration, more polarization and politicization as indications of a more adversarial political climate. They suggest that Dutch politics is best described as 'pendulum consociationalism', a mixture of consensual and adversarial styles, with the mixture constantly being adjusted to changes in the electoral climate (Pennings and Keman, 2008, pp. 174–6).

This brings us back to the debate over what caused Dutch elites to prefer cooperation over competition. *If it was pillarization that necessitated the politics of accommodation, how may we explain a continuation of accommodationist practices, even in some dynamic mixture, after the pillars have crumbled?* We suggest that the importance of pillarization has been overemphasized by most authors. It was this emphasis that led to the puzzle of increasing pillarization after the pacification of 1917, and it is this emphasis that now leads to the puzzle of continued consociationalism after depillarization. Pillarization, however, was only one of the threats to stable democracy, and probably not the most important one. Earlier in this chapter we argued that the minority position of *all* the subcultures might have been the crucial incentive for the elites to cooperate instead of to compete. Whatever else

Table 2.2   *The Changing Rules of Dutch Politics*

1917–67 *Rules of the game observed by Lijphart, 1968*	1967–77 *Proclaimed rules of the game observed by Daalder, 1974*	1977–2001 *Rules of the game observed by Van Praag, 1993*	2001– *Rules of the game observed by Pennings and Keman, 2008*
The business of politics	Exposure of 'establishment ideology'	The business of politics	Critical view of bureaucracy and party cartels
Agreement to disagree	Conflict	Agreement to disagree	Conflict on certain issues (ethnic minorities, EU)
Summit diplomacy	Self-determination at the base	Selective summit diplomacy	Selective summit diplomacy
Proportionality	Polarization	Proportionality	Polarization and catch-all-ism
Depoliticization	Politicization	Symbolic politicization	Politicization
Secrecy	Open government	Selective openness	Secrecy with 'open' image building
The government's right to govern with little interference from Parliament	A critique of 'the decline of Parliament', 'the fourth branch of the government'	Politicization of the government's composition	Selective politicization of government's composition

has changed, all political parties are still far removed from a parliamentary majority. This provides the explanation of continued accommodation without pillarization. The political style Daalder observed in 1974 was a temporary aberration, brought about by the fact that depillarization revived hopes, in particular within the Labour Party, of a majority. As soon as the dust had settled, the Social Democrats realized their mistake, abandoned their majoritarian strategy and calls for reform, and resumed traditional consensual practices, culminating in their cooperation with their 'class enemy', the Liberals, in 'purple' coalitions. Similarly, the post-2002 party-political polarization may prove to be a temporary strategy to take the wind out of the populists' sails. After all, the Netherlands remains a country of minorities which entertain no hope of becoming majorities.

3

Political Parties and the Party System

Parties and Consociational Democracy

Political parties featured prominently in the analysis of the development of Dutch consociational democracy, discussed in Chapter 2. Yet, according to Kurt Luther:

> there has to date been no attempt on the part of those concerned with the comparative study of parties to undertake a systematic examination of the operation of parties and party systems in consociational politics. Nor has consociational theory itself ever paid much attention to what I believe to be the central role within consociational democracies of political parties and party systems. (Luther, 1999, p. 5)

In spite of this view, in the Netherlands at least, the relationship between the party system and the system of pillarization and accommodation described in the previous chapter seems obvious. The growth of the Social Democratic and Christian Democratic political parties was tied integrally to the development of the pillars, and the resultant party system reflected the subcultural composition of Dutch society. Luther expects political parties to be strong and dominant in consociational democracies. He sees the parties as the control rooms of the politics of accommodation. Parties are expected to monopolize the relations between the elites of the pillars, not only in politics but also in other spheres of life. To be able to deliver on whatever a compromise with other parties might entail, the pillars' party elites should also be able to control their own pillars. To this end they can be expected to monopolize the right to represent the pillar, without much competition from other parties. Mobilization of the rank and file in party membership is expected to be high, and the parties to be tightly and hierarchically organized. In contrast, any erosion of pillarization can be expected to be accompanied by a weakening of the parties (Luther, 1999). In this chapter we discuss both the party system and the parties' organizational structure to see whether these expectations are borne out by the Dutch experience.

Political Party System

Both numerical and ideological criteria are used to analyse party systems. The number of parties alone has been shown to affect the relations among the parties. Depending on their ideological proximity, however, parties can either be competitors or opponents. For this purpose we will group parties together into ideological party families. This leads us to a discussion of the number of ideological dimensions that structure the Dutch party system.

The Numerical Criterion

The simplest classification of party systems is in terms of numbers – one-, two- or multi-party systems. Giovanni Sartori has expanded on this rough classification by denoting three types of one-party systems, and three types of multi-party systems – 'limited pluralism', 'extreme pluralism' and 'atomized' (Sartori, 1976). Since the development of political parties, the Netherlands has clearly always had a multi-party system. It might be seen as an example of what is known as 'Duverger's law', which states that 'the simple-majority system with second-ballot and proportional representation favours multipartyism' (Riker, 1982, p. 76; see also Duverger, 1959). After the introduction of direct elections for the Second Chamber of Parliament in 1848, representatives had to achieve a majority of the vote in the district. If no candidate did so in the first round, a second round was held between the two candidates who gained the most votes in the first round. Until 1896, some districts elected a single representative, whereas others elected two or sometimes more. Beginning in 1896, all districts were single-member districts, but still with run-off elections to achieve an absolute majority.

The introduction of universal suffrage and proportional representation in 1917 made it easier for even more parties to take part in elections. Table 3.1 shows that, at the first election (in 1918) with proportional representation and universal (male) suffrage, no fewer than 32 parties submitted lists. Of these, 17 exceeded the electoral threshold and gained seats in Parliament. The number of lists increased at the following election, but an increase in the electoral threshold from 0.5 per cent to 0.75 per cent reduced the number of successful parties to 10. The peak number of lists submitted (54) was in 1933; of these, 14 were successful. After that election, parties were required to make a deposit of 250 guilders (equivalent now to €113), which was returned only if a specified percentage (but less than the electoral threshold) of votes was achieved. This reduced the number of lists presented at the last election before the Second World War to only 20, of which 10 were successful.

At the first post-war elections, the number of lists presented tended to be lower than previously, in part because of attempts to restructure the party system. The number of parties in Parliament were also lower than before, with only seven or eight represented. However, in the mid-1960s, when the system of pillarization began to weaken, the numbers began to increase again. Since 1967, in any given election, 20 or more parties have generally submitted lists at the elections, and up to 14 parties have been successful in getting candidates elected.

Just counting parties, however, does not prove to be particularly satisfactory in describing a party system. Some parties are quite inconsequential and hardly deserving of being counted. Thus, Sartori added a criterion of 'relevancy' to the counting operation. A party is relevant if it participates in governing coalitions

Table 3.1   *Number of Parties Contesting the Election and Number of Parties Achieving Representation, 1918–2012*

Year	Number of lists competing	Number of parties achieving representation in Parliament	Percentage of vote won by five (after 1977, three) major parties	Number of seats won by five (after 1977, three) major parties
1918	32	17	87.2	87/100
1922	48	10	87.8	94/100
1925	32	11	88.4	94/100
1929	36	12	89.1	92/100
1933	54	14	83.9	87/100
1937	20	10	84.6	89/100
1946	10	7	86.2	88/100
1948	12	8	87.0	89/100
1952	13	8	86.7	90/100
1956	10	7	91.5	94/100
1959	13	8	91.6	142/150
1963	18	10	87.5	135/150
1967	23	11	78.9	123/150
1971	28	14	71.7	113/150
1972	23	14	73.1	113/150
1977	24	11	83.7	130/150
1981	28	10	76.0	118/150
1982	20	12	83.0	128/150
1986	27	9	85.0	133/150
1989	25	9	81.8	125/150
1994	26	12	66.2	102/150
1998	22	9	72.1	112/150
2002	16	10	58.4	90/150
2003	20	9	73.8	114/150
2006	24	10	62.4	96/150
2010	19	10	55.5	85/150
2012	20	10	59.9	92/150

Source: Data from the Dutch Electoral Council.

or has the 'power of intimidation' or 'blackmail potential'. In the Netherlands, certainly not all the parties can fulfil one of these criteria. After 1918, five parties dominated Dutch politics. The Catholics, Anti-Revolutionaries, and Christian Historicals were, with few exceptions, represented in all Cabinets between 1918 and 1939. Until 1939, the Social Democrats were excluded from the government coalition, but it would be strange not to count them as a relevant party. The Liberals were not particularly strong in this period and were dispersed over more than one party. Counting them as a single group, however, brings the count to five.

After the Second World War, the parties returned, some with new names (KVP, ARP, CHU, PvdA and VVD) and these five (later three as the result of a merger) parties dominated Dutch politics until quite recently. The data in Table 3.1 show the extent of this domination, but also that they are losing their grip. From 1918 to 1963, the Big Five gained between 84 per cent and 92 per cent of the votes cast, and held no less than 87 per cent of the seats in Parliament. In fact, between 1918 and 1967, the three Christian Democratic parties always held 50 per cent or more of the parliamentary seats, so that if considered as a single bloc one might almost describe the system in Sartori's terms as 'one-party-predominant'. However, to do so would ignore some considerable political differences that existed between these three parties in the past, and Sartori counted each of the Christian Democratic parties separately. This presented him with difficulties in determining his classification system. While at times he drew the line between 'moderate pluralism' and 'polarized pluralism' at four, the five Dutch parties presented an anomaly. Despite there being five parties, however, the Dutch political system was quite stable and thus hardly fitted into his category of 'polarized pluralism'. Thus, at least to an extent because of the Dutch case, he drew the dividing line at a point between five and six.

Perhaps he should have stayed with his original cut-off point, since after 1967 it has not become easier for anyone trying to count the relevant parties in the Netherlands. After 1967, the stranglehold of these five major parties began to loosen, and in 1971 they dropped to only 72 per cent of the vote. Losses by two of the Christian Democratic parties led to the merger of the three into a single new party, the Christian Democratic Appeal, thus reducing the number of dominant parties to three. In part because of this merger, the now three parties (CDA, Labour and Liberal) made a partial recovery in the 1980s, but heavy losses in 1994 reduced their total share of the vote to 66.2 per cent. This percentage rose to some extent in 1998 and 2003, but in the most recent elections it has dropped below 60 per cent. For the first time since 1946, one of the three was not among the three largest parties in Parliament in 2002, and in 2012 the once mighty Christian Democrats dropped to become only the fifth-largest party in the Second Chamber.

Losing their grip on politics implies that other parties have become relevant in Sartori's terms. As the number of MPs provided by the major parties has declined, other parties have been necessary in order to form government coalitions. In 1971, for example, a new party, DS'70, was brought into the governing coalition, and the following year two more new parties – D66 and the Radicals – joined a new coalition. D66 in particular has become a regular partner in governing coalitions (see Table 5.1 on page 147). When the List Pim Fortuyn became the second-largest party in parliament after the 2002 election, its relevance was obvious, since a coalition could hardly have been formed without it. In 2006, no fewer than seven of the ten parties in the Second Chamber were involved in at least some way in the formation discussions, and in the end yet another new party, the Christian Union, entered government. In 2010, the Freedom Party did not officially enter the government coalition, but in a separate agreement lent its support in what has been called 'contract parliamentarism' (see Chapter 5).

During the period of the Rutte I Cabinet, even the SGP might be considered to have become 'relevant'. Sartori did not count the orthodox Calvinist parties as relevant parties, even though the SGP has been represented continuously in Parliament since 1922. However, following the provincial elections of 2011, the government coalition failed to achieve a majority in the First Chamber of Parliament, and was forced to seek support from the SGP. The Rutte II Cabinet holds only 30 of the 75 seats in the First Chamber, which means that it must seek the support of other parties in order to pass its legislation.

With the introduction of contract parliamentarism and the necessity to seek support from non-coalition parties in the First Chamber, it becomes difficult to determine which parties are 'relevant', or more precisely, which are not. In any case, the total number of relevant parties is now somewhere between seven and ten, and in any case far too many for the Netherlands to be included as an example of 'moderate pluralism'. Thus the question arises as to whether the number has increased to such an extent that the system is in trouble. With opinions based to a considerable extent on the unfortunate experiences in the German Weimar Republic and French Fourth Republic, political observers have at times expressed a fear that having too many political parties poses a threat to a stable democracy. The fear has been that when fragmentation is too great, it becomes almost impossible to forge a majority coalition. To what extent this is indeed happening in the Netherlands is a question to which we shall return in Chapter 11.

Party Families

Dealing with up to 10 parties can be challenging to a newcomer to Dutch politics, but Dutch voters seem to handle these large numbers with relative ease. It is clear that some means is necessary to bring structure into such a large number. Two means of providing structure are examined here. First, the parties are introduced as members of party families. The notion of a party family is based on the premise that parties within a family share many ideological aspects (Mair and Mudde, 1998). Though they are distinct entities, they may be seen as variations on a common theme, such as Christian democracy, social democracy, liberalism and so on. Families can place parties into groups, but something is also needed to connect the groups. This is most often done by attempting to order parties into a limited number of ideological dimensions, the most familiar of which is the left–right dimension. This forms the second means of providing structure, but first we look at the families.

Christian Democrats

As was described in Chapter 2, the growth of political parties was tied integrally to the development of the pillars. For the Protestants, organization was a result in no small part of the efforts of the nineteenth-century leader, Abraham Kuyper, a master organizer who founded or helped to found many of the most important institutions within the pillar. He was responsible for the organization of those orthodox groups that had broken away, in part with his help, from the Dutch Reformed Church into the *Gereformeerde* churches. He was also responsible for setting up a newspaper to be the mouthpiece of the movement, and a university – the Free University of Amsterdam – to train an intellectual elite. In 1879, he founded the first mass political party of the Netherlands – the Anti-Revolutionary Party (ARP).

The purpose of this movement, and its associated institutions, was the emancipation of those orthodox Calvinists known in the nineteenth century as the '*Kleine Luyd*en'. Kuyper argued that sovereignty was given by God and could best be exercised through the Orangist monarchy. Opposition to the idea of popular sovereignty, first introduced into the modern world by the French Revolution, led to the choice of the name Anti-Revolutionary Party.

Catholics had perhaps even more reason than the orthodox Calvinists to organize an emancipation movement. They had at times been denied political rights and the freedom to practise their religion openly; in Amsterdam and other older cities, one can still visit their 'hidden churches'. The southern, and predominantly Catholic, provinces of North Brabant and Limburg had never been given equal status within the Republic and were governed as semi-colonies (*Generaliteitslanden*). Steps were taken in 1798 and 1848 to guarantee the freedom of religion, but the Catholics had to wait until 1853 before it became possible to re-establish the church hierarchy.

Catholics were elected to Parliament in the nineteenth century, but it was only at the beginning of the twentieth century that the first Catholic political party appeared. The Roman Catholic State Party was established in 1926. With the support of the church hierarchy, this party was able to become, and remain, virtually the only party for Catholics. After the Second World War, the party was re-established with a new name, the Catholic People's Party (KVP). Opportunity for membership was formally extended to non-Catholics, but it continued to be almost exclusively Catholic. In no small part owing to the efforts of the Catholic clergy, the Roman Catholic State Party and its successor the Catholic People's Party were essentially unchallenged within the Catholic pillar, and functioned as the political arm of the Catholic movement.

Protestants, however, have always been more prone to schism. From 1892 to 2004, there were two main religious denominations within the Protestant pillar – the

Dutch Reformed and the *Gereformeerden*. Politically, it did not take long before a conflict within the Anti-Revolutionary Party led to the establishment of a new party. At the end of the nineteenth century, controversy arose within the Anti-Revolutionary Party concerning the place of the Dutch Reformed Church. This problem was compounded by disagreement over one of the major political questions of the day – the extension of the franchise – as well as the question of the independence of parliamentary politicians from external party organizations. Those opposed to the expansion of suffrage left the party and eventually formed the Christian Historical Union (CHU). This party tended to draw its support from conservative elements within the Dutch Reformed Church, but, as will be shown in Chapter 4, it was never as successful in mobilizing as large a proportion of the believers of that church as the Catholic and Anti-Revolutionary parties were within their related church groups.

Although these three parties were by far the most important of Dutch religious parties, numerous other such parties have been founded. None of those that sprang up within the Catholic pillar were of lasting duration, but this was not so for the Protestants. Small, usually orthodox Calvinist parties have long had a place in Dutch politics. The oldest of these is the Political Reformed Party (SGP), which was founded in 1918 and has been represented in the Second Chamber of Parliament continuously since 1922. The party came about as a result of disagreements within the *Gereformeerde* movement (including a group within the Dutch Reformed Church) over the question of separation of church and state, and the possibility of cooperation with the Catholics. The party remains ultra-conservative in many of its positions, in particular on moral and ethical issues. It might have gone almost unnoticed among such a large number of parties, except that it has been newsworthy because of its discussions concerning the political role of women. In 2005 the courts ruled that the government subsidy for the party had to be stopped because of its discrimination against women. After much prayer and deliberation, the party amended its rules in 2006 to allow women to become members, but expressed the view that women should not have leading positions, either in the party or in representative bodies. However, pressure following a 2010 decision by the Supreme Court of the Netherlands forced the party to rescind the formal requirements that women could not become candidates for office. At the 2014 municipal elections, the first female candidate of the SGP was elected.

Other Protestant parties have emerged since the Second World War. Yet another disagreement over theology led to a walkout from the *Gereformeerde* church and the establishment of a new church with its own political party, the Reformed Political League (GPV). The party just missed achieving the electoral quotient in 1952 and ensuing elections until representation was achieved in 1963. It then held at least one seat until merging into the Christian Union in 2000 (in the party's official Dutch name, the two words are written with no space between them). Political issues and electoral considerations seem to have replaced theological disputes as the source of new parties in the Christian Democratic family. In the late 1960s and early 1970s, electoral support for the Catholic People's Party and the Christian Historical Union declined rapidly (see Chapter 4). Stimulated at least in part by these vote losses, discussions concerning the formation of a unified Christian Democratic party were accelerated. Various forms of cooperation led eventually to the formation of a single parliamentary caucus and a combined list of candidates in 1977. The success of the combined list swept away any final reservations, and in 1980, just slightly more than 100 years after the founding of the Anti-Revolutionary Party, it merged with the Christian Historicals and Catholics to form the Christian Democratic Appeal (CDA).

Disapproval over this merger and opposition to the liberalization of abortion legislation seem to have been the main impetuses for the founding in 1975 of the Reformed Political Federation (RPF). Though less homogeneous than the other Protestant parties, it succeeded in achieving representation in Parliament from 1981 until it put aside its differences to merge with the GPV to form the Christian Union in 2000. In addition to orthodox splits, a few leftist parties also emerged from within the ranks of the Christian Democratic parties. The most important of these descendants was the Radical Party (PPR), which originated in 1968 when four members of Parliament bolted from the Catholic Party. They were soon joined by leftist-oriented ex-members of the Anti-Revolutionary Party and were led to their greatest electoral success in 1972 by a former ARP member, Bas De Gaay Fortman. Though the party may be said to have had its origins in one Christian Democratic party, and its best-known leader came from another Christian Democratic party, the PPR soon lost any clear religious identification and came to be considered a secular leftist party. In 1989, it became one of the partners in the Green Left party (see below). Also involved in this merger was the short-lived Evangelical People's Party, founded in 1980, which had held one seat in Parliament from 1982 to 1986.

Socialists and Social Democrats
The historian Ernst Kossmann wrote 'Socialism came too soon to the Netherlands' (Kossmann, 1978, p. 345). By this he meant that when the ideology of socialism arrived via Germany, conditions were not ripe for a mass socialist movement. The economy, which had initially reached its height because of trade, was in the middle to late nineteenth century based mainly on agricultural production (see Chapter 9). With late industrialization, no large industrial proletariat existed in which socialism could take root. Instead, the first support for working-class movements was found among artisans, urban skilled workers, canal- and peat-diggers, and economically depressed farmers and agricultural labourers. In fact, it was a northern, rural district that sent the first socialist representative, Ferdinand Domela Nieuwenhuis, to Parliament in 1888.

When an industrial proletariat did begin to develop, the socialist movement found itself thwarted by the earlier efforts of Calvinists and Catholics. Workers who maintained their religious beliefs were organized into their respective organizations, including trade unions and political parties. The socialists could only appeal to the non-religious, who while growing in number were still only a minority of the population. Nevertheless, socialists did produce organizations that paralleled and rivalled those of the religious groups, such as newspapers, trade unions and youth organizations.

The first socialist political party was established in 1882 and adopted a programme that was modelled on the, predominantly Marxist, Gotha Programme of its German counterpart. However, as a frustrated Domela Nieuwenhuis moved towards anarchism, a new party, the Social Democratic Workers' Party (SDAP), was established in 1894. It also took its ideological inspiration from German socialists, relying on the more reformist programme adopted by the German Social Democratic Party at the congress in Erfurt in 1891. Though modest in its beginnings, it eventually emerged as the dominant social democratic party. After half-hearted and futile revolutionary gestures in 1918, the party gradually became less revolutionary, and in the 1930s rejected revolutionary reactions to the Great Depression. It turned more towards plan socialism, and in putting forward a national plan to deal with economic problems showed its desire and willingness to cooperate within the system with other parties. In 1939, two social-democrat ministers finally entered the government.

Together with all parties apart from National Socialist Movement (NSB), the party was banned during the German occupation. Following the war, the party re-established, dropping the remainder of its Marxist trappings and changing its name to the Labour Party, or literally, Party of Work (PvdA). By doing so it hoped to produce a 'breakthrough' (*Doorbraak*) that would broaden its appeal and increase its electorate. Despite the new party becoming a regular participant in government coalitions, it still has never come close to obtaining a majority of the vote, generally attracting between a quarter and a third of the vote. In 1995, party leader Wim Kok called on the party to 'shake off its ideological feathers' and move further towards the centre of the political spectrum. Though few elements of a pure socialist ideology can be found in the party today, adherents of the party are still referred to as either socialists or social democrats.

Socialists, like Protestants, have often been troubled by schisms within their ranks. The earliest important break occurred at the beginning of the twentieth century when a group was expelled from the SDAP and in 1909 organized what was to become the Communist Party in the Netherlands (CPN). This party first won representation in Parliament in 1918 and achieved its highpoint in the first election after the Second World War when it won the support of 10 per cent of the electorate. It remained continuously in Parliament until 1986, when disagreements between 'reformers', who were particularly concerned about such issues as women's emancipation, and the more traditional members, who held to a stricter Marxist–Leninist line, led to a split in the party. Both groups failed to obtain sufficient votes to achieve representation in Parliament at that election, and in 1989 the party joined with three other small leftist parties to form the Green Left.

Another splinter party was established during the Cold War (1957) out of protest against the militarism of both the East and West. The name chosen clearly indicated the orientation of the party: Pacifist Socialist Party (PSP). It was represented in Parliament between 1959 and 1989, when it too merged into Green Left.

Though most of the parties that split from the main social democratic party are more radical, there has also been a split to the right. In the 1960s, a group calling itself 'New Left' and calling for closer adherence to socialist principles gained considerable influence in the Labour Party. In reaction, a group of more pragmatic members walked out and formed Democratic Socialists '70 (DS'70). The party had, however, only a short-lived success; it gained eight seats in Parliament and even participated in the governing coalition in 1971 but subsequently lost electoral support and was disbanded.

The final party in this family did not arise out of the Labour Party, but emerged from a split within the Communist Party. A group of Maoist dissidents broke away to form the Socialist Party in 1972. Its first successes were at the local level. Only after five unsuccessful attempts did it finally enter Parliament in 1994. It uses the name Socialist Party, but should not be confused with the Labour Party (in Dutch, the confusion does not exist, since both are more well known by their abbreviations – SP for the Socialist Party and PvdA for the Labour party).

The SP has been described as a leftist-populist party. Its populism is found primarily in its anti-elite attitudes (De Lange and Rooduijn, 2011). For example, for a time the party used the catchy slogan, 'Vote Against', symbolized by a splattered tomato. Though it is not opposed to European cooperation, it is anti-EU in the sense that it opposes transferring national powers to European institutions and the formation of a European superstate. And, while it is not anti-immigration, it decries the fact that the question of integration was left to the parties on the right. The SP calls for mixed neighbourhoods, including young and old, rich and poor, and native and foreign born; in recent years, the party has moderated its views, and expressed a willingness to accept governmental responsibility. Prior to the 2012 election, the party leader, Emile Roemer, was even seen as a potential Prime Minister, but so far such possibilities have not materialized. The party has been described by some as extreme left, and its success in recent elections has raised concerns about the polarization of the party system and the consequences for the stability of the political system as a whole (see Chapter 11).

A Particular Shade of Green

One would think that a party that includes 'left' in its name should be placed in the socialist family. Indeed, in terms of social and economic policy, it well might be included. However, it is the first part of its name 'Green Left' (since 1993 the words have been written closed up in the official Dutch name) that warrants giving it a somewhat separate status. In his discussions of the emergence of post-materialist attitudes in industrialized societies, Ronald Inglehart predicted the emergence of such post-materialist parties, and even mentioned D66 (see below) as being among the first such parties in Europe (Inglehart, 1977, p. 250). D66, however, though long conscious of its image as an environmental party, did not adopt the 'Green' nomenclature. This left the possibility open for the party that resulted in 1989 from the merger of four existing parties – the Communist Party, the Pacifist Socialists, the

Radicals, and a small religious party, the Evangelical People's Party. They chose the name Green Left to symbolize their old (leftist) and new (green) orientation. In fact, some observers have accused the party of being an unripe tomato – green only on the outside, but red at heart.

The degree of 'redness' has continued to be disputed, also within the party. During the period of the Purple coalition (1994–2002), with the CDA in disarray after its electoral defeat in 1994, the Green Left was often seen as the most vociferous opposition party. After that period, party leaders such as Femke Halsema and Jolanda Sap moved the party towards the centre. Prior to the 2006 election, Halsema indicated a willingness to join a coalition, and in 2010 she participated in early discussions concerning a possible 'purple-plus' coalition, but this partnership did not emerge. In 2011, when the Freedom Party refused to support the government proposal to continue its presence in Afghanistan with a police training mission, the VVD and CDA were forced to look to other parties in Parliament (see Box 10.1 on page 257). Now under the leadership of Jolande Sap, the parliamentary party, together with D66 and the Christian Union, took the controversial step of supporting the proposal. This grouping then became known as the Kunduz coalition. In April 2012, when the government fell after the Freedom Party refused to accept budget reduction proposals, the Kunduz coalition re-emerged with proposals that were in time to avert a fine from the European Union for violation of the Stability and Growth Pact. These actions, however, seem to have contributed to the loss of support for Green Left at the elections of 2012, leaving the party to again debate its future course.

Liberals
From the founding of the Dutch Republic in the sixteenth century until the beginning of the nineteenth century, political conflict regularly centred on divisions between sections of the urban patriciate and the 'Orangists' – the supporters of the House of Orange who could be found predominantly among the lower classes of society and among the more orthodox Protestants. However, with participation in politics limited, there was little need for organizations to mobilize and channel political activity, and within the urban elite various ideological trends could be identified. Nevertheless, this elite produced a social and political system that, at least by the standards of the time and the surrounding countries, could be considered quite tolerant. The revolutionary struggle for freedom of religion was not quickly forgotten, and while certain outward manifestations of Catholicism were restricted or forbidden, the individual's right to believe as she or he chose was generally respected. As noted in Chapter 1, this open climate attracted many groups from abroad, including French Huguenots and English Separatists.

This liberal social and political climate became the breeding ground for the philosophy of liberalism that became increasingly important politically at the middle of the nineteenth century. Under the leadership of Johan Rudolf Thorbecke, a new Constitution, which provided for a directly elected Chamber of Parliament and for ministers responsible to Parliament, was drawn up in 1848. During the latter half of the nineteenth century, Liberals were prominent both in politics and in many areas of social life, such as the universities, the media and business. As mentioned in Chapter 2, the Liberals were never highly organized, and some authors have questioned whether one can speak of a Liberal pillar. Nevertheless, they were sufficiently important politically and socially to provide a common foe against which the Protestants, Catholics and Social Democrats could pit themselves in their struggle for equality.

Lacking a mass movement and mass organization, the influence of the Liberals declined sharply after the introduction of universal suffrage and proportional representation. Prior to the Second World War there were various Liberal parties, but even working together they seldom managed to gain more than 10 per cent of the vote. After the war, one of the Liberal parties re-emerged as the Party of Freedom, while another joined the new Labour Party. However, Pieter Oud and his followers soon left the PvdA and together with the Party of Freedom formed a new party in 1948 – called the People's Party for Freedom and Democracy (VVD).

Until 1972 the image of the party remained associated with the urban patricians of the past, and support for the party continued to hover around the 10 per cent figure that had been traditional for Liberals before the war. However, under the leadership of Hans Wiegel the party began to change its image. Rather than making an intellectual liberal appeal, Wiegel attempted to broaden the base of the party. He fought against the large size of government brought about by the welfare state. Though perhaps still inspired by nineteenth-century liberal principles of *laissez-faire*, and still viewed as liberal on certain social or ethical questions such as abortion and euthanasia, in twentieth-century economic terms the party had become the most conservative of the major Dutch parties.

With secularization and the decline of the Christian Democrats, the VVD emerged from the 2010 election as the largest party in Parliament, albeit with only just over 20 per cent of the vote. For the first time since 1918 a liberal, Mark Rutte, became the new Prime Minister. The party grew at the 2012 election to 26.6 per cent of the vote (41 seats in the Second Chamber), its best result ever, and Rutte again became Prime Minister.

The second member of the Liberal family can better be viewed as an adopted member than a true offspring. D66 did not emerge as a member of any particular political family, but as an attempt in 1966 to 'explode' the existing party system. The party was begun by a group of Amsterdam intellectuals, who called their party Democrats '66. As the years passed the date has remained, but the name is generally shortened to simply D66. The party pushed for constitutional reforms that would produce a more 'democratic' political system; for example, the direct election of the Prime Minister, and a district system of election to Parliament. It led in the abolition of compulsory voting in 1970, but has otherwise had little success in gaining support for reforms (see Chapter 4). The party has experienced wide swings in support over the years, but seemingly has achieved a permanent spot in the party system. To do so it has moved from being simply a reform party to one generally described as progressive-liberal, in contrast to the VVD, which is seen as conservative-liberal. In the European Parliament, D66 has joined the VVD in the Liberal parliamentary group, even though D66 is one of the most pro-EU parties and the VVD has grown more sceptical about European integration.

Populist Right

Parties of the extreme right have seldom been of great electoral importance in the Netherlands. In 1931, admirers of Mussolini and Hitler founded the National Socialist Movement (NSB), which, under the leadership of Anton Mussert, achieved its peak of electoral success in 1935 when it gained 8 per cent of the vote nationwide at the provincial elections. One can only speculate on what might have happened to the party if the Germans had not invaded. During the occupation, the NSB was the only political party not banned by the Germans. However, it was declared guilty of treasonous activities and banned by the government in exile in London. After the war the party did not return and many of its former members were prosecuted.

In the 1960s a party emerged that was often referred to, even by its leader, as a rightist party. The *Boerenpartij* ('Farmers' Party') had its roots in the dissatisfaction of farmers. Ideologically the party is somewhat difficult to locate; its opposition to governmental intervention, especially in agriculture, and its commitment to law and order and traditional principles help to justify its placement here. Its electoral success, however, may have been more related to dissatisfaction with the pillarized system than with sympathy with its right-wing populist approach. The leader of the party, Hendrik 'Farmer' Koekoek, appealed to voters who were dissatisfied with the system and with the dominant political parties. The party reached its electoral zenith in 1967 with seven parliamentary seats, but was beset by internal divisions and departed from Parliament in 1981.

Between then and 2002, various attempts were made to begin a populist movement on the right. These attempts generally played on fears and hatred directed at the immigrant workers who had originally been imported to support the economic boom of the 1960s. The size of such radical groups was in general smaller in the Netherlands than in some other European countries, but because of the low electoral threshold (see Chapter 4) such parties were twice able to elect a representative to Parliament. In 1982, the so-called Centre Party elected Hans Janmaat to Parliament. After internal party conflicts, Janmaat was ejected from the party in 1984 but retained his seat in Parliament. He founded a new party, the Centre Democrats (CD), but neither party was able to achieve representation in 1986. Janmaat returned to Parliament in 1989 but was ignored and ostracized by the other members. His party was unable to gain enough votes to retain a seat in 1998 and he disappeared from the Second Chamber.

Janmaat was not an inspiring or popular leader, and could thus easily be ignored and even prosecuted for his statements. However, this did not mean that there was no unrest in the electorate that could be capitalized on by the right person. That person was Pim Fortuyn, who single-handedly produced the greatest success for a new party in the history of the Netherlands. Pim Fortuyn was a publicist and part-time professor who entered politics in the autumn of 2001 (see Box 2.1 on page 28). His appeal was based on disgruntlement with the Purple coalition that had governed for eight years, and a feeling among parts of the electorate that their views were being ignored, particularly on questions related to immigration and the integration of immigrants into Dutch society. While some observers found parallels with parties in France, Belgium and Austria, Fortuyn himself rejected such comparisons alongside any attempts to label him and his party as an extreme-right movement. Even though he was assassinated nine days before the election, his party entered Parliament with 26 seats and joined the Christian Democrats and Liberals to form the new coalition. However, suffering greatly from internal dissension, the party was soon dropped from the coalition, lost heavily at the 2003 elections and disappeared from Parliament at the 2006 elections. The party was disbanded on 1 January 2008.

The legacy, if not in name then certainly in many respects in terms of appeal, was carried on by two dissidents from the Liberal Party. In September 2004, after clashes with the other members of his parliamentary caucus and with the party leader, Geert Wilders left the party, but retained his seat. He began to form a new 'movement' rather than a party, though this was not easy since, because of his provocative statements on Islam (such as the example already mentioned of calling the Quran a fascist book) he was guarded around the clock. To participate in the elections of 2006, he registered with the Electoral Council (*Kiesraad*) under the name Freedom Party. The name was reminiscent of the Party of Freedom founded in 1946 which became part of the Liberal Party in 1948. For Wilders, the Party of Freedom was the last true liberal party because in his view the Liberal Party had become too much of a social-liberal party. His party is unusual in that it has no organization; that is, no local divisions and no members. The law requires that a party has members, so the membership consists of Wilders himself and the Group-Wilders Foundation. Nevertheless, donations and volunteers are welcomed. In choosing to register his own party, he rebuffed various former Fortuyn supporters who had hoped to form a new party on the right (Lucardie, 2008; Lucardie et al., 2008). See Box 3.1 for a list of Dutch political parties.

For a time Wilders faced competition from another populist right party, also headed by a former Liberal Party politician. During the Balkenende III government, Rita Verdonk served as Minister of Integration and Immigration as a member of the Liberal Party. Having narrowly lost a contest for the Liberal Party leadership, but winning more votes in the 2006 elections than the new leader, she continued after the election to compete for the leadership and was eventually expelled from the party. She set up her own party, which received considerable early support in the opinion polls, but failed to win any seats at the 2010 election (see Van Tuijl, 2011).

BOX 3.1

Dutch Political Parties at a Glance

Parties represented in the Second Chamber 2012

Abbrev.	Full (English) name	Founded	Description
CDA	Christian Democratic Appeal	1973	Major Christian-Democratic party. Formed as a merger of ARP, CHU and KVP (www.cda.nl)
SGP	Political Reformed Party	1918	Orthodox Calvinist party (www.sgp.nl)
CU	Christian Union	2000	Orthodox Calvinist party. Merger of GPV and RPF (www.christenunie.nl)
PvdA	Labour Party	1946	Major social-democratic party. (www.pvda.nl)
SP	Socialist Party	1972	Formerly Maoist, now leftist populist party (www.sp.nl)
GL	Green Left	1989	Environmentalist and leftist party. Merger of CPN, PSP, PPR and EVP (www.groenlinks.nl)
VVD	Liberal Party	1948	Major conservative-liberal party (www.vvd.nl)
D66	Democrats '66	1966	'Progressive-liberal' reform party (www.d66.nl)
PVV	Freedom Party	2004/2006	Originally 'Group Wilders', when founder Geert Wilders left VVD in 2004. The Freedom Party was registered as a party in 2006. Populist and conservative anti-Islam party (www.pvv.nl)
PvdD	Animal Rights Party	2002	Animal rights party (www.partijvoordedieren.nl)
50Plus	50Plus Party	2009	Party protecting the position of older citizens (www.50pluspartij.nl)

Non-family Parties

The reader might hope that discussion of these families would exhaust the possibilities, but the list is not complete, as the Netherlands has never faced a shortage of parties. The electoral laws make it easy to register a name, comparatively easy to get on the ballot, and provide a low threshold for success in achieving representation. Krouwel and Lucardie (2008) counted 63 new parties that took part in the elections held between 1989 and 2006 (including Green Left and the Christian Union that were the result of mergers of previous parties). A few of these parties have achieved success and are worthy of a mention here.

In their typology of new parties, Krouwel and Lucardie find 'advocate' parties to have been the largest group with 18. These parties attempt to represent groups in society that have been overlooked by the established parties. One such group is older voters, and various parties have been formed to promote and protect their interests. In 1994, two such parties – the General Senior Citizens' Association (*Algemeen Ouderen Verbond* – AOV) and the Union 55+ – gained six seats and one seat, respectively, in Parliament. The former was beset with internal difficulties, which led to splits and mergers, but no successor gained representation in 1998. In 2012, a new party, 50Plus, gained two seats in Parliament. Another 'advocate' party has been the Animal Rights Party (the official name is Party for the Animals, but animal rights seems a more familiar designation in English). This party entered Parliament in 2006, obtaining two seats, which were retained at the two subsequent elections. A final party that deserves mention is Liveable Netherlands (*Leefbaar Nederland*). The national party was the outgrowth of a number of local parties, the most prominent of which was Liveable Rotterdam. With Pim Fortuyn leading the list, the party became the largest in the municipal council of Rotterdam. Fortuyn became the list puller for the national list, but after an infamous newspaper interview was forced to step aside (see Box 2.1 on page 28). Without him, the party still succeeded in gaining two seats in the 2002 parliamentary elections. In 2006, the party did not submit a list of candidates and in 2007 ceased to exist.

Dimensionality

Categorizing a large number of political parties into a more limited set of party families is one way of providing some structure for what otherwise might seem a rather large and confusing group of parties. A second means, which is often used by political scientists, and to some extent by voters, journalists and politicians, is to make use of spatial analogies or what are called 'party spaces'. Such a space is defined by one, two, or more 'dimensions'. Whereas party families are essentially categories into which the parties are grouped, dimensions can be used to relate the positions of parties to one another. Parties may be close to or distant from one another in the party space. The dimensions become shorthand way of understanding these relationships between the parties. One such shorthand has already been employed in this book, when in Chapter 2 two basic cleavages in Dutch politics were discussed. Cleavages produce dimensions along which both the opinions and the positions of political parties can be aligned.

One difficulty in the employment of such shorthand is that there is no authority to establish how many dimensions should or will be employed, and what the content of the dimensions is to be (see further in Chapter 4). Yet if the number of dimensions employed is not substantially less than the number of political parties, no simplification or structuring ensues, and without some degree of agreement on the content of the dimensions no communication concerning the relationships between the parties can take place.

Certainly no dimension is employed more frequently, both within the Netherlands and internationally, than the 'left–right' dimension. It is so common that it has already been used in the previous section of this chapter to help define the party families. Somewhat outdated research shows that Dutch voters ranked highly compared with voters in several other countries, in recognition of the left–right dimension, and fairly highly in levels of ideological conceptualization (Klingemann, 1979; Fuchs and Klingemann, 1989). More recent comparative research is not available, but there is no reason to assume that this situation has undergone any radical change.

The ease with which Dutch voters employ the left–right dimension can be seen using by data from the 2012 parliamentary election (see Table 3.2). In Dutch national election studies, respondents are generally asked to place themselves and the various political parties on a left–right dimension; in 2012 they were presented with a scale marked by 11 points, with 0 labelled as left and 10 as right. No fewer than 95 per cent of the respondents were willing and able to place themselves on this scale. When placing most of the parties in 2012, generally only 10–15 per cent of the respondents indicated that they did not know the party, did not know where to place it, or were assigned a missing data code (see Table 3.2, col. 1). Higher percentages (26.1 per cent and 20.4 per cent) were found for the SGP, which is better-known for its religious position than where it stands on the left–right scale, and the Animal Rights Party.

The parties have been ordered in Table 3.2 from top to bottom according to the mean placement by the voters on the left–right scale (see col. 2). With mean placements of 2.44 and 2.55 on the left-right scale, the Socialist Party and GreenLeft are placed closely together on the left. The Labour Party is also placed clearly on the left side of the scale (3.34). Somewhat left of centre is the Animal Rights Party (3.71). The average measure for D66 (4.96) is almost exactly in the centre on the scale. To the right of centre are the three Christian Democratic parties (Christian Union (5.55), CDA (5.73), and SGP (6.24). Finally, the Freedom Party (7.02) and the Liberal Party (7.34) are placed on the right. The latter two have switched positions since their placements in 2010, perhaps reflecting a recognition of some of the policy stands taken by the Freedom Party in previous years.

It is difficult to establish whether these perceptions are correct or not, but one way of checking their accuracy is to compare them with how the members of Parliament who represent these parties place themselves on the same scale. On the eve of the 2006 election, the MPs were asked to participate in research that included this question. More than two-thirds of the members participated in the survey and while the numbers are sometimes small, the results seem to be satisfactory. The mean placements by the MPs can be seen in the final column of Table 3.2. Unfortunately, no member of the Christian Union answered this question, and Geert Wilders, the only representative of the newly founded Freedom Party, did not participate, but the results for the other parties reveal that the ordering of the parties is almost exactly the same as the perceptions of the voters. The Socialist Party, Green Left, and the Labour Party form a group on the left, with D66 somewhat left of centre. The Christian Democratic parties are to the right of centre, placing themselves a little more to the right than as perceived by the electorate, but this may be related to the interpretation of the terms left and right (see below). The MPs of the Liberal Party placed their party the most to the right, but this was before the Freedom Party had entered Parliament. In 2010, a smaller number of MPs participated in a similar survey. The ordering was the same, with a single member of the CU placing his party at the 4.0 position and the two members of the Animal Rights Party placing their party on average at 4.5, only slightly different from where these parties were perceived by the voters (PartiRep MP survey, 2010).

As a shorthand, the terms left and right have both the advantage and disadvantage that they have no prescribed substantive meaning. They are merely a spatial analogy, and the meaning of the terms may change. The origin of these terms is often said to be from the seating arrangements in the Assembly during the French Revolution, in which the radicals sat on the left, and the moderates and aristocrats on the right (Lipschits: 1969, p. 12). In the nineteenth century, the terms, certainly in the Netherlands, referred to the religious convictions on which parties were based. This in turn was based on what the founder of the Anti-Revolutionary Party

Table 3.2 *Voters' Perceptions of Left–Right Position of Political Parties, 2012; and MP placement, 2006*

Party	Percentage unable to place party	Mean placement	Standard deviation of party MPs	Mean self-placement
Socialist Party	10.9	2.44	2.13	1.86
Green Left	10.4	2.55	1.73	2.00
Labour Party	8.1	3.34	1.98	3.38
Animal Rights Party	20.4	3.71	1.89	
D66	14.4	4.96	1.59	4.40
Christian Union	16.8	5.55	2.02	n.a.
CDA	10.0	5.73	1.70	6.14
SGP	26.1	6.24	2.31	7.00
Freedom Party	12.5	7.02	2.85	–
Liberal Party	9.1	7.34	2.12	7.00
Respondents' self-placements	4.5	5.21	2.19	

Sources: Dutch Parliamentary Election Study, 2012; Dutch Parliamentary Study, 2006.

termed the *Antithesis,* the cleavage between believers and non-believers (or pagans, as they were often called) (ibid., p. 49). Parties based on religion (that is, the Bible) were the parties of the right, and those based on secular principles (for example, liberalism, socialism, or communism) were the parties of the left. The major political issue of the day dividing the two blocks was the schools question, which was resolved in the Pacification of 1917 (see Chapter 2).

Only a few voters still employ left and right in the nineteenth-century sense, but this does not mean this dimension no longer exists. With the disappearance of abortion as a prominent issue, euthanasia has become perhaps the prime issue representing this dimension. The first graph in Figure 3.1 presents the placement in 2006 by the members of Parliament on this issue. Here we can see immediately why members for the SGP placed themselves more to the right than did the voters; they have probably used this older definition. In any case, they stand far apart from the other members in opposing euthanasia. Unfortunately, again no member of the Christian Union made a placement, but given the party's views on this issue it surely would have been not that far from those of the SGP. In any case, the CDA is the party that is the next most opposed to euthanasia. At the other end of this scale we find the Labour, D66 and Liberal parties. These were the parties that formed the Purple coalition, which passed the legislation that made euthanasia legal under strictly controlled circumstances (see Chapter 5). Thus we find that the nineteenth-century dichotomy still exists in these placements. At the centre of the scale is a mixture of the parties most to the left (Socialist Party and Green Left) and right (LPF).

Figure 3.1   *Average Self-placement of Members of Parliament on Three Issues Representing Left and Right, 2006*

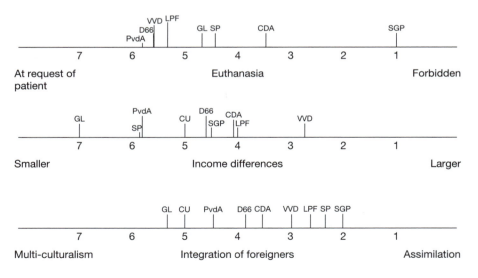

Source: Dutch Parliamentary Study, 2006.

In the twentieth century, after the Pacification of 1917, the *Antithesis* began to lose most of its relevance and was replaced by political issues based first on the ideological division of socialism versus capitalism, economic planning versus economic freedom, and the role of the state. After the Second World War, issues centred on the building of the welfare state. Many issues could be mentioned, but policies to bring about a more level distribution of incomes has been strongly associated with this dimension. Thus a question has long been included in the Dutch studies asking respondents to place parties on a scale related to differences in incomes. As can be seen from Figure 3.1, the mean placements strongly resemble the placements on the general left–right scale, but there are some interesting deviations. The left block of Socialist Party, Green Left and Labour Party is easily identified. In the centre are the Christian Democratic parties (CDA, SGP and Christian Union), but also the LPF. Whereas the LPF was most right on the left–right scale, the Liberal Party is most right on this issue.

It was the socio-economic dimension of left–right that dominated the twentieth century. As will be shown in Chapter 5, government coalitions were generally constructed along this dimension. Beginning perhaps as early as the 1980s, there is evidence of convergence in the positions of the major political parties along the left–right dimension (Pennings and Keman, 2008; Keman and Pennings, 2011). This convergence undoubtedly made it easier to form a coalition of Labour, the Liberal Party and D66 (the so-called Purple coalition) in 1994, but the formation of this coalition weakened the meaning of the socio-economic left–right dimension (Aarts and Thomassen, 2011).

Various authors pointed out that the convergence of the major parties would open up areas in the ideological issue space for new political parties. In particular, it was predicted that the movement of the Liberal Party towards the centre would open the possibility of new, populist parties on the right (Pellikaan and De Keijser, 1998; Thomassen, 2000; Andeweg, 2001). Without the opposition of Labour and Liberal, left and right no longer had meanings as clear as they once had been. In terms of the dimensionality of the Dutch party system, the reaction of the CDA was also important, as it was faced with the choice of fighting battles along the religious–secular divide, or accepting the policies introduced by the Purple coalition. Because the potential electoral gains were minimal (see Chapter 4), and since to antagonize the secular parties might only solidify their cooperation, the CDA put up little opposition. In effect, this further reduced the importance of the religious–secular dimension in Dutch politics.

Almost on cue, Pim Fortuyn arrived to fill the void created on the right when the Liberal Party cooperated with Labour. Some of his appeal was based on discontent among the citizenry about the poor performance of public and health services, but the most important aspect of the 'new politics' was the introduction of the politics of multi-culturalism to the political agenda (Van Praag, 2003; Pellikaan et al., 2003, 2007). This potential issue had, by tacit agreement, been kept off the political agenda by the traditional parties. The issue was therefore difficult to incorporate into the two-dimensional structure just described. Analysis of political party manifestoes indicates that multi-culturalism introduced a new dimension of conflict to Dutch politics (Pellikaan et al., 2003), and analysis of voter opinions showed that attitudes towards immigration and assimilation (together with attitudes towards the treatment of criminals) formed a third dimension, in addition to the socio-economic and ethical dimensions (Van Holsteyn et al., 2003).

Kriesi and his associates have provided theoretical support for the emergence of this new dimension in the Netherlands and elsewhere (Kriesi et al., 2008). They argue that its emergence is a product of the process of globalization. This process produces 'winners' and 'losers': the winners are those whose personal life-style and career opportunities are expanded by globalization – in particular, these are the better educated; and the 'losers' are those whose jobs are threatened by the outsourcing of jobs on the one hand and the influx of immigrants on the other – these are primarily the less well educated. A new *cultural* dimension thus emerges that has 'integration' versus 'demarcation' as its polar positions. 'Integration' refers to a 'universalist, multiculturalist or cosmopolitan position' on issues such as European integration and immigration, versus 'demarcation' that is in favour of 'protecting the national culture and citizenship' (ibid., p. 11). They argue that this new dimension can exist as a separate new dimension or be 'embedded' in the cultural dimension previously defined by the religious-secular dimension. This dimension has been labelled by others as the 'cultural' dimension (Pellikaan et al., 2007) or the 'libertarian–authoritarian' dimension (Aarts and Thomassen, 2008).

To examine the impact of this dimension on the party space, the placement by the members of Parliament on a scale represented by 'Newcomers should be allowed to preserve the customs of their own culture', and 'Newcomers should completely adjust to Dutch culture' can be examined. The ordering of the parties differs from the ordering on the previous two dimensions. Green Left and the Labour Party are found on the side of 'multi-culturalism', with D66 and the CDA to the right of the centre. Later studies using election manifesto data find D66 to be much more on the multicultural side of the dimension (for example Pennings and Keman, 2011). The Liberal Party is found further to the right. This ordering is similar to that of the ordering on the issue of income differences, but other parties are not found in similar positions. The Christian Union is located between Green Left and the Labour Party, but it is on the right that a new combination is found. On income differences, the LPF was in the centre, but is now found on the right with a score of 2.67. However, somewhat surprisingly, the placement of two other parties (the Socialist Party and the SGP) is even further to the right.

Since this study was conducted, the LPF has disappeared and the Freedom Party has emerged as the party most opposed to immigration, especially of Muslims. This party is thus seen as the far right on this dimension, but on the socio-economic left–right dimension, the party has taken a position more to the centre or even to the left. Its unwillingness to accept budget reduction provisions that would lead to higher unemployment and a loss of purchasing power among senior citizens led to its withdrawal of support for the Rutte I Cabinet and thus to its fall. In the election of 2012, the party positioned itself as the most anti-EU party, an issue that, according to Kriesi et al. (2008) is associated with the 'integration–demarcation' dimension.

For decades, political scientists have differed on the question of whether one, two, or now three, dimensions are necessary to represent the Dutch party space. To an extent the disagreement is on how strong a difference must be in order to designate it as a separate dimension, or whether, as Kriesi et al. would say, it is 'embedded' in another dimension. The left–right dimension is clearly the dimension most used by scholars, the media and the general public. We have shown above that the Dutch voters are clearly familiar with this dimension and able to use it in helping to understand spatial relationships between the parties. However, the terms 'left' and 'right' are themselves devoid of ideological content; they are empty vessels that can be filled in various ways. No one would argue that the dominant means of giving them content through most of the twentieth century and into the twenty-first is in terms of issues related to the socio-economic dimension.

Yet the left–right dimension is not coterminous with the socio-economic dimension. This can be seen most clearly by the placement of the LPF, and more recently the Freedom Party. These parties have been called 'extreme right', but such a classification is not based on the socio-economic dimension. We saw above that the LPF placed itself in the centre of the issue of reduction of income differences, and that the Freedom Party takes a leftist position on some major issues. Their classification of 'extreme right' is based on the cultural, or 'integration–demarcation' dimension. On that issue, the Socialist Party, which on socio-economic issues is clearly to the 'left', is also found on the 'right' – based, for example, on positions such as favouring measures to prevent ethnic minorities from clustering in the major cities (*gedwongen spreiding*). So far, neither the Freedom Party nor the Socialist Party has been able to project an image that captures both positions. The Freedom Party is more associated with the right on the 'integration–demarcation' dimension, whereas the Socialist Party is associated with the left on the socio-economic dimension. Van Der Brug, De Vries and Van Spanje argue that, given the distribution of issue preferences of the Dutch electorate, there is room for a new party that more clearly combines left on socio-economic issues with right on issues of integration and multi-culturalism (see Van Der Brug et al., 2011).

Finally, the Christian Union and the SGP are also often referred to as parties of the right. This designation is not based on either the socio-economic or 'integration–demarcation' dimensions, but on the oldest of the three dimensions, religious–secular. It is true that the importance of this dimension is diminishing as the proportion of the electorate holding conservative views on issues such as abortion, euthanasia, and gay marriage declines. Yet the Christian Union participated in the Balkenende IV Cabinet, and support of the SGP in the First Chamber was essential at times for the Rutte I Cabinet. The concessions, for example, to maintain the current level of child payments that these parties were able to obtain in the budget agreement of 2013, indicate that parties based on the religious dimension are still a force to be reckoned with.

Thus, whereas the 'left–right' dimension can be useful as the simplest representation of the Dutch party space, and may be satisfactory for normal discourse, there is tension when attempting to force all the parties onto this single dimension. What confuses matters is that the Green Left and more importantly the Labour Party anchor the left of all three interpretations. The other parties then fan out from these anchors, producing vectors with different parties at the opposite pole. Depending on how much overlap one is willing to tolerate in these vectors, one can choose a one-, two- or three-dimension solution. Despite the overlap, for a full understanding of the Dutch party space, all three dimensions are necessary.

Party Organization

King (1969) has outlined a number of functions that political parties perform within the political system. Among these are:

1   Structuring the vote.
2   Integrating and mobilizing the mass public.
3   Recruiting political leaders.
4   Organizing the government.
5   Formulating public policy.
6   Aggregating interests.

To carry out these functions, political parties find it useful, perhaps imperative, to have an organization.

Party Structure

Given the importance of organization for political parties, it is perhaps somewhat surprising that there are hardly any guidelines in Dutch law, or constraints specifically related to party organization. With the recent exception of the laws on subsidies for political parties, discussed below, there has been a reluctance to treat political parties as separate or distinct entities. Parties are organized under the same law that governs other sorts of clubs and voluntary associations. These require that associations have members, but as was seen with the Freedom Party, a minimum of two is apparently sufficient. There is no mention of political parties in the Constitution, and even the 1989 Electoral Law refers only to political groupings; before 1956, the names of the groupings (that is, parties) were not even placed on the ballot. The names of parties must be registered with the Electoral Council, which determines whether a party of this name already exists or whether the name might cause confusion with other parties.

It is somewhat surprising that despite the large number and diversity of political parties and the lack of legal guidelines, there is considerable similarity in the organization of the parties. The Freedom Party is especially notable because it represents an exception. In almost all cases, parties have chosen the mass member-ship form of organization (this is reinforced by the requirement of at least 1,000 members in order to receive government subsidies). Moreover, they have followed an organizational model in ways that are quite similar, with here and there variations on a theme.

This organizational model parallels the territorial structure of the Dutch state (see Koole and Van De Velde, 1992), which is organized somewhat hierarchically into 408 municipalities (as of 1 January 2013), 12 provinces and the national state (see Chapter 8). At each of these levels, representatives are chosen for legislative bodies – municipal councils, provincial legislatures and the Second Chamber of Parliament. Since candidates must be selected at each of these levels, it is not surprising that party organizations also exist at each of these levels. The election for the Second Chamber tends to complicate matters, however. As we shall see in Chapter 4, formally the election to the Second Chamber is carried out in 20 electoral districts. This means that not all boundaries for these districts coincide with the boundaries for the provinces, as some provinces include more than one electoral district. Parties therefore tend to have local divisions at both the provincial level and the level of the electoral district, the latter being important only because of its national significance.

The grassroots level of the major parties is composed of the local branches. Most parties refer to the municipality, though, depending on the size of the municipality, there may be more than one local branch, or it may be necessary to combine municipalities in order to have sufficient local members. The Socialist Party forms an exception by not referring to the municipality, but to a working area. In most parties, these local organizations are indeed branches of the national party. However, the orthodox Protestant parties have more a federal structure. The SGP and the Christian Union refer to electoral associations (*kiesverenigingen*). The Christian Union is a union of these local associations.

Again, with the exception of the Freedom Party, all major parties have some sort of regional organization. This tends to correspond to the provinces, since parties must select candidates for the provincial legislatures. Most refer to the provinces in the names of the regional organizations, but the Labour Party refers instead to a '*gewest*'. Another exception is the Liberal Party, whose more important regional organization (the '*kamercentrale*') is organized along the lines of the electoral districts for elections to the Second Chamber. For this party, the provincial organization consists of the *kamercentrales* within the province. The Liberal Party also maintains water district associations, which correspond to a water control board.

At the national level, all parties have a party congress, which is generally the highest organ within the party. An exception is the Socialist Party, which designates a Party Council consisting of the chairpersons of the local branches and the members of the national executive board as its highest organ. For the largest parties, a congress may consist of between 800 and 2,000 participants, although a record 5,000 attended the party congress of the CDA that was called to approve collaboration with the Freedom Party to form a government in 2010. In general, the party congress is concerned with the position of the party in the long term; it meets once a year or once every two years, though special meetings may be called to ratify a new electoral manifesto, to make the final determination of the list of candidates, or to approve participation in a government coalition.

Traditionally, the participants at a party congress have been delegates elected by the local branches. D66 was one of the first to extend participation to all members of the party. After sustaining heavy losses at the 1994 and 2002 elections, the major parties have opened up their party congress to wider representation. Now members of the Labour Party, Liberal Party, and CDA, as well as Green Left and SGP, have the right to attend their party congress. The party congress of the Socialist Party continues to follow the traditional pattern of delegates from the local branches, supplemented by the members of the national executive board. As a federation of local branches, the party congress of the Christian Union consists of representatives from the local branches. The number of representatives is dependent on the size of the local branch, but the voting is by local branch, not by individual members.

As well as these three levels within the organization, some parties maintain additional organs within the party, in part to maintain the older principle of representation rather than direct influence of the members. The Labour Party has both a Members' Council (*Ledenraad*) and an Association Council (*Verenigingsraad*) that can issue advice within the party. In addition to the party congress for all members, the Liberal Party also has a Congress of Representatives, to which is reserved the right to amend the statutes and regulations of the party. The SGP also has an advisory council consisting of delegates from the provincial associations.

Each party has a national Executive Board, generally consisting of between seven and fifteen members. The largest, with a maximum of 26 members, is for the CDA; the CDA therefore has a smaller group of seven that is chosen from this larger group and deals with the day-to-day activities of the party. The Executive Board, with the exceptions noted below, is chosen by the party congress. Prominent exceptions have been the election of the party chairman by a vote of the membership. This is another example of attempts to give more influence to the membership. The CDA introduced direct election in 1997, but did not hold an actual election until 2002. The Liberal Party held its first election for the party chairmanship in 2003, and the Labour Party in 2005 (Lucardie and Voerman, 2011).

In addition to these subunits within the party, based on geographical representation and arranged hierarchically, parties have committees or organizations for particular groups within the party. Larger, more established, parties have semi-independent organizations for young people, and most have an organization for female members. Most also have a special organization for those party members who represent the party on municipal councils or in provincial legislatures, or for those who hold executive positions at these levels. In some parties these internal party organizations have direct representation on the party council and/or the party executive.

Finally, most parties have at least two organizations, generally structured as foundations (*stichtingen*) that do not belong formally to the party organization but are associated closely with it. These are a research foundation and an institute supporting democracy and democratic parties abroad. The first serves as the intellectual satellite for the party, producing books, reports, and other documents to provoke discussion of the party ideology. The second carries out activities designed to strengthen democracy and democratic parties in Eastern Europe and the Third World. One reason that all parties have such organizations is that the law providing subsidies to political parties earmarks funds for those organizations designated by the parties to carry out these functions.

Party Membership

All political parties are voluntary associations made up of members (though the Freedom Party has only two). The parties themselves may establish the criterion for membership. D66 makes no mention of an age requirement in the statutes of the party, but all others set a minimum age, ranging from 14 (CDA), to 16 (Green Left, Labour, Animal Rights Party and Socialist Party), or to 18 (Christian Union, SGP, Liberals). While parties once required all members to hold Dutch citizenship, more recently this requirement has been broadened by some parties (CDA, Labour, and Socialist Party) to include those residing in the Netherlands. All parties require that a member supports the principles upon which the party is based. This need not be exclusive, as only the Socialist Party explicitly forbids a member to also be a member of another party (Den Ridder, forthcoming).

The only formal duty of a member is to pay dues (see below). In return, a member earns the right to participate in the internal decision-making processes of the party and becomes eligible to be nominated as a candidate of the party. In addition, a member receives a party publication and access to a protected part of the party website. Parties also organize educational courses and training sessions, and may arrange social activities and outings for members and their families (ibid.).

In contrast to Luther's expectation on the basis of consociational theory, compared with most other European countries Dutch political parties organize only a small proportion of the electorate (Van Biezen et al., 2012). Even during the 1950s, when pillarization may be said to have reached its zenith, membership in the Catholic Party was seldom more than one-fifth of its vote, and the figures for the Anti-Revolutionaries hovered at just over 15 per cent. The Social Democrats have never had a membership that equalled 10 per cent of the number of votes cast for the party.

Part of the explanation for low membership levels may lie in the definitions used. During the period of pillarization, large numbers of voters in these groups clearly identified themselves with the pillar and the associated party. In a 1954 survey, fully 27 per cent of the population claimed party membership (Donner and Kan, 1956), whereas informed estimates put membership at about 15 per cent. There may be many reasons for over-reporting, but one surely must have been that people 'felt' themselves to be members, even though they did not pay dues.

Until about 1970, national party headquarters did not hold complete or accurate information concerning membership, so that figures before that date are not particularly reliable. Only after parties became more centralized and membership lists more computerized did the figures become other than rough estimates. The high point in party membership was reached in the mid-1950s, with approximately 750,000 members (Voerman and Van Schuur, 2011), but during the turbulent years of the 1960s membership dropped to approximately 400,000. Since then the decline in membership has been less dramatic, with figures running at between 300,000 and 450,000 members. Between 1990 and 2001, the number of party members declined steadily from just under 360,000 to less than 300,000. With the excitement surrounding the 2002 elections, membership rose from 290,448 at the beginning of 2002 to 310,483 one year later. Since then, membership numbers have varied between 300,000 and 320,000, with higher numbers in election years. As of 1 January 2013, 315,109 members of political parties could be counted, just under 2.5 per cent of the electorate. Table 3.3 presents the membership of each of the parties as of that date. It also indicates membership as a percentage of the total number of valid votes cast for the party.

Long-term trend figures would show that the size of membership for the three long-standing major parties has declined substantially since about 1980. When the three constituent parties merged into the CDA in that year, the new party could claim about 150,000 members. This was already far below the figures that the three had held at their height – KVP, 300,000–400,000; ARP, just under 100,000; CHU,

Table 3.3   *Party Membership as at 1 January 2013; and 2013 Membership as a Percentage of the Party Vote 2012*

Party	Membership 1 January 2013	2013 membership as percentage of 2012 vote
Christian Democratic Appeal (CDA)	59,126	7.37
Labour Party (PvdA)	55,564	2.37
Liberal Party (VVD)	35,362	1.41
D66	23,344	3.08
Green Left	23,896	10.86
Socialist Party	44,815	5.04
Christian Union (CU)	24,067	8.17
Political Reformed Party (SGP)	29,648	15.07
Animal Rights Party	12,519	6.87
50Plus	5,768	3.25
Freedom Party	2	–
Total	**315,109**	**2.48/3.33**[1]

Note: 1. First figure is based on the total electorate; second on the number of votes cast in the 2012 election.
Source: Membership totals: www.rug.nl/dnpp. Percentages are own calculations.

almost 50,000 – but in spite of a gain of 1,000 members in 2002, by 2013 membership had been reduced to under half that number, at 59,126. Until 1989, the numbers for the Labour Party fluctuated around 100,000, but a loss of 5,000 in 1990 and 12,000 in 1991 started a trend that did not level off until 1996, by which time the party was down to about 61,000 members. Membership declined slowly to about 57,000 in 2002, recovered somewhat thereafter, but by 2013 had fallen to 55,564. Though membership of the Liberal Party took a dramatic jump under the leadership of Hans Wiegel, rising from 41,000 members in 1972 to a high of almost 103,000 under his successor Ed Nijpels in 1982, the party slipped to under 60,000 by 1990, and by 2013 was down to 35,362.

A declining vote may have been more important than declining membership in convincing the Green Left parties to merge, but the two were certainly related. The membership at the time of the 1998 parliamentary election of just under 14,000 was less than the membership of the Communist Party itself as late as 1980. Moreover, in the 1970s the Radicals also had well over 10,000 members, a level also approached by the Pacifist Socialists in 1979. Nevertheless, its prominence as opposition party during the years of the Purple coalition proved profitable in terms of membership and by 2013 it had grown to over 23,000.

D66 has had the greatest roller coaster ride in party membership of any party in post-war history. In the year of its founding it claimed 1,500 members. However, after its initial success waned in 1974 it dropped to only 300 members and there was serious discussion about disbanding the party. It recovered, however, and in 1981 reached a peak of over 17,000 members. In subsequent years, membership declined to as few as 10,000, but recently years the party has once again seen a remarkable recovery and now boasts 23,344 members.

There are exceptions to the general history of low and declining membership rates. The Socialist Party made strong efforts to organize at the local level and was able to increase its membership. In 2002, at least in part as a result of the prominence of the leader of the party, Jan Marijnissen, as an opponent of Pim Fortuyn, the party was able to add more than 9,000 members. It has continued to grow and has now surpassed the Liberal Party by almost 10,000 members, making it the third-largest party in terms of members. The small, fundamentalist Calvinist parties are also not so small if one looks at their membership figures. The SGP and the Christian Union have levels of membership that are around 40 per cent to 60 per cent of that of the four largest parties. The success of these parties in organizing their supporters is seen by looking at the third column in Table 3.3, showing 2013 membership as a percentage of the 2012 vote. The orthodox Protestant parties have a committed core of voters and have by far the highest percentages of any party; and the Animal Rights Party also seems to have a committed core. Electoral fortune and misfortune, as well as the size of the membership, affect the ratios for other parties, and the poor electoral results for Green Left and the CDA led to relatively high figures. Overall, membership as a percentage of the total electorate was 2.48 per cent, or 3.33 per cent if based on the number of the votes actually cast in 2012.

Party Finances

Political parties are organizations, and organizations need money to carry out their functions. Dutch political parties have modest budgets, with no party having an annual budget of more than €10 million. Yet even with budgets running at between €3 million and just under €10 million for the major parties, money has to be found from somewhere. Because there is always worry in a democracy concerning the role and influence of money in politics, it is important to know what the sources of party finances are and what is the legislation governing them.

Membership Dues

Katz and Mair have argued that it is a characteristic feature of modern political parties that they are less concerned about the size of party membership than parties once were (Katz and Mair, 1995). This does not, in general, seem to hold for Dutch parties, as these remain quite concerned with maintaining as large a membership as possible. Members are important not only because they provide activists to mount election campaigns, but also because they are an important source of income for the parties.

In setting the level of membership dues, the party must find a balance between setting the dues low to maximize the number of members and obtaining the income necessary to carry out party activities. Green Left has the lowest rate of €12 per year, though members are encouraged to give more. The Socialist Party, Animal Rights Party, 50Plus, and the SGP all have dues of between €20 and €25 per year. Dues for the Christian Union and CDA are, respectively, €52 and €59 annually. The annual rate for the VVD is €110.50, but discounts are available for younger and older members and other members of a household. The Labour Party and D66 have different rates according to income. For D66, the scale runs from €60 for those earning up to €18,000 to €300 for those earning over €90,000. The Labour Party has more gradations in its scale, with the lowest rate beginning at €24 for those earning less than €5,000 and rising to €563 for those earning more than €100,000.

In a report prepared by the Ministry of the Interior in connection with impending legislation, it was estimated that in the year 2000, membership dues accounted for 46.4 per cent of income across all parties. Koole (2011) reports figures for 2008 indicating that dues comprised between 10 per cent and 74 per cent of the income of the various parties. The lowest figure was for the Socialist Party, which, as we shall see, has a unique source of income; and the highest is for D66. The figures for the major parties, PvdA, CDA, and VVD, were 60 per cent, 55 per cent and 45 per cent, respectively. Given these figures, it can be said that, in general, membership dues make up the largest single source of income for Dutch political parties.

Government Subsidies

With declining memberships in many countries, including the Netherlands, government subsidies have become increasingly important as a source of income for political parties. Many countries have felt that political parties perform such important functions for the democratic political system that it is justifiable to provide support out of general funds. Important questions that must be considered are: who will be qualified to receive a subsidy; how large the subsidies will be; for what purposes they will be provided; and how the amounts will be allocated.

In order to receive a subsidy in the Netherlands, a party must hold at least one seat in either the First or Second Chamber and have at least 1000 members. This latter requirement is somewhat unusual, as it is not found in other countries. It again stresses the importance of membership for Dutch parties, since not only are membership dues an important source of income, but the number of members will also influence the amount of government subsidy. As noted above, the Freedom Party has only two members and is therefore not eligible to receive these subsidies.

In addition, the legislation imposes restrictions on the parties with respect to non-discrimination. The subsidy for a party can be withdrawn if it is determined by a court that the party is guilty of some form of discrimination. This occurred in 2003, when the Reformed Political Party (SGP) was found guilty of discrimination because women were not allowed to be members (see above). On 1 January 2006, the Minister of Home Affairs stopped the subsidy for the party, costing the party about €800,000 of its annual budget of €1.4 million. On 24 June of that year the party voted to change the party statutes to refer to membership of 'persons' rather than 'men'. The party also appealed against the ruling by the minister in the administrative court, and after a ruling by the Council of State the subsidies for 2006 and 2007 were restored. By then the party had about a dozen female members.

In the Netherlands, government subsidies for political party activities began in 1971. Technically these were not provided to the parties themselves, but to specified institutes or foundations affiliated with the parties. In 1972, the first subsidies were for the scientific think tank foundations that each party set up to prepare policy statements and carry out research. In 1975, subsidies were provided to affiliated organizations to organize educational and training activities for the party, and in 1976, the youth organizations associated with the parties received subsidies (Koole, 2011, p. 226).

After a decade of discussion and deliberation, a new law went into effect on 1 July 1999 that marked a major departure in the provision of governmental funds for political parties. It was one of the few pieces of legislation that specifically mentioned parties, and moved from indirect to direct subsidies. While the subsidy was now made directly to the party, the activities that could be performed with these funds were enumerated in the law. These included the first six items in the list below; in 2005, legislation expanded the list to include the last four. Most important, these include not just those that might be seen to have an educational benefit for the general population, but also those that are directly related to the success of the party in recruiting members and representatives, and running campaigns. The list was retained in the 2013 legislation, so the activities that are now subsidized are:

1   Political education and training.
2   Information for members.

3 Maintenance of contacts with sister parties outside the Netherlands.
4 Support of education and training activities for the cadre of sister parties outside the Netherlands.
5 Conduct of political research.
6 Stimulation of political participation among the youth.
7 Recruitment of members.
8 Involving non-members in the activities of the party.
9 Recruitment, selection and supervision of political representatives.
10 Activities in connection with election campaigns.

The amounts allocated for these activities are a direct subsidy to the party organizations. In addition, indirect subsidies continue to be provided for the research institutes of the parties and for the youth organization of the party. The legislation also provides for a subsidy to organizations associated with the parties that support democratic parties in Eastern Europe and the developing world.

The amount of government subsidies has risen from approximately €2 million at the beginning to about €15.5 million in 2013. The amount is low by international standards. According to Lucardie et al. (2010), the size of direct subsidies to political parties in the Netherlands amounted to less than one euro (€0.93) per inhabitant, compared with between one and two euros for Ireland, France, and Belgium, and between five and six euros per inhabitant for Germany and France. This again demonstrates the relatively low monetary resources available to parties in the Netherlands.

Those parties that qualify receive a basic amount of €178,384 and an additional €51,740 per parliamentary member. This constitutes 80 per cent of the amount available; the remaining 20 per cent is distributed by dividing €1,953,202 euros by the total number of members of all political parties and then distributing the amount proportionally. The subsidies for research institutes, for youth organizations, and for party organizations dealing with foreign activities are determined in a somewhat similar fashion.

For the three traditional major parties, PvdA, CDA, and VVD, government subsidies accounted for 29 per cent, 43 per cent, and 42 per cent, respectively, of their annual budget for 2008 (Koole, 2011). The percentage was highest for the Party for the Animals (61 per cent), but also relatively high (50 per cent) for the Socialist Party. The lowest figures were reported for D66 and Green Left, with 20 per cent and 25 per cent, respectively.

Gifts and Donations

After losing its subsidy in 2006, the SGP asked its members and supporters to make donations to the party and received approximately €400,000 for the election fund and €300,000 for the 'subsidy stop fund'. This is an example of an established party that became temporarily dependent on donations. For new parties, donations can also be of vital importance. A new party hardly has the time to set up a large organization with a number of dues-paying members that would support an election campaign, and since it has not yet won a seat in Parliament it is not eligible for government subsidies. Thus reliance on donations and sponsors becomes almost the only ready source of funds. This became evident in the election of 2002, when Pim Fortuyn depended on gifts. The party and its election campaigns in 2002 and 2003 were reportedly financed primarily by Fortuyn's business friends. In 2003, an outcry occurred when it was rumoured that a real estate owner, who had become chair of the party, planned to provide €10,000,000 to cover the costs of the campaign. However, no such amount ever emerged. For the 2006 campaign, a businessman donated €300,000 to the Animal Rights Party that was used to broadcast a series of radio spots featuring prominent figures from the world of entertainment (Van Praag, 2007, p. 105). As was noted above, Geert Wilders has opted for an organization without members, and is thus totally dependent on donors to finance party activities, including campaigns.

In addition to gifts, businesses may sponsor activities of political parties. The Liberal Party congress in 2001 was sponsored by Mercedes Benz, a bank, and an internet company. The party has also made use of fundraising dinners (Lucardie, 2003). Sponsoring and donations have become increasingly relevant because of the rise of new political parties. Established parties also have foundations that make donations to the party. For example, in 2010, the VVD reported receiving €891,000 from four foundations.

The increasing importance of donations, both for new and older parties, dissatisfaction with the existing legislation, as well as criticism from the Council of Europe and the Organization for Security and Co-operation in Europe, led to the adoption of new legislation in 2013. The purpose of this legislation is to provide greater transparency concerning the finances of political parties. Legislation passed in 1999 for the first time provided that gifts to political parties should be reported, but no sanctions for failure to do so were mandated. This has been changed in the new legislation. Parties are now required to provide a yearly report to the Minister of Finance regarding a) subsidies received; (b) gifts received; (c) other income; (d) the financial resources of the party; and (e) the debts owed by the party. All gifts of €4,500 or more must be listed and include the name and address of the donor. Debts greater than €25,000 must be reported, again with information concerning to whom the amount is owed. Failure to provide the requisite information can lead to a fine of up to €25,000.

To oversee this new legislation, a Commission for the Oversight of Political Party Finances (*Commissie toezicht financiën politieke partijen*) has been established. The three members of the commission are appointed by the Minister of the Interior for a term of four years. The Commission will provide advice to the Minister concerning the administration and enforcement of the law.

A special type of 'donation' to a party will presumably fall under the new legislation. Various political parties request or demand that elected officials 'donate' part of their salary to the party; this is sometimes called a 'party tax'. Most parties, including D66, CDA, Labour, the Animal Rights Party, the Christian Union, Green Left and the Socialist Party (Dragstra, 2008, p. 309), have some sort of provision along these lines. For most parties, the remuneration received by the office-holder goes first to the individual, who then makes a tax deductible donation to the party.

The Socialist Party, however, makes the greatest demands on its representatives and employs a different arrangement. Candidates for office sign an agreement requesting that their remuneration be transferred immediately to the party. For members of the Second Chamber and European Parliament, the representatives then receive a modal salary plus expenses from the party (similar arrangements are made for members of municipal councils, provincial councils and aldermen). These arrangements have at times been controversial, both within and outside the party. In recent years, at least one alderman, some members of municipal councils, and one member of Parliament have left the Socialist party because of the requirement. At least one Minister of the Interior has attempted to end the arrangement, by declaring that the remuneration would no longer be transferred to the party, but only directly to the MPs. For ideological reasons, this arrangement is important to the party, but it also provides an important source of income. In 2011, the Socialist Party reported having received €3,251,100 (40 per cent of its annual budget) from its office-holders. Party 'taxes' are also an important source of funds for the Labour Party, which in 2011 received €1,074,350 (11 per cent of income) from its politicians.

Future Questions
The 2013 legislation is a step towards greater transparency concerning the sources of funding of political parties. At the present time, there is no reliable information concerning gifts to political parties, though for the older, established parties, gifts other than the party taxes on office-holders are probably relatively modest.

While this legislation is seen as a step in the right direction, many potential loopholes remain, and when defending the law in the First Chamber, the Minister admitted that it was not watertight. In particular, there was criticism that the law does not apply to local branches of parties, so that it would be simple to donate to these rather than to the national party. The Minister promised to introduce new legislation to remedy this situation.

Another potential loophole relates to the possibility of setting up foundations that could receive anonymous donations, but then pass them along to the parties. Or these foundations could plan and run their own campaign on behalf of a candidate or party, via what in the USA would be called 'independent expenditures'. The legislation also does not cover internal campaigns that are being used more frequently for the choice of the party chairman or list puller. It is not clear how such campaigns will be financed (see also Koole, 2011). Implicitly, in passing the legislation, decisions were made concerning the amount and sources of donations. In any case, no restrictions were placed on the amount that an individual could give, nor on who might give (individuals, businesses, trade unions and so on) either domestic or foreign. These questions may yet arise again in the future. The sanction provided (€25,000) may also not be sufficient to ensure transparency. At one point in the parliamentary debate, the Freedom Party threatened to simply pay the fine rather than provide the required information. Finally, there can also be concern over the enforcement of the legislation. The Commission mentioned above is not independent, and can only advise the Minister. It is not impossible that there is no political advantage to the Minister to enforce the law if it had detrimental effects on his/her own party.

Parties and Elections

Candidate Selection – the List

Earlier it was explained that political parties in the Netherlands are considered to be voluntary associations and are covered only by the laws that regulate such organizations. What makes political parties unique among voluntary associations is that they present lists of candidates at elections. To have a party name placed above a list of candidates, that name must be registered with the Electoral Council. Lacking any legislation to determine how candidates are to be selected, the parties are free to determine their own internal procedures, and considerable diversity is found (Hillebrand, 1992). Parties allow only party members to participate in the process of selecting candidates. D66 experimented with allowing non-members to participate in regional caucuses that nominated candidates for the European Parliament election of 2004, but because of costs and sensitivity to manipulation, immediately abandoned the practice (Lucardie and Voerman, 2007, p. 81).

The size of the party delegation in Parliament has an influence on the procedure, with larger parties facing greater challenges than smaller ones. If a party has only a few representatives, the main task is simply to find the best-qualified candidates to be placed at the top of the list. However, when the number of representatives becomes large (approximately between 20 and 50 MPs), the pressure to 'balance' the parliamentary group becomes greater. 'Balance' takes two forms, which are not always complementary. On the one hand, there is the desire to obtain expertise within the parliamentary caucus in as many policy areas as possible; this will make the caucus more effective in holding the government accountable. During the period of *verzuiling,* some larger parties reserved 'quality seats' for representatives of the affiliated interest associations of the pillar (see also Chapter 6). No longer are seats reserved for such affiliated associations, but depending on the party, there may be a perceived need to have trade unions, agriculture and/or business represented. On the other hand, there is pressure to have the caucus reflect the composition of the electorate, or at least the electorate of the party. This has been strongest in demands that there be some element of gender balance within the caucus. Each party also now ensures that members of various ethnic groups are included on the list; even the Christian Democratic CDA has placed Muslims on its list (see also Chapter 2). As mentioned above, there may also be concern for regional representation. Balance can also mean that there is pressure to have additional younger representatives or merely that there be more new blood so that the caucus does not become too stodgy.

Giving more influence to either the members or the regions generally conflicts with the goal of balance within the list, and parties have altered their selection procedures to reflect which of these goals is perceived as most important at the time. The party that has consistently chosen for democracy is D66, which has always placed the ultimate decision in the hands of the members, though in 1986 a committee was introduced into the procedure that presents a recommended list to the members. Other parties were under pressure to democratize their procedures during the 1960s and 1970s (Koole and Leijenaar, 1988). In practice, democratization meant decentralization, and the result was a strengthening of the position of the regional 'party barons', who sometimes seemed more intent on obtaining a high place on the list for 'their' candidates and rewarding party service than concern for the quality or balance on the list (Hillebrand, 1992). This led to a return to procedures that were more centralized (Koole, 1992; Leijenaar and Niemöller, 1997).

By the 1990s most parties followed a fairly similar procedure, much of which continues to be followed. The party executive board calls (sometimes even through newspaper advertisements) for individuals to submit their candidacy and for the local parties to make candidate suggestions. The board also installs a more-or-less independent committee, which examines the qualifications of the candidates and may hold interviews with a large number of potential candidates. The committee can attempt to achieve a balance of age, experience, gender, region, expertise, religious or ethnic background, or whatever characteristic is of importance to the party. Then, either the committee advises the party executive board on the ordering of candidates or the board determines the ordering of the candidates itself. Once the selection committee has made its recommendations and the party executive board has established its ordering, the idea of party democracy is kept alive by submitting the list to the various local party organizations and to the party congress for final approval. However, it is not surprising to note that the impact of the party congress is minimal. Occasionally minor changes have been imposed, but a large party congress is hardly the place to negotiate an entirely new ordering (Lucardie and Voerman, 2007).

One difficult factor facing these committees and the executive board is how to deal with incumbent members of Parliament. In the past, incumbent MPs had an extremely strong position and, if they so desired, were reselected almost automatically. In recent years, parties have become more concerned about MPs remaining in office for too long, or about the need to rejuvenate the parliamentary delegation. MPs are no longer certain of their positions and are subjected to an evaluation of their performance. The leader of the parliamentary party is generally involved in this evaluation.

Major losses by the larger established parties in 1994 and 2002 led to a period of democratization within Dutch parties (Lucardie and Voerman, 2011). This is particularly evident in the changes in procedures for the selection of the first name on the list of candidates – the so-called list-puller. These developments justify the special consideration given to them in the following section. Attempts to give more influence to party members in the selection of the numbers two and lower on the electoral list have been less dramatic, and less successful. The party congress for the Green Left voted down a proposal that would have provided for election by the membership, preferring to keep the decision-making power in its own hands.

The party congress of the Labour Party also voted down a proposal to allow the members in each province to elect a candidate to the list. The CDA has provided somewhat more opportunities for the membership by allowing all members who attend the party congress to have a vote, rather than the system of delegate selection that had been in place in the past. The Liberal Party has introduced the most far-reaching changes by making it possible for all members to attend the party congress and to vote on the candidates by mail, telephone, or via the internet, by allowing members to elect not only the list-puller but also the party chairman, and making it possible in principle to hold a referendum among party members on an important question. These reforms have, according to Lucardie and Voerman (2011), made the party the most internally democratic of the parties. However, it is not yet clear how much has changed within the parties. With only rare exceptions, the list as recommended by the party leadership has been approved.

Geert Wilders' Freedom Party makes no pretence of maintaining democratic internal procedures. In selecting candidates, Wilders and his appointed advisers make the determination. He has attempted to avoid the problems faced by Pim Fortuyn's LPF, but he has nevertheless had to see various members of Parliament resign because of scandals and controversies. In 2012, at least two of the names on the original list of candidates were forced to withdraw before the definitive list was submitted.

At times the party executive of other parties have also had to intervene in the selection process. In 2006, both CDA and Labour had placed candidates of Turkish origin on their list, but controversy arose on whether genocide had been committed by Turkish forces in Armenia in 1915. The party standpoint was that genocide had occurred, but this has never been recognized by the Turkish government, and the Turkish candidates refused to accept the party position. The respective party executives of the parties removed them from the list of candidates. In anger, the Turkish Forum called on Turkish–Dutch voters to boycott these two parties and vote for the number six on the D66 list who refused to take a position on the issue. Her 35,564 preference votes were enough to jump her past number three on the list and elect her to Parliament (Lucardie and Voerman, 2011).

Finally, it should be noted that the lists do not lose their importance after the election results have been determined; they remain in effect until the subsequent election. There are no by-elections under the Dutch system. If a vacancy occurs, it is filled by beginning at the top of the list and continuing down until a candidate on the list accepts election. This means that it is possible to leave Parliament but still return later. Sometimes this return is already planned when the vacancy occurs: since 2006, it has been possible for an MP to leave Parliament for 16 weeks for reasons of pregnancy or an illness, and then return.

Candidate Selection – the List-Puller

Party regulations have almost always specified different procedures for this selection than for the candidates from the second place onwards down the list. With exceptions and developments to be discussed below, the choice of the list puller has often been even more centralized than the selection of the other candidates. In some cases, a party leader has simply anointed his successor (for example, the Labour Party in 1986 and 2002, and D66 in 1998). In other cases, it has effectively been the parliamentary party that has selected a new party leader. This happens often because the list-puller at the election has become the parliamentary leader of the caucus. If a resignation occurs, the caucus selects its new leader, who then virtually automatically becomes the list-puller at the next election. The shifts in leadership of the CDA between 1994 and 2002, from Elco Brinkman to Enneus Heerma to Jaap de Hoop Scheffer to Jan Peter Balkenende, is an illustration of this.

Given this background, it is somewhat surprising to see the extent to which the parties have opened up this selection process. Since 2002, several parties have introduced internal elections by the membership of the list-puller. Actually, the first such election was held by Green Left in 1993. Two 'duos' competed for the leadership, with the combination Brouwer/Rabbae gaining 51 per cent of the vote. The party suffered badly in the election of 1994 and a disappointed party temporarily abandoned the experiment. However, after the election of 2002 in which Pim Fortuyn gained so much notoriety and several traditional parties suffered badly, pressure mounted to 'democratize' the parties and give the membership a greater say in the selection of the leadership.

The Labour Party was one that had lost heavily and, under the leadership of party chair Ruud Koole, who himself had been chosen on a platform of returning more influence within the party to grassroots membership, the new leader was elected by a vote of the membership. The winner of the vote was Wouter Bos, who then led to the party to a remarkable recovery in the January 2003 election. Bos was unopposed in 2006. When he resigned in 2010, he proposed Job Cohen as his successor and when no opposition to Cohen emerged, he became the list-puller. On his own resignation in February 2012, the party again held an internal election and Diederik Samsom was elected as the leader.

The new regulations adopted by the Liberal Party in 2003 called for a direct election of the party list-puller by the membership. This resulted in a particularly divisive struggle within the party between Rita Verdonk (known as 'Iron Rita' because of her strict policies on immigration as a Cabinet minister) and Mark Rutte. Rutte won with 51.5 per cent of the vote, but at the subsequent parliamentary election he suffered the indignity of receiving fewer preference votes than Verdonk (Lucardie and Voerman, 2007, p. 81). Eventually Verdonk was forced to leave the party and formed her own movement, and Rutte went on to become Minister-President and was unopposed for the party leadership in 2010 and 2012.

While D66 has been a champion of democratic reforms, only once has it held an internal election for the leadership. In 2006, Alexander Pechtold did battle with Lousewies Van Der Laan for the list-puller position. This race also included personal attacks on opponents and the result was close, with Pechtold gaining 53 per cent of the vote of the members. Rather than continue a conflict within the party, as was happening in the Liberal Party, Van Der Laan retired from politics (ibid.).

After 10 years of discussion following losses at the 1994 election, the CDA in 2003 adopted party rules that provided for a vote of the membership for the list-puller. However, since no candidate emerged to challenge Prime Minister Balkenende, no such election was held until 2012. After suffering heavy losses at the 2010 elections, Balkenende retired as leader of the party. The leadership of the party was then shared by Maxime Verhagen (deputy prime minister in the Rutte I Cabinet), Ruth Peetoom (party chair), and Sybrand van Haersma Buma (leader of the parliamentary caucus). When Verhagen announced that he would not be a candidate for Parliament at the 2012 elections, Buma announced his candidacy for the position of list-puller. He faced strong opposition, but won in the first round with 51.4 per cent of the vote of the members.

In 2012 Green Left finally again held a party vote for the leadership, though with little enthusiasm. The party congress had voted in March 2005 to elect the list-puller by a vote of the membership, but under the leadership of Femke Halsema, no election had been held. After her resignation from Parliament, she was succeeded by Jolanda Sap. She was challenged in 2012 by fellow MP Tofik Dibi, and while she easily defeated him, gaining 84 per cent of the vote, the internal division of the party was at least in part the cause of the poor showing of the party at the election, and she was forced out a few weeks later by the party chairman and executive board.

Since five major parties have now conducted internal elections for the list-puller (and in some cases list-pullers for other elections and for party chairperson), it is possible to speak of a trend. There might have been more cases, except that it has become clear that incumbents are seldom challenged within their party. Koole has argued that the 'Fortuyn revolt' of 2002 was instrumental in the adoption of initiatives within Dutch parties to provide more internal party democracy. He notes that all of the internal elections were 'introduced after a severe electoral loss in the previous years', although loss was a 'necessary, but not sufficient' condition, since not all losses led to such elections. Such elections also did not guarantee electoral success. The reason often given by the parties was an attempt to 'revitalize party life', to 'break down the one-sided top-down character of internal decision making, to satisfy wishes of emancipated party members, or to make party membership more attractive'(Koole, 2012).

A Decline of Parties?

The history of political parties in the Netherlands has also been closely related to both pillarization and depillarization (Andeweg, 1999). During the period of pillarization, the role of the political party was well defined; parties were tied directly into the network of newspapers, broadcasting, trade unions, employers' organizations and other organizations that made up the pillar. The political party was not so much a separate organization as the political arm of the pillar, defending its interests in politics. However, the expectation voiced by Luther, and quoted at the beginning of this chapter, that these parties would hold monopoly positions, is not borne out. With the exception of the Catholics, there have often been parties that competed with and challenged the position of the dominant party in the pillar. Even during the heyday of pillarization, only a small minority of voters were members of a political party, and even fewer participated in the activities of the parties. This also seems to contradict the expectation that such parties would recruit a large percentage of followers to become members of the party. Single-issue action groups can at times mobilize far more citizens than political parties are able to do on a more permanent basis.

At first glance, the expectation that depillarization would result in a weakening of the parties is borne out, though a decline of parties has also been observed outside formerly segmented societies. Nevertheless, the role of parties in facilitating communication between voters and their representatives has largely been taken over by radio and television. Professional public opinion polling organizations often provide quick, but reasonably accurate, indications of how the public views a particular political question or issue. Election campaigns are increasingly media events rather than grassroots ones, and the organization of campaigns is increasingly in the hands of professional consultants. Parties are also criticized for failing in the exercise of their aggregation function. No longer do they have a clear political ideology; instead of a clear set of political principles, party manifestoes have become a pot-pourri of hundreds of statements on all possible issues, lacking any unity: 'The only thing holding party programmes together is the staple' (Tromp, 1985). Krouwel (1996) has found empirical evidence that many of the accusations are true, and that Dutch parties are moving towards becoming 'catch-all' parties. In 2002, the List Pim Fortuyn became the first example of a new phenomenon, which might be called a 'candidate party'; that is, a party based strongly on the appeal of a specific candidate. This phenomenon has been followed by Geert Wilders' Freedom Party.

Yet concerns remain, both within and outside the parties. The loss of members is often taken as a sign that Dutch political parties no longer play an important role in people's lives. Such trends have been observed in the comparative literature, as well as a trend towards a more limited role for party members. Different terms have been applied to the new types of political party, such as 'electoral professional organization' (Panebianco, 1988), 'modern cadre party' (Koole, 1994), or 'cartel party' (Katz and Mair, 1995). The expansion of both the size of governmental subsidies and the purposes for which these funds can be used is another indication of the movement towards 'cartel' parties. Such discussions are particularly acute in the Netherlands, given the extremely low rates of membership. The Freedom Party has demonstrated that certain functions of political parties can be performed without the party actually having members.

In the Netherlands, such trends have been counterbalanced by other developments. In one sense, parties have only just begun to come into their own. During pillarization, the parties acted merely as a subculture's ambassador to the national government, and only recently have they become the independent organizations one generally defines as political parties.

One such defining quality is that parties nominate candidates at elections, and the Dutch parties have tightened rather than loosened their control over the pathways to political office. During the period of pillarization, some parties reserved positions on the list of candidates for representatives of other organizations within the pillar (see Chapter 6); the candidate selection process itself was largely in the hands of the party elite. In the interests of providing balance on the list, people without a long record of party service could be placed on the list. Cabinet ministers were frequently recruited from outside Parliament, and at times even included people with no party affiliation (see Chapter 5). Since the 1960s, however, the grip of parties has become stronger. Internal party democratization and decentralization put candidate selection, including the list-pullers, somewhat more in the hands of the membership. This has made lateral entry more difficult, as the party members stress service within the party in making their selection. All in all, the possibility for a career in politics is now almost completely under the control of the parties. And, because government subsidies are dependent on membership rather than on votes alone, the parties have an incentive to recruit members.

The parties may also have increased their control over the political agenda. In recent years, parliamentary parties have attempted to bind governments to the coalition agreement negotiated by the parties during the Cabinet formation process (see Chapter 5). Parties and party leaders also continue to dominate political discussions; while broadcasting and polling organizations are occasionally successful in placing an issue on the political agenda, the discussion will die without the participation of the parties. More often it is the parties who either generate or sustain political discussions, and the research foundations of the parties can play a role in either internal political discussions or public debates.

It cannot be denied that Dutch parties have changed in the years since depillarization began: they have even fewer members, more state financing and less distinctive ideological profiles, but are more autonomous and more in control of government recruitment and policy. Whether this constitutes a decline of parties is a matter of definition or of expectations concerning the roles that parties should fulfil and how they should fulfil them, but predictions that 'the party's over' (Broder, 1972) are clearly premature for the Netherlands.

4

Elections

Elections form the heart of any democratic system. However, they can be organized in many different ways and this can be important for how the system functions. In Chapter 1 we outlined some of the significant dates and events in the development of democracy in the Netherlands, noting that direct elections and the parliamentary system were introduced in 1848, and that in 1917 universal suffrage for men (and in 1919 for women) was introduced, together with election by proportional representation. The Netherlands is now known for having one of the most proportional systems in the world. This proportionality has reinforced the multi-party system that was considered in Chapter 3 and influences how government coalitions are formed, which will be discussed in Chapter 5.

We begin this chapter by describing how elections are organized and discussing the many attempts that have been made to change the system. The focus will be on the national parliamentary elections; the rules for elections for municipal councils, provincial legislatures and the European Parliament are based on the same principles. In the second part of the chapter, we attempt to explain the patterns of behaviour within this framework: how political parties campaign, and how voters make their choices at elections.

The Electoral System

General Characteristics

Few Shall Be Chosen
While there is no disagreement about the principle that the power of the people to choose their leaders in free elections is essential in a democratic system, there are considerable differences among democracies in the degree to which the principle is applied. For example, the USA seems to apply what might be called the 'elective principle'; that is, leaders should be elected directly by the people unless there is some good reason not to do so. Thus there are numerous elective offices at the local, state and national levels, and for all three branches of government: legislative, executive and judicial. The Netherlands, on the other hand, applies an 'appointive principle'; that is, offices are filled by appointment unless there is good reason not to do so. Only

representatives to legislative bodies (municipal, provincial, national and European) and water control boards are elected by the people, and even then the First Chamber of Parliament is elected only indirectly, as its members are elected by the representatives to the provincial legislatures. Members of the executive branch are selected by other means. As described in Chapter 5, it is the parliamentary parties who select the members of the government, who are then formally installed by the monarch. At the provincial level, the governors, who are still called 'King's Commissioners', are appointed by the national government. Despite various attempts at change, mayors are still not elected directly by the voters, but also are appointed, albeit with advice from the municipal council (see Chapter 8). For most Dutch citizens it is therefore almost unthinkable that judges might be elected rather than appointed.

Absence of Geographical Representation
During the nineteenth century, elections to the Second Chamber of Parliament always involved geographical representation. Immediately prior to the introduction of universal suffrage in 1917, there were 100 single-member districts and the law required that the winning candidate in the district receive an absolute majority of the vote, in a system very similar to the one used currently for French presidential elections. If no candidate received a majority in the first round, a vote was taken on the top two candidates in a second round. It is important to note that numerous parties and groups participated in these elections, and that single-member districts did not inhibit the development of a multi-party system (see Chapter 3). Even under the district system, up to eight parties or groups were represented in Parliament.

With the introduction of a list system of proportional representation, district representation was abandoned. Eighteen (now 20) electoral districts were created, but for the determination of the distribution of seats in the Second Chamber of Parliament the country is treated as a single electoral district. The districts are important only for administrative reasons. They come into play in determining which individuals within a party are elected to Parliament. However, if the party has submitted the same list in each district, or has formally linked the lists in a specified procedure, even this potential impact is effectively negated. Otherwise, the actual selection is carried out within the districts in a quite complicated procedure (see Box 4.1 on page 106).

Where geographical distribution does occur, it is primarily a result of internal pressures within the party. Local party organizations push for a high place on the list for 'their' people. Some parties, notably the Labour Party, have at times attempted to stimulate a relationship between MPs and the district in which they were formally chosen, but this has never been particularly successful. However, there is no evidence that regional identification has any significant impact on the choice of party and even within the party: in 2006, only 9 per cent of voters stated that they had chosen a candidate on the list because he or she was from the local area or region (Van Holsteyn and Andeweg, 2010). Thus, geographical representation exists only in so far as the parties deem it important in their nominating procedures.

Extreme Proportionality

With no geographical representation, the purpose of the election is to determine how many seats each of the lists on the ballot is to receive. There is no special electoral threshold that a party must cross in order to achieve representation in Parliament. The only threshold is the electoral quotient formed by dividing the number of valid votes cast at an election by the number of seats (150) in Parliament (see Box 4.1). This amounts to only 0.667 per cent of the vote. Since the electoral districts play no role in determining the number of seats allocated to each party, this means that, depending on the turnout, approximately 60,000 votes nationwide are sufficient to gain a seat.

The absence of a special threshold other than the electoral quotient and the treatment of the entire country as a single 150-member district, underlines that the Dutch electoral system is one of the most proportional systems in the world (Taagepera and Shugart, 1989, p. 196). The proportional distribution of seats is as close as possible to the proportion of the vote that the parties have achieved, and as one of the 'rules of the game', proportionality has become an important feature of Dutch political culture (see Chapter 2). It is one of the few aspects of the electoral system that is enshrined in the Constitution itself and affects all attempts to alter or reform the system, as will be seen below.

Legal Requirements

Ballot Access

Parties that wish to appear on the ballot of a district must submit a list of candidates in that district. Although any party of significance will participate nationwide in all districts, it is quite possible to submit a list in fewer districts. For example, in 2006, 11 parties did not submit lists in all districts, and in 2012, six smaller parties did not submit a list in the new district of Bonaire. In recent years, the importance of the districts has been further reduced by allowing parties under certain conditions to submit the lists for all 20 districts at a central office in The Hague. These lists must be supported by written declarations of support from 30 eligible voters, who must have signed the declaration in the presence of the mayor of their municipality (or his or her appointed representative). For parties not represented in Parliament, a deposit of €11,250 is required regardless of the number of districts in which the party submits a list. The deposit is returned if the party receives 75 per cent of the national electoral quotient, which amounts to roughly 0.5 per cent of the total vote. In 2012, 10 parties did not achieve the required percentage of the vote and lost their deposit. Since an incumbent party is not required to pay a deposit, it cannot lose it, even if it fails to achieve the electoral quotient, as did the List Pim Fortuyn in 2006.

A party may submit the same or a different list of candidates in each of the electoral districts. Most parties will have some degree of overlap, especially at the top of the list. Since the 1950s it has become standard practice for parties to place the same name at the top of the list in each district; this top candidate is the electoral leader of the party and is known as the 'list-puller'. His or her job is to pull the party to victory, and with the growing role of the media in campaigning, the importance of the 'list-puller' has increased, becoming in many respects the personification of the party (at least for the duration of the campaign). Since the top names are submitted in all 20 districts, it is obvious that there is no legal requirement for a candidate to be resident in the district in which he or she is a candidate.

Voter Eligibility

As noted above, universal male suffrage was introduced in the Netherlands in 1917, and this was extended to women in time for the election in 1922. In 1917, the age requirement was set at 25; this was lowered to 23 in 1946, to 21 in 1963, and to 18 in 1972. Suffrage is dependent on holding citizenship in the Netherlands, with the exception that citizens of EU countries and non-nationals who have lived legally in the country for five years are eligible to vote in municipal elections.

Eligible voters are registered automatically by the municipality in which they reside. Not less than two weeks before the election, each eligible voter is sent a card showing the nearest voting station. The voter need only appear with this card on the appointed day to obtain a ballot paper and cast a vote. After a successful experiment in 2006, in which about 10 per cent of voters cast their votes at a polling station other than the one to which they had been assigned, it is now possible to vote at any voting station within the municipality; to vote outside the municipality, a special voting pass must be requested 14 days (written) or five days (oral) prior to the election. No absentee ballots are issued, but since 1928 it has been possible to vote by proxy. Proxy can be assigned in two ways: by making a written request to the municipality, or more simply by signing the card that was sent and giving it to a family member or friend. The latter may only cast the proxy vote when casting his or her own vote, and may receive the proxies of only two voters. Dutch citizens living abroad are eligible to vote in parliamentary elections and in elections for the European Parliament. However, they must take the initiative to register themselves with the municipality of The Hague.

The Simple Act of Voting

The burden on a Dutch voter at any election is minimal, since only a single choice must be made. Under the list system of proportional representation, the candidates are listed in a column (or columns) under the name of the party (before 1956, the party names were not listed on the ballot, making the situation somewhat more complicated for the voter). The ballot itself may appear somewhat intimidating, since generally between 15 and 25 parties participate in parliamentary elections (see Table 3.1 on page 60). This complicates the task for the voter only slightly, however, since the parties are ordered on the ballot by the size of their current representation in Parliament. For parties having no parliamentary representation, the order is determined by lot. For elections to the Second Chamber, a party may list up to 50 names on the ballot, or, if it has more than 15 members in Parliament, a maximum of 80.

Before 2006, most municipalities made use of voting machines, but in that year a group calling itself 'We do not trust voting machines' created a public discussion that eventually led the Ministry of the Interior to ban the use of one brand of voting machine. As a result, 34 municipalities were forced to revert to paper ballots for that election. In October 2007, the Junior Minister of the Interior revoked the approval of all voting machines, and in May 2008 the Cabinet announced that for present time paper ballots would be reinstated. In 2013 a commission was set up to investigate how and under what conditions voting by machine could be reintroduced, but for now the famous red pencil to fill in the circle corresponding to the name of the desired candidate has returned. This single, simple act completes the voting process.

Preference Votes
As was seen in Chapter 3, it is the party that determines the order of the candidates on the list. This is the order in which the party hopes that the candidates will be elected. There is only one possibility for voters to break through this ranking. Most voters cast their vote for the first name on the list, the 'list-puller', but it is also possible to vote for any of the other candidates on the list. Such a vote is called a 'preference vote' (*voorkeurstem*); that is, this person is preferred to the candidates above her or him. Whether or not one casts a preference vote has no influence on the number of seats the party will receive, since the votes for all candidates on the list are totalled to determine the distribution of seats. It can, however, have an impact on which of the candidates is actually elected. In an attempt to give voters a greater influence and perhaps increase interest in elections, new legislation came into effect for the 1998 election that lowered the percentage of the electoral quotient a candidate needed to be elected whatever his or her place on the list (assuming the party had a right to that seat) from 50 per cent to 25 per cent. In general, parties have discouraged the casting of preference votes and in some cases have even gone so far as to require candidates to sign agreements that they would refuse election if chosen in this fashion.

The number of voters casting 'preference votes' has been rising, however. In the 1950s, the percentage of voters voting for someone other than the first name on the list was only 3–4 per cent, in the 1960s and 1970s this percentage was generally around 10 per cent, but in the 1990s it rose to approximately 20 per cent. In 2002, the leaders of the Labour and Liberal parties were not popular and the number of preference votes rose to the current record of 27 per cent. In 2006, the percentage of preference votes was also high (23 per cent), in part because, for the first time, a list-puller failed to receive the largest number of votes for his party, when Rita Verdonk (number two on the Liberal Party list) outpolled list-puller Mark Rutte. In 2010 and 2012, the percentages of preference votes fell back to 16 per cent and 19 per cent, respectively.

There can be a wide range of reasons for a voter not to vote for the first name on the list. The unpopularity of the leading candidate or dissatisfaction with the campaign are obvious ones; however, the foremost reason seems to be a preference for a female candidate within the party of choice; between 30 per cent and 40 per cent of respondents in election studies have indicated that this was their reason (Van Holsteyn and Andeweg, 2010). Some members of ethnic groups seek out a group member on the party list to whom to give their vote. As mentioned above, regional candidates are mentioned in less than 10 per cent of cases.

Despite the numbers having risen and the threshold being lowered, preference votes continue to have only a relatively small influence on who becomes a member of Parliament. From the end of the Second World War until 1998, under the 50 per cent rule, only three candidates were elected by preference votes who would not have otherwise been elected according to their placement on the list. The new 25 per cent threshold has increased the influence of preference votes, and in the 1998–2012 period nine candidates were elected in preference to the ordering of their parties' lists.

Turnout

In the agreement of 1917 that led to universal male suffrage with proportional representation in 1918, it was reasoned that if all men (as noted above, women's suffrage followed in 1919, taking effect in the 1922 election) were to have the vote, then each vote should have equal weight. Yet if some citizens chose not to vote, one could hardly determine what the proper proportions were to be. Thus it seemed only logical to require citizens to exercise this new right, and a form of 'compulsory voting' was introduced. Voters were not actually forced to vote, but were required by law to present themselves at the polling station on election day. Virtually all voters complied, and once there they also tended to cast their vote. At 11 national elections between 1925 and 1967 the average percentage of votes cast (based on eligible voters) was 94.1 per cent.

The legal compulsion to vote was discussed on numerous occasions in Parliament, and in 1970 the law was finally repealed. The impact was far greater than had been anticipated; turnout at the first non-compulsory election (for provincial legislatures) was only 68.1 per cent, and at the municipal elections in the same year an even lower figure was achieved, of 67.2 per cent. Turnout at the first parliamentary election without compulsion in 1971 was 79.1 per cent. Figure 4.1 shows the level of turnout since the repeal of compulsory voting.

What emerges most clearly from Figure 4.1 is that since Dutch voters are no longer obliged to vote at elections, a clear distinction in turnout has emerged for the different elections. When compulsory voting was in effect, the turnout for provincial and municipal elections was only marginally less than for national elections. After the repeal of compulsory voting, however, turnout at all levels fell, and at times it has seemed that there was a general downward trend. At parliamentary elections, turnout hovered at or slightly above the 80 per cent level until the 1980s, after which it appeared to decline. A low point was reached in 1998 when the turnout was 73.3 per cent. However, in 2002, perhaps because of the excitement generated by Pim Fortuyn, it rose to 79.1 per cent. When elections became necessary only eight months later, many thought that it would fall again, but it actually rose further, to 80.0 per cent, and then to 80.4 per cent in 2006. However, in 2010 and 2012 it slipped again, to 75.3 per cent and 74.6 per cent, respectively.

At the municipal level, turnout was for some time about 10 per cent less than for parliamentary elections, but in recent elections the gap has increased. In 2010, only 53.5 per cent turned out at the municipal elections, even lower than the percentage that turned out for the provincial elections the following year (55.9 per cent). Until 1982, turnout at the provincial level had been similar to that for municipal elections, but since then a gap ranging up to 15 per cent has opened. The higher turnout in 2011 may have been because of the expectation that these elections would decide whether the governing coalition of VVD, CDA, and Freedom Party would achieve a majority in the First Chamber (see Chapter 6). Elections for the European Parliament have never ignited the enthusiasm of Dutch voters, and turnout has always been lower than for domestic elections. Until the election in 2004, there was also a clear downward trend in turnout for these elections. Turnout rather unexpectedly bounced back to 39.1 per cent in 2004 (from

Figure 4.1   *Voter Turnout after Repeal of Compulsory Voting, 1970–2012 (percentages)*

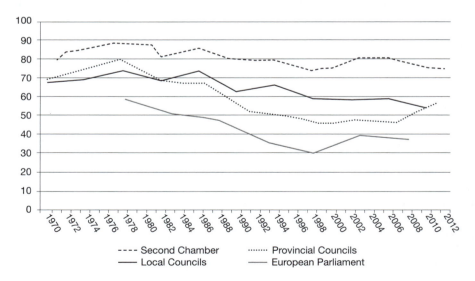

the low of under 30 per cent in 1999), only to fall again to 36.9 per cent in 2009. Both the 2004 and 2009 figures remained under the European averages of 45.5 per cent and 43 per cent, respectively.

Determining the Results

As mentioned above, the first step in counting the votes and determining the results is to calculate the electoral quotient. This is found by dividing the number of valid votes cast by the number of parliamentary seats to be divided (150). Each multiple of the electoral quotient entitles a party to an additional seat. However, when each party has received the seats to which it is entitled, not all of the 150 seats will have been allocated. The votes for parties that did not meet the electoral threshold and the votes a party has above one multiple of the threshold, but less than the next multiple, have been lost in the process. The seats that remain after parties have been allotted their multiples of the electoral quotient are the so-called 'remainder seats' (*restzetels*). These seats are then distributed among the parties that have exceeded the electoral quotient, according to the method of largest average (the so-called d'Hondt method).

Use of the d'Hondt method gives a slight advantage to larger parties. To an extent this is compensated by a feature of the electoral law introduced in the 1970s. Parties are allowed to register that their votes are to be combined with other parties for the purpose of the original allocation of seats. This alliance is announced on the ballot and the parties are thus treated as a single unit for the purpose of the initial distribution of parliamentary seats. Once this distribution has been determined, the law provides additional procedures for determining how the seats are to be divided proportionally between the partners. By combining their lists, smaller parties can in essence be treated as part of a larger unit for the distribution of seats. This offers a greater advantage to smaller parties, and as result such parties have formed alliances more often than have larger parties. In recent elections, combinations of the orthodox Calvinist parties and those on the left have been common. Before 2012 this had not changed the outcome of the vote, but in 2012 the combination of the Socialist Party and Green Left cost the Labour Party a seat when the final tally was made (see Box 4.1).

Reforming the Electoral System

The electoral system has remained remarkably unchanged since its introduction in 1917, despite suffrage being expanded to include females, and the voting age being lowered several times. The enlargement of the Second Chamber in 1956 from 100 to 150 had the side-effect of lowering the electoral quotient from 1.0 per cent to 0.67 per cent. Compulsory voting was abolished in 1970, and in 1998 the threshold for election by preference votes was lowered from 50 per cent to 25 per cent. Otherwise, the system has remained intact.

BOX 4.1

Distributing Parliamentary Seats, 2012

Number of valid votes: 9,424,235

Number of votes needed to secure a seat
  (valid votes/150 seats = 'electoral quotient'): 62,828.23

Party	A Number of votes	B Multiples of electoral quotient	C Average votes per seat if remainder seats were allocated	D Average C after assignment of first remainder seat	E Final number of seats
VVD	2,504,948	39	62,623	61,096	41
PvdA, SP, GL	3,470,499	55	61,973	*unchanged*	57
[PvdA	2,340,750				38]
[SP	909,853				15]
[GL	219,896				4]
PVV	950,263	15	59,391	unchanged	15
CDA	801,620	12	61,663	unchanged	13
D66	757,091	12	58,237	unchanged	12
CU/SGP	491,366	7	61,420	*unchanged*	8
[CU	294,586				5]
[SGP	196,780				3]
Animal Rights	182,162	2	60,720	unchanged	2
50Plus	177,631	2	59,210	unchanged	2

Note: Party alliances are italicized.

- **Distributing seats to parties/alliances**

Step 1   The electoral quotient is determined by dividing the total number of valid votes by the 150 seats in the Second Chamber. In 2012 the electoral quotient was 62,828.23.

Step 2   For each multiple of the electoral quotient, a party or alliance of parties receives one seat (column B). All other participating parties received fewer votes than the electoral quotient and therefore received no seats. The number of seats allocated to a party in this step is listed in column B. Since only 144 of the 150 seats are allocated, there are 6 'remainder seats' still to be allocated.

Step 3   The number of votes in column A is then divided by the value of column B plus one seat to determine what the average number of votes per seat would be if the first remainder seat were to be allocated to this party/alliance. This average value is listed in column C.

Step 4   The party with the highest average, in this case the VVD, is assigned the first remainder seat.

Step 5   For the party that has received the remainder seat, step 3 is repeated to determine the average number of votes per seat if this party were also to receive

→

→

Step 6
the next remainder seat. The averages of the other parties remain unchanged (column D).

The party with the highest average, in this case the PvdA, SP, GL (GreenLeft) alliance, is assigned the next remainder seat.

Steps 5 and 6 are repeated until all remainder seats have been distributed. In this case the PvdA, SP, GreenLeft alliance received 2, the VVD received 2, the CDA and the CU (ChristianUnion)/SGP alliance each received 1.

- **Distributing seats to parties within an alliance**

Step 7 For those parties that have linked their lists in an alliance (in this case PvdA, SP and GL, and CU and SGP), the seats that have been allocated to their alliance must be distributed among them. The distribution among the parties in an alliance follows a procedure similar to the one just described: an intra-alliance electoral quotient is calculated based on the number of votes cast for the alliance and the number of seats now allocated to the alliance (for PvdA/SP/GL it was 60,885, and for the CU/SGP it was 61,420). Each party in an alliance receives a seat for each multiple of the intra-alliance electoral quotient (in the PvdA/SP/GL alliance, 38 seats go to PvdA, 14 to SP, and 3 to GL, with 2 remainder seats. In the CU/SGP combination, the Christian Union receives 4 and the SGP 3 seats, leaving 1 remainder seat. Remainder seat are allocated to the party with the largest *remaining* number of votes after subtracting its multiple of the electoral quotient from its number of votes. In this case, the SP, GreenLeft, and ChristianUnion each receive 1 remainder seat. The final number of seats for each party are listed in column E of the table.

- **Distributing seats to district lists within a party**

Step 8 For those parties that have not linked their district lists (that is, submitted lists that differ in each district – in 2012 these were the PvdA and SP), the seats that have been allocated to them are distributed among their district lists. Again, the procedure is similar to the one described above for allocating seats to parties/alliances. An intra-party electoral quotient is calculated based on the number of votes cast for the party and the number of seats received by the party. Each district list receives a seat for each multiple of the intra-party electoral quotient. Any remainder seats are allocated on the basis of the system of largest *remainders*.

- **Assigning seats to candidates on the list**

Step 9 Now that we know the number of seats a party has won in a particular district, or nationwide if a party has linked its district lists, candidates can be assigned to those seats. Candidates who have received more than 25 per cent of the national electoral quotient (15,707 votes in 2012) nationwide are declared elected regardless of their position on the list in the district in which they received the most votes (27 candidates, but 26 of them would also have been elected because of their positions on the list).

Step 10 The party's remaining seats in a district are assigned to the remaining candidates on the district list, in the order of that list. Candidates who win a seat in more than one district are declared elected in the district in which they received the most votes.

This should not imply that there has been no discussion of possible reforms to the system. Since the 1950s there has been a concern that the voters are not sufficiently connected with national politics, and in particular that there was not enough contact between the members of Parliament and the voters. As early as 1958 a special commission noted recurrent criticism that nationwide proportional representation weakened the contact between representatives and the electorate, thus possibly leading to reduced interest in politics among the electorate. Moreover, the voter had little influence on the composition of the executive branch. In 1966, a new political party emerged, D66, which had as one of its primary goals the passage of reforms to the electoral and political system. This party has been at the forefront of the drive for electoral reform in the ensuing decades.

Since the Second World War, no fewer than seven major governmental commissions investigated the system and made recommendations. A National Convention has been convened and a Citizen Assembly was called. The most prominent of the proposals that have been made by these bodies and others include: direct election of the Prime Minister (or of the *formateur*), direct election of the mayors of municipalities, the introduction of a referendum, and the introduction of a district system of electing the Parliament, generally as part of a mixed system along the lines of the German system.

The introduction of a binding referendum came close to adoption in 1999, when it carried the Second Chamber by the necessary two-thirds vote to amend the Constitution. However, in the First Chamber, the Liberal Party was unable to enforce party discipline, and its former leader, Hans Wiegel, cast the deciding vote that killed the amendment. To appease D66, at that time a member of the Cabinet coalition, a temporary law was passed to provide a non-binding referendum. However, the legislation expired in 2005 and no referendum was ever held under the law. A new attempt was initiated in 2013 by MPs from the Labour Party, Green Left and D66. A proposal to revive the non-binding referendum was passed and sent to the First Chamber. In addition, a proposal was presented to amend the Constitution to make a binding referendum possible. In 2005 a special national referendum was held on the proposed European Constitution (see Box 10.2 on page 260).

The direct election of mayors was almost passed in 2006. Again, to make this possible, a two-thirds majority in both Chambers of Parliament was necessary. And again, it was the First Chamber (ironically itself not directly elected) that thwarted this attempt at constitutional revision. This time it was the members of the Labour Party, led by former party leader and ex-Cabinet minister, Ed Van Thijn, who voted against the amendment. His opposition was not to the amendment, but rather to the legislation that would have ensued subsequently which would have provided for direct election. Despite his party at one time supporting direct election, Van Thijn now preferred election by the municipal council.

All attempts to reform the electoral system by introducing some variation of the German mixed model of districts and proportional representation ('Mixed Member Proportional') have not even come this close to adoption. The crucial element is the effect on proportionality and the effect of an electoral threshold on smaller parties. Proportionality is grounded in the Constitution, so any proposal that affects this principle must be passed by Constitutional amendment. In 2003, the Minister for Constitutional Reform proposed an electoral system modelled on, though not identical to, the German and New Zealand examples (Van der Kolk and Thomassen, 2006) The voter would have two votes, one for the district and one for the national list, and the distribution of seats would have been based on the national vote. By having multi-member districts, it was hoped to avoid the problem of *Überhangmandate* (that is, supernumerary seats that are necessary when a party has won fewer seats under nationwide proportionality than it has candidates who have won district seats). This was necessary because the Constitution sets the number of seats at 150 and the government hoped to avoid the necessity of amending the Constitution. This proposal was withdrawn when the minister in charge resigned from the Cabinet after the proposal to elect mayors was rejected. It is interesting to note that the Citizen Assembly that was called by the minister's successor listed the absence of electoral districts as one of the strengths rather than one of the weaknesses of the current electoral system.

Thus, after more than 60 years of discussion, very little has changed in the electoral system. In Chapter 11 we return to the subject of reform and examine public support for a number of reform measures. In this chapter, since elections to legislative bodies continue to form the core of the participation of the citizens in Dutch democracy, we turn now to how campaigns and elections are conducted and how the voters determine for which party or candidate they will vote. Election results for the first election after World War II and for all elections from 1963 through 2012 are reported in Table 4.1.

Campaigning

The procedure that parties must follow to produce a list of candidates on the ballot has been described above. However, getting on the ballot is one matter, but a major, perhaps the main, objective of any political party is to have representatives elected to office. To convince the electorate to vote for its candidates, the party conducts an election campaign. In the Netherlands, campaigning at the municipal and provincial level is quite simple. The municipality provides billboards on which the parties can display their posters, while some party supporters still place them in their windows at home. Party workers distribute flyers, either door-to-door or in shopping streets and at markets. Meetings are held with candidates or take place as debates between candidates.

Even at the national level, campaigns are not extensive, in part because they are low budget affairs. Table 4.2 presents estimates of the war chests that the parties had available for the 2012 parliamentary election. These figures represent an approximate 14 per cent increase over the estimated figures for the two previous elections, and almost a doubling of the amounts that were available in the 1990s. After the

Table 4.1 *Election Results for 1946 and all Elections from 1963 through 2012 (percentages of valid vote)*

	1946	.....	1963	1967	1971	1972	1977	1981	1982	1986	1989	1994	1998	2002	2003	2006	2010	2012
Religious																		
KVP	30.8		31.9	26.5	21.8	17.7												
ARP	12.9		8.7	9.9	8.6	8.8												
CHU	7.8		8.6	8.1	6.3	4.8												
CDA							31.9	30.8	29.4	34.6	35.3	22.2	18.4	27.9	28.6	26.5	13.6	8.5
SGP	2.1		2.3	2.0	2.3	2.2	2.1	2.0	1.9	1.7	1.9	1.7	1.8	1.7	1.7	1.6	1.7	2.1
Christian Union[1]			0.7	0.9	1.6	1.8	1.0	2.0	2.3	1.9	2.2	3.1	3.3	2.5	2.1	4.0	3.3	3.1
Orthodox Catholic					0.4	0.9	0.4											
Left																		
Labour (PvdA)	28.3		28.0	23.6	24.6	27.3	33.8	28.3	30.4	33.3	31.9	24.0	29.0	15.1	27.3	21.2	19.6	24.8
Green Left[2]	10.6		5.8	6.5	7.1	11.0	4.3	6.7	6.5	3.3	4.1	3.5	7.3	7.0	5.1	4.6	6.7	2.3
Socialist Party (SP)									0.5	0.4	0.4	1.3	3.5	5.9	6.3	16.6	9.8	9.7
Liberal																		
VVD[3]	6.4		10.3	10.7	10.3	14.4	17.9	17.3	23.1	17.4	14.6	20.0	24.7	15.4	17.9	14.7	20.5	26.8
D66				4.5	6.8	4.2	5.4	11.1	4.3	6.1	7.9	15.5	9.0	5.1	4.1	2.0	6.9	8.0
Right																		
Populist Right[4]			2.1	4.8	1.1	1.9	0.8	0.1	0.8	0.4	0.9	2.5	0.6	17.0	5.7	5.9	15.5	10.1
Niche																		
Pensioners[5]												4.5	0.5					
Animal Rights																1.8	1.3	1.9
Retailers					1.5	0.4												
Other																		
Receiving seats					5.3	7.1	0.7							1.6				1.9
Not receiving seats	1.0		1.6	2.6	2.1	1.0	1.5	1.8	0.9	0.9	0.9	1.8	1.9	0.8	1.2	1.1	1.1	0.8

Notes:
The elections of 1948, 1952, 1956 and 1959 are not included in this Table.
1. Christian Union since 2002; previously GPV 1952–98 and RPF 1981–98 (both Orthodox Protestant).
2. Green Left since 1989; previously CPN (Communist) 1948–86, PSP (Pacifist) 1959–86, PPR (Radical Left) 1971–86, and EVP (Evangelical Left) 1981–6 before
3. PvdV (Party for Freedom) in 1946.
4. BP (Farmers' Party) 1959–77; CD (Centre Democrats/Centre Party) 1981–98; LPF (List Pim Fortuyn) 2002–03; PVV (Freedom Party) 2006–.
5. AOV 1994–8; Unie55+ 1994; 50Plus 2012.

Table 4.2 *Estimated Campaign Budgets, 2012*

Party	Approximate campaign expenditure per vote	Approximate expenditures 2012 for party (€)
CDA	1,600,000	1.99
PvdA	2,200,000	0.94
VVD	2,275,000	1.09
SP	1,600,000	1.76
Green Left	900,000	4.09
D66	875,000	1.16
Christian Union	400,000	1.38
SGP	400,000	2.03
Animal Rights Party	290,000	1.59
50Plus Party	150,000	0.84
Freedom Party		n.a.
Total	**11,165,000**	**1.31**

Source: First column, Van Praag and Walter, personal communication. Second column, own calculations. Freedom Party has been excluded from calculation of totals

Freedom Party has been excluded because no information is available, the total figures show that the parties spent somewhat more than one euro per voter in 2012. No party spent more than around four euros, in part because of the extremely poor showing of the Green Left. By comparison, in the US presidential election, held two months later, the teams for the two major candidates collected and spent approximately US$1 billion each, approximately US$16 per vote cast. Before the amounts in the Netherlands increased, Germany was estimated to spend about 15 times the 'per vote' amount, and the UK about five times as much (Van Praag, 2003).

The amounts available to the parties come from the dues paid by the members, from fund-raising among the members, and from the subsidies provided by the government, as the latter may now also be used for campaigns. Each year, the parties set aside a portion of their income to be used at an upcoming election. Thus, if elections are held more frequently than the legal four-year cycle, parties may be struggling for funds. As described in Chapter 3, the new law governing party finance requires parties to disclose the names of donors of large amounts. However, these lists will not be long, since large donations are still quite rare.

One reason that the amounts have remained low is related to the question often posed in the literature concerning whether campaigns really matter to the outcome. For a long period in the Netherlands the answer was that they mattered very little. During the period of pillarization (that is, until approximately 1967) there were not too many votes to be won during an election campaign. Voters belonging to a particular pillar tended to vote for the associated party, and were not greatly inclined to switch to a party of another pillar. On average, only 5 per cent of seats changed hands at elections between 1948 and 1963 (see Figure 4.3 on page 129). Campaigns were not costly because they were aimed more at mobilizing the faithful and retaining their support than at converting and obtaining new votes. The strategies may be described more as defensive than offensive, though this may have applied more to the religious parties than secular ones.

By current standards, attitudes towards campaigning were quite reserved. A survey conducted in 1954 showed that 55 per cent of voters were opposed to the idea that 'candidates at the elections attempt to visit as many people as possible in order to clarify in a personal conversation what they will do if they are elected' (Donner and Kan, 1956). The primary reasons mentioned for such opposition was that the voter might be influenced (!) or bought off, or that easy promises might be made that could not be kept.

The organization of the campaign was also reasonably simple. Campaigns were generally run directly by the party organization: 'A number of well-meaning amateurs gathered after office hours to discuss the question of political propaganda for their party' (Hoogendijk, 1971, p. 207). No special research was carried out and no marketing strategy formulated (Brants et al., 1982). The campaign consisted mainly of organizing speakers to appear at meetings of party supporters. Since within each pillar there was also at least one newspaper and a radio/television organization that supported the party, there was little need for efforts to attract media attention.

The 1960s brought changes that would have a major impact on election campaigns. First, there was a change in the electorate: fewer people voted along traditional lines (see Table 4.3 on page 118), and more people became floating voters. The number of seats changing hands between 1967 and 1986 was generally close to or greater than 10 per cent, doubling the average in the previous period (see Figure 4.3 on page 129). The Christian Democratic parties, who were losing votes most heavily, adopted even more defensive strategies, whereas the Labour and Liberal parties (together with several new parties) employed strategies that attempted to woo new voters. Second, the pillars began to crumble. Organizations that had been part of the pillar became more, or even fully, independent. This independence meant that they could no longer be counted on to support the party in campaigns. Third, technological developments, such as the introduction of television and the rise of public-opinion polling organizations, reinforced the first two changes and provided new opportunities for parties to communicate with voters. As a party committed to political change, D66 was also instrumental in leading the way in introducing new elements into election campaigns. Since the 1960s, foes have decried and friends have lauded the 'Americanization' of campaigning.

While attitudes are not as reserved now as they were in 1954, the techniques employed in campaigns by Dutch parties still tend to lag behind those of many other countries. The political scientist, Hans Anker, who has had experience in election campaigns in the USA, the Netherlands and other countries, evaluated the techniques employed by the parties in 1998. He noted that, when one party employs a new electoral technique the other parties tend to follow suit in the subsequent campaign. For example, the Labour Party began a more extensive use of electoral research (both survey and focus groups) in 1994, and the other parties followed in 1998. A new element in the campaign of 1998 was the focus on a central theme in the campaign by the CDA and Labour parties. Other new features were the use of conference calls among the campaign strategists, computer presentations with beamers, and training volunteers in the substantive message of the campaign; also, all parties now have websites. However, Anker saw the Netherlands as being under-developed in such campaign techniques as fundraising and direct mail, opposition research, rapid response, media monitoring, grassroots activities and endorsements (Anker, 1998). Though his comments were made at the end of the twentieth century, with the exception of the limited usage of new social media (see below), little has changed in the twenty-first.

One thing that *has* changed, though, is that election campaigns seem to be becoming more aggressive. During the period of *verzuiling,* campaigns tended to be defensive. As voters loosened their ties with the parties and more votes could poten-tially be won, there was more reason to consider running an aggressive campaign. The Socialist Party had taken steps towards negative campaigning in 1998 (Anker, 1998, p. 123), but it was Pim Fortuyn who more than anyone changed the style of campaigning in the Netherlands. He was blunt and outspoken, and not afraid to make the attacks personal (Van Praag and Brants, 2007, p. 15). In 2006, even the CDA, which had traditionally been defensive in its campaign strategy, became more aggressive, accusing the Labour leader, Wouter Bos, of flip-flopping (ibid., p. 18).

Despite the anecdotal evidence, Walter and Van Der Brug, who analysed the party broadcasts from 1981 to 2010, concluded that there has been no increase in negative campaigning. Three elections in this period were identified as having been above average for negativity – 1982, 1994, and 2006. The 1982 election followed the breakup of the coalition of CDA, D66, and Labour, the stormy existence of which came to an end after only 260 days in office. In 1994, the Liberal Party ran an unusually negative advertisement, and three new parties, who were highly critical of the previous government, entered Parliament. In 2006, the Freedom Party made its breakthrough and other right-wing parties tried to capture the legacy of Pim Fortuyn (Walter and Van Der Brug, 2013).

Walter and Van Der Brug found support for the commonly held hypothesis that the multi-party system of the Netherlands, combined with the necessity for coali-tion governments, places restraints on parties to go negative. Parties are not only vote-seekers, but also office-seekers; that is, they seek the power of office, in this case participation in the governing coalition. To criticize a party heavily during the election campaign may make it difficult or impossible to cooperate in a coalition after the election. Thus support was found for the hypothesis that parties with low coalition potential were more likely to go negative. Related to this, parties that are found to be distant from the median party position on the left–right scale are more likely to go negative. Opposition parties and parties that are losing in the polls also tended to be more negative. Mixed evidence was found for hypotheses that parties with less experience in governing, and new parties, were more likely to broadcast negative advertisements.

There is one element of Dutch campaigns that is not generally found in other countries. Since 1986 it has become customary for parties to submit their election manifestoes to the Central Planning Bureau (which uses the name 'Netherlands Bureau for Economic Policy Analysis' on its own English-language website), a semi-independent government agency that calculates the economic and fiscal (and since 2010 also the environmental) consequences of the proposals within the manifestoes. Results are then compared with the programmes of other parties. In 2012, ten parties submitted their economic plans to the Bureau. The parties may themselves determine which plans are to be evaluated and which not, so that the evaluation of the total of proposals of a party is not always valid. For example, in 2012, the plans submitted by the Freedom Party received a positive evaluation, yet the proposal for the party for the Netherlands to leave the European Union and withdraw from the euro was not included (Van Holsteyn, 2013). Nevertheless, in a campaign, such as in 2012, in which economic questions play an important role, these plans and the evaluation by the Central Plan Bureau take on significance. Parties are generally able to find something positive in the evaluation and point to this with pride during the campaign.

Election Campaigns in the Media

As election campaigns in the Netherlands tend to be short and must be run on low budgets, there is heavy reliance on the media. The earliest and most direct subsidy of political parties was the provision of free radio and television time. By law, a party that has submitted a list of candidates in each of the 20 electoral districts is granted 20 minutes of radio time; 10 blocks of one minute are provided across six radio stations, plus one block of 10 minutes is provided on one of these. For television, six blocks of three minutes are provided on the three public television channels during the campaign. Funds are also provided to cover some of the costs of technical support needed to produce these programmes. The broadcasts are made during the last three weeks before the election. For those parties that elect representatives to Parliament, the government provides free radio and television time during the years between elections. In recent years, 8 hours 30 minutes of television time and 35 hours of radio time has been made available for distribution among the parties.

No party can rely exclusively on such limited exposure, but additional exposure is not generally obtained by purchasing time slots to broadcast advertisements. Before 1998, broadcasters, both public and commercial, refused to sell television time to political parties. In 1994, neither the parties nor the national broadcasters had dared to break through the long-standing taboo, but in that year, the Socialist Party purchased television time on some local stations. This set the stage for the breakthrough in 1998 as, long before the campaign began, this party had announced its intention to purchase broadcasting time. For some time it was uncertain whether the national broadcasters would be willing to sell time for political commercials, but finally the commercial station SBS, as well as the organization that coordinates the sale of time for advertising on the public channels, agreed to do so. The timing of these decisions came so late that, aside from the Socialist Party, only D66 produced and aired a commercial. In 2002, several parties had plans to broadcast radio and television spots in the days immediately preceding the election. However, these plans were cancelled when the campaign essentially stopped after the assassination of Pim Fortuyn on 6 May. Since 2003 spots have become an accepted part of campaigns, but their growth has not been dramatic. In 2012 only three parties, Liberal, Labour, and D66, made television spots a major part of their campaigns, and with expenditure of approximately €750,000, €400,000, and €200,000, respectively, these efforts must be considered relatively modest. All parties, with the exception of the SGP and the Freedom Party did, however, make use of radio spots, primarily because of the lower costs (Van Praag and Walter, personal communication).

Lacking funds for extensive television advertising, parties are highly dependent on free publicity to bring their message to the voters. One way of achieving this is by doing something newsworthy, and part of the campaign strategy is devoted to creating newsworthy events. The evening news programmes on the public channels are produced by an organization that is independent of the broadcasting organizations. Two commercial channels now also produce evening news programmes. All attempt to provide a balance of coverage among the major parties. For the smaller parties, virtually any coverage received is disproportionate to their size. The parties that do have an advantage are the coalition parties, since the activities of the ministers and the Cabinet are news in themselves and therefore are virtually guaranteed coverage (Kleinnijenhuis and De Ridder, 2007, p. 121).

The other opportunity for free publicity is to appear in programmes produced by the various broadcasting agencies. One might assume that parties that have their roots in the pillarized system are at an advantage here – the ties between political parties and broadcasting organizations were described in Chapter 2 (see Figure 2.2 on page 36). Broadcasting organizations have their own news teams and produce news programmes that are longer than the evening news broadcasts and are intended to provide background information. During campaigns, such programmes devote considerable attention to the most recent campaign developments and analysis of these. There is no legal obligation for these broadcasting organizations to provide equal time to all parties or to remain neutral, yet the amount of support provided for an allied party is minimal. Depillarization is evident here, and there is strong pressure for these organizations to avoid clear bias. With changes in the organization of broadcasting taking place in 2013, there will be fewer broadcasting organizations and the ties with the old pillars will become even weaker. No broadcasting agency announces a preference for a particular party or endorses a party, and pressure to maintain a fairly neutral position has increased since organizations of different backgrounds now work together, taking turns in producing a daily news analysis programme. Television broadcasts tend to devote less coverage to smaller parties than do newspapers.

During the campaign, many television programmes include discussions or debates by representatives of various parties. The media have strong control over who is invited to such programmes and the format of the discussion or debate. In 2012, four different broadcasting organizations organized a total of at least eight debates for various combinations of parties in the short period between 22 August and election day on 12 September. With more and more voters determining their choice close to election day, televised debates have become increasingly important to the parties. The debates are important not only because they are a source of free publicity, but also because they reach a large number of voters. In the Dutch Parliamentary Election Study, 2012, 29 per cent of respondents reported that they had seen one or more of the debates in their entirety, and an additional 48 per cent reported having seen fragments of at least one debate. It is possible that respondents here are also referring to fragments that were reproduced in news programmes, but even in that case it is clear that the debates are reaching a wide audience.

It is difficult to place a monetary value on the free publicity that debates and news programmes provide for the parties. One research project attempted to estimate the monetary value of such programmes. Based on estimates of what the production costs would have been, it was estimated that, in the campaign of 2003, 'free' publicity had a monetary value of approximately €4,275,000 (Van Den Broek, 2003). At the time, this amount was almost equal to the total that the parties themselves had available for the 2003 campaign.

Though the old media still dominate, it is hardly surprising that the new media have seen themselves brought into election campaigns. According to the Central Bureau of Statistics, in 2011 the Netherlands had the highest percentage of households with internet access in Europe (94 per cent). The use of the internet continues to increase and the Dutch are highly active in the social media. In 2013, 7.9 million Dutch citizens made use of Facebook (of these, 5 million did so daily); 7.1 million used YouTube; 3.9 million were on LinkedIn; 3.3 million used Twitter; 2.0 million Google+; and 1.2 million were on the Dutch social networking website, Hyves (Newcom). In percentage terms, as of March 2011, the Netherlands was world leader in the use of Twitter (26.8 per cent) and LinkedIn (26.1 per cent) (ComScore). It was therefore inevitable that the political parties would feel a need to have a presence on the internet and make use of it in election campaigns.

The parties began to be active on the internet in 1994, and by 1998 each had its own website. However, 2002 produced something of a breakthrough, as that year and in 2003 the websites became considerably more attractive and received more attention. In 2002, the website of the LPF received 550,000 hits (Kleinnijenhuis et al., 2007). In 1998 the list-pullers were less prominent on the websites than on television, but by 2002, with the exception of the SGP, Livable Netherlands, and the SP, all the list-pullers had their own sites, as did a number of candidates. In 2006, the parties set up special sites for the elections, though these still were basically 'digital election folders' (Van Santen, 2007).

This period is often referred to in the literature as Web 1.0; that is, communication that is one-way and top-down. Parties and candidates used the internet to disseminate information to voters. By the 2006 election, and especially in 2010, the social media, which are referred to as Web 2.0, had emerged. Web 2.0 is characterized by collaboration, communication and sharing. There is the possibility for interaction between candidates and voters. Hyves was first used in 2006 (ibid.). In 2010, the innovations were Twitter and YouTube. In January 2009, only 16 members of Parliament had a Twitter account, but by January 2011 no fewer than 90 had an account. In 2010, almost all of the parties had their own channel on YouTube. Two exceptions were the Freedom Party (which was also absent on Hyves and Facebook) and the SGP, the latter because it was not possible to shut the channel down on Sundays. The parties placed a total of 406 clips on YouTube in 2010. The CDA had the most (121), followed by the Labour Party (98) and the Liberal Party (69); the Animal Rights Party had only four (Walter and Van Praag, 2012).

Despite these efforts by the political parties, there is little evidence that use of the social media has had more than a minimal impact on the voters and the election outcome. The social media still reach far fewer voters than do the old media, especially television. The new social media are not reaching a new audience, as those who visit websites or follow parties and candidates on the social media are often those who are already interested in politics. There is still little interaction between candidates and voters, and the information flow continues to be primarily in one direction. One study has claimed that, within most parties, those candidates who score higher on a Social Media Indicator received relatively more votes, but this applied to candidates below position 5 on the list, and therefore had little impact on the election (Effing et al., 2011). The limited resources that are available to Dutch political parties make it impossible to carry out a web campaign of similar magnitude as that of, say, Barack Obama in the USA. Use of the internet in the Netherlands is still in its infancy and it is not likely to reach puberty, let alone maturity, in the near future.

Electoral Behaviour

From a Structured to an Open Model

Despite a long history of having many political parties, Dutch voters were not accustomed to listening to the appeals of various parties or shopping around to find the most appealing party, but voted to a considerable extent according to their social group. In fact, between the introduction of proportional representation and some point in the mid-1960s, the Netherlands was what Rose and McAllister described as a

> classic example of a structured system of multi-party competition, because the electorate has been determined along two dimensions, religion and class, each sustaining separate political parties ... [W]hen the electorate is *determined*, voting reflects the persisting structure of society [and not the] voluntaristic choice of individuals, or transitory influences of a particular election, such as the personality of a party leader. (Rose and McAllister, 1986, pp. 12, 8)

The structure of voting during this period closely followed the lines of class and religion. In Chapters 2 and 3 we saw how those divisions produced five major political parties, each more or less associated with one of the 'pillars'. These parties (KVP, ARP, CHU, PvdA and VVD, or their predecessors) dominated the electoral process generally by capturing 90 per cent of the vote. In 1956, during the heyday of pillarization, the KVP gained the votes of more than 90 per cent of all Catholics who attended mass regularly; a similar percentage of practising *Gereformeerden* supported the ARP (and most who did not voted for one of the minor orthodox Calvinist parties). Practising members of the Dutch Reformed Church were not so uniform in their voting behaviour, however. The CHU was never able to capture more than two-thirds of this group, despite the party being made up almost exclusively of regular-church-going Dutch Reformed members. The ARP also attracted Dutch Reformed voters; the orthodox members also voted for the smaller Calvinist parties while the more nominal members tended to vote along class lines for Labour or Liberal. This was also true for those who professed no religion: the working class voted Labour, and the middle class Liberal. Not only could voting behaviour be explained to a considerable extent by this simple model (see Table 4.3) – voters were also quite consistent from one election to another in their choices. If one treats the two Protestant parties as part of a single bloc, voter consistency during this period has been estimated to be as high as 85–90 per cent (Houska, 1985). Only slightly more than 10 per cent of the seats in Parliament changed hands after elections.

Because of two developments, all this began to change in the 1960s. First, the religious and class composition of society has changed dramatically since then.

Table 4.3   *Sizes of Groups and Voting Behaviour According to Structured Model, 1956 and 2012*

	Size of group			Voting behaviour	
	1956	*2012*		*1956*	*2012*
Practising Catholic	30	6	Voting KVP/CDA	95	24
Practising Dutch Reformed	12	2	Voting ARP/CHU/CDA	63	28
Practising PKN		4	Voting CDA	93	43
Practising *Gereformeerd*	10	2	Voting ARP/CHU/CDA		23
Secular working class	33	25	Voting Labour	68	47
Secular middle class	15	58	Voting Liberal	32	36
	100%	97% (other = 3%)			
	982	1656			

Sources: 1956 – Lijphart (1974); 2012 – Dutch Parliamentary Election Study, 2012.

Whereas in 1956 practising Christians comprised a majority of the population, by 2012 they made up just a seventh of it. The size of the secular (that is, non-church-going) working class has fallen from about a third of the population to about a quarter. The tremendous growth has been in the secular middle class, which has quadrupled in size from 15 per cent to about 60 per cent of the population.

The second development is that not only has the size of the groups changed, but voting patterns within each group has also altered, again fairly dramatically (see Table 4.3). For Protestants, the vote for the ARP and the CHU has been combined, and for all three religious groups after 1977 the associated party is the CDA. The extraordinary ability of the KVP and the ARP, during the period of pillarization, to mobilize voters from their respective religious groups led to the more than 90 per cent support rates mentioned above. These figures dropped in subsequent elections to only 24 per cent and 28 per cent (!), respectively, in 2012. The merger of the Dutch Reformed and *Gereformeerden* into the Protestant Church in the Netherlands (PKN) clouds the interpretation somewhat. Just over 40 per cent of those who defined themselves as PKN in 2012 voted for the CDA, whereas among those who continued to define themselves as *Gereformeerd*, only 23 per cent voted CDA and much larger percentages voted for the orthodox Christian Democratic parties.

The secular parties have also lost their hold on their potential groups of voters. Whereas two-thirds of the secular working class once voted for the Labour Party, in 2012 this had dropped to just over a third, which actually was an improvement over its results in 2010. The percentage of the vote for the Liberal Party has remained the most stable, however, with percentages only in the twenties and thirties. Its results in 2012 were a high point, but in general its growth in recent decades has been more a result of the increased size of the secular middle class group than its increased popularity within the group.

The obvious conclusion is that the 'structured model' of voting behaviour has lost any ability to understand voting behaviour. In 1956, 72 per cent of the electorate voted according to this model, but by the 2006 election this had fallen to 28 per cent, a level only slightly better than would be achieved by random voting. Not only has the percentage dropped, but the contribution to its explanatory power has also shifted. In Chapter 2, a distinction was made between three true pillars (Catholic, Protestant and Socialist), and a possible fourth (Liberal). In 1956, 93 per cent of the votes following the structured model went to the parties of the 'true' pillars and only 7 per cent from those voting for the Liberals. In 2006, those from the secular middle class voting for the Liberals accounted for 38 per cent of the vote along structured lines, and in 2003 this percentage was even higher (43 per cent). The drop in overall percentage from 72 per cent to 28 per cent, combined with this shift to a substantial portion consisting of secular middle-class Liberal voters, not only weakens the importance of the structured model but also changes its meaning substantially. Therefore, no attempt has been made to calculate a percentage for subsequent elections. It simply no longer provides a useful model for understanding Dutch voting behaviour.

Ideology and Issues

The demise of group identification as the primary factor in explaining voter choice does not mean that voters have had nothing to guide them in determining their vote. According to Van Der Eijk and Niemöller, identification with an ideological position replaced identification with the social group, so that left–right turned out to be the most important determinant of voter choice (Van Der Eijk and Niemöller, 1983, 1987). They showed that most voters were able to place themselves and the political parties on a 7-point or 10-point left–right scale, and that a large number of people voted for the party closest to themselves on such a dimension. In Van Der Eijk and Niemöller's view, this single left–right ideological dimension was both dominant and sufficient for understanding voting behaviour.

Other observers have been less convinced that a single dimension provides a satisfactory representation of the Dutch ideological issue space. Luyten and Middendorp showed that voters did not employ a single definition of left–right, but seemed to use a two-dimensional structure (Luyten and Middendorp, 1990; see also Middendorp, 1991). In Chapter 3, we discussed the question of the 'dimensionality' of the political party system, and it was argued that at least two, and now possibly three, dimensions are needed in order to understand this system. The analysis here begins with the consideration of two dimensions: the socio-economic left–right dimension and the religious–secular dimension. Since 2002 and Pim Fortuyn, these two dimensions may not be sufficient to understand voting behaviour, so a possible third dimension must also be considered.

As a reaction to the strictures of a smallest distance model based on a single dimension, Irwin and Van Holsteyn introduced what they termed the 'heartland model' (Irwin and Van Holsteyn, 1989b). This model was based on the two dimensions of socio-economic left–right and religious–secular. Two questions from the Dutch Parliamentary Election Studies have been used to operationalize these two ideological dimensions. The issue selected as being most indicative of the socio-economic dimension is the position of the voter on the question of how great the differences between high incomes and low incomes should be. The secular–religious dimension was first based on a question concerning abortion, but as that issue diminished in importance, it was replaced in the election studies by euthanasia. The question that has been included since 1986 concerns whether individuals should be able to receive the help of physicians to end their lives on request, or whether euthanasia should be forbidden in all circumstances (see also Box 7.1 on page 207). In the surveys, respondents were asked to place themselves on 7-point scales, so a combination of 49 responses that can be displayed as a matrix is possible.

To understand voting behaviour, it is necessary also to determine the placement of political parties in this space. The alignment of the political parties on such dimensions has also been discussed in Chapter 3. Based on the analysis there, it is possible to define areas within the matrix that correspond to the positions of the three traditional major parties. For example, the Labour Party ideology has favoured both the reduction of income differences and the extension of possibilities for legal euthanasia. The Liberals have also favoured the liberalization of euthanasia, but do not support a reduction in income differences, or even argue that these differences have become too small and should be increased. The Christian Democrats have traditionally opposed euthanasia, but because they attempt to draw from all classes in the population they tend to take a broad, centrist position on the question of income differences. Each of these combinations of issue positions has been used to block out an area in the two-dimensional space. These areas are referred to as the 'heartland' for the respective party. It is within this area that the party could expect to win a substantial portion of the vote (see Irwin and Van Holsteyn, 1989b, 1999). The area not defined as heartland, which is located at the centre of the two-dimensional space, is labelled the 'battlefield'. Lacking no clear ideological identification with a party, this is the space in which one would expect the competition for votes to be strongest. The heartlands and the battlefield are shown in Figure 4.2.

To show the changes that have taken place within the electorate since the introduction of the heartland model, the percentages of the electorate that have placed themselves in each of the areas are shown for 1986 and the two most recent elections, in 2010 and 2012. A comparison of the percentages shows both stability and change. The percentages for the Labour and Liberal heartlands are quite stable; figures for other years would show some variations, but in general the pattern over a quarter

Figure 4.2 *Heartlands and Battlefield Based on Economic and Ethical Issue Dimensions, 1986, 2010, 2012*

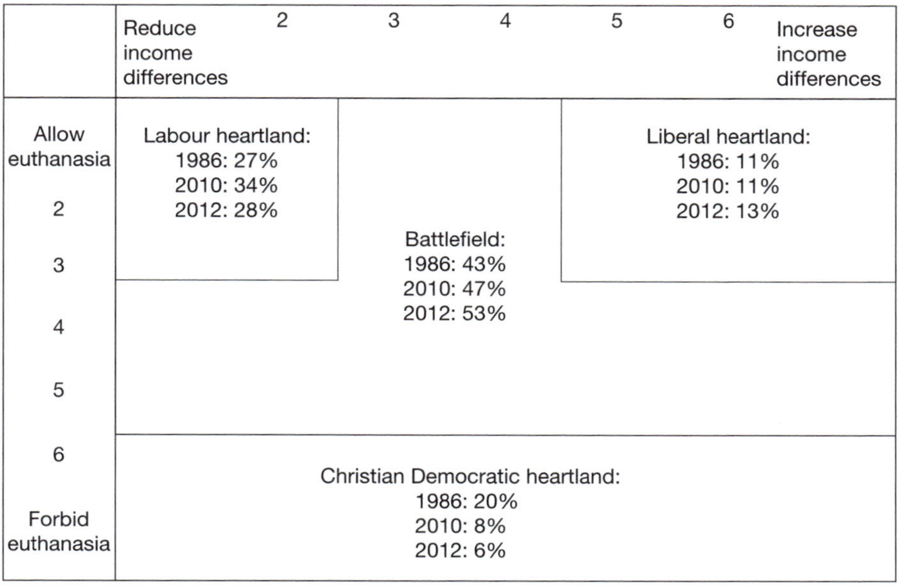

Source: Dutch Parliamentary Election Study, 1986, 2010, 2012.

century has been of stable patterns of opinion. This cannot be said for the Christian Democratic heartland. In 1986, 20 per cent of the electorate placed themselves in this area, but in the most recent election years, this percentage had fallen to 8 per cent and 6 per cent, respectively. This decline means that the CDA has a much smaller base of ideologically sympathetic voters on which to draw. With the Christian Democratic heartland declining and the Labour and Liberal heartlands remaining stable, it is obvious that the size of the battlefield has increased. There are thus more voters who are not clearly aligned ideologically with one of the major parties.

By naming the heartlands for the three major parties, it was expected that these parties could count on large percentages of support within these areas. Table 4.3 (see above) reports the percentages of the vote for all parties in each of the heartlands and the battlefield for the election of 1986 and the two most recent elections of 2010 and 2012. The figures for 1986 show that this expectation was justified. In its heartland, the Labour Party received the support of 66 per cent of the voters. The Liberal Party and CDA did not do quite as well, but still succeeded in receiving majority support (55 per cent and 56 per cent, respectively) within their heartlands. However, an examination of the figures for the most recent elections reveals that just as the model based on religious identification has lost its explanatory power, the power of the heartland model, or at least the interpretation of it, has also been altered dramatically. Only the Liberal Party has maintained its dominance in its heartland – and even increasing to 63 per cent in the 2012 election. By contrast, the Labour Party fell from the 66 per cent figure in its heartland in 1986 to only 28 per cent and 39 per cent of the vote in 2010 and 2012, respectively. It has faced strong competition in these and other recent elections from parties on the left, in particular the Green Left and the Socialist Party, and to a degree from D66. More disturbing for the model is the support found for the Freedom Party and the Liberal Party in Labour's heartland in recent elections. The support for the Freedom Party may be an indication that a new dimension is necessary in order to understand voting behaviour. Such a dimension will be investigated below.

The losses for the CDA within its heartland are even more dramatic. Even within its greatly diminished heartland in 2010 and 2012, it was only able to capture 22 per cent and 13 per cent of the vote, respectively. The small core of voters who remain opposed to euthanasia are now the supporters of the small, orthodox Calvinist parties. In 2012, these two parties received 61 per cent of the vote of those in this area. The weakness of the CDA in its own heartland is also revealed by the fact that in the most recent elections, the Labour Party has received as many votes as, or more than, the CDA.

Despite a declining base of religious supporters and ideological adherents, the CDA was able to maintain its position and even to become the largest party in Parliament between 2002 and 2010, by winning votes in other heartlands and in particular the battlefield. In 1986, during the heyday of the Lubbers Cabinets, the CDA gained the largest percentage (36 per cent) of the votes in the battlefield. This was true in 2002 and 2006 and almost so in 2003 (figures not shown in the table), but in 2010 and 2012 this was not the case, as it gained only 16 per cent and 10 per cent of the battlefield, respectively. In these elections, it has been the Liberal Party that has gained the largest percentage in this area (see Table 4.4).

Table 4.4 *Electoral Choice within the Ideological Heartlands and Battlefield, 1986, 2010, 2012*

Election year	Labour heartland			Liberal heartland			Christian Dem. heartland			Battlefield		
	1986	2010	2012	1986	2010	2012	1986	2010	2012	1986	2010	2012
PvdA	66	28	39	14	9	10	20	22	13	29	16	22
VVD	6	9	12	55	52	63	6	4	6	20	26	31
CDA	9	9	6	21	8	4	56	19	13	36	16	10
D66	5	7	4	8	9	11	2	2	0	11	11	14
Gr.Left	11*	9	5	2	4	2	1	0	1	3	7	2
Orth. Calv.	0	1	0	0	1	0	15	43	61	0	2	2
SP		18	18		4	4	2	5	4		10	8
PVV		17	10		11	8		5	0		9	5
PvdD			4			0			1			2
Other	3	1	3	2		1	1	1		1	2	2
Total	100%	99%	99%	100%	98%	100%	100%	101%	99%	101%	99%	98%
N =	315	707	358	127	212	161	243	150	72	524	954	665

Notes: * For 1986, the constituent parties (PPR, PSP, CPN, and EVP) that later formed the GreenLeft have been added together;** rounding errors.

Source: Dutch Parliamentary Election Study, 1986, 2010, 2012.

The heartland model was based on the dominance of three major parties in their own areas of a two-dimensional issue space. This dominance no longer holds. All three of the parties now face stiff competition, not only in the battlefield, but also within their own heartlands. In fact, one can no longer really speak of heartlands as the domain of these parties. Instead, the heartlands have become mini-battlefields in themselves. The parties must fight within the heartland for votes as well as attempt to win votes in other heartlands and in the battlefield. To understand this, other factors influencing voting behaviour must be examined. The first to be examined is the new dimension discussed above.

A New Dimension

In Chapters 2 and 3 we discussed changes in the dimensionality of the ideological issue space for Dutch political parties. We noted that the nineteenth-century definition of left–right has faded in importance as the major issues of abortion, euthanasia, and gay marriage have essentially been resolved. The twentieth-century definition involving socio-economic issues retains importance, but has now been joined by a new interpretation of left–right that has been referred to as a 'cultural' or 'authoritarian–libertarian' dimension (Pellikaan et al., 2007; Aarts and Thomassen, 2008), or 'integration–demarcation' dimension (Kriesi et al., 2008). As early as 1994, the Dutch Parliamentary Election Study found that issues related to minorities and refugees had exceeded unemployment as the issue uppermost in the minds of the electorate (Aarts and Thomassen, 2008, p. 216). This may have been related in part to the efforts of the Liberal leader, Frits Bolkestein, to place such matters on the political agenda. In an analysis of the 1994 election it was noted that this issue may have reinforced some existing ideological positions, but was dismissed as not being important enough to warrant description as a separate dimension (Irwin and Van Holsteyn, 1997, p. 113). Apart from Frits Bolkestein, the parties avoided conflict over such issues, but in 2002 Pim Fortuyn forced them on to the electoral agenda and all parties were forced to react (see Chapter 2; see also Otjes, 2011).

In attempting to operationalize this new dimension, two aspects can be considered. Virtually all observers would surely agree that attitudes towards immigration, especially whether immigrants to the Netherlands should be allowed to retain elements of their own culture or should adapt to Dutch culture, are indicative of a voter's position on this dimension. Fortuyn was instrumental in shifting the political agenda by giving voice to those who felt foreigners should adapt. Geert Wilders has been even more vociferous in his demands that immigrants assimilate into Dutch culture. A question from the Dutch Parliamentary Election Studies can be used to operationalize this aspect of the new dimension. The question asks respondents to place themselves on a 7-point scale with 'allow immigrants to keep their own culture' at one end and 'adjust to Dutch culture' at the other. To examine whether this new dimension cuts across the two dimensions of the heartland model, the seven points have been re-coded into three categories: a category including those on

Table 4.5 *Attitudes towards Immigrants and Electoral Choice within the Ideological Heartlands and Battlefield, 2012*

	Labour heartland			Liberal heartland			Christian Dem. heartland			Battlefield		
	Keep own culture	Middle	Adjust	Keep own culture	Middle	Adjust	Keep own culture	Middle	Adjust	Keep own culture	Middle	Adjust
PvdA	41	47	25	24	11	4	40	13	0	29	20	20
SP	27	16	13	0	4	2	10	3	4	6	10	6
Gr Left	19	1	0	5	1	0	10	0	0	7	2	0
D66	5	5	1	14	12	7	–	–	–	22	17	3
CDA	1	5	11	0	5	4	10	11	17	9	11	8
Orth. Calv.	–	–	–	–	–	–	30	61	75	3	1	3
VVD	4	13	16	57	63	65	0	8	4	20	30	42
Freedom	0	4	26	0	4	18	–	–	–	0	4	13
Animals	2	5	4	–	–	–	0	3	0	3	2	1
50+	0	3	5	0	1	2	–	–	–	0	1	4
Other	0	2	0	–	–	–	0	3	0	1	1	1
Total	99	101*	101	100	101	102	100	102	100	100	99	101
N =	75	160	103	21	83	57	10	38	24	146	335	184

Note: * Where total is not exactly 100, this is due to rounding errors.
Source: Dutch Parliamentary Election Study, 2012.

the side of the scale that would allow immigrants to retain their own culture (18 per cent); those with a moderate position (positions 4 and 5 on the scale, 48 per cent); and those most demanding of immigrants to adjust to Dutch culture (34 per cent). The voting behaviour for each of these three categories can be examined within each of the areas of the heartland model.

Results from the 2012 election show the importance of this new dimension in at least three of the four areas of the heartland model. Since votes in the Christian Democratic area went predominantly to the Christian-Democratic parties and no votes were recorded for the Freedom Party, this issue has had very little impact within this heartland. However, within the Labour heartland the impact has been substantial: among those with the most permissive views, the Labour Party received just over 40 per cent of the vote and no fewer than 87 per cent supported a party of the left (that is, Labour, Green Left, or Socialist Party). On the other hand, among those in the Labour heartland who demanded that immigrants adjust to Dutch culture, only 25 per cent voted for the Labour Party and the combined vote for the left was only 38 per cent. The Freedom Party received no less than 26 per cent of the vote, and the Liberal Party and CDA added 16 per cent and 11 per cent respectively.

In the Liberal heartland, the Liberal Party vote varied only between 57 per cent and 65 per cent across the three categories, but the deviations from this dominant pattern were strongly affected by attitudes towards assimilation. The 65 per cent vote for the Liberal Party was among those with the strongest demands to assimilate, but the party faced competition among those with these views from the Freedom Party, which received only 18 per cent of the vote. On the other hand, among those who would allow immigrants to maintain their own culture, 24 per cent supported the Labour Party. This pattern is equally clear in the battlefield area. Those who would allow the maintenance of an immigrant's own culture generally supported parties of the left, whereas those who demand adjustment tended to favour the Freedom Party and the Liberal Party.

A second operationalization of this dimension relates to European integration. Recall that Kriesi et al. (2008) have labelled this new dimension the 'integration–demarcation' dimension, clearly referring to European integration, even though they stress the issue of immigration for the Netherlands. Aarts and Thomassen (2008) also include the issue of European integration as an element of this new dimension. This is an issue that had never been high on the political agenda, as all major parties had traditionally been supportive. Nevertheless, some observers have seen it as a potential 'sleeping giant' waiting to be awakened by the proper individual or party (see Van Der Eijk and Franklin, 2004; Van Holsteyn and Den Ridder, 2005; De Vries, 2007a, 2007b). Fortuyn also did not emphasize this issue, but in the aftermath of his success the other parties became unsure of how to deal with the ratification of the European Constitution and called for a national referendum (see Chapter 10). Despite the defeat of the European Constitution, the issue did not emerge as a major matter for debate in the 2006 election – though it hardly seems completely coincidental that the parties most opposed to the Constitution (the Socialist Party, the Christian Union, and Wilders' Freedom Party) were the biggest winners in

2006. Wilders attempted to capitalize on this issue in 2012, entitling the party mani-festo '*Their* Brussels, *Our* Netherlands'.

Recent Dutch national elections studies have included a 7-point scale with '[European integration] should go further' at one end and 'has gone too far' at the other. In 2012, 33 per cent felt European integration should go further; 23 per cent chose the middle position, and 44 per cent felt integration had gone too far. By looking at the voting behaviour of those with these attitudes within the areas of the heartland model, we can understand how this new dimension is becoming important in understanding voting behaviour.

As with immigration, this issue plays no role within the Christian Democratic heartland, but is important in the other three. In the Labour heartland, not only does an opinion that European integration has gone too far lead to votes for the Freedom Party, but it helps to explain the distinction between voting for the Labour Party or Green Left and support for the Socialist Party. The latter received slightly more than 20 per cent of the vote in this heartland among those who had middle views or felt integration had gone too far, but only 10 per cent among those who felt European integration should go further. Within the Liberal heartland, it is the competition between the Liberal Party and the Freedom Party that takes place along this dimension. The Freedom Party gains almost no votes among those who are in favour or are in the middle on this issue, but just over 20 per cent among those who are opposed. Further competition for the Liberal Party in its heartland appears at the other end of the scale, with D66 obtaining almost 20 per cent of the vote among those who feel European integration should go further. This pattern is repeated in the battlefield, with D66 doing better among those who favour more European inte-gration, and the Freedom Party doing better among those who feel it has gone too far (see Table 4.6).

Thus there are indications that the new 'cultural' or 'integration–demarcation' is replacing the older religious–secular dimension in importance for understanding voting behaviour. The religious–secular dimension is important for a declining number of votes, though for these voters it is dominant and the new dimension has little impact. For other voters, this new dimension, whether in the form of immi-gration or European integration, is becoming more important. In particular, those voters who are on the left in socio-economic terms, but on the right in cultural terms, must make a choice as to which of the two dimensions will be predominant. The heartlands have become 'mini-battlefields', with competition occurring along this new dimension. The choice among the parties competing within the Labour and Liberal heartlands and within the battlefield are also affected by a number of short-term factors. It is to these factors that we now turn.

Short-term Factors

Religious and class identification, as well as ideological identification, can be seen as 'long-term' factors related to voting behaviour. That is to say, they are

Table 4.6 *Attitudes towards European Integration and Electoral Choice within the Ideological Heartlands and Battlefield, 2012*

	Labour heartland			Liberal heartland			Christian Dem. heartland			Battlefield		
	Should go further	*Middle*	*Gone too far*	*Should go further*	*Middle*	*Gone too far*	*Should go further*	*Middle*	*Gone too far*	*Should go further*	*Middle*	*Gone too far*
PvdA	54	40	30	6	16	9	17	10	10	19	23	23
SP	10	22	21	0	5	4	8	0	4	6	12	9
Gr Left	13	3	1	2	0	2	8	0	0	4	2	1
D66	5	9	1	19	5	4	–	–	–	21	12	7
CDA	3	9	6	5	3	4	8	40	8	11	13	7
Orth. Calv.	–	–	–	–	–	–	58	40	69	2	2	1
VVD	9	8	14	66	68	57	0	10	4	32	27	34
Freedom	3	3	16	2	0	21	–	–	–	1	6	11
Animals	3	5	4	–	–	–	0	0	2	2	1	2
50+	0	2	5	2	3	0	–	–	–	1	2	3
Other	0	0	2	–	–	–	0	0	2	1	1	2
Total	100	101*	100	102	100	101	99	100	99	100	101	100
N =	100	65	171	67	37	56	12	10	48	273	165	218

Note: * Where total is not exactly 100, this is due to rounding errors.
Source: Dutch Parliamentary Election Study, 2012.

generally determined well in advance of a particular election. As long as their impact is strong, the results of elections should exhibit considerable stability. This has long been the case in the Netherlands, as can be seen in Figure 4.3. In the 1950s, the structured model produced low levels of electoral volatility and generally only slightly more than 5 per cent of the seats changed hands at the election. During this period, volatility at the individual level was equally low, with perhaps no more than 10–15 per cent of voters switching parties between elections (Mair, 2008). As the structured model described above began to lose its grip, volatility in the Netherlands began to increase, but the major jump began in the 1990s, with a peak in 2002 when more than 30 per cent of parliamentary seats changed hands. At the present time, as much as a third of the electorate changes parties between elections. The percentage of voters who reported always voting for the same party fell in the space of just over two decades from a half in 1981 to under a third in 2003 (Van Der Kolk, 2000, p. 96; Dutch Parliamentary Election Study, 2003) and researchers have given up asking the question. Volatility is now high by European standards, and no fewer than three of the 11 most volatile elections across Europe between 1950 and 2006 were recent Dutch ones – 1994, 2002, and 2006 (Mair, 2008).

As these long-term factors have declined in importance and voters actually have to make choices, they have begun to postpone their decisions concerning the vote. As late as 1986, 70 per cent of voters reported that they knew months in advance for which party they would vote, and only about 10–12 per cent reported that they decided only in the days just before the election. Since then, more and more voters have postponed their decision. In 2010, the Dutch Parliamentary Election Study reported that only 31 per cent of voters knew months before for which party they would vote, and a greater percentage (42 per cent) only decided in the final days

Figure 4.3 *Electoral Volatility, 1946–2012 (% of seats changing hands)*

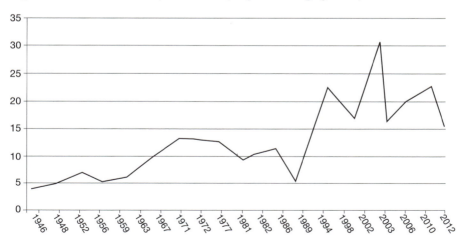

before the election. No fewer than 14 per cent stated they had only decided on election day itself. For 2012, the pollster Maurice de Hond reported a similar figure (15 per cent) deciding on the election day itself, but added that no fewer than 30 per cent had decided in the previous 48 hours (De Hond, 2012).

Choice Sets

One reason that Dutch voters are postponing their decisions is that they no longer associate a single party with their position in society or their ideological convictions. Rather than always voting for the same party, they must now make a choice among a set of parties. Van Holsteyn and Den Ridder (2008) have attempted to understand the magnitude of these choice sets by making use of a set of questions posed in the Dutch Parliamentary Election Studies. Respondents are asked to indicate on a scale from 1 to 10 what the chance is that they will vote for each of the parties in the future. Van Holsteyn and Den Ridder estimated that, in elections between 1994 and 2006, only about 30 per cent of voters indicate that there was only a single party for which they would consider voting. Using a slightly different method of calculating the choice set of voters, a similar distribution was found for 2010. Only 31 per cent gave a value of 8 or higher to a single party; 33 per cent gave a high score to two parties; and 30 per cent gave a high score to three or more parties (6 per cent gave no party a score of 8 or higher). Those with only a single party in their choice set have less difficulty in reaching a decision, and 70 per cent indicated that they knew what their decision would be well before the last days before the election. On the other hand, among those with three or more parties in their choice set, about half report making a decision in 2010 only in the last days or on election day itself. In addition to the number of parties in the choice set, the strength of feelings towards the parties also affects the timing of the decision. Those who have no strong feelings towards any of the parties (and have given no party a score of 8 or higher) are the most likely to decide at the last minute; about half made their decision in the last days before, or actually on, election day (data for 2012 are not available).

With far more votes and seats 'up for grabs', parties must now compete more for the votes they receive, and the Netherlands has moved towards a more open, almost unstructured, model of electoral competition. The campaign, while short in the Netherlands, has taken on increased importance, and short-term factors have become more important, for example, the importance of election debates has been discussed above. Other short-term factors will be considered here.

Retrospective Voting

As both the parties and the electorate have become depillarized sociologically and depolarized ideologically, governmental performance has begun to emerge as a short-term factor influencing voter choice. This can be seen in Figure 4.4, which

"thrown the rascals out"' (Mair, 2008), meaning that there has always been some overlap between the outgoing and incoming coalitions.

Evidence has emerged that those who are satisfied with government economic performance vote retrospectively for the government coalition partners, particularly the party of the Prime Minister, whereas those who are dissatisfied vote for opposition parties (Irwin and Van Holsteyn, 2008). By the 1980s, the parties had become aware of this, and in 1986 the CDA coined a clever slogan to combine the popularity of the Prime Minister with improvement in the economy: 'Let Lubbers finish his job'. That election was unusual, since the governing parties indicated prior to the election that they would continue the coalition if the voters provided a mandate. Though the Liberals lost as many seats as the CDA won, the coalition was able to return. Another election after which the governing coalition was able to return was 1998; D66 lost 10 seats, but both of the other coalition partners were rewarded and the coalition returned with five seats more than previously (see Figure 4.4).

However, rewarding a coalition is clearly the exception to the rule, and the degree of punishment is generally far greater than the rewards. The election that first made it clear that Dutch voters would punish a governing coalition was 1994, when only 14 per cent felt the impact on the economy had been favourable, and 32 per cent felt it had been unfavourable (Van Holsteyn and Irwin, 2003). The CDA lost so many seats at this election that it became possible to exclude it from the new Cabinet (the so-called Purple coalition of Labour, Liberal and D66). Since then, with the exception of 1998, governing coalitions have tended to lose fairly heavily at elections.

One should, however, never maintain the illusion that economic performance is the only consideration in retrospective voting. It is not always the economy and it is stupid to presume that it is. This point was brought home to the parties with a vengeance in 2002. Buoyed by the strong economy in the previous years the Purple coalition parties again entered the 2002 election campaign with confidence. Data from the election study of that year indicated that the electorate remained positive concerning the performance of the government. Two-thirds thought that the government had had a favourable impact on employment, and 52 per cent thought there had been a favourable impact on the economy in general. However, by the time of the 2002 election, the economy was no longer uppermost in the minds of the voters. Only very small percentages mentioned anything to do with the economy as being among the most important problems. Pim Fortuyn was able to activate latent discontent in the electorate on issues such as crime, the quality of health services, and policies towards asylum-seekers into unprecedented success for his party and equally unprecedented losses for the coalition parties (Van Praag, 2003).

A final note on the importance of governmental performance concerns the distinction between how performance affects an individual voter personally and how it affects the economy in general. In the literature on voting behaviour, this is the distinction is referred to as *pocketbook* voting versus *sociotropic* voting. While it is often assumed that the way that economic performance affects an individual personally is more important in influencing the vote, generally the opposite has been found to be true. Results from the Dutch Parliamentary Election Studies give an indication as to why this is the case. Respondents are more likely to place blame on the government for its effects on the economy in general than for the effects on his or her personal financial situation, and thus be more likely to cast a vote regarding the general economic impact rather than any impact on him or her personally. At the same time, results from 2012 also show that governmental performance effects on the personal financial situation were particularly negative in that year. Researchers will therefore need to examine these results carefully to determine the extent to which both evaluations influenced the vote in 2012.

Party Leaders

The weakening of social attachments and ideological identification as clear indicators of voter choice has led increasingly to charges that voters no longer vote for a party and its ideas, but for the attractiveness of the leader. Of course, even before dealignment took place, it was at times argued that political leaders had an impact on the vote. Names such as Drees, Zijlstra, De Gaay Fortman, Van Mierlo and Wiegel are frequently mentioned in this context. More recently it might be Bos, Marijnissen, Rutte, or Samsom.

Perhaps no individual leader has had as great an impact on the vote as Pim Fortuyn in 2002. Fortuyn is also of special interest because he was the leader of another party before he organized his own list. This allows us to separate the impact of the person and the party more clearly, at least for this case. When he switched from Liveable Netherlands to his own list, support for the former dropped precipitously, whereas support for his new list was even higher than support for Liveable Netherlands had been (Van Holsteyn and Irwin, 2003). Clearly the voters had stuck with the person and not with the party. Of course, in this case both were newcomers to the political stage, and even such evidence does not separate the personality of the candidate from the message he or she is espousing.

It is a major challenge for researchers to sort out to what extent voters have voted for an individual or for a party. The voters themselves have no doubt; invariably, when asked in surveys they indicate overwhelmingly that they vote for a party. In a 2006 study, Van Holsteyn and Andeweg concluded that the electorate still vote overwhelmingly for a party rather than a candidate. Of those who cast a preference vote in 2006, no more than 11 per cent indicated that they would have voted for this candidate had he or she been on the list of a different party (and even this number may be inflated by the number of voters who supported Rita Verdonk). When combined with the list-pullers, no more than 9 per cent of Dutch voters would have followed their favourite candidate to another party, and the remaining 91 per cent would simply have found another candidate on the list for whom to vote (Van Holsteyn and Andeweg, 2010, p. 122). Such results indicate minimal impact of leaders and candidates. Yet the importance of the candidates mentioned above implies that the matter is not so simple. The problem is to sort out the impact of the party from that of the person, as the two are often closely tied together. It is fairly easy to show that voters who like a candidate also like his or her party, and those who dislike a candidate also dislike that candidate's party, but what is the direction of causality?

Whatever the causality, on balance, parties would certainly prefer to have a popular candidate leading the list than an unpopular one. This can be illustrated by the fate of the Labour Party at the 2002 and 2003 elections. In 2002 the popular prime minister, Wim Kok, retired and was succeeded as party leader by Ad Melkert. Melkert was far less popular than his predecessor, scoring 25 points lower on average on a 101-point feeling thermometer scale. The Labour Party campaign strategy had been to focus on Melkert as the next Prime Minister, but this was clearly a major mistake. By focusing on the candidate and not the party message, when the candidate became a liability, a recipe for disaster had been found and the party lost heavily. Melkert resigned soon after the election and was replaced by Wouter Bos. Bos was personally more popular (by 20 points on average) than Melkert. At the 2003 elections, the Bos focused on the message of the economy, and the Labour Party was able to regain much of the vote that had been lost in the previous year.

Sorting out what leads to popularity and unpopularity is also not an easy matter. Pim Fortuyn was a candidate voters either loved or hated. No fewer than 20 per cent gave him the lowest possible score on the 101-point scale. However, 14 per cent gave him a score of 75 or higher, and it was among these people that votes were found. Yet, even in this case, it would appear that the message is more important than the individual. Personally Fortuyn was brash, arrogant, disrespectful, and blatantly homosexual, though also provocative and intelligent. But analysis has shown that the evaluation he received from voters was based more on his message than it was for other top party candidates (Van Holsteyn and Irwin, 2003). Voters were attracted by his message concerning immigration, integration, and related issues.

In more recent election studies, respondents have been asked to evaluate the parties and leaders on an 11-point scale. In 2012, the highest average score went to Prime Minister Mark Rutte (6.71). It is not unusual that the Prime Minister receives the highest score, which can often be translated into success in an election. An exception to this would be Jan Peter Balkenende, whose popularity in three previous elections had played out by 2010, when his average value fell to only 5.39, below that of five other party leaders. In 2012, Rutte was followed closely by Labour leader Diederik Samsom, with an average score of 6.30. Alexander Pechtold (D66) and Emile Roemer (Socialist Party) also had average scores of above 6.0. At the other end of the spectrum, Geert Wilders (Freedom Party) received an average score of only 3.01. This was in part because of the exceptional percentage (20 per cent) of respondents who gave him the lowest possible score of 0 on the 11-point scale; no other leader of a political party had more than 3 per cent with such a low score.

To win votes for a party it is virtually essential that the leader has greater popularity than the party, as little help will be provided by a leader who is less popular than his or her party. To make this comparison, the scores on the 'feeling thermometer' for the parties have been compared with the scores for the party leaders. Table 4.7 compares these scores and reports the percentages for the party leaders that are higher, equal or lower than the scores for their respective party.

Table 4.7 *Comparisons of the 'Feeling Thermometer' Scores for Party Leaders and their Respective Political Party, 2012*

	Party leader higher than political party	Party leader same as political party	Total higher than party leader	
Van Haersma Buma v. CDA	39	25	33	101%*
Samsom v. PvdA	45	35	21	101%
Rutte v. VVD	57	31	13	101%
Roemer v. SP	55	31	14	100%
Wilders v. Freedom Party	34	43	22	99%
Pechtold v. D66	46	34	20	100%
Sap v. Green Left	45	28	27	100%
Slob v. CU	43	34	23	100%
Van der Staaij v. SGP	47	33	20	100%
Thieme v. Animal Rights Party	42	35	23	100%

Note: * Where total is not exactly 100, this is due to rounding errors.
Source: Dutch Parliamentary Election Study, 2012.

In general, individuals are viewed more positively than parties, but this was especially so in 2012. All the party leaders had percentages that were higher for their own popularity than for their party's. Nevertheless, important distinctions can be made. The scores of more than 50 per cent who rated the party leader more popular than the party for Rutte (VVD) and Roemer (SP) are comparatively high, not only for 2012, but also in comparison to previous elections. The problems for the CDA, which were seen in the analysis of the structured vote and in the heartland, were compounded in 2012 because the party was not able to field a popular candidate as leader. Van Haersma Buma had only 39 per cent seeing him as more popular than his party, and since his average score (5.48) was a full point lower than that for Rutte and Samsom, neither the party nor its leader were evaluated particularly highly. Geert Wilders has the highest percentage for whom an equal score for the party and its leader was given, indicating (not incorrectly) that the respondents saw little distinction between the party and its leader in his case.

While the importance of having a popular leader is surely evident, exactly how and when it is translated into electoral success is still undetermined. The VVD with Mark Rutte achieved excellent success in the 2012 elections, but while Emile Roemer is shown here to have been quite popular, his party ultimately had no electoral gains in 2012. Voters are convinced that they vote for the party, but they clearly are influenced by who is putting the message of the party forward. With so many options available to them, often with relatively minor differences in substance, the packaging and the messenger can have an influence. A good product, poorly packaged, will do poorly, but packaged well it will sell.

Strategic Voting

Most theories of voting behaviour proceed on the assumption that the voter casts a vote for his or her favourite party. This is called *sincere voting;* the voter decides which party is best and casts the vote accordingly (Rosema, 2004, 2006). However, for at least 150 years it has been known that there may be reasons for a voter to cast a *non-sincere* vote; that is, for a party other than the most preferred party. In 1869, Henry Droop formulated the 'wasted-vote hypothesis', which applied in single member majority vote electoral systems. In such systems, a vote can be wasted if it is cast for a party or candidate who is not in the running to win. In such a case, in order not to waste the vote, the voter should cast a vote for one of the two candidates or parties that have a chance of winning. Voting for a less preferred party in order to influence who wins the election is known as *strategic voting*, and is a prominent form of non-sincere voting.

Proportional representation has been seen a solution that all but eliminates the 'wasted vote', since if the votes are tallied proportionally, smaller parties can actually win representation in an elected body. Strategic voting should therefore become unnecessary. In his classic study, Anthony Downs (1957) actually saw it as impossible. He saw voting as means for selecting a government, and under proportional representation with coalition governments, it would be impossible for the voter to acquire the requisite information to cast a strategic vote. Purists view strategic voting as the attempt by a voter to cast the vote that breaks a tie. Indeed, in a proportional representation system, such as in the Netherlands, it would be impossible to estimate the chance of determining the final remainder seat that brings a coalition to exactly 76 seats and therefore makes that coalition possible.

Yet, the inability to cast a pivotal vote does not mean that voters in systems of proportional representation may not employ strategic considerations when determining for which party to vote. Voters may attempt to act instrumentally in order to cast a vote that influences an outcome other than the distribution of seats. Various researchers have employed the term *strategic voting* to include all forms of voting in which the voter casts the vote for other than the most preferred party in order to influence such an outcome. This broader definition is used when discussing strategic voting in the Netherlands.

The well-known *bandwagon* (voting for a party because it is the largest) and *underdog* (voting for a party because it needs help) *effects* may be forms of non-sincere voting that have strategic components. However, other forms, which can be either affective or cognitive reactions to poll results, have been identified (Van Holsteyn and Irwin, 2013). A voter can also cast a non-sincere vote in order to attempt to influence the direction that their favourite party is taking. For example, when some members felt that the Labour Party was becoming too centrist, they cast a vote for the Green Left.

The most prominent form of strategic voting in the Netherlands, at least the one that is most often discussed, is *coalition preference voting*. In systems of proportional representation, it is often the case that the outcome of the election does not determine who gains power, and the formation of a government must be regulated in the process of coalition formation. Yet data show that Dutch voters are concerned about which parties form the coalition, and one survey showed that, when asked, more responded that they would prefer to have influence on the composition of the government than the number that wished to influence the composition of the Parliament (Irwin and Holsteyn, 2011) There are increasing indications that a number of voters are attempting to influence the composition of the coalition when casting their vote.

In 2002, research found that 29 per cent of voters cast a non-sincere vote, of which some were surely strategic votes (Irwin and Van Holsteyn, 2012). That research also investigated whether the voters satisfied the conditions that would be necessary to cast a coalition preference vote: 1. having expectations concerning how other voters would vote and what the electoral outcome would be; 2. having expectations concerning the likelihood of various coalition possibilities that could emerge after the election; and 3. having expectations concerning the compromises to be reached in forming a coalition. It was found that Dutch voters were reasonably well-informed concerning the first two, but that nobody, not even the parties themselves, had information concerning the third condition. Nevertheless, the conclusion was that voters probably felt themselves to be sufficiently well informed to cast a coalition preference vote (ibid.).

Since 2002, the term strategic voting has entered the vocabulary of Dutch journalists and voters and is now commonly employed. In the 2012 election, it was prominently discussed. As the campaign developed, the question arose as to whether the Liberal or Labour Party would emerge as the largest party and thus be empowered to take the lead in the Cabinet formation process. It was generally felt that many voters on the left, whose early preference had been for the Socialist Party (and perhaps Green Left) turned to the Labour Party in order to influence the coalition outcome. Pollster Maurice de Hond reported that 17 per cent of respondents in his survey indicated that they had cast a strategic vote, and that without these votes, the Labour Party would have gained 12 fewer seats (De Hond, 2012).

Peter Kanne of TNS-NIPO found a similar number (16 per cent, up from 11 per cent in 2010) of voters who stated that they had based their choice on strategic considerations. He also examined the motivations for voters who had switched their vote in the last days before the election. He found evidence of the various types of non-sincere or strategic voting that have been mentioned here. Among these switchers, 23 per cent said they had done so in order to increase the chances for a particular coalition, and 6 per cent voted to attempt to make a particular coalition have less chance of emerging; 17 per cent voted in order to make one party the largest, and 12 per cent did so to ensure that a party was *not* the largest. These strategic considerations were mentioned far more often by switchers than other reasons such as watching the news and debates (26 per cent), or cue-taking from family members, friends or acquaintances (Kanne, 2012).

BOX 4.2

Voter Assistance Apps

With so many voters facing a choice between up to five parties, it is hardly surprising that they have turned to technology for assistance. The Netherlands was the first country in which what has come to be known as Voter Assistance Apps appeared. The first such application began as a paper and disc version in 1989 and is known as the Stemwijzer (VoteMatch; www.stemwijzer.nl). It went online in 1998 and has since been used at all elections for the Second Chamber of Parliament as well as for municipal and water board elections. In 2006, the newspaper *Trouw* collaborated with political scientists at the Free University of Amsterdam to develop Kieskompas (www.kieskompas.nl). In 2012, the producers of Stemwijzer developed a new version called Stemtracker. These are the three most popular general voter aids, but a large number of specialized aids have since been developed.

The purpose of all these aids is to provide information to the voter concerning his/her own issue positions compared with the positions taken by the various political parties. This means that the makers of the aid must in some fashion determine the positions taken by the parties. This is generally based on the election manifestoes of the parties, but in some cases the parties are allowed to comment on the coding that has been done. This has led to questions concerning to what degree the parties can manipulate their responses to become more popular with the voters. It has even been suggested that parties may begin to write their election manifestoes with these voting assistance apps in mind. The Stemtracker introduced a new element by basing the party positions on how the party voted on important legislation.

Both the Stemwijzer and Kieskompas present the voter with 30 statements, which can be answered on a 3-point and 5-point scale, respectively. Stemwijzer then indicates for how many of the statements the voter is in agreement with the various parties. Kieskompas presents the results in a two-dimensional space with left–right and progressive–conservative on the axes. Both the voter and the parties are placed in this space, thus providing the voter with an indication of where he/she stands with respect to the parties. The choice of axes has been somewhat controversial, especially since the Freedom Party is pictured as a centre party.

The use of such apps by the voters has risen rapidly. In 2002 and 2003, the Stemwijzer was used more than 2 million times. In the three most recent elections, this risen to 4.6, 4.2, and 4.85 million in 2006, 2010, and 2012, respectively. In 2010, Kieskompas was consulted 1.5 million times. In the Dutch Parliamentary Election Study 2012, more than 66 per cent of respondents indicated that they had heard of such voter assistance apps, and fully 60 per cent indicated that they had seriously filled in at least one of the sets of questions. Note that such apps avoid making a claim that they provide advice, but concentrate on providing assistance to the voter in determining the choice for a party. How the voters use the information is not known, but in 2012, among those who had consulted a voting assistance app, 12 per cent said that it had had a strong influence on their choice, and an additional 41 per cent said it had had some influence. This amounted to 27 per cent of all voters who indicated that they had at least to an extent used the information from the app in making their decision. One set of

→

→

researchers has claimed that, in 2006, the Stemwijzer accounted for a shift of approximately five seats at the parliamentary elections (Akse et al., 2010). In other research
on that same election, researchers concluded that there was bias in the 'advice' given
by the Stemwijzer, and that the CDA and Freedom Party gained an advantage over the
Liberal and Labour parties (Kleinnijenhuis et al., 2007, p. 144).

Conclusion

The Netherlands has gone from what can be called a structured system of voting
behaviour, based on religion and social class, to an open system. Some structure
in this open system is provided by the ideological differences between the parties.
However, these differences seem to be declining and the electorate also may be
becoming less polarized along ideological lines. This means that other factors, often
shorter-term ones, are becoming more important in influencing voting behaviour.
At times, the performance of the government has had an impact on the electorate.
In 2002, a new face with new issues emerged on the scene and strongly influenced
the results. Though Pim Fortuyn and his party have disappeared from the political
scene, others have picked up the gauntlet. The Dutch electorate has become quite
volatile, as evidenced by the gains made on both right and left in recent elections.
What motivates Dutch voters is becoming more difficult for both observers and the
politicians themselves to understand.

5

The Core Executive

The Coalition Imperative

Dutch government is coalition government. As a result of such factors as socio-cultural minorities, a multi-party system and proportional representation, which have been discussed in the three previous chapters, no single party has ever controlled a majority of seats in Parliament, or come sufficiently close to try to govern the country as a single-party minority government. This simple fact has important consequences for political life in the Netherlands. In this chapter we discuss how governing coalitions are formed before turning to the consequences of coalition government for the functioning of the Dutch core executive.

Building the Governing Coalition

'Dutch Without Government', 'Power Vacuum in The Hague': Dutch politics does not often attract the attention of the international press, but when it does it is often with headlines such as these in connection with the formation of a new government. Any hint of episodes of anarchy would be an exaggeration, but the suggestion that the interregnum between two Dutch governments is both important and different from the practices relating to the transfer of power in other countries is undoubtedly correct.

Important as they are, elections seldom have a determining impact on the formation of a government. First, despite a general trend towards bipolar party systems in Europe, the Netherlands is one of five countries in which parties still do not cluster into two blocs that usually alternate in government (Mair, 2008, 2011). Parties announce their intention to form a coalition only occasionally before an election; for example, if they want to continue the governing combination, but such proto-coalitions do not always gain a majority and, if they do not, they considerably complicate the building of a new governing coalition. Examples are from the 1972 election, when PvdA, D66 and PPR had formed a 'progressive' electoral alliance, winning enough votes to deprive the Christian Democrats of a majority but without obtaining one themselves; and from the elections of 1981 and 2003, when the Christian Democrats and the Liberals fell short of a parliamentary majority, thus thwarting their plans to continue their partnership in government.

Second, the election outcome usually leaves several options open. After the 2012 elections, for example, numerically speaking, 2,047 different single-party governments and combinations of parties were possible, 1,006 of which could have commanded a majority in Parliament. Third, parties may sometimes claim a right to be included in the new governing coalition on the basis of their electoral results, but in practice a party that has 'won' in the election may lose the government formation. If we look at all the governments formed immediately after elections since 1945, 33 of the parties in the new coalition had made electoral gains and 31 had suffered electoral losses. There is not even a guarantee that the largest party will be part of the governing coalition.

Constitutionally, it is not necessary that the electorate be consulted before forming a new government after the previous one has collapsed. In 1963, a coalition was formed between the three Christian Democratic parties (KVP, ARP and CHU) and the Liberal Party. Two years later, this Cabinet fell and a new coalition of KVP, ARP and Labour was formed. A year later, this Cabinet too was gone and a coalition of KVP and ARP filled in the time until new elections were held in 1967. Thus three coalitions of quite different political composition had governed the country, only the first coalition having been formed following an election. The public reaction to this episode is often suggested to have led to a new unwritten constitutional rule that a new government can be formed only after elections; that it is 'unhygienic to change partners without changing the sheets'. Since 1967, many changes in the formation and functioning of the Dutch core executive have taken place; however, this is not one of them. Replacing one government with another fully powered one without having first held elections was exceptional even before 1967. Both before and after 1967 the most common resolutions of a Cabinet crisis are mediation or the continuation of part of the coalition (in Dutch: *rompkabinet*) as a caretaker Cabinet preparing for early elections (Andeweg, 2008, pp. 261–2).

Because of the weak link between election outcome and government formation, the interregnum between the resignation of the old Cabinet, and the swearing in of the new one, remains one of the most important but also one of the most controversial times in Dutch politics.

Procedures of Cabinet Formation

The negotiations for a new governing coalition are presided over by a *formateur* (a politician appointed to organize the formation of a coalition government) or by one or more *informateurs* who attempt to find points of agreement in potential coalition partners). The distinction between *formateurs* and *informateurs* is of little significance. Originally, only *formateurs* were appointed, but since the Second World War, often because of complicated inter-party relationships, no *formateur* has succeeded in forming a government at the first attempt. This made the office of *informateur* more attractive, as information about the various options left open can always be gathered, whereas a government cannot always be formed immediately. Thus the political risks involved in being an *informateur* are far less than those inherent in the position of *formateur*. In practice, however, *informateurs* no longer confine themselves to the gathering of information (*informateurs* who do restrict themselves to that task are now sometimes called *verkenners*: explorers), and it has become customary for *informateurs* to leave only the recruitment of new ministers to a *formateur*, who is the Prime Minister designate.

Until the formation of the Rutte I government in 2010, *formateurs* and *informateurs* were appointed by the monarch (see Box 1.3 on page 21 for other details about the monarch's political role). Before making such an appointment, the Queen in those days would consult all party leaders. If a likely coalition emerged from these consultations, the Queen would follow the advice of the party leaders and appoint a politician from one of the potential governing parties, usually the largest one, as *(in) formateur*. If the political situation was more complicated, she would first appoint a less partisan politician (such as the vice-president of the Council of State) as *informateur* to explore which combination of parties was most likely to succeed in forming a coalition. If trust between the potential governing parties was too low for them to accept an *informateur* from one of the parties, a duo or troika would be appointed. In this way, the monarch sought to avoid making politically controversial decisions, but as soon as the appointment was made public, the appointee's past was scrutinized, like examining the entrails of a sacrificial beast by Roman augurs, or the opinions of a candidate for the US Supreme Court, for any sign of a coalition preference. In exceptional cases the monarch has been known to intervene personally. For example, when, in 1981, an elder statesman from the CDA appeared on television to criticize his own party leader for refusing to accept the political reality that CDA and VVD no longer had a governing majority, he was immediately appointed as an *informateur*. In 1994, a three-party coalition was needed for a majority government, but the CDA leader vetoed a CDA–PvdA–D66 combination, the D66 leader vetoed a combination of CDA, VVD and D66, and the VVD leader vetoed a coalition of VVD, PvdA and D66. When this impasse was reported to Queen Beatrix by the *informateur*, she publicly ignored his advice and appointed the leader of the Labour Party as the new *informateur*, the only one who had not yet vetoed any combination. The monarchs involved probably saw it as their role to ensure that the process of forming a new government was not unduly delayed, but such personal interventions were inevitably criticized as reflecting personal political preferences. This was certainly the case in 2010 when, after the formation of a coalition of VVD, PvdA, D66 and Green Left failed, negotiations were initiated to form a minority government of VVD and CDA, supported in Parliament by a majority coalition of these parties and the populist Freedom Party. This created considerable controversy within the CDA, and when Freedom Party leader Geert Wilders estimated that division within the CDA would deprive the coalition of its majority, the *informateur* reported to the Queen that this attempt had also failed. While the Queen was still considering her next move, the leaders of CDA, VVD and the Freedom Party suddenly decided to resume their negotiations. Queen Beatrix was not amused and appointed the vice-president of the Council of State (and a member of the Labour Party) as *informateur* to see if the these negotiators were now serious. In contrast to the monarch's general role, this intervention actually delayed the formation process, and was widely interpreted as a sign of the Queen's personal displeasure regarding the inclusion of Mr Wilders (a staunch critic of her televised Christmas messages of goodwill and tolerance) in a governing coalition.

It may be no coincidence that soon after this episode, Parliament restricted the monarch's role in the formation of a new government to the constitutionally prescribed swearing in of the new ministers. On 27 March 2012, a majority approved a proposal by D66 to amend the Standing Orders of the Second Chamber to introduce a new procedure for appointing *formateurs* and *informateurs*. Only the VVD and the Christian parties opposed the amendment. According to the new rule, within a week following the start of a newly elected Parliament, it must convene to appoint an *(in) formateur* and to formulate that *(in)formateur*'s commission. This process is repeated each time an *(in)formateur* reports, until a new government is formed. The idea dates back to 1971, when Parliament approved of a resolution introduced by Catholic MP Kolfschoten. The current rule, however, does not merely allow for a parliamentary appointment of *(in)formateurs*, but makes it mandatory. Only when a government terminates prematurely is Parliament not obliged to appoint an *(in)formateur.* Sceptics pointed to the possibility that no majority can be found for the appointment of a particular *formateur*, as happened on the single occasion that Kolfschoten's resolution was implemented, and some predicted that the monarch's role in the formation process would soon be revived. In 2012, however, the new procedure operated smoothly. This may be because the leaders of the two largest parties, VVD and PvdA, decided to join forces shortly after the election results were known, transforming an otherwise complicated situation into a relatively straightforward one. It may also be because the Speaker of the Second Chamber carefully prepared for the new procedure and actually assumed part of the monarch's role herself. Immediately after the elections, the Speaker met all the party leaders and appointed a prominent politician from the largest party, the VVD, as an 'explorer' to prepare the plenary debate in Parliament. On the basis of his report, the Second Chamber appointed two *informateurs* (one Liberal, one Labour), and when they had completed their task, the Second Chamber, at their recommendation, appointed the Prime Minister designate, Liberal leader Mark Rutte, to act as *formateur* and present the new government to the Queen to be sworn in. So the new procedure is not that different, except for the roles of the monarch and the Second Chamber. Symbolically, the *(in)formateurs* now operate from an office in the buildings of the Second Chamber that has appointed them rather than in the First Chamber.

Whoever appointed them, and wherever they are located, before a new government can be sworn in *(in)formateurs* must seek answers to four questions, in roughly the following order:

- Which parties are to form the new Cabinet?
- What will be the content of the new government's programme?
- How will ministerial portfolios be distributed over the governing parties?
- Who will be nominated as ministers?

At any of these stages, the negotiations may derail. Often a new (*in*)*formateur* or even a team of (*in*)*formateurs* will be called upon to get the train back on the tracks, and on average three such rounds of negotiations are needed before a new government can be sworn in. The most notorious case was the formation of the CDA– VVD government in 1977, which took nine attempts involving a total of 11 (*in*) *formateurs* and a change of participants when, after 163 days, negotiations between Labour, CDA and D66 broke down irreparably.

The (*in*)*formateur's* first and most important task is to determine which parties will be invited to the negotiating table. His (so far there has only been one female infor- mateur) choice is restrained by the fact that some combinations of parties may not be able to muster the support of a majority in Parliament, and by the relations between the parties. Between 1959 and 1994, VVD and PvdA excluded each other as coali- tion partners, which had the effect of reducing the options to either a centre–right or a centre–left coalition. Thus CDA (and before the merger of the Christian Democratic parties the largest of the three, KVP) became the pivotal party in coalition forma- tions. Between 1945 and 2013, 34 *formateurs* and 40 *informateurs* were appointed from the ranks of the Christian Democrats, against 13 and 20 from the Labour Party, two and 10 from the VVD, and just two *informateurs* from D66. The Dutch political scientist Hans Daudt has argued that the Christian Democrats have a natural prefer- ence for the VVD, as neither party advocates radical change while the Labour Party does. Only in cases of 'dire necessity' will the Christian Democrats enter into a coali- tion with the Social Democrats. Such a necessity can be numerical (when a coalition with the Liberals has no majority) or political (when unpopular measures are deemed to be necessary that will gain social acceptance more readily when coming from a government in which the Labour Party participates) (Daudt, 1982). Critics of Daudt's thesis, on the other hand, have pointed out that the Christian Democrats attract voters who share a common religion, but who have very different socio-economic positions and interests. The political strategy of the Christian Democrats has, therefore, always been a careful balancing act to satisfy all factions within the party. To govern only with the VVD would sooner or later lead to dissatisfaction with the left wing of the Christian Democrats. Officially, the Christian Democrats proclaim to have no prefer- ence for either of the two combinations, and between 1945 and 2013 they took part in as many centre–left coalitions as centre–right ones. Since Labour and the Liberals ended their mutual exclusion in 1994, the CDA has lost its pivotal position and the options available to (*in*)*formateurs* have increased.

Once the combination of parties is settled, the negotiations start in earnest. The leaders of the parliamentary parties (and not the party chairmen, as in Belgium) represent the prospective governing parties in these talks, sometimes including other MPs in the process. Usually, the new government's policy programme is most likely to require protracted negotiations and cause occasional conflict. The resulting coali- tion agreement (*regeerakkoord*) has been described as a codification of mistrust, because the issues on which the parties expect to disagree dominate the agenda during the negotiations. The result is a package deal with the compromise in different policy areas sometimes favouring different parties. If no compromise can be reached on an issue, the parties may agree on a procedure for further negotiations, or they may opt to depoliticize the issue by setting up a committee. Dutch coalition agreements are among the most elaborate of such documents in countries with a coalition government, along with the coalition agreements in Belgium, Norway and Portugal (Müller and Strøm, 2008, p. 173), and they have become more detailed and extensive agreements over time, from just over 3,000 words in the first such documents in the 1960s to the 36,000 words of the 1998 coalition agreement, the most elaborate so far (Timmermans and Andeweg, 2000, p. 374). In 2010, the government had two coalition agreements: one for the two parties in the minority government, VVD and CDA (24,600 words), and one between these two parties and their partner in the parliamentary majority coalition, the Freedom Party (6,900 words).

By means of the coalition agreement, the parties in the coalition increasingly try to bind the ministers to the parties, and the parties to one another. It is a kind of political contract that holds the coalition together. Thus political conflicts that bring down coalition governments in other countries may, to some extent, be prevented in the Netherlands before the government takes office (but see Timmermans, 2003). Sometimes, however, the coalition agreement contains compromises that allow different interpretations, or policy proposals that are rendered out of date by later economic or international developments. If such conflicts cannot be resolved by the Cabinet, it may offer to resign. This does not necessarily imply the termination of the coalition and early elections, especially when the next scheduled elections are still distant. An *informateur* will usually be charged with the task of mending the rift; this is known as a 'glueing attempt', which in fact comes down to a return to the government formation arena and negotiations regarding an amendment to or update of the coalition agreement. In this way, five post-war Cabinet crises were resolved and the Cabinet resumed its task. In 1999, for example, D66 accused the VVD of being an unreliable partner when the proposal for a binding referendum, which had been decided in the coalition agreement, was deprived of the needed two-thirds majority in the second reading by the defection of one Liberal senator. This led to a Cabinet crisis that was resolved after three weeks of mediation by an *informateur* when the parties agreed to restart the procedure to amend the constitution to allow *a binding* referendum, and in the meantime temporarily introduce a *consultative* referendum for which the Constitution did not need to be changed (see Chapter 4). In 2005, another rejection of a constitutional amendment by the Senate, also proposed by a minister from D66, similarly led to a renegotiation of parts of the coalition agreement, this time without the help of an *informateur* (see Chapter 4). In 2012, shortly after the new government took office, a storm of protest within the Liberal party forced the coalition parties to renegotiate the agreement's paragraph on housing policy, also without appointing a new *informateur.*

After the parties have agreed on a programme, the (*in*)*formateur* and the party leaders turn their attention to the distribution of seats in the Cabinet, which is normally a matter of proportionality. If a satisfactory proportional distribution of ministerial posts cannot be achieved, inequalities may be compensated for at the level of junior ministers (called *staatssecretarissen*, or state secretaries). The Prime

Minister customarily comes from the largest governing party. While there are occasional disagreements about the number of portfolios to which each party is entitled, the matching of portfolios to party preferences may be more difficult. The parties' preferences need not conflict – Christian Democrats are overrepresented in the list of post-war ministers of Agriculture and Education, the Liberals have often occupied Economic Affairs, and the Social Democrats have shown a preference for Social Affairs. The puzzle is sometimes complicated when all parties claim prestigious posts such as Home Affairs, or seek to avoid particular portfolios such as Defence. Though formal Cabinet committees are of little importance in the Dutch core executive, an effort is often made to have all the governing parties represented in each of the main policy areas (socio-economic affairs, foreign policy, infrastructure and so on).

Finally, once the portfolios have been apportioned, the government has to be staffed with ministers and junior ministers. Party leaders put forward names only for their own party's ministers, but these must be acceptable to the coalition partners. However, vetoing an appointment from another party may not be without consequences: the attempts to form a centre–left coalition in 1977 finally failed when the Social Democrats blocked the appointment of a prominent Christian Democrat as Minister of Economic Affairs. Ministers need not be recruited from Parliament, but if they are, they are constitutionally required to give up their seat in Parliament. This feature of the Dutch Constitution has important consequences for the policy-making culture of the Cabinet, as we shall see later in this chapter. The incompatibility of ministerial office and membership of Parliament is one of the few aspects of government formation regulated by the written Constitution.

Once all four questions have been answered, the *formateur* nominates the new ministers for appointment by royal appointment and swearing in by the monarch. There is no formal end to the Cabinet formation in the form of an investiture vote in Parliament. The Second Chamber may invite *(in)formateurs* to account for the formation's progress, and soon after being sworn in the Cabinet presents its policy programme to be debated in the Second Chamber (since 2007 also in the First Chamber), but the political *fiat* to the new government is given by the parliamentary caucuses of the new coalition, and in some parties by the party conference, rather than by Parliament as such. The procedures we have described so far are extrapolated from government formations in recent years; the traditions and customs that determine the procedures are evolving continuously and could be set aside at any time if required by political expedience.

Critique and Attempts at Reform

The way in which governments are formed in the Netherlands has frequently provoked criticism, one complaint being that too much time is wasted. In 1998, the formation of the second Kok government took 87 days, despite there being no change in the party composition of the government. By Dutch standards this was not excessively slow: if we disregard the formation of interim Cabinets, the average post-war coalition took almost 84 days to put together, with variations ranging between the 1948 speed record of 31 days and the unparalleled 208 days of 1977 (see Table 5.1). Since the Belgian government formation of 2010–11, which took 541 days, this is no longer the most protracted formation in Europe, but in general, the interregnum between governments lasts longer in the Netherlands than elsewhere (De Winter and Dumont, 2008, pp.130–1).

Table 5.1 *Cabinet Formation, 1945–2012*

Date installed	Prime Minister	Duration of formation (days)	Composition+	Status++
24-06-1945	Schermerhorn*	47	*PvdA*/KVP/ARP/np	
03-07-1946	Beel I	47	PvdA/*KVP*/np	mw
07-08-1948	Drees I	31	*PvdA*/KVP/CHU/VVD/np	sm
15-03-1951	Drees II	50	*PvdA*/KVP/CHU/VVD/np	sm
02-09-1952	Drees III	69	*PvdA*/ARP/KVP/CHU/np	sm
13-10-1956	Drees IV	122	*PvdA*/ARP/KVP/CHU	sm
22-12-1958	Beel II*	10	ARP/*KVP*/CHU	mw
19-05-1959	De Quay	68	ARP/*KVP*/CHU/VVD	sm
24-07-1963	Marijnen	70	ARP/*KVP*/CHU/VVD	sm
14-04-1965	Cals	46	PvdA/ARP/*KVP*	sm
22-11-1966	Zijlstra*	38	*ARP*/KVP	m
05-04-1967	De Jong	49	ARP/*KVP*/CHU/VVD	mw
07-07-1971	Biesheuvel I	69	*ARP*/KVP/CHU/DS70/VVD	mw
20-07-1972	Biesheuvel II*	22	*ARP*/KVP/CHU/VVD	m
11-05-1973	Den Uyl	163	PPR/*PvdA*/D66/KVP/ARP	sm
19-12-1977	Van Agt I	208	*CDA*/VVD	mw
11-09-1981	Van Agt II	108	PvdA/D66/*CDA*	sm
29-05-1982	Van Agt III*	17	D66/*CDA*	m
04-11-1982	Lubbers I	57	*CDA*/VVD	mw
14-07-1986	Lubbers II	52	*CDA*/VVD	mw
7-11-1989	Lubbers III	61	PvdA/*CDA*	mw
22-08-1994	Kok I	111	*PvdA*/D66/VVD	mw
03-08-1998	Kok II	87	*PvdA*/D66/VVD	sm
22-07-2002	Balkenende I	66	*CDA*/VVD/LPF	mw
27-05-2003	Balkenende II	123	D66/*CDA*/VVD	mw
07-07-2006	BalkenendeIII*	7	*CDA*/VVD	m
22-02-2007	Balkenende IV	92	PvdA/CU/*CDA*	mw
14-10-2010	Rutte I	127	CDA/*VVD*/(PVV)	m(mw)
05-11-2012	Rutte II	47	PvdA/*VVD*	mw(m)

Notes: * interim Cabinet intended for short duration;

+ party of Prime Minister in *italics*; np = non-partisan;

++ mw = minimum winning; sm = surplus majority; m = minority.

During the post-war period, on average, about one month per year has been spent on government formation. This is sometimes seen as detrimental to effective government. In general, however, the problem of a power vacuum should not be overstated, since during an interregnum the previous Cabinet continues as a caretaker government and retains all its powers, though controversial legislative proposals may have to wait until the new government is sworn in. Moreover, the long duration of government formation is accounted for primarily by negotiations over a detailed government programme that is intended to prevent later conflicts, and a long interregnum is often perceived as the price that has to be paid for Cabinet stability. As D66 leader Thom De Graaf put it during the 1998 government formation: 'Better a week more now, than a year less later.'

Figure 5.1 presents the duration of each Cabinet, expressed as days in office as well as days in power; that is, not counting its days as a caretaker government while negotiations are under way for a new government. Under two sets of circumstances it is possible for a Cabinet to be in office for somewhat more than four years: (i) the Cabinet was formed after early elections that were not held in May, the regular election month; and (ii) a Cabinet remains in office after elections until a new Cabinet is formed. Between 1945 and 2012 there were 28 governments, being in power for an average of 791 days (or two years and two months). However, six of these 28 Cabinets were interim governments, intended to be in office for only a short period prior to new elections. If such Cabinets are excluded, the average Dutch Cabinet was in power for 967 days (or two years and eight months).

Most Dutch people would therefore probably agree with Gladdish, who noted that the relatively long interregnums in the Netherlands 'are scarcely a pathological feature, since the system depends upon the patient reconciliation of the ambitions of a number of minority parties; and they do not connote the kind of government instability associated with the French Fourth Republic' (Gladdish, 1972, p. 344). However, there is concern that government stability has declined alarmingly since 2002. To some extent the concern is justified; in the decade following 2002, the only government that did not terminate prematurely was the Balkenende III interim cabinet, which was not intended to last long. However, it is also caused by the contrast with the two preceding decades of unprecedented government stability: between 1982 and 2002, Prime Ministers Lubbers and Kok led five cabinets that were in power for an average of 1,358 days, compared with five cabinets averaging 601 days between 2002 and 2012. If we compare the latter average to the average days in office before 1982 (686 days), there is still a decline, but the contrast is not as stark.

A much more serious criticism of the whole procedure is its lack of democratic legitimacy. Until recently, the involvement of the monarch in the formation of governments symbolized the undemocratic nature of the process, but even since 2012 the fact remains that 'voters propose, politicians dispose'. Elections have little impact on which coalition is formed. This is the Achilles heel of the Dutch political system, and several reforms have been proposed over the years to remedy the situa

Figure 5.1 *Cabinet Duration, 1945–2010*

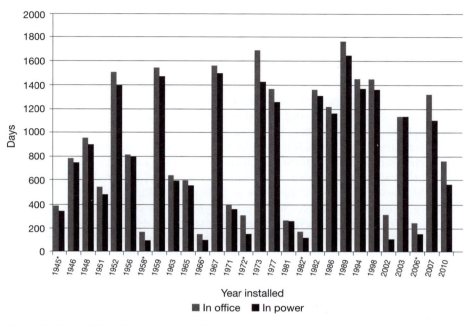

Year installed
■ In office   ■ In power

Note: * = Interim Cabinet intended for short duration.

tion. All such proposals have sought to increase the government's democratic legitimacy by moving the coalition negotiations from after to before the elections, but they have tried to achieve this end by different means. The proposed reforms can be divided roughly into two categories: those modelled on the British example; and those inspired more by the American system of government.

The 'British' reforms have concentrated on the party system rather than on the institutions of government. In a celebrated essay, a then young Social Democrat, later Mayor of Amsterdam and Minister of Home Affairs, Ed Van Thijn, argued that in Dutch politics the displeasure of the voters cannot be channelled into 'turning the rascals out', as opposition votes are not concentrated on an alternative government party but are dispersed over many parties. In such a system, according to Van Thijn, an inherent tendency exists for the extremes to grow at the expense of the centre, until the centre is crushed between extremist anti-system parties. To avoid such a Weimarian showdown, he advocated remodelling the party system along British lines (as they existed at the time he was writing), in which the pendulum of power could swing back and forth freely according to the electorate's preferences (Van Thijn, 1967). Lacking a two-party system, the Dutch parties ought to form two blocs or pre-election coalitions, so as to offer the voter a clear choice between two competing alternatives. It was hoped that, eventually, these blocs would transform into parties. Van Thijn's dreams of a bipolar party system were inspired by the heavy losses that the centrist Christian Democratic parties had begun to suffer at that time. The feeling that the Christian Democrats would gradually be reduced to electoral insignificance was reinforced by growing discord within the Catholic Party. Talks were soon under way between the Social Democrats and smaller left-of-centre parties about a single, broadly-based Progressive People's Party. In the 1971 election campaign, these 'progressive' parties presented a shadow Cabinet, but they came nowhere near a parliamentary majority. In 1972 the progressive parties negotiated a joint manifesto before the election, but, as we have already seen, in a protracted government formation they were forced to accept Christian Democratic participation in 'their' Cabinet. The reform was then watered down: if the leftist pre-election coalition did not achieve a parliamentary majority, it would govern only if it could have a majority of the seats in Cabinet. Gradually even this 'majority strategy' proved unworkable, however, and the reform of the party system has now been forgotten. The reform failed because the Christian Democrats did not disappear. On the contrary, the Christian Democrats were able to set aside old rivalries between Catholics and Protestants to form a unified party, whereas the Progressive People's Party never materialized.

The proposed 'American' reforms involved radical institutional changes, and would have transformed the Netherlands almost into a presidential system. The intellectual godfather of this type of reform, Leiden Professor of Law Jan Glastra Van Loon (1964), started from the familiar assumption that proportional representation may lead to an adequate reflection of popular political opinion in Parliament, but provides few incentives to form pre-election coalitions. However, proportional representation has become so ingrained in Dutch political culture, and is so central to consociational democracy, that the reintroduction of a majoritarian electoral system was not seen by Glastra Van Loon as a feasible option. Instead, he suggested giving the electorate the right to choose the Prime Minister: parties, or pre-election coalitions of parties, could nominate a candidate, and the office of Prime Minister would go to the party or coalition with the plurality of votes in the parliamentary election. This would considerably strengthen the position of the Prime Minister, but stop short of a presidential system. Van Loon's ideas formed the basis of more radical proposals put forward by D66, the party that originated from discontent with the way in which governments are formed in the Netherlands. It called for a separate, direct election of the Prime Minister and the abolition of ministerial responsibility. In 1969, a Government Advisory Commission recommended a moderate version of the D66 proposal and, in combination with the introduction of multi-member districts into the electoral system, that version was put formally before Parliament several times from the 1970s to the 1990s, but each time without success (see Chapter 4). When Dutch politicians noted the consequences of such a reform when it was introduced (and withdrawn again later) in Israel, even its advocates began to lose enthusiasm.

Coalition Theory and Dutch Cabinets

If election results cannot predict the outcome of the formation process, can political science? Most theories view coalition formation as a game in which players act rationally to maximize their own interests. The two most important assumptions are that political parties seek to maximize power; that is, to capture as many ministerial positions as possible, and/or that political parties want to transform as much of their programme as possible into government policy. The first assumption leads us to expect political parties to form coalitions in which they have to share ministerial posts with as few other political parties as possible. Hence 'minimal-winning' coalitions will be formed that contain no parties that are not necessary for obtaining a parliamentary majority. Interestingly, before 1967, most Dutch coalitions contradicted such theories by being 'surplus-majority' rather than minimal-winning (see Table 5.1).

This Dutch 'deviation' can be explained in several ways. The first explanation points to the fulcrum position of the Christian Democrats and, before this party submitted a combined list in 1977, of the largest of its predecessors, the Catholic Party. As we have seen, this position was reinforced for many years by the mutual exclusion of VVD and PvdA. This enabled the Christian Democrats to play off the parties to its left and right against each other, and explains in part why it was represented in government continuously from 1918 to 1994. As De Swaan pointed out, still speaking only of the Catholic Party:

> the most effective way to exploit this position was for it ... to carry the advantages of a pivotal position into the government coalition itself. By including both Social Democrats and centre-right parties, the Catholics could play both sides against the middle at every cabinet meeting. (De Swaan, 1982)

Parties have thus been added to the coalition even if they were not necessary to obtain a parliamentary majority. This observation is an interesting improvement over existing rational choice coalition theory, because it takes into account that what is rational for one party need not be rational for another, and that a centre or pivotal party is in an excellent position to impose its conception of rationality on the other players.

As Table 5.1 shows, since 1966 surplus-majority coalitions have become more the exception than the rule, and De Swaan's explanation does not account for the disappearance of the theoretical deviation. Another explanation does account for the emergence after 1966 of minimal-winning coalitions. In Lijphart's original theory, elite cooperation was a reaction to pillarization (see Chapter 2): the more parties represented in the governing coalition, the better, in terms of elite cooperation. 'Executive power-sharing or grand coalition' is mentioned as one of the basic principles of consociational democracy, and the occurrence of surplus-majority coalitions is an indicator of consensus democracy. Of all the characteristics of consensus government, this is the only one that he found to have declined in the Netherlands (Lijphart, 1989, p. 147). Indeed, in the two decades of pillarization (1946–66) 70 per cent of the governing coalitions contained parties that were not needed for a parliamentary majority; in the two decades of depillarization (1967–86) the percentage of surplus-majority coalitions dropped to 22 per cent, and if we restrict ourselves to the first two post-pillarization decades (1987–2006) only 17 per cent of the coalitions were larger than necessary (or even fewer if we include the coalitions formed since 2006). It is surely not accidental that the decline of the oversized coalition has coincided with the erosion of pillarization. It should be pointed out, however, that the definition of minimal-winning and surplus-majority is based on the number of parties and their seats in Parliament. Prior to 1977, the major Christian Democratic parties – KVP, ARP and CHU – often collaborated, but remained three distinct parties. In 1977 they merged their lists at the election. If we were to treat them as a single party prior to the merger, the calculations would be quite different. If the three were counted as a single unit in all Cabinets in which all three were represented, oversized coalitions would always have been the exception, and the shift away from surplus-majority coalitions would not be as impressive (Andeweg, 2008, 257–8).

Another deviation from coalition theory, minority government, has long been absent from the Netherlands, except in the form of caretaker governments (see Table 5.1). This is a puzzle in itself, as there are few institutional obstacles to minority government – a new Cabinet is not subject to an investiture vote; there are parties near the centre, at least on the socio-economic left–right dimension, that would be well-positioned to negotiate support for *ad hoc* majorities in Parliament (see Chapter 4); and the structure and procedures of Parliament provide ample opportunity for non-governing parties to exercise influence (see Chapter 6). In 2010 this changed, when the Rutte I government took office as a minority government with ministers from VVD and CDA, controlling 52 seats in the Second Chamber. However, it was a minority government that had negotiated structural support from the Freedom Party, giving it a 76-seat majority in the 150-seat Second Chamber. As mentioned above, an additional coalition agreement listed the policy concessions to the Freedom Party – primarily in the field of immigration and integration, in return for its support. Freedom Party leader Wilders met with the Prime Minister and the leader of the Christian Democrats each Monday to discuss the Cabinet's policies and to prevent conflicts. The category of minority governments has always included both 'pure' minority governments and 'quasi' minority governments, but it is claimed that this latter category is growing (Bale and Bergman, 2006). That the Rutte I government was a minimal-winning parliamentary coalition rather than a true minority government is illustrated best by the fact that the government immediately resigned after the Freedom Party withdrew its support when a combination of economic crisis and EU budgetary requirements necessitated renegotiating parts of the coalition agreements.

However, the Freedom Party did not support the government on all issues: foreign policy and European integration were notable exceptions. On such issues, the cabinet was a true minority government, cobbling together *ad hoc* coalitions, as that with the Labour Party on EU rescue packages for the Greek economy, and with D66 and Green Left on sending a police training mission to the Afghan province of Kunduz. A further complication was that VVD, CDA and PVV had a narrow majority in the Second Chamber, but not in the First Chamber. Despite intensive campaigning and strategic manoeuvring, this did not change when the new First Chamber was elected in 2011. This necessitated further bargaining for the support of the orthodox Protestant SGP in the Senate. Interestingly, the Rutte II government that took office in 2012, while having a comfortable majority in the Second Chamber, is also a minority government in the Senate, prompting renewed debate about the existence and powers of the indirectly elected Upper House (see Chapter 6).

The second assumption of coalition theory, that parties prefer government policy to conform to their own programme as much as possible, leads us to expect that parties prefer to team up with the parties that are nearest to them ideologically. One operationalization of this hypothesis is that coalitions are ideologically 'closed'; that is, they consist of neighbouring parties on the dominant ideological dimension. Until 1994, almost all Dutch coalitions did indeed leave no gaps on the socio-economic left–right dimension. The mutual exclusion of VVD and PvdA gave the Christian Democrats the leverage needed to prevent the two secular parties from using their parliamentary majority to liberalize abortion and introduce other policies on ethical issues. Irritation over this effect of their parties' antagonism on the socio-economic dimension finally brought a group of politicians from PvdA, VVD and D66 together for more-or-less regular meetings in an upmarket hotel in The Hague. None the less, few observers at the time saw those dinners as harbingers of a secular coalition. Yet, after one of the most complex of recent government formations, PvdA and VVD did end their mutual veto in 1994 and, together with D66, formed 'the Purple coalition' (so named because this is the colour that results from mixing the colour of the Social Democrats, red, with the colour of the Liberals, blue). Several Dutch political scientists had gone on record during the government formation process predicting that a purple coalition would not come about, in part at least because it would not be an ideologically 'closed' coalition. PvdA and VVD were far apart on the socio-economic dimension, and both were ideologically closer to the CDA, which was excluded, than to each other. The leader of the Liberals, Frits Bolkestein, seemed to agree when he characterized the newly-formed Purple coalition as an 'all party government without CDA', or as the Lubbers IV government without Lubbers.

Of course, the Purple coalitions (Kok I, Kok II, and Rutte II, though that coalition did not adopt the purple label) did consist of ideological neighbours if we accept the religious–secular dimension as the basis for ordering the political parties (see Chapter 3). Many 'purple' policies would not have been possible if the Christian Democrats had participated in government. Shortly after the Kok I government took office Sunday shopping was allowed; in 1998 homosexual marriages were introduced; prostitution was legalized in 1999; and liberal legislation on euthanasia was passed in 2001. The first Purple coalition clearly showed that the religious–secular dimension was still relevant at the time.

On the other hand, and notwithstanding the significance of the policy departures just mentioned, the greatest political controversy over moral issues of the post-war era, the conflict over abortion, had already been 'resolved' in 1981 by a coalition of CDA and VVD through a classical Dutch mixture of depoliticization and compromise. And while the first Purple coalition legalized euthanasia, the conflict had effectively been resolved much earlier by the judiciary (see Box 7.1 on p. 207). By then, and certainly since then, the socio-economic dimension should be considered the most relevant dimension for day-to-day politics, and the agenda of the Purple coalition was definitely concerned more with economic issues than with moral questions. One searches in vain for policy proposals in the latter area in the coalition agreement of the Rutte II Cabinet. To that extent, the deviation from the expectation of a closed coalition is real. Whatever the explanation of these 'purple puzzles' (Andeweg, 2011), it does not follow from standard coalition theory, and predicting the outcome of Dutch coalition formations remains a hazardous undertaking.

Collective and Collegial Government

The Position of Prime Minister

The coalition nature of Dutch governments has important consequences for Cabinet decision-making. If Cabinets are placed on a scale from prime ministerial government to collegial government, Dutch Cabinets are clearly positioned towards the collegial end of the scale. In fact, the Netherlands ranks second only to Switzerland in terms of collegiality of leadership (Baylis, 1989). In a 1955 English-language article, Hans Daalder wrote about Dutch ministers serving *with*, not *under*, a Prime Minister. It had taken him over an hour to convince the journal's editor that this was not a foreigner's linguistic mistake, but a correct reading of Dutch Cabinet practices.

Compared with his British, French or even his German colleagues, the Dutch Prime Minister has very few formal powers. He draws up the agenda and chairs all meetings of the cabinet and its committees, and he casts the deciding vote when there is a tie. But the Prime Minister does not appoint the ministers; instead names are put forward by party leaders and agreed on in negotiations between the parties. The Prime Minister cannot remove a minister or 'reshuffle' the Cabinet by assigning ministers to other portfolios without the formal approval of the whole Cabinet, and without the consent of the leaders of the affected ministers' parties. The Prime Minister of the wartime government in exile twice dismissed a minister without even consulting the Cabinet, but he was criticized immediately for such 'Persian constitutional morals' and after the war a parliamentary inquiry rejected the claim that the Prime Minister should have the power of dismissal. Though the Prime Minister is entrusted with the task of coordinating Cabinet policy, he has no authority to settle conflicts between ministers, unless they agree to his arbitration. He cannot give any directives to ministers. In 1994 the Cabinet's standing orders were amended to give the Prime Minister the authority to put a proposal on the Cabinet agenda even when the departmental minister concerned is opposed, but only if he has the support of the Cabinet. So far, regular proposals to further extend the Prime Minister's powers, in particular with regard to the Dutch role in EU policy-making, the coordination of disaster relief, and matters pertaining to the royal family, have not resulted in any strengthening of the Prime Minister's formal position.

The staff of the Prime Minister is relatively small. He heads the Department of General Affairs, but most the civil servants work in the Government Press Office, the Communication Service, on the staff of the independent Scientific Council for Government Policy. The Prime Minister's Office proper consists of only 10 to 12 people who act as advisers to the Prime Minister, plus some assistants. Apart from its small size, the most striking feature of the Prime Minister's Office is that it consists of only career civil servants, with just one political assistant. The Cabinet Secretariat is also part of the Prime Minister's Office, but has a semi-independent position. Apart from the Cabinet Secretary, the Secretariat is run by a handful of young civil servants on loan for a few years from other departments.

Despite the Prime Minister's paucity of staff and formal powers, there is a feeling among many Dutch commentators that the Dutch government also shows signs of the 'presidentialization' that has been reported for other European countries (Fiers and Krouwel, 2005), though the use made of this position varies considerably with the personality of the Prime Minister and the political situation of the moment. At least three factors are often mentioned as contributing to a strengthening of the Prime Minister's position: increased media attention, the ever-increasing demand for policy coordination, and European integration. Since Prime Minister De Jong (1967–71), the Prime Minister gives a weekly press conference and a television interview in which he or she explains and defends the Cabinet's decisions. While this may have enhanced the Prime Minister's public profile, it is less clear how this external role has strengthened his influence over decision-making within the Cabinet. To some extent, the same argument applies to the Prime Minister's role in the increasingly important European Council meetings. The Treaty of Amsterdam gave the Prime Minister a formal position with regard to the formulation of the common foreign and security policy of the EU, which is more of a change in the Netherlands than in other EU countries, but the Dutch position in EU decision-making is formulated in an elaborate system of inter-departmental committees with the Cabinet and its European Affairs Committee at the apex (see Chapter 8). However, occasionally the Prime Minister may have to make compromises during summit meetings without any opportunity to consult the ministers concerned. Though the Prime Minister cannot afford to go consistently against the opinions of the departmental ministers on such occasions, it is plausible that European integration has had a modest impact on his position within the Cabinet in this way. It is less evident how a greater need for policy coordination automatically strengthens the position of the Prime Minister other than through wishful thinking. As mentioned above, the Prime Minister has not been given effective new powers in this respect. Prime Minister Balkenende said as much in a memorandum on his department's budget in 2007: 'The expectations about the power of the Prime Minister are not matched by his real and by his formal position.'

Collegial and collective government has long historical roots in the Netherlands. With the possible exception of the first two or three decades after 1813, the Dutch never experienced absolute monarchy. In Chapter 2 we mentioned Daalder's critique of Lijphart's 'self-denying prophecy', based on the tradition of elite bargaining and compromise dating back to the early days of the Republic of the Seven United Provinces. Consociational practices, whether they date back to 1579 or to 1917, are less conducive to a monocratic premiership than is majoritarian democracy. After all, the Prime Minister, being only one individual, could belong to only one of the pillars. The tradition of collegial and collective government is constantly reinforced by the coalition character of Dutch Cabinets. In a coalition Cabinet the jealousy of the other governing party (or parties) provides a powerful antidote to any monocratic ambitions harboured by the Prime Minister. Many of the institutional constraints mentioned above, such as his inability to staff or reshuffle his own Cabinet, or to take policy initiatives, stem from the circumstance that Cabinet members from other parties will only accept the Prime Minister's leadership as long as he is acting as leader of the coalition and not as leader of his own party. All this would have changed if the proposal to introduce a directly elected Prime Minister had succeeded.

Traditions and coalitions are not the only factors contributing to the culture of collegial and collective Cabinet government. The Dutch Cabinet is not merely a coalition of political parties, but also a board of department heads. All departmental ministers (but not junior ministers) are members of the Cabinet, and even ministers without portfolio (such as the Minister for Development Cooperation) *de facto* represent a part of a department. Departmental ministers enjoy a strong position. In Chapter 7 we discuss at length the degree to which Dutch policy-making can be characterized as corporatist, one of the consequences of which is a high degree of autonomy for the various policy sectors. Each department has developed its own network of interest groups, quangos (quasi non-governmental organizations), advisory bodies and specialized parliamentary committees. Ministers define their role primarily as being the head of a department, and, as a consequence, the Prime Minister is constrained not only by political envy of other governing parties, but also by the departmental jealousy of individual ministers. Even against the Prime Minister, ministers jealously guard their departmental turf, sometimes even in a literal sense. The most celebrated example concerns the Den Uyl government, which was divided over the building of a particular dam as part of the Delta works to protect the Province of Zeeland from flooding. Prime Minister Den Uyl decided that he wanted to see the estuary where the dam was being planned, and commissioned a customs cutter to take him there. By chance, the Minister of Public Works, who was responsible for the Delta works, heard about this, managed to get hold of a faster ship, and chased the Prime Minister out of his 'territorial waters'. In another case, during the Summer of 1990, several proposals for administrative and political reform were again discussed, both in a parliamentary committee and in Cabinet. One suggestion, to give the Prime Minister more room to manoeuvre when representing the country at international summits, immediately prompted a threat of resignation by the Minister of Foreign Affairs, a fellow party member and close political associate of the Prime Minister.

A final factor worth mentioning in this respect is the Cabinet's small size. Not even the literature on group dynamics provides us with an exact cut-off point, but common sense dictates that true collective and collegial decision-making is inversely related to Cabinet size. The number of Cabinet ministers has risen from just nine in 1917 to 16 (and 17 junior ministers) in the 1973–7 government. Since then, the number of ministers has been reduced somewhat: the 2010 Rutte I government had the smallest Cabinet for many years, containing just 12 Cabinet ministers, including the Prime Minister; the Rutte II government contained just one more minister. Junior ministers, seven in the Rutte II government, have no voting rights in Cabinet, and are invited to attend only whenever the Cabinet discusses matters relevant to their portfolio. Only since 1998 do junior ministers formally act as their Cabinet minister's substitute when he or she is absent, but even then they have no vote when the Cabinet meets. On average, since the Second World War, Cabinets have consisted of 15 Cabinet ministers. Most countries' Cabinets have more than this number, the average being above 20 (Blondel and Müller-Rommel, 1997).

In the resulting culture of collegial government, Cabinet meetings are far from merely ritual occasions. The average post-war Dutch Cabinet minister has spent 20 to 30 hours a month in plenary sessions of the Council of Ministers, compared with six to nine hours a month for his or her French or British counterparts. The annual total number of mornings, afternoons and nights during which the Cabinet meets has gradually increased from 75 in the immediate post-war period to about 125 in the 1970s. In 1976, the Den Uyl Cabinet probably set a record by meeting on 163 mornings, afternoons or evenings for a total of 478 hours. Since then the frequency of meetings has declined. In these meetings many matters are considered and an average of 25 decisions are taken. Moreover, these decisions are far from being simply rubber stamps; a careful reading of the minutes for some of the years for which minutes are available (they are accessible after 20 years) shows that approximately one in five decisions differs from the original proposal put to Cabinet.

The Politicization of the Core Executive

Given the fact that all Cabinets are coalitions of political parties, it is surprising that the Dutch Cabinet remained a relatively apolitical, technocratic body at least until the 1960s. Before then, ministers regarded themselves primarily as departmental chieftains, and most conflicts in Cabinet were caused by divergent departmental interests. Several factors may account for this relative lack of politicization. First, we must again mention consociational democracy; if stable government was threatened by subcultural strife, the Cabinet had to remain aloof from the daily political squabbles – it had to be depoliticized to be acceptable to all pillars. Sayings about ministers such as 'The closer to the Crown, the less partisan', or 'The sounds from the Tourney Field only faintly reach the Salle de Trêves, where Cabinet usually meets' (Drees 1965, p. 22) about Cabinet decision-making, testify to this depoliticization. Ministers had little or no contact with the parliamentary party that had nominated them. When Jelle Zijlstra (later Prime Minister) was appointed Minister of Economics in 1952, as a political novice he sought the advice of his party's leader in Parliament. The latter declined 'because they had separate responsibilities'. To symbolize the apolitical nature of their office, during debate in the Second Chamber of Parliament the ministers are seated in a separate section, facing the members of Parliament (see Chapter 6).

A second factor contributing to depoliticization has been the relatively non-political nature of ministerial recruitment. Even before the incompatibility of ministerial office and a seat in Parliament was written into the Constitution, it was customary for a member of Parliament to resign his seat on being raised to government rank. Moreover, ministers have often been recruited from outside Parliament. Of all ministers appointed between 1848 and 1967, only 35 per cent had parliamentary experience (Secker, 1991, p. 198). The selection criteria were often more technocratic than political: a banker or economist at Finance, a lawyer at Justice, someone with trade union credentials at Social Affairs, a farmer or farmer's son at Agriculture and so on. This 'rule' has not been adhered to without significant exceptions. In the post-war period purely non-political specialists have become rare – a few non-partisan diplomats at the Foreign Office, for example – but as late as the 1970s most government formations produced rumours that one or two ministers had hastily to become party members before taking the oath of office. Even as recently as 2002, this was true for all LPF representatives in the Balkenende I Cabinet, some of whom even retained their membership in another party for some time. Even though most ministers had been active politically prior to their appointment to the Cabinet, they were not recruited mainly for their political experience, but for their expertise in the policy area for which they were to assume responsibility. Even Prime Ministers have not always been the political heavyweights one would expect in that position. Between the introduction of parliamentary democracy in 1848 and 2013, 41 individuals have served as Prime Minister; 19 of these had not been a member of Parliament, and 18 had not previously been a Cabinet minister (such as, most recently, Prime Ministers Balkenende and Rutte). With the exception of the Labour Party, the governing parties have often preferred to keep their leader in Parliament. As late as 1973, Norbert Schmelzer, a former leader of the Catholic Party, remarked: 'Being the parliamentary leader of the largest governing party is a much more influential, powerful, and creative function than being Prime Minister.'

A third factor contributing to the emphasis on a minister's departmental rather than political role, is the absence of a 'Cabinet ministériel' of political appointees, as exists in France, Belgium and Italy. Only recently have most ministers had a political adviser, but they function primarily as the minister's liaison with his or her party, or, in the case of deputy Prime Ministers, to help coordinate the ministers of the deputy Prime Minister's party within the government. As in the UK, ministers are briefed on Cabinet papers primarily by their department, and these departmental briefings are based on rather narrow interpretations of the department's interest. If the civil servants involved do not think their department will be affected by a proposal, however politically controversial it may be, they have been known to advise their minister not to take part in the deliberations.

The effect this has had on Cabinet decision-making is that it was, and to some extent still is, frowned upon when a minister joins a debate in which his or her department has no stake: 'One is not going to pester one another unnecessarily', one minister remarked. Recurrent violations of this tacit agreement of 'non-intervention' sometimes meet with a collective reprisal from the other ministers. On the basis of the nearly verbatim minutes for some of the years for which they are available, it can be shown that about four-fifths of all contributions to debates in Cabinet could be traced to the speakers' departmental interests. Even if we correct the calculations for the fact that the Prime Minister's portfolio includes everything, and that junior ministers are only allowed to participate when their portfolio is at stake, less than a quarter of all the contributions bore no relation to the ministers' departments (Andeweg, 1990, p. 27).

Beginning in the 1960s, several developments nevertheless point to a politicization of the Cabinet, one of the few 'rules of the game' of the politics of accommodation that appears to have changed (see Chapter 2). In the first place there has been a change in the recruitment of ministers. As mentioned above, only 35 per cent of all ministers appointed between 1848 and 1967 had been members of Parliament, but between 1967 and 2013 the proportion of ministers with prior parliamentary experience rose to 69 per cent (Secker, 1991, p. 198 and authors' own calculations). If political experience is defined more broadly, including other offices at the national and subnational level, a similar pattern of politicization can be observed. Expertise in the policy area for which the new minister will assume responsibility continues to be important, but increasingly in combination with political experience. From 1967 onwards, more ministerial appointees had political experience than technical expertise (Bakema and Secker, 1988). The year 1967 is usually associated with the beginning of the end of pillarization, and it may be that with the demise of pillarization the need for 'government above politics' has also declined.

A similar timing of politicization can be observed in the recruitment of Prime Ministers. Between 1946 and 1967, the choice of Prime Minister was part of the negotiations during the formation of a new coalition. Three out of 10 Cabinets in this period were chaired by a Prime Minister who did not belong to the largest governing party in terms of parliamentary seats (Drees I, Drees II and Zijlstra; during Drees III the Prime Minister's Labour Party had the same number of seats as the KVP). No Prime Minister in this period can be regarded as the leader of his party, with a possible exception of Drees. De Jong (1967–71) was the last Prime Minister who was not his party's leader, and his successor, Biesheuvel (1971–3), was the last Prime Minister whose party was not the largest in the coalition. Since then, the premiership has fallen virtually automatically to the largest party in the coalition, and this party then nominates its own leader. The leaders of the other parties' contingents in the Cabinet usually become deputy Prime Ministers, but here we find more exceptions. The choice of Prime Minister has also become more of an issue during election campaigns, with television debates between the leaders of the largest parties being dubbed 'Prime Minister's debates', and this too has been interpreted as a sign of presidentialization (Fiers and Krouwel, 2005). Being his own party's leader, the

Prime Minister is indeed probably in a stronger position *vis-à-vis* his own party and its other ministers than he was before, but the same is not true for his relations with the other coalition parties and their ministers. Any hierarchical intervention on his part may actually have become less legitimate in their eyes as a result of his leadership of a rival party, the more so now that, because of the same politicization, the Prime Minister finds himself surrounded by ministers with a higher political profile than before, and by deputy Prime Ministers who are often their party's leaders too.

A final indication of the Cabinet's politicization is the appointment of junior ministers in departments led by a Cabinet minister from another party, presumably to monitor that minister's actions on behalf of his party. In Cabinets between 1948, when the office of junior minister was first introduced, and 1967, on average 59.5 per cent of all junior ministers were teamed up with a Cabinet minister from another party. Between 1967 and 1987 this rose to 65.6 per cent, and reached 76.6 per cent between 1987 and 2013. It is sometimes argued that in practice these political 'watchdogs' may also turn out to be political 'guide dogs', but even in that case the role of the junior minister is to represent one political party within a department allocated to another political party.

In a second development since the 1960s, the coalition agreement has gradually gained in importance as a political contract (Timmermans, 2003). Here the 1963 coalition agreement marks the beginning of the politicization of the Cabinet. For its time, the agreement was uncommonly detailed in that year and the governing parties considered themselves bound to it; the agreement was also referred to more often than in previous Cabinet meetings. In the nearly four years of the De Quay Cabinet (1959–63), the Cabinet minutes mentioned the government programme only six times. During the less than two years of the Marijnen Cabinet (1963–5) the programme was mentioned at least 28 times in the Cabinet minutes. Subsequently, Cabinet ministers have been known to refer to the coalition agreement as 'the Holy Bible'. One study of budget cutbacks in the 1970s and 1980s shows that only targets set in the coalition agreement were actually met (Toirkens, 1988).

A third contribution to politicizing the Cabinet is the elaborate system of weekly political consultations that has developed, in which party leaders meet with the party's ministers to prepare that week's Cabinet meeting. In the 1950s and 1960s, for example, the entire Cabinet met once a week informally for dinner. Only on the day of the Cabinet meeting itself did ministers from each governing party lunch separately. As a first sign of the politicization of the Cabinet it became customary for the parliamentary leader of a governing party to attend his party's ministers' lunch. The lunch then became so important that decisions were seldom taken in the Cabinet's morning session. In 1973 lunch was replaced by a dinner on the eve of the Cabinet meeting, during which a party's ministers, junior ministers, the party's leader in the Second Chamber of Parliament, and more recently also the party's leader in the First Chamber and the party chairperson, would discuss the next day's Cabinet agenda. Occasionally, party discipline is enforced and the decision taken by Cabinet differs from the one that would have emerged had all ministers followed their individual judgement.

The open surge barrier in the Scheldt estuary is probably the biggest monument to the politicization of the Dutch Cabinet. After the 1953 floods it was decided to close the estuary completely with dams that would reduce the risk of another inundation. In the early 1970s, as the time approached to build the final and largest dam at the mouth of the Easterscheldt, conservationists argued against the construction of a dam and in favour of a surge barrier that would be open to the tides in fair weather, but could be closed in case of a storm. The Den Uyl Cabinet (1973–7) had to choose between the less-costly closed dam, advocated by the government's own specialists, and the much more expensive open surge barrier. The cabinet was a coalition of coalitions: 10 ministers from PvdA, PPR and D66 formed a 'progressive' bloc, and six ministers from KVP and ARP a Christian Democratic bloc. If all ministers had followed their own judgement, all Christian Democratic ministers and a minority of the progressive ministers would have constituted a Cabinet majority in favour of simply closing the estuary. Within the progressive bloc, however, the majority in favour of the open surge barrier used the Thursday-evening dinner to impose its will on the other progressive ministers. When, on the eve of the crucial Cabinet meeting, the Social Democratic Finance Minister gave in to party pressure, the ranks had closed and a whipped vote produced a 10 to six majority in favour of the open surge barrier, adding two billion guilders and an extra eight years to the project (Kohl, 1986). Other, though less spectacular, examples of the politicization of the Cabinet could be given. As we shall see in the next chapter, this development is closely linked to changes in the relationship between government and Parliament.

Despite the growing influence of the parties on the Cabinet, it is probably still fair to say, as former Prime Minister Drees did in 1965, that 'functional [that is, departmental] conflicts tend to be more important than political conflicts' (Drees, 1965, p. 25). Nevertheless, today's ministers wear two hats, and this does complicate decision-making from time to time. In 1989, the Lubbers II Cabinet fell because of a disagreement with the VVD over the financial aspects of an environmental protection plan. Most of the Liberal ministers in the Cabinet had treated this issue as a purely interdepartmental conflict in which they did not want to take sides, while their parliamentary party was treating it as a political conflict. Only after it was too late did they realize they were wearing the wrong hats. It has proved particularly difficult to improve coordination mechanisms inside the Cabinet because of the combined problems of departmental envy and political jealousy. In the 1965 government formation the party leaders agreed that the new Cabinet should have a 'presidium' or inner cabinet, consisting of the Prime Minister and one minister from each of the other governing parties. This would facilitate political coordination, and was acceptable to all governing parties, as they would all be represented in this presidium. It was, however, not acceptable to all departments, as some departments would, but others would not, be represented. At the very first meeting of this Cabinet it was voted down because of departmental jealousy. Strengthening the Prime Minister to improve coordination between departments is less controversial among ministers, because the Prime Minister has no departmental interests. Any suggestions in this direction, however, meet with political jealousy from the other governing parties.

The fact that the Dutch Cabinet is both a board of departmental ministers and a coalition of political parties also has its advantages. Ministers are moderated in their pursuit of narrow departmental interests by political cross-pressures. Parties are kept informed about departments headed by ministers from other parties through the fact that junior ministers from one party are appointed to a department of another party's minister. Deadlocks may be broken by transforming a departmental issue into a political one, or vice versa. For years, trench warfare between the departments of Justice and of Internal Affairs prevented a planned reorganization of the Dutch police force; only after the governing parties agreed to a political solution in 1989 could the reorganization be realized. Similarly, for decades, abortion seemed an insoluble political conflict until the Van Agt I Cabinet (1977–81) delegated the search for a compromise to the two departmental ministers involved (Justice and Health). Thus depoliticized, it proved easier to find a solution on which new legislation was eventually based.

In the past, the consensus-seeking that is so characteristic of consociational democracy took place in all sorts of institutions throughout society. The breakdown of pillarization has not led to a demise of consensus-seeking, but it seems to have concentrated consensus-seeking in the Cabinet. The fact that the Cabinet has become a dual institution in which both sectoral interests and political ideologies have to be reconciled, has increased its importance in the Dutch political system. It has also reinforced the tradition of collective and collegial government. In that sense, the Dutch Cabinet probably comes closer to the ideal of Cabinet government than governments in many other countries.

6

Parliament

Separation of Powers within a Parliamentary System

Once sworn in by the monarch, the Dutch Cabinet is dependent for its survival on the continued confidence of a majority in the States-General, the bicameral Parliament of the Netherlands. If the fact that Parliament can dismiss a government is to be taken as the defining factor for a parliamentary system, then the Netherlands must be placed in this category. Nevertheless, there are features of the Dutch Constitution that are more characteristic of presidential systems than parliamentary ones. In discussions among Dutch constitutional experts and parliamentary historians, the focus is on the question of whether the relationship between the Crown and the States-General is 'monistic' or 'dualistic'. 'Monism' refers to the absence of a clear distinction between Parliament and Cabinet, as one would expect in a parliamentary system, whereas 'dualism' describes the situation in which government and Parliament have distinctive roles and responsibilities, more akin to the separation of powers one would expect to find in a presidential system.

One important feature indicating this dualistic relationship was mentioned in the previous chapter: the position of government minister is incompatible with membership of Parliament. MPs who are recruited as ministers must resign their seats. A second dualistic feature emphasizes the independence of the Cabinet. The Cabinet is sworn in by the monarch, and while it is dependent on parliamentary support for its survival, no formal vote of investiture in Parliament is required.

The architecture of the Lower House of Parliament symbolizes this dualism. Ministers are seated in a separate section, facing the MPs, on chairs unadorned by the parliamentary seal, and debate is primarily construed as debate between Parliament and Cabinet. The MPs are seated in a semi-circle opposite the government and, if interruptions are made, speakers must turn their backs to their fellow MPs and face the Cabinet. While such features are insufficient to remove the Dutch system from classification as a parliamentary system, there is certainly some ambiguity present. Most Dutch observers have concluded that the system could in their terms best be described as one of 'limited dualism'.

A similar ambiguity is evident in other attempts to classify the Dutch Parliament. Nelson Polsby, for example, has drawn a useful distinction between parliaments as transformative institutions and parliaments as arenas. In transformative parliaments, the internal institutional structures and procedures affect the behaviour of the MPs and the outcome of the legislative process. Parliaments of the arena variety do not affect policy-making in this way, but offer a platform on which outside forces, primarily governments and political parties, may try to exert their influence. Polsby describes the US Congress – a parliament in a system of separation of powers – as a transformative institution, and the British House of Commons – a parliament in a parliamentary system – as an arena. Given the Dutch attempt to combine aspects of both parliamentary and presidential systems, it is not surprising that Polsby describes the Dutch Parliament as a moderately transformative institution (Polsby, 1975, pp. 292, 296).

In this chapter we shall discuss the position of the States-General *vis-à-vis* government in the light of these theoretical dichotomies. We shall argue that there has been a long-term development from parliament as an institution to parliament as an arena, but that this development is incomplete, so that the contemporary States-General appears to be several things: institution, arena and market. But first we shall introduce briefly the Dutch Parliament's organization and procedures.

Parliamentary Organization and Procedures

While the Dutch Parliament is still officially called the States-General, and proudly celebrated its 500th anniversary in 1964, it bears little resemblance to its feudal and Republican predecessors, neither in its organization nor in its powers. The current Parliament is organized into two Houses, in parliamentary committees, and in parliamentary party groups. It has extensive powers with regard to both legislation and the oversight of governmental actions.

The Structure of Parliament

Bicameralism

Though the First Chamber (or Senate) was introduced during the short-lived union with Belgium, after the latter's independence the First Chamber remained (see Chapter 1). Since then, the bicameral structure of the Dutch Parliament has been controversial, and proposals to eliminate it have frequently been made. Until now, however, such proposals have never met with success, in part because the First Chamber would have to assent to its own abolition.

The 75 Senators are not elected directly by voters, but by the 566 members of the provincial legislatures, whose votes are weighted by the size of their province's population. The members of all the provincial legislatures form an electoral college by which the First Chamber is elected under a system of PR very similar to that used for the Second Chamber. The political parties present their lists of candidates to this college and strict party discipline is enforced during elections. There is no electoral campaign, and the outcome of an election in terms of party composition is a foregone conclusion except for an occasional rebel or an honest mistake (in 2011, D66 lost a seat because one of its provincial councillors used a blue pen to vote rather than the required red pencil). If the electors deviate from their party's instructions, it is by casting an intra-party preference vote. It is symptomatic of the party control over this 'election' that the threshold for such preference votes taking effect was doubled when the number of preferences increased in recent years. Despite their election by the provincial legislatures, members of the First Chamber in no way represent the various provinces, and the Senate constitutes no exception to the absence of any form of territorial representation in the Netherlands.

Since a constitutional revision in 1983, the 'elections' for the First Chamber are no longer staggered: the entire Senate is elected at the same time. This election takes place every four years, soon after the newly elected Provincial Councils have first met. As the provincial elections all take place simultaneously, but do not coincide with the elections for the Second Chamber, the political composition of the two chambers can be different. This may produce 'divided government': a government supported by a majority in the Second Chamber, but facing an opposition majority in the First Chamber. Early in the twentieth century, a few governments found themselves in this situation, but between 1918 and 2010 governing parties always controlled a majority in both Houses. Three factors may account for this long stretch of congruent majorities. First, as discussed in the previous chapter, until 1967 Dutch coalitions were usually 'oversized', providing the government with a safety margin should the composition of the First Chamber be very different. Second, with pillarized loyalty producing extremely low electoral volatility in those years, fluctuations in the outcome of provincial elections (and thus elections for the First Chamber) and elections for the Second Chamber were most unlikely to exceed that safety margin; especially as, third, proportional representation was used for both the First and Second Chambers. With the decline of the surplus-majority coalition, and with the rise of electoral volatility after 1967, it is more surprising that it took until 2010 for 'divided government' to appear.

After the 2010 elections it was quite a challenge to form a government with a majority in the Second Chamber, resulting in the minority government with a majority coalition in the Second Chamber (see Chapter 5). The coalition did not have a majority in the First Chamber, but this did not worry the negotiators too much; together, VVD and CDA already had 35 seats in the First Chamber, and the government's support party, the Freedom Party, was not yet represented in the Senate at all. It seemed likely that this party would do well in the next provincial elections, which would lead to a newly composed First Chamber, only six months after the Rutte I government took office. For the first time, many voters realized that the provincial elections would also determine the composition of the Upper House, and after a long downward trend, turnout actually went up. The Freedom Party indeed entered the Senate with 10 seats, but this was not enough to offset the losses of the CDA. The coalition fell one seat short of a majority, necessitating further deals to acquire the support of the orthodox Protestant SGP. After the premature end of the Rutte I government and the 2012 elections, a coalition of VVD and PvdA was formed, also without a majority in the First Chamber, at least until the provincial elections of 2014. The Rutte II government sought to avoid gridlock by negotiating *ad hoc* deals with opposition parties in the Second Chamber in the hope that they would be able to deliver their colleagues' support in the First Chamber. At the same time, 'divided government' rekindled the debate about the Senate's purpose and its powers.

There is no denying that the official titles of 'First' and 'Second' Chamber are misleading, and that the 'First' is secondary in importance. In contrast to the full-time members of the Second Chamber, Senators are part-time politicians, usually meeting for only one day a week. They have no personal staff, and their remuneration (€25,000, plus expenses) is about a quarter of that of a member of the Lower House. While the First Chamber has the same powers of governmental oversight as the Second Chamber, it concentrates almost exclusively on legislation. However, lacking the right to initiate or amend bills, the First Chamber is formally restricted to either vetoing or accepting bills. To its critics, the Senate can do no good. If it accepts the legislative proposals already approved by the Second Chamber, it is said to be redundant; and if it rejects legislative proposals it is accused of encroaching on the primacy of the directly-elected Second Chamber. In defence of the First Chamber, it is often argued that it acts as a '*Chambre de reflexion*', primarily judging the constitutionality, consistency and practicability of bills. The problem is that the First Chamber is also a political institution, peopled by party politicians, with senators from governing parties sometimes grudgingly accepting bills that they consider to be unsound, and senators from opposition parties voting against bills that pass muster in a technical sense for political reasons; it is relatively rare for the parliamentary parties in the Second and First Chambers to take different positions on a bill.

The debate about the position of the First Chamber has gained in importance recently, not only because of 'divided government', but also because the First Chamber has assumed a more activist role.

Figure 6.1   *The Senate's Impact on Legislation, 1952–2011*

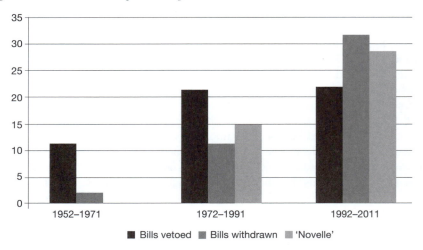

Source: www.eerstekamer.nl.

As the number of bills has been relatively constant over the years, the absolute numbers for the three 20-year periods shown in Figure 6.1 are comparable. The number of bills that have been vetoed by the Senate may not be very high (56 over 60 years), but numbers have clearly increased since 1972. Some of these vetoes attracted considerable attention. In 1976, a few Liberal Senators were opposed to the length of pregnancy during which abortion would be allowed under new legislation initiated (among others, by a fellow Liberal MP) and approved by a majority of the Second Chamber, including their own party. When these Senators voted with the opponents of the bill, it was rejected. In 1999, a proposal to introduce a referendum (see Chapters 4 and 5) entered its second reading in the First Chamber; the proposal was strongly disliked by the VVD but the party had accepted it as part of the coalition agreements of the Kok I and Kok II governments. As with all constitutional amendments, this change needed a two-thirds majority in the second reading, and the votes of all the governing parties' Senators were needed to meet this requirement. It fell one vote short during 'Wiegel's Night', so-called after the Liberal Senator who broke ranks. This episode even led to a brief Cabinet crisis when the main advocate of the referendum, D66, accused the VVD of not keeping its promises. Similarly, during 'Van Thijn's Night' in 2005, the proposal to abolish the constitutional requirement that local mayors must be appointed by the central government, failed to get the required two-thirds majority in the second reading when the Labour caucus in the First Chamber opposed the amendment despite it being supported by the party leader and caucus in the Second Chamber (see Chapters 4 and 8). And in 2012, after heavy lobbying by Jewish and Muslim organizations, the Senate rejected a ritual slaughter ban introduced by the Animals' Rights party. The bill had been approved by 116 votes to 40 in the Second Chamber. The number of vetoes has not increased further in recent decades, but this may be a result of the rise in the number of bills that have been withdrawn during the legislative process in the First Chamber, from just three in 1952–71 to 33 in 1992–2011. Some of these bills were withdrawn because the government that had introduced them had been replaced, but at least half of the withdrawals were caused by senatorial objections (see www.eerstekamer.nl). In addition, over the years, the First Chamber has created a *de facto* right of amendment for itself by putting a bill's deliberation on hold until the government had received the Second Chamber's approval for an additional bill, giving in to senatorial objections to the original bill. Some of these amending bills (*novelles*) merely serve to correct technical errors that were discovered by Senators in the original, but others result from substantive objections. It is only the latter type of *novelle* that is included in Figure 6.1 and its use has been increasing rapidly since the 'usurpation' of this right in the 1970s.

While senatorial self-restraint makes it unlikely that an opposition majority will censure a government, the growing activism of the First Chamber may prevent a government without a majority in the Senate from implementing fully its legislative programme. Although this has led to calls for outright abolition of the First Chamber, this most radical reform is unlikely to gain the two-thirds majority needed. Another reform would give the Second Chamber the power to override a Senate veto, effectively transforming the current absolute veto into a suspensive one and changing the request for the amendment of bills into suggestions for improvement. Such debates about the Senate's existence and proper role indicate that its importance should not be underestimated, but with regard to parliamentary oversight and even for most legislation, the Second Chamber is still of greater importance and therefore the focus of the remainder of this chapter.

Parliamentary Committees

Committees play an important role in the functioning of the Dutch Parliament, and of the Second Chamber in particular. Between 1848 and 1953, with only minor modifications, a simple committee system was in effect. The Second Chamber was divided into five general committees, composed three times a year by the drawing of lots. Each committee examined all bills submitted and, after consideration, each committee assigned a *rapporteur* to convey its findings to a central committee consisting of all the committee chairpersons and the Speaker.

After 1888, more specialized select committees gradually developed alongside these five standing committees. Finally, in 1953, the old standing committees were abolished and the select committees took over the consideration of bills. There are probably two causes for this development: first, it was felt that the ever more detailed and technical proposals from the government required a level of specialization from MPs that could not be guaranteed by randomly composed committees; and, second, the more general political discussion of new bills had gradually moved from the standing committees to meetings of the newly developing parliamentary parties.

Today there are about 24 committees in the Second Chamber, all but a few of which are permanent. The committee system reflects the structure of the bureaucracy, with each ministerial portfolio (apart from that of the Prime Minister) being monitored by a parliamentary committee. In addition, there are a few committees with more general tasks, such as the Committee on Government Expenditure, the Committee on Petitions and Citizens' Initiatives, and the Committee on European Affairs (see Chapter 8), and a few committees with more specialized tasks, such as the Committee on the Intelligence Services (containing only the leaders of the parliamentary parties, who are sworn to secrecy). A few committees have an internal task, such as the Presidium, and the Committee on Parliamentary Procedures. Except for these latter committees, committees have a function with regard to both legislation and oversight of government activity. However, when a particular government action seems to deserve more extensive scrutiny, a temporary committee or a special Committee of Parliamentary Inquiry may be set up exclusively to investigate a particular policy.

Officially, the Speaker appoints the members of committees, but in practice he or she is given little choice. The partisan composition of committees is roughly proportional to the strength of the parties in the Chamber, though special consideration is given to the smaller parties. These smaller parties are often given some latitude in the choice of the committees on which they wish to serve. Once the party composition is known, the leader of each parliamentary party nominates the party's representatives. Proportional representation also dictates the distribution of committee chairpersons over the parties, and chairpersons may come from opposition as well as government parties. The leaders of the parliamentary parties meet informally to discuss which party will get which chair.

Parliamentary Parties

Despite their obvious importance, little is formally regulated about parliamentary parties. The Second Chamber's Standing Orders define a parliamentary party merely as 'all Members who have been declared elected on the same electoral list'. Blocs of seats, office space and speaking time in debates are all allotted to the parliamentary parties roughly in proportion to their size, and it is left to them to allocate seats and offices, and to select the spokespersons in parliamentary debates. The parliamentary parties also receive subventions to hire staff contingent on their size. This state funding of parliamentary parties consists of over €24 million (Budget 2013). Roughly two-thirds of the money goes to the parliamentary parties as such, and one-third to individual MPs, who are each entitled to one full-time assistant. The chairpersons of the parliamentary parties receive a higher salary than ordinary MPs, with the bonus being proportionate to the size of their parliamentary party.

In addition to these formal rules of Parliament, each parliamentary party has its own rules about its organization and the obligations of its members and staff (Elzinga and Wisse, 1988). Some parliamentary parties have elaborate written standing orders. In most parties, the parliamentary party meeting is the highest authority; it usually meets at the beginning of each parliamentary week behind closed doors, but often in the presence of staff members. In its first meeting after elections it chooses its chairman and an executive board from among its members. The larger parliamentary parties also have an internal system of committees more or less mirroring the Parliamentary committees. MPs are expected to abide by the decisions of the parliamentary party meeting, even if they were not present; if they feel they cannot follow the party line, they have to give advance warning to the parliamentary party executive board. Some parliamentary parties also require their members to seek permission from the chairperson or the relevant internal committee before making use of an individual MP's parliamentary rights, such as putting a written question to a minister.

Nevertheless, an MP who decides to leave the parliamentary party is under no constitutional obligation to give up his or her seat, despite moral pressure, or even formal party rules, to do so. Such splits do occur, but they are relatively rare; between 1945 and 2013, 44 MPs left the parliamentary party that had nominated them and remained in Parliament. Given the fact that more than 3,000 MPs have been declared elected in this period, this amounts to a mere 1.4 per cent. This is surprisingly low, considering that there are no formal obstacles to setting up one's own parliamentary party. A breakaway faction needs only to notify the Speaker in order to be recognized as a separate parliamentary party; no minimum number of MPs is required to qualify as a parliamentary party, which is the case in many other countries.

Parliamentary Procedures

Legislation

The Constitution stipulates that legislation is a joint venture of Crown and States-General. With the exception of a few bills that can be introduced only by the government (most notably the Budget), both ministers and Second Chamber MPs have the right to initiate legislation. While there are no formal or informal limitations on the introduction of private members' bills, the number proposed is quite small and in practice the vast majority of bills originate in the Cabinet. During the readings in the Second Chamber, members may introduce amendments that can be adopted by a simple majority. If a minister has introduced a bill, the government is allowed to alter (or even to withdraw) its proposal up to the final vote being taken in the Second Chamber. After passage the bill is then referred to the First Chamber where, as noted, it can only be adopted or rejected (or withdrawn by the government or the sponsoring MP).

Once adopted by both Houses, a bill must be signed by the monarch and countersigned by a minister before it is promulgated. In 1976, the Minister of Justice, a Christian Democrat, threatened to withhold his signature from a private member's bill liberalizing abortion. Although such a refusal is constitutional, political conflict or even crisis would undoubtedly ensue. So far, no such incident has occurred; in the case just mentioned the rejection by the Senate of the proposed bill headed off an otherwise inevitable conflict. A refusal by the monarch to sign a bill has even more potential for a constitutional crisis. The Constitution does not provide for a 'Belgian' solution (in 1991, the Belgian King Baudouin temporarily abdicated to avoid a crisis over his refusal to sign an abortion bill), and in the few cases that have become known the government preferred to have no legislation rather than an open constitutional conflict (see Box 1.3 on page 21).

Constitutional Revision

The procedure for changing the Constitution is only slightly more complicated than that for passing legislation. According to the constitutional procedure, after a constitutional amendment has been adopted by an ordinary majority in both Houses, Parliament is dissolved and new elections are held to give the electorate an opportunity to voice its opinion on the change. The newly elected Parliament must then adopt the amendment by a two-thirds majority. Theoretically, this gives the electorate a voice and potential veto. In practice, parliamentary dissolutions for reasons of constitutional revision are timed to coincide with regular parliamentary elections; amendments are first adopted at the end of a parliamentary period immediately preceding a regular election. Discussions of constitutional amendments have never played a role in election campaigns, and it is unlikely that the electorate is even aware that it is passing judgement on constitutional amendments as well as electing new representatives.

Dutch legislative procedures do not deviate widely from what is customary in most parliamentary systems. There is, however, one aspect that may be more idiosyncratic. In most countries, bills die after a dissolution of Parliament. In the Netherlands, once introduced, bills never die (Van Schagen, 1997). On average, about 250 bills are introduced each year and take 14 months before they are adopted by the Senate. However, there is no official time limit to the legislative process for a particular bill, the record being 26 years! That bills can survive governments or Parliaments may seem a minor detail, but its importance lies in the fact that the government is usually not under any time pressure with regard to its legislative programme, and therefore has no need to intervene in the agenda of Parliament. It is the Speaker and the Presidium of the House who set the agenda, without the kind of government interference that is customary in most parliamentary systems. Table 6.1 gives an overview of the use made by the Second Chamber of its various parliamentary rights. The table shows no overall increase in legislative activity; the number of private member bills has risen slightly, but the number of amendments has decreased significantly. The pattern with regard to parliamentary oversight is very different.

Oversight

Parliamentary oversight is based on Article 42 of the Constitution: 'The Government shall comprise the King and the Ministers. The Ministers, and not the King, shall be responsible for acts of government.' It is to Parliament that the ministers are thus responsible. Parliament can ask for information, which the government is not allowed to refuse except for reasons of state. Written questions are the most widely used means of obtaining information; oral questions (or, more accurately, oral answers to written questions) also exist, but are used more for political purposes than the acquisition of factual information. When these questions are answered during the regular Tuesday question hour, they may lead to supplementary questions and a short debate. The political purpose of parliamentary questions is most pronounced in urgent debates, during which there is an opportunity for other MPs to join the debate once the minister has answered the question of one of their colleagues. There are two types of urgent debates: interpellations that formally require the consent of a majority of parliament; and 30-member debates, so called after the number of MPs whose consent is required. Since the introduction of the latter category the number of urgent debates has increased dramatically.

In terms of oversight, there is no formal distinction between the First and the Second Chambers, but in practice it is the Second Chamber where most of the relevant activities take place. In addition to collecting information by standing or special committees, each House also has the power to call for an official Parliamen-

Table 6.1 *The Second Chamber's Use of Assorted Parliamentary Rights, 1956–2012 (average per year during four-year periods)*

Period	Meetings		Legislation			Oversight		
	Plenary	Committee	Total number of bills	Private member's bills	Amendments introduced	Written questions	Urgent debates	Resolutions introduced
1956–60	74	273	(258)	0	101	228	6	–
1960–64	79	354	(252)	1	187	268*	5	20
1964–68	58	368	(282)	1	130	621*	3	63
1968–72	87	639	(276)	7	262	1389*	15	171
1972–76	100	597	(274)	3	493	1498*	12	249
1976–80	94	736	(303)	5	728	1532*	15	639
1980–84	96	1124	(322)	4	1483	1305*	15	831
1984–88	102	1286	(266)	7	1460	1011	15	597
1988–92	99	1078	(264)	3	1085	736	12	872
1992–96	100	1051	(276)	6	1030	990	9	535
1996–2000	103	1429	(254)	6	1188	1571	8	898
2000–04	97	1367	(269)	10	n.a.	1692	9	1118
2004–08	102	1475	(262)	13	n.a.	2147	37	1470
2008–12	107	1594	(251)	11	510	2902	61	2643

Note: The number of 'bills introduced' encompasses bills introduced by the government and private members' bills.

Sources: Asterisked data from G. Visscher (1998); all other data until 1999 from Central Bureau of Statistics, Statistical Yearbook (The Hague, various years); data for 1999–2004 from Rijksbegroting, Hoofdstuk 2 Hoge Colleges van Staat, Art. 3 Wetgeving en Controle Tweede Kamer, various years; data since 2004 www.tweedekamer.nl.

tary Inquiry. An *ad hoc* Parliamentary Committee is then set up, with far-reaching powers: hearing witnesses under oath, and even imprisoning witnesses who refuse to testify. In the history of the Dutch Parliament only 20 such Parliamentary Inquiries have been held, probably because a majority in Parliament is needed for the setting up of an Inquiry. Attempts to give minorities of a fifth or a third of the members the right to a Parliamentary Inquiry have been vetoed by the First Chamber, even though that House itself has never held an Inquiry.

Parliament may adopt resolutions (*moties*) at any time; for example, when it deems a minister's answer to be unsatisfactory. Any MP is allowed to introduce a resolution as long as it is seconded by at least four other MPs. Resolutions adopted are not binding on the government, and ministers do occasionally ignore them. On several occasions during the Vietnam War, the Second Chamber adopted a resolution requesting the Foreign Affairs Minister to register protest with the American government, but the long-serving and wily Minister Luns always refused to do so.

It is generally accepted that a motion of no confidence, if adopted, cannot be ignored and must result in the resignation of the minister or of the Cabinet as a whole, or in the dissolution of Parliament. This rule is not found in the Constitution. Actually, nowhere does the Constitution mention that the Cabinet needs the confidence of Parliament, and votes of confidence do not even exist. Perhaps for that reason, Parliament has in the past occasionally used other means to unseat a minister, such as the rejection of his budget, or lowering his salary by one, very symbolic, guilder (€0.5). Sometimes it is not even clear whether a resolution is a censure motion or not. One case achieved such notoriety that a play was written about it: in 1966, during 'Schmelzer's Night', the Cabinet stepped down after a resolution had been adopted criticizing the government's financial policy, even though the Catholic Party leader, Norbert Schmelzer, who led the critics, always maintained that it was not intended as a motion of no confidence. In another case, the adoption of a resolution led to a debate on whether or not it was a motion of no confidence. To end the confusion, the MP who had introduced the controversial resolution introduced a second one, stating that the first motion was indeed intended to censure the government. The House then rejected this second resolution. The ambiguity over censure motions has no real significance, but does symbolize the fact that the Dutch parliamentary system has a touch of separation of powers.

For all instruments for oversight (parliamentary questions, urgent debates, resolutions), Table 6.1 shows considerable increases in their use. Some speak of 'motion inflation' or the unwarranted calling of urgent debates in response to media hypes, and fear that the more frequent use of such instruments may blunt their impact. Others attribute the more frequent use to improved staffing, or to individual MPs' need to impress the nominating committee of their party. Whatever the causes and effects, the development does point to a changing relationship between parliament and government.

Executive–Legislative Relations

From Institution to Arena

The institutional characteristics of the Dutch Parliament, and the formal powers of 'the' Parliament *vis-à-vis* 'the' government were shaped before political parties were formed. Parliament has changed little since 1848, whereas the first political party, the ARP, was founded only in 1879 (see Chapter 3). Before disciplined parties were formed, there was no coherent majority in the Second Chamber to sustain 'its' ministers for the duration of a Parliament. Instead, more or less *ad hoc* majorities had to be put together on each issue. In the absence of parties, the King continued to determine the composition of Cabinets to a considerable extent. This royal (and indirectly, through the monarch, even divine) legitimation in a sense 'elevated' the Cabinet above Parliament. The separation of powers was further emphasized because the very position of Parliament *vis-à-vis* the King and his ministers was one of the major political issues of the period between the shaping of Parliament and the forming of political parties.

When political parties developed around the start of the twentieth century, they gradually wrested the power to form a government away from the monarch. When, for example, the Queen tried to reinstate royal Cabinet formation in 1939, her ministers were censured at their first appearance in Parliament. In the latest stage of this development, the monarch was removed from the government formation process completely in 2012 (see Chapter 5). However, for a long time the parties in Parliament remained content with their control over the formation of Cabinets, and did not extend their influence to the government once formed.

In the previous chapter we mentioned the originally rather apolitical recruitment criteria for ministers, the taboo on contacts between ministers and their fellow party members in Parliament, and so on. There we also discussed possible causes of this curious self-restraint on the part of the parties in Parliament, such as the 'rules of the game' of consociational democracy. Here it is important to note that the notion of Parliament as an institution, as a collective body, confronting another institution, the government, survived the formation of disciplined political parties longer than in many other countries. However, as the basic unit of Parliament was no longer the individual member but the parliamentary party (or *fractie*, as it is referred to in Dutch), conflicts between ministers and their own parliamentary party were not uncommon. In the post-war period, at least two Cabinet crises resulted from such intra-party conflict. In 1951, the Liberal Party in Parliament introduced a motion of no confidence aimed at the plans for the decolonization of Dutch New Guinea by the Liberal Minister of Foreign Affairs. This led to the resignation of the entire Cabinet. In 1960, the Cabinet resigned when the ARP introduced a motion of no confidence in reaction to the plans of its own Minister of Housing. However, when individual ministers have been forced to resign because of criticism in Parliament, the victim's party has normally chosen to replace the minister rather than escalate the conflict into a full-blown Cabinet crisis. After all, the minister was often a political outsider, and the parliamentary party had not been consulted in advance about the issue that led to the unfortunate minister's downfall. The prestige of the party was thus not at stake.

In Chapter 5 we also described how the Cabinet was gradually politicized from the 1960s onwards. Ministers without previous parliamentary experience have become less common; weekly consultations between a governing party's ministers and its parliamentary leaders have been set up, and the coalition programme has gained in importance, binding not only the ministers but also the parliamentary parties making up the government majority. As far back as 1979, 68 per cent of all MPs interviewed in a survey agreed with the statement that 'Government policy is formed in close consultation and cooperation with the parliamentary parties in the governmental majority.' Of all MPs, 84 per cent agreed that 'More than in the past, the government is dependent on what the parliamentary parties in the governmental majority want.' It is difficult to gauge actual party unanimity accurately as roll calls are rare and thus possible dissenters are not registered. The Proceedings (*Handelingen*) of the Second Chamber normally record the votes of parliamentary parties rather than of individual MPs. The Dutch political scientist Wolters has argued that this practice suggests a low level of intra-party dissension, and cites estimates of party unanimity of 92–98 per cent during the 1967–71 Parliament (Wolters, 1984, pp. 182–5). Between 1998 and 2008, the Second Chamber took 14,532 votes (on bills, amendments and motions), and in only 67 of these votes (0.46 per cent) did at least one MP break party ranks (Simon Otjes, personal communication). This high level of party unity in parliamentary votes is caused primarily by the fact that MPs belonging to the same party tend to have very similar views on important political questions. Even when an MP disagrees with his or her party, most MPs feel that they should still toe the party line, unless a matter of high moral principle is involved. Party discipline, in the sense of threats of sanctions against dissenters, is rarely necessary to maintain a united front (Andeweg and Thomassen, 2011). Party discipline is probably most important in governing parties when agreements made between the parties during the Cabinet's formation or the weekly consultations are at stake, as these are more likely to deviate from MPs' personal preferences. The government can therefore count on a loyal and firm majority; on average, less than one government bill per year is defeated in the Second Chamber.

As a result, the characteristic lines of conflict are now between parties rather than between the institutions of Parliament and government, pitting ministers and MPs of one party against (ministers and) MPs of another. Of these lines of conflict, the one between ministers plus MPs of the governing parties on the one hand, and opposition MPs on the other hand, is most visible, but also rather sterile in terms of policy outcome. By definition, the opposition is a minority, and as such it is powerless apart from the rare occasion when a wedge can be driven between the governing parties. Conflicts between the governing parties, in both government and Parliament, are much more interesting, as the outcome is less predictable and directly affects government policy.

This shift has reduced the importance of the elements of a separation of powers in the Dutch Constitution. In the language of Dutch constitutional lawyers, executive–legislative relations have become more 'monistic' and less 'dualistic'. This development has had important consequences. Since 1965 we have seen a new type of Cabinet crisis in which the Cabinet falls after a conflict along party lines within the Cabinet (for example, in 1965, 1972, 1977, 1982, 2002, 2006 and 2010). Moreover, individual ministers are less often censured by a parliamentary majority. Between 1946 and 2009, 5.1 per cent of ministers were forced to resign, but from the 1960s to the 1980s ministers seemed immune to parliamentary censure (Bovens et al., 2010). In the past, a parliamentary party accepted, albeit grudgingly, the forced resignation of one of its appointees. Since ministers tended to be prominent party members, and since the parliamentary party was consulted and involved in the preparations of Cabinet decisions, to repudiate a party's minister is to repudiate that party itself. If a minister were to be forced to withdraw from the Cabinet, his or her party would be more likely to withdraw from the coalition, thereby bringing down the whole Cabinet. This would force the other coalition parties to choose between criticism of an individual minister and the survival of the Cabinet, with generally predictable results. The best-known case in which this mechanism prevented the censure of an individual minister occurred in 1977, when a Catholic Minister of Justice was accused of being responsible, through personal negligence, for the escape of an alleged (later convicted) war criminal. The spokesman for one of the other coalition parties, the Social Democrats, doubted the minister's capability to lead a department, but refused to support a motion of no confidence:

> We have judged this minister as Minister of Justice. He is more. He is the Deputy Prime Minister, he is a member of this Cabinet. As such he is a partner in compromises that we have made. That is what we have to consider. That is what is on the scales. If we weigh that, we can come to no other conclusion [than to refrain from censuring this minister]. (Proceedings of the Second Chamber, 1976–7, 23 February 1977, p. 3418; *authors' own translation*)

Only if the minister's own parliamentary party decides that he has become a liability and refuses to defend him against attacks from other parties, have individual ministers felt forced to resign. As long as the minister can count on the support of his/her own party, he or she cannot be ousted: the minister apologizes to Parliament and continues in office. The use of apologies to escape accountability has been denounced as a development towards a 'sorry democracy' (Van Thijn, 1998). In general, the separation of powers has decreased, and the Dutch system has moved towards a more typical parliamentary system. Today, Parliament is less an institution confronting other institutions and more an arena in which political parties attempt to influence public policy. This development is sometimes depicted as one of the factors contributing to a 'decline of Parliament'.

Parliament as a Marketplace

The Dutch Parliament has a third feature. In addition to the constitutional institution and the political arena, Parliament may take the form of a marketplace in which social interests are traded. Because of the electoral system, regional interests have little impact on parliamentary behaviour, but socio-economic interests are well-represented, and their representation does not necessarily coincide with party membership. In the parliamentary marketplace, departmental ministers and specialized MPs of all parties join forces to defend their common sectoral interests against the tradespeople with other interests, and in particular against the Minister of Finance. The Minister of Agriculture, together with all the parties' spokespersons on agriculture in Parliament defending farmers' interests, used to be a prime example. This coalition was known as the 'Green Front' long before 'green' took on another meaning, and by no means stands alone. Parliament as a marketplace takes its place in the neo-corporatist policy networks that will be described in Chapter 7.

The emergence of Parliament as a marketplace is more difficult to date than its development as an arena, though clues to its timing may be found in a few related developments. In the first place, during pillarization political parties, and in particular Christian Democratic parties, attempted to appeal to a socio-economic cross-section of the electorate by putting candidates on their list who came from various interest groups that were associated with the same pillar: so-called 'quality seats'. This practice became possible only after the introduction of proportional representation and the list system of candidate nomination in 1917. By its very nature, this encouraged MPs to operate as 'stallholders' for the interest group involved. The 'quality seats' are a symptom of the general emphasis placed on specialization and specialists in Dutch political decision-making, which is also evident in the parliamentary marketplace.

Another important factor was the replacement of the non-specialized by specialized Parliamentary Committees in 1953. These specialized Committees consist primarily of MPs who are experts in the policy area concerned, sometimes because of prior activities in one of the relevant interest groups. As can be seen in Table 6.1 above, the number of committee meetings has increased substantially. These specialized committees are the market stalls where the specialized tradesmen from the governmental majority and the opposition jointly discuss market strategy for their common interest. These changes, implemented in 1917 and 1953, indicate that Parliament as a marketplace seems to have coexisted with both Parliament as an institution and Parliament as an arena.

The Coexistence of Institution, Arena and Marketplace

To complicate matters further, even Parliament as an institution has not vanished completely. Actually, from a normative point of view the institutional perspective still seems to dominate the interactions between ministers and MPs There appears to be a remarkable gap between 'is' and 'ought' in this respect, as can be seen from Table 6.2.

Table 6.2   *MPs' Opinions on Executive–Legislative Relations, 2006 (percentages)*

	Who should	Who actually does
	determine the broad outlines of government policies?	
Parliament	43	16
Government	35	17
Government plus parliamentary parties in the coalition	12	51
Government plus 'social partners'	4	5
Others	6	11
Total	100	100
N =	113	110

Source: Dutch Parliamentary Study, 2006.

Despite 51 per cent of the MPs interviewed in 2006 agreeing that policy is largely determined by the government plus the parliamentary parties belonging to the governing majority (as one would expect in a Parliament operating as an arena), only 12 per cent are of the opinion that policy ought to be determined in this fashion. This pattern can be observed within all parliamentary parties, though the parties with the most experience in government – CDA, PvdA and VVD – appear to be less critical of Parliament as an arena.

Parliament as an institution is not confined to the normative level only. There has been, for example, a revival and redefinition of the Parliamentary Inquiry. Eight of the 20 parliamentary inquiries held so far date back to the second half of the nineteenth century. After 1887, the Parliamentary Inquiry fell into abeyance for nearly a century, with just one exception; to make up for the absence of Parliamentary oversight during the years of the Second World War, an Inquiry was held in 1947–8 to investigate the government's activities in exile. Since the 1980s, 11 new Parliamentary Inquiries have been started (see Table 6.3). The nature of the Parliamentary Inquiry has also changed; whereas the nineteenth-century inquiries dealt primarily with social problems (contagious cattle disease, working conditions in factories and so on), recent inquiries have tended to investigate government fiascos and policy failures. In line with this new purpose, it has become possible for Inquiry Committees to summon incumbent ministers to testify.

There has been a similar increase in the number of investigative parliamentary committees that do not have the full powers of a formal Parliamentary Inquiry: two-thirds of the 36 such committees in the 1945–2013 period have been set up since the 1990s. Some of these investigative committees are to collect information on which to base a decision of whether or not to begin a Parliamentary Inquiry, while others have a similar exposure and impact as a Parliamentary Inquiry (such as the committee that reported in 2008 on the negative effects of the government's many reforms of the Dutch education system). The increasing attention towards

Table 6.3 *Parliamentary Inquiries, 1983–2013*

1983–4	Government interference in the shipbuilding industry
1986–8	Housing subsidies
1987–8	Failure to develop a new tamper-proof passport
1992–3	Implementation of social insurance programmes
1994–6	Criminal investigation of organized crime
1998–9	The crash of an EL AL cargo plane on to an Amsterdam apartment block
2001–02	Fraud with government building contracts
2002–03	The fall of Srebrenica
2011–12	Government response to the financial crisis
2013–	Public housing corporations
2013–	Purchase of defective high-speed trains

Parliament's oversight role, already referred to above in the discussion of parliamentary questions, urgent debates and motions, is also evident in other developments. In 2000, an annual 'Accountability Day' (*Verantwoordingsdag*; the third Wednesday of May) was introduced, on which the Second Chamber debates the annual reports of the various government departments and a reaction to these reports from the General Accounting Office. In 2002, the Second Chamber created its own Research Office, in large part to support Parliamentary Inquiries and investigative committees.

This renewed attention on Parliament's role in oversight has to some extent even reversed the trend towards the 'sorry democracy' mentioned above. Even though no ministers have been voted out of office by a formal censure motion, since the 'revival' of the Parliamentary Inquiry in the 1980s the number of ministers who were forced to resign increased once more (Bovens et al., 2010).

The fact that separation of powers seems to have survived primarily with regard to oversight indicates that the kind of issue most likely to be dealt with by Parliament as an institution is a scandal or a policy fiasco. Parliament might also take this form when its position as a constitutional institution is at stake (as when the government tries to cut the budget of the States-General), when novice ministers do not abide by 'the rules of this House', or when ministers are reluctant to give an MP the information he or she is asking for. Whereas Parliament as an institution survives primarily with regard to parliamentary oversight, Parliament as a marketplace can be observed when it is dealing with legislative proposals, particularly with bills that are more technocratic than ideological in nature. This is illustrated by the fact that opposition parties usually support government proposals when it comes to the final vote.

Figure 6.2 shows the annual average percentages of governing parties and of opposition parties supporting that year's government proposals. Since the late 1980s, the percentage of parties in the governing coalition supporting the government's proposals gradually increased from just over 60 per cent in the early 1960s to close to 100 per cent since the late 1980s. This is in line with the tightening of the relations between a parliamentary party and the government ministers from that

party that were discussed above. More surprising is that the support for government proposals from the opposition shows a similar development; since the early
1990s, between 80 per cent and 90 per cent of the opposition parties have voted
in support of the government's proposals. In a detailed study of the fate of some
3,000 bills that were discussed in Parliament between 1963 and 1986, Gerard Visscher found that the most oppositional of the opposition parties in those years – the
Communist Party – supported 84 per cent of all government proposals (Visscher,
1994, pp. 375–6)! This is not because Dutch opposition parties are lacklustre, but
because their MPs can influence the bills before they come to a final vote. Nearly
half of all bills are changed before they reach the Statute books, and as the nature of
some bills does not allow for changes (for example, proposals to ratify a treaty), this
is an underestimation of the impact of the parliamentary process on the content of
government proposals (Visscher, 1994, p. 196).

The committee stage is of special importance in this respect, because within the
Parliamentary committees MPs act more as policy specialists than as partisans. In
both the 1979 and the 1990 Parliamentary Study, about 80 per cent of the MPs interviewed agreed with the statement 'As a rule, the parliamentary party allows one
considerable freedom of manoeuvre in Parliamentary Committees'. Within Committees, the distinction between MPs from the governing majority and from the opposition is therefore less important, and suggestions by opposition MPs are not rejected
automatically. As a result of the deliberations during the committee stage, the
government will often change its proposal by taking on board some of the comments
and criticisms made by committee members, including opposition MPs. Of the bills

Figure 6.2   *Average Support for Government Proposals from Government and Opposition
Parties, 1947–2012*

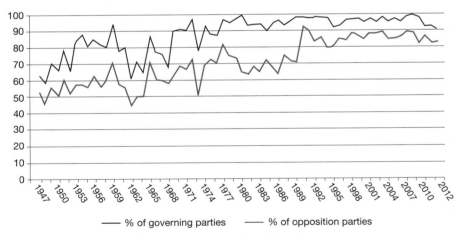

Note: Freedom Party is treated as an opposition party during Rutte I government.
Source: www.tweedekamer.nl; calculations by Harmen van der Veer.

analysed in Visscher's study, some 45 per cent were changed by the government itself (Visscher, 1994, p. 200). In addition, if we look at the government's reaction to formal amendments, the government did 'advise against' (the parliamentary term for the strongest form of government disapproval) 68 per cent of all opposition amendments, but it registered no objections to 13 per cent of those amendments, and even adopted 7 per cent of them (ibid., p. 261). An agreement between policy specialists within the committees may carry over into the much more partisan plenary sessions: in the 1972, 1979, 2001 and 2006 Parliamentary Studies there was widespread agreement among MPs (between 80 per cent and 96 per cent) with the statement 'As a rule, one votes according to the advice of the specialist'. In this way the marketplace transforms into the arena, and through this mechanism opposition amendments are not without prospect when they come to a vote: 11 per cent of such amendments in Visscher's study gained majority support, against 17 per cent of the amendments introduced by a governing party (ibid., p. 293).

Thus it would seem that Parliament 'shifts gear' between arena (whenever the item on the agenda is politically controversial, and in plenary sessions for the television cameras), marketplace (with regard to new legislation that is of a technical or routine nature, particularly in the specialized Parliamentary Committees), and institution (when Parliament deals with a policy failure, as in Parliamentary Inquiries) (Andeweg, 1997b). This idea that Parliament can 'shift gears' between institution, arena and marketplace was put to MPs in recent Parliamentary Studies. As can be seen from Table 6.4, in 2006 a large majority of Second Chamber MPs agreed that in general the best description of the relationship between government and Parliament is in terms of a political arena (ministers plus parliamentary parties of the governing coalition versus the opposition). That about one in five MPs still describes the relationship as one between the institutions of Cabinet and Parliament is a sign of the continued importance of the doctrine of separation of powers in the Dutch Parliament. As expected, Parliament as an institution supervising the government as such has survived primarily with regard to inquiries. However, in the 1990 Parliamentary Study, the difference between institution and arena was clearly more marked: in that study, 73 per cent of the MPs perceived Parliament as an institution to be the dominant mode of executive–legislative relations when it comes to Inquiries (against 56 per cent in 2006), and 25 per cent pointed to Parliament as an arena (against 39 per cent in 2006). Apparently, the increased emphasis on parliamentary scrutiny has not stopped the ascendancy of Parliament as a party-political arena (see Van Vonno, 2012).

In view of widespread complaints about the 'over-specialization' of MPs and the 'sectorization' of Parliament, it is surprising that very few mention the marketplace as the dominant mode of executive–legislative relations in general. We expected this mode to be mentioned more frequently with regard to departmental budget debates, for the reasons outlined above. Indeed, Parliament as marketplace was mentioned more often with regard to budgetary proceedings, but still only by 7 per cent of MPs. A possible explanation is that, when it comes to a vote in Parliament, parties

Table 6.4   *MPs' Perceptions of Executive–Legislative Relations, 2006 (percentages)*

	Best description of the relationship between government and Parliament		
	In general	*In debates on departmental budgets*	*During affairs and inquiries*
Cabinet v. Parliament (Parliament as institution)	21	17	56
Cabinet plus parliamentary parties in coalition v. opposition (Parliament as arena)	76	76	39
Sector specialists (MPs plus ministers) v. other sector specialists or generalists (Parliament as marketplace)	3	7	6
Total	100	100	101
N =	110	110	109

Source: Dutch Parliamentary Study, 2006.

unite behind their specialist, and MPs therefore possibly make no distinction between marketplace and arena. We should also take into account that the representation of sectoral interests is considered undesirable, and rather than admit that it nevertheless does take place, MPs may prefer to use the normatively more attractive label of Parliament as an institution. However, we should also not discount the possibility that the complaints about overspecialization and sectorization are exaggerated, or at least outdated: it is interesting that the marketplace was still mentioned by 30 per cent of MPs as the best description of the relationship between government and Parliament in budget debates in a 1990 study, but only by 7 per cent in 2006. Between these two studies, Parliament reorganized its committee system to create fewer (20 instead of 40) and less specialized committees, precisely to combat excessive sectorization.

Parliament and the People

As in any parliamentary system of government, the Dutch Parliament is a linchpin between civil society and the government. As a consequence, MPs are not only involved in executive–legislative relations, but also in relations between Parliament and the people. These latter relations are usually described under the heading of 'political representation'. This is not the place for a discussion of the merits of the various meanings attached to 'representation' in the literature, but we shall use three dominant perspectives on representation to discuss the relations between Dutch MPs and voters: descriptive representation; policy representation; and constituency work.

The constitutional provision that 'The States-General represent the entire Dutch people' is sometimes read as meaning that Parliament should be representative of the population in socio-demographic terms. Parliament has never been a microcosm of Dutch society, but there have been three important developments that have made its composition more varied and, indeed, more representative. The first of these developments is the gradual replacement of MPs from the aristocracy and the *haute bourgeoisie* (often from a small number of families) by MPs from a variety of social class backgrounds (Secker, 2000). A related shift has been from an overrepresentation of the professions to an overrepresentation of the public sector (teaching, civil service). For the most part, this development took place in the first half of the twentieth century, and is clearly associated with the widening of the suffrage and the development of mass political parties.

A second development is the increase in the number of female MPs. In 1918, Suze Groeneweg (Labour) was the first woman to be elected to the Dutch Parliament, but it took almost 60 years before more than 10 per cent of MPs were female. From 1977 onwards this number has risen sharply, from 12 per cent in 1977 to 20 per cent in 1983, to a third in 1994, after which the percentage of female MPs appears to have reached a plateau at around 40 per cent (with a record 64 female MPs – 43 per cent in May 2010). While it is still not as high as in some Scandinavian countries, the Netherlands offers evidence of the strong correlation between party-list PR (see Chapter 3) and a high percentage of female MPs. There is no legal quota, but some parties on the left voluntarily use a quota when they nominate candidates. On average, female candidates are given higher positions on the party lists and receive more preference votes than male candidates: in 2012, 34 per cent of all candidates were female, but 39 per cent of all elected MPs were female.

The third and most recent development is that recent Parliaments have also included MPs coming from one of the immigrant communities. In November 2013, there were 14 MPs (nearly 10 per cent) with a non-Western immigrant background in the Second Chamber, including five MPs with a Moroccan background and four of Turkish descent (see also Chapter 2).

In other respects there has not been much change in the social-demographic composition of Parliament. Despite a temporary increase in the number of MPs with no more than primary or secondary education in the Interbellum, Parliament is currently dominated by university graduates, just as it was in the nineteenth century. Although the level of education has risen in the population as well, Parliament is not representative in this respect, which has given rise to concern over an emerging 'diploma democracy' (Bovens and Wille, 2010; see also Bovens and Wille, 2012; Hakhverdian et al., 2012; Waterborg et al., 2012). Secker links this high level of education to the professionalization of MPs, aided by the fact that improved salary conditions have transformed MPs into full-time functionaries (Secker, 2000). Thus there is a risk that the old hereditary caste of politicians has been replaced by a new political class, albeit a demographically more heterogeneous one.

Indeed, some pundits perceive a widening 'gap' between an introverted political class that is out of touch and an increasingly disgruntled electorate (see Chapter 11).

This would lead us to expect that Dutch MPs would adopt a 'Burkean' role of independent trustees rather than the role of a delegate, faithfully representing the opinions of their voters. Since 1972, the Dutch Parliamentary Studies have asked MPs how they would act in case of a disagreement with their party's voters.

However, the development of MPs' role orientations seems to be in the opposite direction (see Table 6.5). In 1972, 71 per cent of MPs would act as a trustee, following their own judgment rather than that of their voters, but the proportion of trustees declined over the years, to 49 per cent in 2006. The number of delegates following their voters rather than sticking to their own view, has increased from 7 per cent to around 20 per cent. We should be careful in interpreting these figures. This typology of representative roles originated in the USA, and it may not travel well to the Netherlands, with its presence of strong parties and absence of constituency voting. The fact that a third of the MPs answered 'it depends' to the question of what they would do in the case of a disagreement between them and their voters adds to these concerns.

Another approach to issue representation is to see how representative Parliament is of the electorate, not in terms of demographic characteristics, but in terms of positions taken by MPs and voters on a range of important issues (Figure 6.3).

If we look at where voters and MPs position themselves on an 11-point left–right scale, we see a remarkable congruence in the two distributions. The median voter and the median legislator are at an identical point on the scale. This is not the case for some of the more specific (7-point) issue scales, however. Parliament is still quite representative of the electorate when it come to the issue of income equality, though the voters are clearly more inclined to take the most extreme pro-equality position. Income equality is closely associated with the dominant interpretation of left–right in socio-economic terms (see Chapters 3 and 4), but the other issues are not, and this affects voter–MP congruence (Thomassen, 1999). On euthanasia, the median legislator is also towards the liberal end of the scale, but more than half of the voters take the most liberal position compared with only 13 per cent of MPs. The lack of congruence is even clearer on the issues least associated with a left–right split in any interpretation: on crime, on multi-culturalism, and especially on European integration, the distributions of MPs and of voters are quite different, with

Table 6.5   *Representative Role Orientations, 1972–2006 (percentages)*

	1972	1979	1990	2001	2006
Delegates ('follow party voters')	7	7	10	21	19
Politicos ('it depends')	22	29	34	40	32
Trustees ('follow own judgement')	71	64	56	40	49
Total	100	100	100	101	100
N=	141	129	130	129	104

Source: Dutch Parliamentary Studies.

the MPs being less strict with regard to crime, less insistent on the complete assimilation of immigrants, and less sceptical about European integration. It seems to be no coincidence that the 2002 electoral landslide centred on multi-culturalism and crime (see Chapter 2), and that the 2005 referendum surprise was regarding the EU (see Chapter 10).

Figure 6.3   *Issue Congruence between Voters and MPs, 2006*

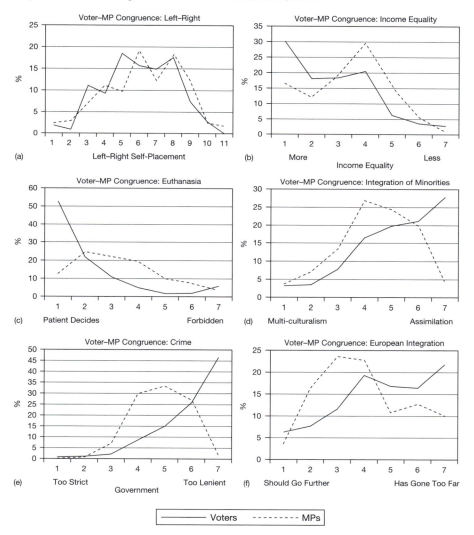

Sources: National Election Study, 2006 (voters); Parliamentary Study, 2006.

Figure 6.3 compares the issue positions of all voters with those of all MPs, and gives no indication of the congruence of a party's MPs and its voters. On average, the MPs of a party are one point (on a 7-point scale) removed from the average party voter, but there are differences between parties and issues. Surprisingly, CDA MPs are the least representative of their party's electorate on euthanasia, and most representative on multi-culturalism. Liberal MPs represent their voters best on crime and multi-culturalism, but are least representative on income equality. Labour MPs are most representative of their electorate on income equality, and least representative on European integration and on crime. On crime, however, the difference between the means of voters ands MPs was 1.26, much less than it has been in the past. As Thomassen wrote about the issue of law and order:

> In the early seventies PvdA MPs took a position that was almost the opposite of their voters … However, the voters got their revenge. Almost twenty years later … the PvdA voters were on the average still where they were two decades before, but their representatives had moved to that position as well. It took the voters almost twenty years to close the gap, but they finally did, not because the ideological framework had changed, but because of the increasing salience of this particular issue that had been neglected by the political elite for such a long time. (Thomassen, 1999, p. 55)

In the coming twenty years, a similar mechanism may also force MPs to adapt their positions on multi-culturalism and on Europe.

Finally, an aspect of political representation that is an increasingly important part of an MP's life in almost any other country is almost absent in the Netherlands – dealing with individual voters' problems (Andeweg, 2012). If Dutch MPs have any contact with individual voters, this usually deals with general policy issues rather than with particular complaints. One reason for this Dutch exception is the small size of the Dutch Parliament relative to the population; with more than 100,000 inhabitants per MP, of the EU member states, only Germany and Spain have smaller Parliaments (Norton, 2002, p. 15). However, a more important factor is the simple fact that, in other countries, contacts with individual citizens take place for the most part in MPs' surgeries or other forms of constituency work. With the whole of the Netherlands effectively forming a single electoral district (see Chapter 4), MPs do not have a constituency, and voters do not have 'their' Congressman or MP to write to. Parliament as an institution has established mechanisms to compensate for the lack of constituency work. Citizens may write to Parliament directly with complaints about government services, and a Committee on Petitions and Citizens' Initiatives deals with these complaints. The number of such complaints has declined since the 1990s to about 200 per year, probably because Parliament itself has set up an Ombudsman, which has developed into a well-known institution receiving thousands of complaints each year (see Chapter 7). To facilitate direct citizen input into policy-making, since 2006 the Second Chamber has allowed for citizen initiatives: petitions on issues that have not been the subject of parliamentary decisions in the previous two years and that have been signed by at least 40,000 citizens will be debated in a plenary session with the minister concerned present. While several citizen initiatives (curtailing the bio-industry, better treatment for Lyme disease, allowing active euthanasia for the elderly who are not ill, raising state pensions, for example) did gain access to the Second Chamber's agenda in this way, most have been rejected because the issue had recently been debated in Parliament. However, such facilities for citizen complaints and citizen initiatives do not alter the fact that Dutch MPs primarily spent their time on legislation and oversight rather than on contact with individual citizens.

Perhaps we should not overemphasize this lacuna in political representation. It is a curious paradox that, compared with most Parliaments where MPs spend much more time on constituency work, trust in the Dutch Parliament remains high and shows no sign of a decline (see Chapter 11). Introducing some form of electoral district is often proposed as a means of bringing Dutch MPs and citizens into more regular contact with each other, but it is interesting to note that when, in 2006, a Citizens' Assembly was asked to review the electoral system, it listed the absence of electoral districts as one of the strengths rather than one of the weaknesses of the current system. Apparently, Dutch citizens do not want or expect their MPs to engage in constituency work.

7

The Policy-Making Process

'An Orchestra with No Conductor?'

Policy-making in the Netherlands has been likened to 'an orchestra with no conductor' (Gladdish, 1991, p. 144). In the preceding chapters we have discussed the considerable fragmentation that characterizes the political arena in the Netherlands: a country of minorities, a multi-party system, coalition government, a formally weak position of the Prime Minister, strong parliamentary committees in a bicameral Parliament, and so on. To the resulting political fragmentation, this chapter adds functional decentralization or sectorization (in Dutch: *verkokering*) because of the way in which the bureaucracy is organized and how interest groups are involved in the policy-making process. Civil servants and interest groups are not the only actors in the policy-making process that are not recognized formally by the Constitution; the courts are also increasingly active as policy-makers, adding yet another player to this arena.

Corporatism

After consociationalism, (neo-)corporatism is probably the best-known characteristic of Dutch governance. There is no consensus in the literature on the exact definition of corporatism or neo-corporatism, but we need not enter that debate: in a meta-analysis of 23 attempts to measure the degree of corporatism in 24 industrial democracies, the Netherlands showed a high degree of corporatism on all scales but one, taking fourth place if the data are averaged (Siaroff, 1999). A recent study of developments in corporatist policy formation in small north-west European countries between 1990 and 2006 mentions the Netherlands as one of the countries where there have been ups and downs, but no structural change in this respect (Woldendorp, 2011). For our purpose it suffices to define corporatism as an empirical relationship between interest groups and the government that is based on exchange (influence for support) and cooperation rather than competition. Thus pressure groups no longer observe their definitional limits of organizations attempting to influence governmental policy-making *from the outside* without taking part in the decision-making or accepting responsibility for the resulting policies; instead, organized interests are incorporated into the policy-making process and defend the outcomes to their members. The theoretical boundaries between the roles played by political parties and by interest groups are blurred.

Organized Interests

The existence of strong, well-organized interest groups is an important precondition for a corporatist model of policy-making to work. One indicator of interest-group strength is inclusiveness or 'density'; that is, the proportion of actual members among the sector of the population that an interest group claims to represent. In this respect there seems to be at least as much variation as in other countries. A few professions operate as a closed shop; for example, lawyers, accountants, and medical doctors; and high density is also achieved by interest groups representing organizations rather than individuals. The Dutch Association of Municipalities (VNG), for example, organizes all 408 potential members. Of all large business enterprises, 90 per cent are member of an employers' association. The percentages are lower for associations of small companies (about two-thirds: Van Rijt-Veltman, 2010) and farmers (about half: SER, 2010).

For comparative purposes, the membership density rate of the trade unions is often used as an indication of corporatism. Until the 1970s, about 40 per cent of all workers were members of a trade union, but this dropped quickly to 24 per cent in 1990 and has fluctuated since then. These percentages are low, especially when compared with those of other so-called corporatist states such as the Nordic countries (70–90 per cent), Austria (42 per cent) or Belgium (54 per cent) (SCP, 2001, p. 155). The relative lack of inclusiveness is evident in most sectors of the economy. It is highest among government employees (40 per cent) and in construction (36 per cent), and lowest in financial institutions (14 per cent), trade (13 per cent), and hotel and catering (12 per cent). It is no accident that the latter sectors are those in which many women work, often part-time. The typical trade union member is still an older male worker with a full-time job.

However, low density rates may not be a good indicator of the strength of Dutch trade unions. Legislation dating back as far as 1927 and 1937 gives the government the power to make the result of wage negotiations between trade unions and employers' associations binding for that particular branch of industry, regardless of whether workers are members of trade unions or whether a firm is affiliated with an employers' association. When, in 2004, one company's employees agreed to a return to a 40-hour work week, the courts declared this agreement illegal because working conditions had to be negotiated by the social partners, not by a company and its employees! In practice, about 80 per cent of the labour force falls under a collective wage agreement, and so far it has been exceptional for the government not to declare a collective agreement binding (see Chapter 9). Since 1966, negotiations between unions and employers' associations have resulted in the employers paying the unions a fee per employee (10 Dutch guilders at first – the 'union tenner' (*vakbondstientje*)– an average of €18 in 2012), which cannot be used to finance actions against the employer, such as a strike for representing not just their own members, but all employees (Delsen, 2002, p. 12). Moreover, the downward trend in trade union membership may not be representative of the willingness to join interest groups in the Netherlands; for example, the membership of consumer organizations almost doubled between 1980 and 2006 (Van den Berg and De Hart, 2008) (see also Chapter 1).

Next to density rates, the cohesiveness of organized interests is also an indicator of strength, as a single unified trade union is a stronger party in corporatist arrangements than several competing trade unions. At first sight, interest-group cohesiveness does not seem to be very impressive: there are not many interests that are represented by a single organization. In the past, pillarization often resulted in separate Catholic, Protestant and 'general' (sometimes split into Socialist and Liberal) organizations for any particular interest (see Chapter 2). Depillarization has reduced the number of separate organizations for the same interest, but many remnants of that era still persist. There are now two large trade union federations: the Federation of Dutch Trade Unions (FNV), a 1976 merger of the Socialist and Catholic trade union movements with 1.2 million members in 2012 (64 per cent of all trade unionists); and a much smaller Protestant Christian National Trade Union (CNV) with a membership of about 341,000 (18 per cent) (Statistics Netherlands). Both of these organizations represent a cross-section of both manual and non-manual workers, with the CNV attracting relatively more white-collar workers. In addition to the FNV and the CNV there are several small, independent unions (such as for the police and the military, which left the CNV umbrella organization in 2012) but, with the exception of a few white-collar organizations (combined in a union for Middle-level and Higher Personnel (MHP) with 132,000 members in 2012, or 7 per cent of all trade union members), they rarely play an important role.

The process of mergers has gone further for the peak organizations representing large and medium-sized companies (Visser and Hemerijck, 1997, pp. 87–90). As early as 1968, two secular employers' organizations combined to form the Association of Dutch Companies (VNO), and in 1970 their Catholic and Protestant counterparts formed the Dutch Association of Christian Employers (NCW). In 1997, these two merged into VNO-NCW. This is the most important employers' organization, but it has no monopoly. In addition to a few specialized organizations (such as for the metallurgical industry, or for banks), there are also rival organizations for smaller firms (MKB Nederland) and for farming (LTO Nederland). The cohesion of the employers' interests is further affected by a few large companies, often multinationals (Philips, Unilever, AkzoNobel, and so on), that are members of VNO-NCW, but prefer to lobby the government directly and negotiate their own in-company agreements with the unions.

Such divisions, however, have not necessarily weakened the strength of the interest groups. Through their integration within a pillar, they once enjoyed close relations with a political party, giving them an additional channel of influence. In contrast to the ideological diversity among French or Italian interest groups, pillarization did not lead to much competition among pressure groups, and it was there-fore better to speak of parallel rather than rival organizations. Each organization had its own constituency, without much hope of converting members from its counter-parts in other pillars. Depillarization appears not to have led to increased compe-tition among interest groups, at least not to the same degree as among political parties. In general, they work together to protect the interests for which they stand. Within the trade union movement, for example, Christian unions were sometimes created from above in order to take the wind out of the socialists' sails, but such rivalry no longer plays a part. The CNV tends to be more moderate than the FNV, but it is rare for the CNV to sign an agreement that is rejected by the FNV, or for the FNV to go on strike without at least the tacit approval of the CNV. And the three main employers' organizations (VNO-NCW, MKB and LTO) have set up a joint Council of Central Business Organizations (RCO) for those occasions on which they want to present a united front to the government and the trade unions.

PBO and Advisory Councils

The incorporation of interest groups into the policy-making process has been facil-itated by the creation of advisory boards, tripartite councils and quangos. Dutch corporatism is often illustrated by reference to a project for the public-law organi-zation of economic activity (*Publiekrechtelijke Bedrijfs Organisatie*, or PBO), first initiated by the German occupiers (see Chapter 1) and continued in the post-war years with the Social and Economic Council (SER) as its best-known and most important organization. The intention of the PBO was that the government would transfer some of its responsibilities to independent regulatory commissions in which representatives of employers and workers, together with government appointees, would regulate their particular sector of the economy. The plan was to develop a matrix of 'vertical' organizations encompassing all companies that contribute to a particular product (such as a dairy product board) as well as 'horizontal' organiza-tions comprising all companies in a particular branch of industry (such as a retail board). Companies paid a mandatory contribution to these boards, which not only advised the government on new policy proposals, but also issued binding regula-tions (for example, the percentage of fat in skimmed milk) for which the govern-ment bears no responsibility. However, the PBO project has been a major failure. Despite the efforts of a special Cabinet minister for PBO, boards were set up in only a few economic sectors, most notably in the food and agriculture sector. In the 1990s, the most powerful of these boards, the Agriculture Board, was discontinued after internal conflict. In 2012, without much resistance, the government moved to abolish the 18 PBO boards that were still in existence.

The Social and Economic Council was intended as the capstone of the PBO structure, but despite the demise of the product- and branch-boards, the SER, which in 2010 celebrated its 60th anniversary, remains a central institution in any discussion of Dutch policy-making (Dankers et al., 2010). It is often described as a tripartite organization, but this is only partially correct. It is tripartite in the sense that it consists of three components of equal size (11 seats each), but 'tripartite' would more usually imply that the government is also represented, together with employers' associations and trade unions. This is not the case with the SER, in which the third element consists of 'Crown members' who are appointed by the central government, but who act independently. These Crown members are mainly university professors, specializing in macro-economics and labour relations. As experts, they may have a moderating effect on the debate between clashing interest groups, but they cannot take the government's place when the exchange of influence for support, so central to corporatist policy-making, takes place. When it comes to bargaining between the government and socio-economic interests, the SER, despite being a showcase of corporatism, plays no role. Paradoxically, it is a formally bipartite institution, the Foundation of Labour set up by employers' organizations and trade unions, that often serves as a meeting ground for government and interest groups. If the SER plays a significant role in policy-making, it is because of its advisory role.

The SER is part of a much larger conglomerate of advisory bodies. A 1977 study of advisory councils by the Scientific Council for Government Policy (itself an advisory board), found no fewer then 402 such councils with over 7,000 members, three-quarters of them having been recruited from organized interests, with over 90 per cent of the advice given being unanimous. The study sparked a debate about the use of such councils and the role of interest groups in the government's advisory system (Oldersma, 1997, 1999). In 1997, a framework law on advisory councils set out a list of criteria aimed at reducing the number and size of the councils, and at distinguishing 'advice' (expertise) and 'consultation' (interest representation). In 2010, 26 permanent advisory councils were registered under this framework law, but the total number of advisory bodies is estimated at 200 (BZK, 2010). Advice is also more non-committal; since 1995, the government is no longer obliged to ask the SER for advice before taking a decision in the relevant policy area, and in 2011 the government announced that it would no longer give an official reaction to all advice it receives.

In reality this change has been less radical than it might seem; in 1977, half of the 402 advisory councils were found to be dormant (that is, they no longer met) in any case, and the small number of remaining councils hides the fact that many of them operate with various sub-councils for specific policy fields. The SER has more than 20 committees (not counting sub-committees and temporary working groups), the Advisory Council on International Affairs has four committees, and so on. Finally, the distinction between interest representation and expertise may also be more formal than real, as expertise is often gathered while working for organized interests. And even the abolition of the government's legal obligation to consult the SER may not have diminished its influence, as it is now free to concentrate its activities on its own priorities and on those issues on which it can achieve unanimity (Koole and Daalder, 2002, p. 36). Nevertheless, there is no denying that a substantial restructuring of the government's advisory system has taken place.

policy-makers into a consensual style, corporatism eventually degenerated into immobilism. During the 1970s and early 1980s there was increasing polarization between employers and trade unions. Meanwhile, their continued incorporation into policy-making institutions provided them with the veto points to block any policy change. It is this period that led to increasing criticism of the 'viscosity' of policy-making, and to calls to restore the 'primacy of politics' over pressure groups, which resulted in the reform of the system of advisory councils discussed above.

These reforms do amount to an institutional weakening of the incorporation of interest groups into the institutions of policy-making, and together with a continued polarization between trade unions and employers would result in Visser and Hemerijck's category of 'corporatist disengagement'; that is, a pattern of governance in which both the institutions of corporatism and the willingness to seek consensus are absent. However, partially in reaction to the government's new-found assertiveness, and partially in response to rising unemployment and low profitability, the trade unions and the employers' associations once again found a compromise in the 1982 Wassenaar Accord and in subsequent agreements (see Chapter 9). This resumption of corporatist behaviour, but with a much lower degree of institutional incorporation of organized interests, brings us full circle, and back into the category of 'innovative' corporatism. It is this more informal variety of corporatism that has been given credit for the exceptional performance of the Dutch economy in the late 1990s, and which has become known, both at home and abroad, as 'the polder model'.

We should be careful not to make too much of the 'polder model'. Jaap Woldendorp, for example, denies the appearance of a 'polder model' from 1982 onwards. He focuses on the strategies of the government and of the social partners, and argues that they varied with the circumstances, and that it was rare for the government, the employers, and the trade unions to all opt for non-confrontational strategies at the same time (Woldendorp, 2005; Woldendorp and Delsen, 2008). Visser and Hemerijck (1997, p. 180) look more at the result than at the strategies of the individual players, but also caution against speaking of a model. First, it was not the result of any grand design, but the net outcome of various small steps and reactions to new circumstances: the Wassenaar Accord was only recognized as the harbinger of a new pattern of policy-making with the benefit of hindsight. Second, the pattern of policy-making varies from one policy field to another, even within the broadly defined area of socio-economic policy (ibid., pp. 182–5). The 'polder model' applies to industrial relations in particular, but with regard to social security the trend is more towards 'corporatist disengagement'.

The mixture of institutional and behavioural corporatism can be very different in other policy areas. The incorporation of interest groups into policy-making appears to be less extensive in policy areas presided over by regulatory rather than spending departments, departments that date back to before the development of the welfare state. For example, policy-making with regard to public health has many characteristics of the 'polder model', with the 2013 'care agreement' often being compared with the 'social agreements' in the socio-economic domain. Attempts by the government to create 'a green polder model' – that is, a similar pattern of consultation for decision-making about major infrastructural projects such as the enlargement of Schiphol Airport or the high-speed railway – have generally foundered on a lack of consensus between environmentalists and economic interests. Apart from infrastructural projects, however, more than 70 'covenants' have been negotiated to reduce pollution (Van Waarden, 2002, p. 59). In 2013, the SER took the lead in inviting environmentalist organizations to negotiate an 'Energy Agreement for Sustainable Growth'. Policy-making in other fields, such as foreign policy (see Chapter 10) is very different from Dutch socio-economic policy-making (see Chapter 9).

Although, as we have just argued, Dutch corporatism has changed rather than disappeared, there are those who suggest that its end is nevertheless nigh. Lei Delsen, for example, points out that an important change in socio-economic corporatism that is not captured in Table 7.1 is its decentralization. Whereas in the 1950s detailed agreements were reached at the central level and implemented almost uniformly with the aid of the government in all sectors and firms, today's central agreements allow considerable variation at both sectoral and company levels. Collective wage agreements, for example, today are often mere frameworks for more detailed agreements at lower levels. This, it is felt, provides the flexibility that is needed because different economic sectors face different forms of international competition. However, such decentralization not only produces inequality among both workers and companies, which may undermine solidarity within the employers' associations as well as within the trade union movement , it also reduces the visibility of the organized interests at the central level. Sooner or later this will create legitimacy problems that will force the leaders of the interest groups to take up a more radical position and abandon their current consensus-seeking style (Delsen, 2002, pp. 170–1) if they are not outbid by political entrepreneurs mobilizing those who are disillusioned with their own interest organizations (Jones, 1999, p. 179). Such a scenario is not implausible. In 2011–13, for example, the FNV came close to collapse when its leadership eventually gave up its long-time opposition to raising the age of retirement. The resulting compromise was accepted by the majority of the unions within the federation. However, the two unions that rejected the agreement together represented a majority of the FNV membership. The difference between radical and moderate unions thus exposed a flaw in the FNV's constitution, plunging the organization into a conflict that many feared it would not survive. Eventually, after several mediation efforts and the resignation of the leading protagonists in the conflict, the FNV was restructured and, for the time being, has found a new balance between pragmatist consensus seeking and radical activism.

On the other hand, there are few signs of a terminal weakening of the corporatist style of policy-making. The Wassenaar Accord followed a period of increased polarization between trade unions and employers in the 1970s. And after 'the long year of 2002', the mood again became more critical of consensus politics, until the Rutte II Cabinet invested heavily in negotiating agreements with interest groups in domains such as macro-economic policy and healthcare. Such fluctuations are often attributed to economic circumstances, or to the composition of the Cabinet: participation of the Labour Party tends to reinforce corporatism (Woldendorp, 2005), and its lack of majority support in the First Chamber also helps to explain the Rutte II Cabinet's corporatist strategy.

The Sources of Corporatism

The question of whether we should expect a gradual erosion of corporatism, or merely trendless fluctuation, is an important one (Hemerijck and Visser, 2002; Van Der Meer et al., 2003), its answer depending on what, and how enduring, are the sources of Dutch corporatism.

Corporatist Ideology

One explanation of Dutch corporatism views it as the outcome of corporatist ideology. It is pointed out that corporatism is an important feature of Christian Democratic, and particularly of Catholic, political philosophy. The Catholic principle of subsidiarity requires the government to devolve decision-making to the lowest possible level. Dutch Calvinists developed the notion of 'sovereign spheres' in society, created by God and subordinate only to God, in which the government should not interfere. While the Catholic principle is more hierarchical than the Calvinist idea, both call for organized interests to be involved in policy-making in their own spheres of interest, and to shoulder responsibility for the resulting courses of action. The Dutch Social Democrats had already adopted the idea of 'functional decentralization' in their programme of planning (rather than 'nationalization') in the 1920s and 1930s. During the Interbellum, proposals for corporatist representation in Parliament were discussed within the Labour Party. Even Dutch liberalism, being more organic than individualistic in its ideological origins, did not object much as long as corporatist institutions were not imposed, but could emerge voluntarily. After 1945 there was some predictable argument about the exact role of the state and the voluntary nature of corporatism, but a consensus soon developed and a junior minister, and later even a Cabinet minister, was appointed to develop the PBO on the foundations created during the German occupation. If these ideological roots constitute the sources of Dutch corporatism its days seem to be numbered. The Liberals have grown rather critical of corporatism, and they are the driving force behind attempts to reduce the number and role of advisory councils. The Christian Democrats continue to stress the importance of 'the societal meso level' (*maatschappelijk middenveld*), that is, of organized interests, but in government with the Liberals they do not always follow corporatist strategies. The same is true of the Labour Party: when the secular 'Purple coalition' took over in 1994, one of its stated goals was to reduce the power of that same societal meso level. Moreover, if Dutch policy-making is still corporatist, it is not because of the ideologically inspired PBO which, as we saw above, had only very limited success. As Van Waarden suggests: 'It is a bit like with consociationalism: pillarization has gone, but consensualism is still mostly in place. In the process, corporatism has dispensed with the Catholic clothes it wore for a while. The body underneath, the older and more republican tradition of a well-organized civil society, engaged in self-regulation and ordering of markets, has emerged more clearly again' (Van Waarden, 2002, p. 64).

A Small Domestic Market

Another explanation comes from the idea that the Netherlands is a small state. The small state argument is a dangerous one, however; it has also been used, for example, to account for consociational democracy by suggesting that small states only have small problems, and can therefore afford the luxury of consociationalism. In his book *Small States in World Markets,* Katzenstein (1985) offers a less simplistic argument. He points out that small states have small domestic markets, making them dependent on the international market. In an open economy, and the Netherlands most certainly qualifies as such (see Chapter 9), the government is relatively powerless to steer the economy and the option of protectionism would be suicidal. According to this argument, open economies can only adapt to world market changes, and as such adaptations are in the interest of all parties involved (government, employers, trade unions), this facilitates their cooperation. Corporatism is therefore functional in the case of an open economy. The fact that those most closely involved in the creation and maintenance of 'the polder model' regularly mention the need to remain internationally competitive lends credence to this argument. If true, reports of the demise of Dutch corporatism are premature. However, critics have also argued the opposite – that globalization, and European integration in particular, increasingly deprives the Dutch government of the means to 'oil' the corporatist machinery with subsidies, tax measures or manipulation of the exchange rate (see, for example, Delsen, 2002, p. 171). The widespread use of a corporatist policy-making style in other policy areas than macro-economic management adds doubt that the openness of the Dutch economy alone can account for Dutch corporatism.

A Cultural Explanation

A third explanation is cultural in nature (Kickert, 2003). In Chapter 2 we noted that corporatism and consociationalism are interrelated: both are characterized by consensus-seeking rather than competition. We discussed how Daalder argues that the elite culture of consensus goes back to the days of the confederal Republic, but the very term 'polder model' suggests even older historical roots, evoking as it does associations with the cooperation within the medieval water control boards set up to protect new polders against the water (see Chapter 1). Prak and Van Zanden (2013) argue that, for the past thousand years, the Netherlands has been characterized by a combination of three factors that together make up the 'polder model': well organized social groups (from guilds to trade unions); institutional facilities for deliberation and cooperation (from water control boards to the SER); and a rough equality of power among the various social groups combined with 'a shadow of hierarchy' – that is, the existence of a party that would take the lead in bringing the groups to the negotiating table (from the province of Holland to the current core executive). Almost inevitably, such a long history has left its imprint on Dutch culture, and this culture of consensus is not only found at the level of the decision-making elites. Newspapers routinely refer to *harmonie model, overleg economie* (consultative economy), or *polder model*, and citizens are more likely to recognize referrals to employers associations and trade unions as 'the social partners' than as 'pressure groups'. The word 'compromise' has no negative connotation, and the untranslatable *maatschappelijk draagvlak* (literally, 'societal weight-bearing surface') is a household term to connote the need for government policies to have widespread support from organized interests and citizens. In his comparative study of work-related values, Geert Hofstede has found Dutch (together with Scandinavian) culture to be among the least 'masculine' in the world, with an emphasis on interdependence, egalitarianism and solidarity (Hofstede, 2001, p. 286). To the extent that Dutch corporatism is rooted in a mass culture that values cooperation and consensus, it would seem that this policy-making style, in some variety, is not about to disintegrate very soon.

The Bureaucracy

We shall return to the advantages and disadvantages of consensus government in Chapter 11, but in the context of the current chapter it is important to note that one of the unintended consequences of corporatism is that it strengthens the fragmentation of policy-making into various 'Iron Triangles', 'policy networks' or 'policy communities'. Pressure groups fight for one interest only, thereby focusing on a particular policy area without paying much attention to the full range of government activities. This is their proper function, and we should be surprised if it were otherwise. The more these organizations are incorporated into policy-making, however, the more policy-making is sectorized. This sectorization is further strengthened by the structure of the Dutch bureaucracy.

The most striking characteristic of the Dutch civil service is that as such it does not exist, at least not as a unitary and united entity. Government departments are largely autonomous, to such an extent that the development of the Dutch state has been jokingly described as one from the Republic of the Seven United Provinces to the Republic of the Thirteen Disunited Departments. The current departmental autonomy does in fact have historical roots going back to the days of the Republic. During the Republic, the absence of an absolute monarch prevented the development of a strong and centralized bureaucracy; the Republic was a state composed of local offices rather than of central officials (Daalder, 1966, pp. 190–2). It was only during the Napoleonic occupation, and under King William I's subsequent reign, that a hesitant and modest beginning was made towards building a bureaucratic apparatus. When ministerial responsibility was introduced in 1848 (see Chapter 1), political parties and coherent government majorities were still to develop, and it was individual ministers who oversaw the building of their own departmental bureaucracy. Once suffrage was widened and parties developed that joined in governing coalitions, the notion of collective responsibility gained importance. By that time, however, departmental autonomy had become firmly entrenched. It was not until 1929 that a Civil Service Act regulated at least the formal position of all civil servants across the departments (Van Der Meer and Dijkstra, 2000, pp. 151–3). Moreover, the new departments that developed, mainly as splits from the Department of the Interior, were set up to oversee a particular sector of the budding welfare state. In contrast to the traditional regulatory departments, these new departments were much more in need of specialized knowledge. Among university-trained civil servants, the proportion of (generalist) lawyers dropped from 75 per cent in 1930 to 27 per cent in 1988, while graduates in economics and the social sciences increased in number from just 1 per cent to 35 per cent (Van Der Meer and Raadschelders, 1999, p. 221). A list of departments, the number of civil servants within them and the size of their budgets is shown in Table 7.2.

Thus it was more by historical accident than by any conscious design that the Dutch bureaucracy (like its Scandinavian counterparts) has developed into one of the clearest examples of a 'position system' in Europe (Auer et al., 1996). In a 'position system', people are hired when they possess the skills and prior training required for a particular position, recruitment to mid-career positions is possible, and promotion is not automatic, in contrast to the more common 'career systems' (of, for example, France or Germany) in which civil servants typically enter the bureaucracy after a uniform exam or through meeting other uniform requirements, receive in-house training, start in a low position and are automatically promoted and paid according to seniority. Yet we should not overestimate the effects of these formal differences: once inside the system, a Dutch civil servant learns of vacancies

Table 7.2   *Personnel and Budgets of Government Departments, 2012/13*

Department	Number of personnel, 2012	Budget (millions €), 2013
General Affairs	351	62
Foreign Affairs	2,619	11,778
Security and Justice	26,433	11,197
Interior and Kingdom Relations	9,577	5,068
Education, Culture, Science	3,758	34,075
Finance	29,857	10,927
Defence	70,369	7,777
Infrastructure and Environment	12,385	9,911
Economic Affairs, Innovation and Agriculture	9,185	5,229
Social Affairs and Employment	2,156	30,225
Public Health, Welfare and Sports	4,020	15,711

Sources: Personnel figures: Ministry of the Interior, *Jaarrapportage Bedrijfsvoering Rijk*, 2012.
Budget figures: Ministry of Finance, *Miljoenennota 2013*, 2012.

before they are advertised, and heads of departmental units may prefer applicants with some administrative experience to complete outsiders. As a result:

> The Dutch public service is basically a professional public service: the public servant generally stays in the administration and builds up his/her career there by successively holding different and increasingly important positions. (Ziller, quoted in Auer et al., 1996, p. 65)

However, a remaining difference between the Dutch system and a career system is that the focus on position implies both that the power to hire is decentralized to those who are able to judge the specialized expertise needed in a particular position, and that new recruits tend to be specialists rather than generalists.

Once appointed to a particular department, a civil servant may move up to higher-level positions, but those positions tend to be within the confines of that department, and often within a single directorate. Occasionally civil servants are recruited from organized interests, but more often they are drawn directly from the universities. There are sometimes clear links between particular universities and departments: thus, Infrastructure attracts many engineers from the Technical University at Delft; Economic Affairs employs a large number of economists trained at Erasmus University in Rotterdam, and the Justice Department has recruited many graduates from the Leiden University Law School. The recruitment of departmental specialists has important consequences. Experienced observers can detect distinct departmental cultures, even in dress, ranging from jeans at Education and Culture to pin-striped suits in the Foreign Office. One study found a relatively low incidence of classic Weberian role orientations in the newer welfare state departments such as Public Health, Education, and Social Affairs, whereas such role orientations prevailed in older departments such as Interior and Justice (Eldersveld et al., 1981, p. 85).

Moving from one department to another can therefore be like moving into a quite different world. It takes some time to become familiar with the acronyms by which Directorates, Sections and Bureaux within a department are known. The structure of departments also varies: in an attempt to counteract excessive internal sectorization, some departments (for example, Education and Justice) have set up a 'management council' consisting of the permanent secretary and the directors-general, in which the directors-general no longer act as the heads of the main units within the department, which they still do in other departments (Van Der Meer and Raadschelders, 1999, p. 210). Some departments concentrate on policy-making (for example, Economic Affairs) and are top-heavy with officials in the higher grades, while other departments dealing with many purely administrative tasks (such as Interior) or even some implementation functions (such as Finance) put more emphasis on the medium and lower grades. To add to this confusion, a particular position may have quite different functions: for example, the Permanent Secretary in the Department of Economic Affairs is his/her minister's top adviser on macro-economic policy, whereas the equivalently named colleague at Finance is the top manager of the administrative apparatus.

Differences in recruitment, culture and structure cannot help but leave their mark on the resulting policies. Lawyers refer to 'Thirteen Legal Families' to indicate that each department has its own predilection for using specific instruments. Older departments maintain a preference for legislation, while newer ones rely more on regulation, permit systems or subsidies. It has been argued that this variety reflects profound differences of opinion about the government's proper role in society, with some departments clearly being more interventionist by nature than others.

Compared with the central government's administrative apparatus in other European countries such as the UK or Germany, the Dutch bureaucracy is relatively small (Van Der Meer and Roborgh, 1993, pp. 107–10), and while its small size might be expected to add some coherence or make coordination easier, this is not in fact the case. The small size of the bureaucracy is not the result of 'small government', but rather of 'big government' delegating many tasks to semi-autonomous and autonomous agencies and organizations. To a large extent this is a legacy of pillarization (see Chapter 2), but this culture of delegation is not confined to policy areas where pillarized organizations were, or still are, active. For example, the Netherlands must be one of the few countries where road signs are not put up and maintained by the government. Instead, the government has delegated this task, and the necessary funds, to, among others, the automobile club ANWB. Such arrangements are quite common. As Theo Toonen aptly remarks, 'We would probably call it "agencyfication" these days' (Toonen, 2000, p. 176). This is not to say that the more recent international administrative fashions (new public management, next steps and so on) could have no further impact on the Dutch bureaucracy. Since the 1980s there has been a trend towards 'core departments' – that is, departments that confine themselves to policy-making or general administration, and delegate all executive tasks. This delegation consists both of giving more autonomy to departmental units that nevertheless still fall under ministerial responsibility (agencies [*agentschappen*] such as the Immigration and Naturalization Service of the Justice Department, the National Archive of the Department of Education and Culture, or the Meteorological Institute of the Department of Infrastructure), and of giving responsibility for governmental tasks to so-called autonomous administrative bodies (*zelfstandige bestuursorganen,* or ZBOs, such as the Bureau for Driving Licence Testing, the Media Commissariat supervising the media, or the Student Grants Authority) that do not fall under full ministerial responsibility. As there is no generally agreed definition of ZBOs, the estimates of the number of these vary considerably. The government's own register (in 2013) lists 121 such bodies, but Van Thiel reckoned that in 2011 there were more than 600 ZBOs (Van Thiel, 2011). Critical reports in the 1990s about the lack of control over ZBOs by, for example, the General Accounting Office, and in 2004 by an interdepartmental committee, seem to have led to a lesser degree of autonomy, but attempts to bring all ZBOs under a common regime have failed (Van Thiel, 2006, 2011). Because of the trend towards core departments, there has been a decline in the number of departmental civil servants since 1985 (Van Der Meer and Dijkstra, 2011), but fragmentation of the government's administrative apparatus, though more difficult to measure, is likely to have increased.

This fragmentation is not offset by a *grands corps* that crosses departmental boundaries, or by political appointments intended to strengthen the core executive's control over its sectorized apparatus. The first step towards a *grand corps* was the establishment, in 1995, of a General Administrative Service (*Algemene Bestuursdienst*) (Van Der Meer and Toonen, 2005). The chief goal of the General Administrative Service is to increase interdepartmental mobility in the top ranks: the intention is that civil servants remain in one post for seven years. The Service advises ministers on appointments and provides training for 'high potentials'. All civil servants above a particular grade come under the General Administrative Service, but it acts as an employer only for the 'Top Management Group', about 70 highest-ranked officials. Among the higher ranks of the civil service, interdepartmental mobility has clearly increased since the General Administrative Service was set up. In 1996, 54 per cent of all Permanent Secretaries were recruited from within their own government department, as were 63 per cent of all Directors-General – the second highest rank; in 2009, the percentages of internal recruitment had dropped to 43 per cent and 44 per cent, respectively (Steen and Van Der Meer, 2011). However, the General Administrative Service has had only a marginal effect on the fragmentation of the civil service as a whole. Moreover, there have also been unintended consequences. The General Administrative Service emphasizes management skills over substantive expertise. The resulting decline of expertise in a particular policy domain at the top level seems to have been balanced by hiring more external consultants; in 2007, the thirteen government departments together spent €1.2 billion on consultants, compared with €0.3 billion ten years earlier. Apart from the financial aspects, it is interesting to note that hiring external specialists presumably adds to the fragmentation of the Dutch bureaucracy.

The role of the General Administrative Service at the top level would seem to limit the opportunities for political appointments by individual ministers. Political considerations have always played some role in the appointment of civil servants, especially at the highest levels, not so much to ensure that advisers are loyal to a particular minister, but rather as part of the proportional distribution over all major parties so central to consociational democracy (Van Thiel, 2012). This proportion has always been an approximate one, with some departments being dominated by one party (for example, Foreign Affairs by the VVD), but it was viewed as unwise for a minister to surround him/herself only with advisers from his or her own party or from the coalition parties: that would be of no help to the minister in search of consensus and compromise. In this light, it is surprising that Steen and Van Der Meer recently found that, in 2009, 57 per cent of all Permanent Secretaries shared their Minister's party affiliation, compared with 39 per cent in 1989. Moreover, they showed that this was not the result of chance combinations of ministerial appointments and civil servants' careers, but of ministers appointing Permanent Secretaries of their own party: 'In general, it is rare that [a Permanent Secretary] with a party affiliation divergent from the political colour of the ruling coalition is appointed' (Steen and Van Der Meer, 2011, p. 226).

This is just one finding, and the number of Permanent Secretaries is low (14 in 2009), but if corroborated by similar findings for other top-level bureaucrats, this would signal the end of the tradition of proportional patronage and the beginning of a politicization of the civil service. It would fit with recent concerns about the balance between political loyalty and civil rights of bureaucrats, especially as there has been an increasing number of incidents in which high-level civil servants (some of them in the uniform of the police or the armed forces) publicly criticized the government ('t Hart and Wille, 2006). This has led to a series of conflicts between ministers and their top civil servants, and occasional resignations by civil servants. As a result, more emphasis has been given to the need for high-level civil servants to be 'politically astute' as well as technically competent.

Judicial Policy-Making

Increasingly, the judiciary has also begun to manifest itself as a policy-maker. For the purpose of this chapter we use the term 'judiciary' also to include various bodies of administrative appeal, and not just the regular courts as most Dutch jurists would. The regular courts comprise 11 district courts (*rechtbanken*) (each with several subdistrict courts (*kantonlocaties*) for minor cases), four appeal courts (*gerechtshoven*), and the Supreme Court (*Hoge Raad*), is the latter being a cassation court that decides only legal and not factual questions. These courts deal primarily with cases of civil and criminal law. There is no trial by jury in the Netherlands; apart from the subdistrict courts and for summary proceedings, cases are tried before a panel of three to five judges. Nevertheless, the courts only render their decisions *per curiam*; that is, unsigned and without dissenting or concurring opinions. With regard to administrative appeal, there is no single, unified system in the Netherlands, and determining which institution or court is competent in a particular administrative case can be a science in itself that need not concern us here. Recent reforms have created administrative law chambers in the regular district courts for those cases for which the statutes have not assigned a specialized administrative court, but appeal is usually to the Judicial Division of the Council of State rather than to the regular courts of appeal and to the Supreme Court. Finally, there is a National Ombudsman who is taking on a gradually increasing number of cases; in 2012, the Ombudsman published more than 15,000 conclusions. Despite the fact that these conclusions are not binding, they can be of considerable importance; a series of Ombudsman conclusions in effect resulted in new standards for proper police behaviour (Koopmans, 2003, p. 219).

While litigation is still not as popular in the Netherlands as it is in Germany and the UK (let alone the USA) (Blankenburg, 2006, p. 16), the caseload of the courts is rapidly increasing (see Table 7.3). The only exception is the decline in the number of criminal cases, but this is largely the result of procedural changes since 1995. For example, most traffic violations are now treated under administrative law, and a system of community service allows many juvenile offenders to avoid standing trial.

Table 7.3   *Numbers of Decisions by Dutch Courts, 1950–2011*

Year	Civil law cases	Criminal law cases	Administrative law cases
1950	90,365	360,488	12,977
1975	136,049	367,670	35,958
1986	182,539	482,926	46,204
1990	210,765	465,934	51,031
1999	276,000	207,800	58,600
2006	424,700	318,000	68,900
2011	543,100	248,500	72,200

Sources: 1950–90 Cohen et al. (1993); 1991 onwards CBS Statline.

The number of judges has almost tripled, from 453 in 1960 (Cohen et al., 1993, p. 302) to about 2,202 in 2002 (Blankenburg, 2006, p. 27), data demonstrating that the judicialization that can be observed in other Western countries is also affecting Dutch society. The particularly rapid rise in the number of administrative law cases also points to a growing political importance of the courts. The number of civil law cases (for example, when the government is accused of tort) and criminal law cases (for example, on euthanasia; see Box 7.1) with political significance is also increasing.

Dutch constitutional law, however, is unequivocal in its rejection of judicial policy-making. Article 120 of the Constitution explicitly denies the courts the power to review the constitutionality of laws and treaties, making the Netherlands one of the few countries without judicial review. Moreover, according to statute, judges are not allowed to pass judgment on the 'inner value or fairness' of laws, and their decisions are to have no wider application than the specific case before them. It is ironic that the gap between the constitutional 'ought' and the political 'is' is nowhere wider than in the case of the judiciary. However, for four broad reasons, the absence of judicial review and other formal constraints have not prevented the courts from playing a political role.

First, and most important, the Dutch courts have gradually loosened some of the constraints put on them. In this respect, the 1919 *Lindenbaum–Cohen* judgment is still a landmark decision, not unlike *Marbury* v. *Madison* (1803) is for the position of the American judiciary (Van Koppen, 1992, pp. 84–5). In *Lindenbaum–Cohen*, the Dutch Supreme Court ruled that tort is not just based on the violation of a statute, but may also be caused by behaviour 'contrary either to good morals or to the care which is due in society with regard to another's person or property'. Since then the use of extra-statutory criteria has steadily increased. In administrative law, the courts have developed 'general principles of good governance' such as 'the principle of legal certainty', which demands that public authorities should keep their promises and that radical changes of policy should not be introduced at short notice; or 'the principle of proportionality', which implies that decisions by the authorities should be commensurate with both the seriousness of the problem and the interests of those adversely affected by the decision. Some of these principles have since been codified, but the administrative courts continue to apply all of them, regardless of whether they are written into the statute books or not (De Moor-Van Vugt and De Waard, 2006, p. 352). In a study of the 'styles of thinking' within the judiciary, a sample of judges was asked about the relative importance in their professional practice of formal rules, and of general principles of fairness and care. While for some of them both orientations played a part, 78 per cent answered that 'substantive justice' is more important than 'formal justice'. In the words of one judge, 'I think the judge, after he has examined a case, first tries to determine the outcome of the case and subsequently tries to motivate this within the Dutch legal system' (De Groot-Van Leeuwen, 1992, p. 151). The courts have also broadened their competence since the 1970s by liberally interpreting the requirement in many cases that only interested parties can appeal to the courts. By recognizing 'diffuse interests' and class actions, the courts have allowed interest groups to use court action as a new strategy against the government.

Up to now, the courts have stopped short of breaking the ban on judicial review, they but have discharged a first warning shot. When a controversial law was passed to limit the number of years for which a student is entitled to a grant was applied retroactively to some students who were already enrolled, a lower court decided that not even a statute is allowed to be retroactive; the decision was based on a provision in the little known Kingdom Charter that regulates the relations between Aruba, Curaçao and Sint Maarten, and the Netherlands in Europe. The Supreme Court eventually quashed this imaginative decision in 1989, but 'it went out of its way to show the illegality of the measure, before deciding that it had no power to counter an illegality of this kind' (Koopmans, 2003, p. 84). Moreover, in its decision the Supreme Court argued that the increasing 'monism' in the relations between government and Parliament (see Chapter 6) leads to decreasing attention to legal principles in new legislation, and that this development provides grounds for 'a less restrictive' interpretation of the ban on judicial review (Van Koppen, 1992, pp. 88–9). The decision also led to a renewed debate about the desirability of judicial review, and in a proposal by then Green Left leader Femke Halsema to amend the Constitution in order to exempt those articles dealing with civil rights, the franchise, and the prohibition of the death penalty from the ban (Adams and Van Der Schyff, 2006; Van der Schyff, 2010). Halsema's proposal survived the first reading in the Second Chamber in 2004, and in the First Chamber in 2008. The narrow majority in the Senate (37 votes to 36) bodes ill for the chances of obtaining the two-thirds majority required on the second reading to amend the constitution.

A second reason for the growing political importance of the judiciary is that the ban on judicial review applies only to statutes, and not to other types of legislation. Non-statutory regulation has increased over the years. The discrepancy between the limited number of bills that Parliament can process in a given year, and the need for regulation, plus the preference for more flexible forms of regulation than statutes, have resulted in many statutes merely outlining the broad direction of a policy ('framework laws' – *Kaderwetten)* while delegating its detailed contents to decrees (Orders in Council, ministerial resolutions) or legislation by provincial and municipal councils. This broadens the scope considerably for judicial policy-making, as the courts are entitled to review the constitutionality and legality of such non-statutory regulation. The courts have, for example, voided ordinances allowing fluoride to be added to the drinking water, because the Water Supply Act contains no provision for the prevention of tooth decay; and a government decree intended to reduce the income of medical specialists has been declared *ultra vires* (unauthorized) because the statute on which these measures were based did not mention incomes policy as a ground for government interference. The next step in the expansion of the political role of the judiciary has been the combination of the review of non-statutory regulation with the use of extra-statutory criteria mentioned above; in 1986, the Supreme Court ruled that regulations can be set aside not only if they are incompatible with a statute, but also when they are contrary to 'unwritten legal principles'.

The third reason why the judiciary's role has grown is that the Constitution contains another exception to the ban on judicial review. Since 1953, and more unequivocally since 1956, the Dutch Constitution does give treaties and resolutions by international institutions (such as the EU) that have a direct effect on citizens' precedence over domestic legislation (Article 94). Thus the courts can annul statutes that infringe human rights, not with reference to the chapter on human rights in the Dutch Constitution but, for example, on the basis of the European Convention on Human Rights or the International Covenant on Civil and Political Rights. Since the 1980s, the courts have made use increasingly of this possibility. A wide variety of provisions in Dutch statutes have since been struck down, ranging from family law (for example, the veto an unmarried mother had been given in Dutch law over the acknowledgement of the child by the biological father was deemed incompatible with the latter's right to a family life under the European Convention) to social security law, where the courts have struck down provisions giving higher benefits to so-called breadwinners as this was seen as violating anti-discrimination (that is, against women) articles in the International Covenant. It should be noted that international treaties may also limit the Dutch court's room for manoeuvre when an international court, such as the EU Court of Justice (ECJ), or the European Court of Human Rights (ECtHR), has been set up that may override Dutch decisions. For example, in 2007, the ECtHR's decision in *Salah Sheekh v The Netherlands* caused a radical change in Dutch asylum procedures that had been upheld by a range of Dutch courts: no longer could the government rely exclusively on its embassy's reports regarding the political situation in the country of origin, and no longer would an asylum seeker from a group that is known to be at risk in the country of origin have to provide evidence that he or she is also at risk individually.

Finally, political non-decision-making occasionally forces the courts to take on politically controversial issues. While the most controversial issue that the courts have dealt with is without a doubt that of euthanasia (see Box 7.1), it is by no means the only one. The European Social Charter, for example, obliges the government to introduce legislation recognizing the general right of workers, even government employees, to strike, and to specify when strikes are not allowed. Yet, because of political differences, such a law has never reached the statute books. In the meantime, employers have been asking the courts for injunctions to order the trade unions to end particular strike actions, and the judges have developed their own criteria for the acceptability of strikes, taking into account the nature of the preceding negotiations and the social disruption caused by a strike, for example, by railway employees. On the whole, the unions and the employers' associations seem quite happy with the way the judiciary arbitrates industrial disputes, and no one is pressing for legislation any more.

BOX 7.1

Decriminalizing Euthanasia

In 2002, the Netherlands became the first country formally to legalize euthanasia (that is, 'active' euthanasia, not death caused by abstinence or pain relief). The passing of the bill on the Termination of Life on Request and Assisted Suicide marks the provisional end of a typically Dutch story of depoliticization that effectively put the responsibility for the development of a euthanasia policy in the hands of the judiciary. The demand for euthanasia had been on the political agenda since the late 1960s/early 1970s, fuelled by the secularization of society and the advances of medical technology. However, until 2001 the Criminal Code did not recognize euthanasia, and it remained a crime to assist a suicide. The secular parties had long favoured the 'decriminalization' of euthanasia, but the pivotal position of the Christian Democrats until 1994 blocked any movement in this direction.

Several governments sought to depoliticize the issue, at least to remove it temporarily from the political agenda, by asking for outside advice: the Health Council, one of the government's advisory bodies, was asked to advise on euthanasia in 1972 and again in 1982. In addition, ad hoc Commissions were set up to study this thorny issue in 1982 and 1989. The advisers were allowed to take their time (the Health Council produced its report in 1986, four years after it had been requested), but were unable to provide a compromise that was acceptable to all parties. In 1986, D66, while in opposition, tried to force the issue by introducing a private member's bill permitting euthanasia. This put the VVD in an awkward position: ideologically, the Liberals were in favour of the bill's contents, but politically the party was negotiating a continuation of its coalition with the Christian Democrats, who were trying to block the private member's bill. Eventually, a compromise was reached within the coalition: the government produced a proposal that was much closer to the Christian Democrats' position on euthanasia. Together with the private member's bill, this proposal was sent to the Council of State for advice. The Council of State refused to arbitrate, and recommended that the issue was not yet ripe for legislation. In effect, this meant that euthanasia policy was left to the medical association, the prosecutor's office, and in particular to the judiciary (Steunenberg, 1997; Griffiths et al., 1998). Thus the country's highest constitutional advisory body turned the Constitution upside down: instead of being Montesquieu's 'mouthpiece of the law', the judiciary became the legislator in this field.

$\longrightarrow$

208

→

Over the years, the courts developed a set of criteria to decide whether euthanasia by a physician, while still a crime, could nevertheless be excused: the patient's request must be explicit and earnest, made voluntarily and repeatedly; the doctor must diagnose the patient's suffering as unbearable and without hope of improvement; the termination of life should be carried out in a professionally responsible way; and the physician should follow a number of procedural rules, the most important of which are the consultation of at least one other doctor, and notification of the authorities. Eventual legislation in 1993 (curiously, not by amending the Criminal Code, which would have been highly symbolic, but by adding a few clauses to the law on the disposal of the dead) merely codified existing judicial practice and did not address new or remaining moral issues (euthanasia in cases of non-somatic suffering, the termination of the life of patients who are incompetent (for example, demented geriatrics) but who hold an advanced directive written while still compos mentis, specifying the conditions under which they would seek euthanasia, etc.). Again, it was left to the courts to pave the way for legislation. Judicial policy-making on euthanasia has not been without victims: physicians who had to take decisions without clear legal guidelines ran the risk of being prosecuted like criminals, and prosecutors who were reluctant to bring a euthanasia case to trial were forced to do so by the Minister of Justice.

By leaving the initiative to the judiciary, even the secular political parties got a more liberal euthanasia policy than they were requesting. In the Chabot case of 1994, the Supreme Court acquitted a psychiatrist who had assisted the suicide of a middle-aged, physically healthy woman who had requested euthanasia because she was extremely unhappy after her marriage had ended in divorce, one son had committed suicide and her other son had died of cancer. In the Brongersma case, in 2000, the District Court in Haarlem acquitted a physician who had terminated the life of an 86-year-old but still relatively healthy former Senator who had asked for euthanasia simply because he felt lonely and tired of life. These two decisions considerably widened the definition of 'unbearable suffering without any hope of improvement'.

When in 1999 the Purple coalition, relieved of the CDA's veto power, took the initiative back from the judiciary and introduced new legislation, it was originally criticized for acting prematurely; that is, before a consensus had been developed through public debate and case law. But the government used the parliamentary debates on the bill to clarify that 'unbearable suffering' should be interpreted restrictively as resulting from a somatic disease, in exceptional cases from a recognized psychiatric disease, and that despair or unhappiness do not provide legitimate grounds for euthanasia. In 2002, the Appeal Court quashed the original District Court's decision to acquit the physician in the Brongersma case, citing the new law, and later that year the Supreme Court sided with the Appeal Court. In another respect, the new legislation does go further than the courts' jurisprudence: advanced directives are now acceptable as an expression of a patient's request for euthanasia, but only if the physician diagnoses the patient as currently suffering unbearably. Physicians have to report cases of euthanasia to regional 'ethical committees'; only if such a committee judges that the doctor has not met all the legal criteria will they remit the case to the prosecutor's office. In 2012, four out of a total of 3,695 reported cases were brought to the prosecutor's attention. Studies have

→

→

shown that the number of cases of euthanasia first declined after the law took effect (from 3,500 in 2001 to 1,815 in 2005), but that it has been rising considerably in recent years. This is partly explained by a higher percentage of cases being reported (from 54 per cent in 2001 to 80 per cent in 2007) but since then surveys show the reporting percentage to be stable. The percentage of euthanasia requests by patients that have been accepted by physicians has increased (Onwuteaka-Philipsen et al., 2012). Survey research has shown that it also enjoys widespread support among the Dutch population (Van Holsteyn and Trappenburg, 1998; Trappenburg and Van Holsteyn, 2001).

As a consequence, the probability that the euthanasia regime will either become stricter or more permissive is very low. In 2007, the first official evaluation of the law in 2007 found no reasons for substantial changes. The return to power of the Christian Democrats between 2002 and 2012 led to no proposals to abolish the law or to make it more stringent. Ironically, when an Italian minister, Carlo Giovanardi, publicly condemned Dutch euthanasia practices in 2006, it fell to the Dutch Prime Minister and Minister of Foreign Affairs, both Christian Democrats, to protest to the Italian government. On the other hand, in 2012, a citizen's initiative (see Chapter 6) to allow senior citizens to request euthanasia when they were tired of life only got support from a few political parties in Parliament.

Despite this evidence of a growing role of the judiciary in policy-making, the courts themselves occasionally refuse to be drawn into political territory. In 1984, groups of concerned citizens appealed to the court to prohibit the stationing of cruise missiles in the Netherlands (see Chapter 10), but the judge refused, arguing that this was a matter for the government and Parliament, in which he had no right to intervene. In 2003, environmentalist groups failed to persuade the court to order Parliament to legislate immediately to introduce an EU directive on nitrate. In 2012, Freedom Party leader Wilders asked the court to prevent Parliament from taking a decision on the European Stability Mechanism (ESM) before the parliamentary election later that year, but the court refused to be drawn into the domain of government and Parliament. Sometimes, when their decisions create a political uproar, the courts are quick to retract their actions, as the Supreme Court did in the widely discussed *Pikmeer 1* and *Pikmeer 2* cases concerning the criminal prosecution of a local authority and one of its civil servants for illegally dumping contaminated sludge into a lake. In the first judgment, in 1996, the Supreme Court effectively granted immunity from criminal prosecution to local authorities. The decision was immediately criticized in Parliament, which adopted a resolution instructing the government to introduce legislation broadening the possibilities for the criminal prosecution of local authorities. The Supreme Court immediately modified its position, explicitly referring to the parliamentary debate, when it had the opportunity to issue a second judgment in the same case two years later, in which it limited the immunity to situations when a local authority performs a public task that cannot be delegated to a private party (Van Geffen, 2001, pp. 105–13). Such isolated examples, however, do not add up to a Dutch 'political questions doctrine', and there is increasing concern about the judiciary acting as a 'surrogate legislature'.

Of course, government and Parliament can nullify judicial policy-making in most cases by introducing corrective legislation to overrule the courts. This is what eventually happened in the *Pikmeer* case, and with regard to non-somatic suffering as grounds for euthanasia (see Box 7.1). Interestingly, such corrective legislation is relatively rare; one study estimates that, annually, no more than 10 to 20 out of an average of 5,000 Supreme Court decisions meet such a fate, and that such corrective legislation is most common when the courts interfere in taxation policy (Van Geffen, 2001, p. 81). It is more difficult to undo judicial policy-making when the courts base their decision on international law. In the late 1980s, an administrative court's interpretation of an International Labour Organization (ILO) Convention regarding job-related accidents and diseases resulted in considerable financial costs to the government; the government then introduced legislation to revoke the ILO Convention unilaterally , but this step was rejected by Parliament as being too drastic.

Another conceivable political reaction to judicial activism is a reduction in the judiciary's independence. Once appointed, judges can only be removed by their peers before they reach the age of 70, which is the mandatory age of retirement, but there are ample opportunities for making political appointments. In the case of the Supreme Court, for example, the court reports any vacancy to the Second Chamber of Parliament, together with a list of six candidates, ranked in order of the Supreme Court's preference. The Second Chamber subsequently submits a shortlist of three candidates, also ranked in order of preference, to the government, but Parliament's choice is not restricted to the names suggested by the court. The government appoints one of the Parliament's nominees. In the distant past, before 1861, political considerations did play an important role in this process, but paradoxically, with the development of political parties, the appointments have become depoliticized. Since 1945, for example, with only a few exceptions of a non-political nature, the Second Chamber has nominated the candidate at the top of its list as was suggested by the Supreme Court, and the government has appointed that candidate (Van Koppen and Ten Kate, 2003). Occasionally, MPs have voiced concern over the political representativeness of justices on the Supreme Court, but this has not led to changes in the procedures or in the outcome. In 2011, however, the Freedom Party objected to two nominations. One of the candidates, Diederik Abels, had criticized the decision to replace the judges in the trial of Geert Wilders (see Chapter 2) while that trial was still going on. MPs from other parties sympathized with the Freedom Party's objections, and the Supreme Court then changed its nomination. Another candidate, Ybo Buruma, had been active in the Labour Party and had written critically about Wilders. This time the Freedom Party did not find support for its objections, and Buruma was appointed.

A more serious attempt to rein in the judiciary was the establishment, in 2002, of a Council for the Judiciary. This Council advises the government on new legislation, oversees the functioning of the courts (with the exception of the Supreme Court and of the Council of State) and promotes the quality and uniformity of judicial decision-making (Brenninkmeijer, 2006, pp. 54–5). The fact that the Minister of Security and Justice appoints its four members (including two from outside the judiciary) for a six-year term has fuelled suspicions that the Council erodes the independence of the judiciary. In 2012, 700 judges signed a 'manifesto' criticizing the Council for being more responsive to political wishes than to the needs of the courts, appointing new presidents of the courts without consultation, and putting the quality of judicial decisions at risk by the introduction of unrealistic production targets.

Conclusion

Gladdish's characterization of Dutch policy-making as 'an orchestra with no conductor' is hardly an exaggeration, given our description of the consequences of corporatism, the fragmentation of the bureaucracy, and the ascendancy of the judiciary as a policy-maker. The disadvantages, to which we shall return in Chapter 11, of such fragmentation have not gone unnoticed, and with some regularity reforms are proposed to restore 'the primacy of politics' over interest groups, bureaucrats and judges. However, Gladdish is careful not to equate the absence of a conductor with a resulting cacophony. The fragmentation of the political arena, of the corporatist arena, of the bureaucratic arena, and competition from the courts rarely reinforce each other. Occasionally, they even compensate for each other, and we have already mentioned a few examples of this in passing: the government played a crucial role in breaking the stalemate in the corporatist arena in the early 1980s; the judiciary effectively broke the political deadlock on strike legislation and on euthanasia; and the government corrected the judiciary when it went too far in the public's opinion with regard to euthanasia. To describe Dutch policy-making as a system of checks and balances puts perhaps too nice a gloss on its fragmentation, but there can be no doubt that the development 'from government to governance', which is now observed everywhere, has a long history in the Netherlands.

8

Multi-Level Governance

The Territorial Dimension

Since 1982 it has been the official policy of all Dutch governments, regardless of their political composition, to decentralize tasks to subnational authorities that were hitherto performed at the national level. At the same time, these various Cabinets have remained committed to European integration, despite adapting a more sceptical rhetoric (see Chapter 10). In this chapter we shall explore the territorial dimension of Dutch governance to gauge the extent to which policy-making in the Netherlands is not only fragmented horizontally (see Chapter 7), but also vertically across different levels of government.

Subnational Government

Provincial Government

The decentralization that was characteristic of the confederal Republic was abolished during the Napoleonic occupation, never to be reintroduced (see Chapter 1). It is ironic that the once sovereign provinces now form the least powerful of the three layers of government (national, provincial and municipal) (De Vries, 2004). The 12 provinces (see Map 1.1 on page 2) have their own directly elected provincial legislatures and provincial governments but, with the exception of a few policy fields (such as transport infrastructure and environmental protection), their independent impact on policy-making is limited. As an intermediary between local and national authorities, provincial governments deal with other governments rather than with individual citizens (see Nomden, 1999). It has even been argued that the provinces, in a desperate effort to be seen as relevant by the citizens, have recently usurped some tasks of local authorities, as in the field of social policy, while neglecting their less appealing tasks, such as supervising local government's finances (Peters, 2007). Few citizens identify with their province, apart from the northern provinces such as Friesland, with its own recognized language, and the southern provinces. In the 2011 provincial elections, of the total of 566 seats on all provincial legislatures, only seven were won by regional parties. Even the largest of these, the Frisian

Nationalist Party, obtained only four out of 43 seats on the provincial legislature of Friesland. Traditionally there have been differences in political culture, with the Social Democrats stronger in the north-west and the Catholics stronger in the south-east, but these differences are rapidly decreasing.

In recent years, the turnout at provincial elections has fallen far below that in local elections (see Figure 4.1 on page 104), even in 2011, when the fight over a governmental majority in the Senate (see Chapter 6) rekindled some interest in these elections. Calls for the abolition of the provinces have already been heard; and the provinces are criticized for being simultaneously too large and too small. Municipal governments have long felt the need for cooperation and the coordination of their activities with neighbouring municipalities in regions that are smaller than the current provinces. The major cities of Amsterdam, Rotterdam, The Hague and Utrecht often view the provinces as unwelcome representatives of the smaller municipalities that surround them, and hinder city expansion. Since the Second World War, the creation of some form of regional (that is, smaller than provincial) government has been on the political agenda almost constantly (Toonen, 1992). So far, however, fears of complications arising from the creation of a fourth layer of government have prevented any reform. The experiment with a regional authority in Rijnmond (Rotterdam and the area surrounding its seaway), between 1965 and 1986, was even aborted for this reason. As a partial solution, in the 1990s the government suggested the creation of 'urban provinces', including a major city and its smaller neighbours, as split-offs from the current provinces. This would increase the number of provinces, but it would not add to the number of levels of government. To prevent imbalance within these urban provinces, cities such as Amsterdam or Rotterdam were to be separated into parts. It was this aspect of the plan in particular that led to its defeat in referendums in Amsterdam and Rotterdam (with turnouts above 90 per cent!) in 1995 and its subsequent abandonment by the government. Over the years, most local governments have set up various forms of regional cooperation with their immediate neighbours for the collection of refuse, disaster contingency plans, ICT services and so on (Hulst and Van Montfort, 2007). The boundaries of these informal and functional regions rarely coincided, and they were different again from regional cooperation decreed from above, for example for the police. To rationalize this patchwork of regional cooperation, in 1986 the government subdivided the country into 59 'cooperation districts' and ordered the provinces to oversee the transformation of the various functional regions into these new districts (the number of districts was later reduced to 42), but some 20 years later that process had still not been completed: in 2005, there were more inter-municipal cooperations (almost 700) than there were municipalities, and that is not counting the almost 1,200 private-law cooperative arrangements between municipalities (Derksen and Schaap, 2010, p. 199). As a result of this cluttered pattern of proliferation, regional cooperations constitute a *de facto* fourth layer of government, with two important imperfections: powers have been transferred from all-purpose governmental units to specialized functional administrations, trading one coordination problem for another, and powers have been transferred from electorally legitimated local authorities to regional ones that are not accountable to their citizens.

Even though the provinces may be too large to function efficiently as regional governments within the Netherlands, from a European perspective they are too small to be treated on a par with the German *Länder* or Belgian regions. It has been suggested that the whole country should be treated as a single European region, but it is more likely that the current provinces will eventually amalgamate into four or five such regions. Some of the provinces are already increasing cooperation with their neighbours in anticipation of such a development (De Rooij, 2003). Together, the provinces have set up an office in Brussels to lobby for their interests, but in fact this 'House of the Dutch Provinces' consists of four offices: one for the northern provinces (Friesland, Groningen, Drenthe); one for the eastern provinces (Gelderland, Overijssel); one for the western provinces (North Holland, South Holland, Utrecht, Flevoland); and one for the southern provinces (Limburg, Brabant, and Zeeland). Increasingly, these clusters of provinces are referred to as '*landsdelen*' (country parts), but unfortunately these voluntary combinations are different from the ones used by the EU Commission as the highest level of regional administration in the Netherlands (NUTS-1 regions in EU-speak) in which North Holland, South Holland, Utrecht and Zeeland form one region, and different again from a combination the Dutch government proposed in 2012 in which North Holland, Utrecht, and Zeeland were to merge. Thus it would seem that the dogmatic insistence by the government that there should only be two layers of subnational government has resulted in a development towards four such layers: local government; a variety of regions for inter-municipal cooperation; provinces; and *landsdelen* with unclear borders.

Local Government

Toonen has argued that the centralization of the past was possible only because pillarized organizations provided some of the functions that regional governments provide in other countries. After depillarization,

> some new form of regionalisation seems unavoidable in the Netherlands. The country is politically too diverse and administratively too differentiated and interwoven at the same time to be centrally run as if it was one big corporation. The pillarized structure will no longer do the job and cannot and should not be restored ... The provinces as traditional regional government in the Dutch system could very well benefit. (Toonen, 1996, pp. 629–31)

So far, however, even Toonen does not deny that local government is of greater importance. The municipalities rather than the provinces are also the main beneficiaries of the government's policy of decentralization.

Paradoxically, decentralization is also accompanied by centralization. There is centralization in the sense that the government has a long-standing policy of amalgamating small municipalities that are perceived to be lacking the scale necessary for a modern local government, the more so if increasing numbers of tasks are to be decentralized to that local government. In 1900, the country was divided into 1,121 municipalities and this number had declined very little by 1950, when there were still 1,015 municipalities. More than 60 per cent of these had fewer than 5,000 inhabitants. In 2013, however, only 408 municipalities remained (of which less than 1.5 per cent had fewer than 5,000 inhabitants) and the number will decline further in the coming years, even if the Rutte II Cabinet's intention to have only municipal authorities governing at least 100,000 inhabitants is unlikely to be realized.

There is also centralization in that the structure of local government is uniform for all municipalities, from the smallest (in 2013, the northern island of Schiermonnikoog with 948 inhabitants) to the largest (Amsterdam, with a population of 801,847). Municipal councils are directly elected for a four-year term, and they are all elected on the same day. This helps the national political parties in conducting a national campaign for the local elections. In the past, local political parties were important only in the southern provinces. Rather than have one-party systems at local elections in those provinces, the dominant Catholic Party allowed various local parties to represent particular interests or local areas. Local parties can now be found throughout the country, and in 2010 they obtained about 24 per cent of the vote. However, with the exception of these local parties, municipal elections are in essence second-order national elections, and the fate of local chapters of national parties is less dependent on local performance than on how the national party has performed at the national level. In local elections, the standard deviation in the outcome is very low; Marcel Boogers calculates that, on average, the outcome of the election for the local council in a given municipality deviates from the national trend by just over 1 per cent (Boogers, 2010, p. 31).

Depending on the size of the population, the municipal council consists of between nine and 45 members (a proposal to reduce the size of the councils was vetoed by the Senate in 2013). The council elects between two and nine aldermen (not including part-time aldermen), again the number being dependent on the size of the municipality. Together with the mayor, the aldermen form the executive branch of local government. The structure of municipal and provincial governments is almost identical, but differs in important ways from how the national government is organized. The electoral system at the local level is quite similar to the one used for national elections (as described in Chapter 4), and the local executive boards are also coalitions of several parties. Despite such institutional similarities, the style of politics at the local level differs considerably from that at the national level. In larger cities, local government is as politicized as national politics, and the process of coalition formation has come to resemble the national pattern as well, including the use of impartial *informateurs*. Elsewhere, however, attempts in the 1970s to replace 'mirror coalitions' (reflecting the composition of the council at large) with 'majority coalitions' (minimum winning coalitions bound by a common coalition agreement) have largely failed. In most municipalities, all the major parties are represented in government, usually in proportion to their strength on the council (Steunenberg, 1992), though most of them now negotiate a coalition agreement. Van

Stipdonk (2006) calculated that 66 different coalitions were formed after the 2006 elections, with both PvdA and CDA participating in 71 per cent of the local coalitions, and the VVD in 44 per cent. Local parties were included in more than half of all local governments.

Since 2002, aldermen are no longer members of the municipal council, a reform intended to introduce a degree of separation of powers into local politics. Although this latest reform was again imposed uniformly by the national government and legislature, for the first time it allows different municipalities to make different choices with regard to the position of the aldermen, to continue electing them from among council members, or to start recruiting them from among outside candidates. After the 2010 local elections and formation of local governments, 20 per cent of all aldermen were recruited from outside the council, and another 7 per cent even came from outside the municipality (Castenmiller and Van Dam, 2010). It is sometimes claimed that the reform, and the growing number of 'outsider aldermen' has led to an increase in the number of aldermen resigning before the end of their term of office (roughly a third of all aldermen). However, that increase started before 2002 and is probably unrelated to the reform (Aardema et al., 2011).

In other respects, too, there are signs of decentralization of a hitherto excessively centralized system. One such development is in the nomination of mayors. Dutch mayors are appointed formally by the central government from among applicants who in all but a few cases are from outside the town or village concerned. All prospective mayors are party members, and in making appointments it has been customary to try to reflect the national proportions of the major parties, while taking local political circumstances into account. The proportionality can only be an approximate one, lagged because sitting mayors cannot be unseated when their party loses, and marred by controversy over the basis of proportionality (number of mayoral posts for a party, or number of people governed by a mayor from a particular party), which makes a considerable difference (see Table 8.1). Occasionally, national politicians are parachuted into a mayoralty of one of the larger municipalities, but in general mayors are recruited more for their managerial skills or expertise in local government (for example, as an alderman in some other town) than for their political experience. For most occupants of the office, being mayor is a career in which appointment to a larger municipality is regarded as a promotion which brings more prestige as well as a salary increase.

Currently, the mayor is chairman of both the local council and its executive board, in addition to which he or she has a few responsibilities in his or her own right, such as maintaining public order. The mayor's appointment is for a six-year renewable term and, unlike the aldermen, he or she cannot be removed by the council, though, increasingly, mayors resign if they are censured. Despite the power of central government over their appointments and careers, mayors rarely act as agents of central government in The Hague and they are not subject to instructions from above; neither are they part of a bureaucratic hierarchy or mayoral *grand corps*. In fact, their role in local politics can vary widely. In smaller communities the mayor often dominates the council and the executive board, being the only full-

Table 8.1 *Political Distribution of Votes in Local Elections, Council Seats, Aldermen and Mayors Compared with National Parliamentary Election Results, 2010*

	Council % votes	Aldermen		Mayors		Parliamentary elections
		% seats	% aldermen	% municip	% pop	
CDA	15	18	21	33	26	14
PvdA	16	15	17	26	33	20
VVD	16	17	19	26	29	21
D66	8	6	6	6	7	7
GL	7	6	4	2	1	7
SP	4	3	1	–	–	10
SGP/CU	7	7	6	3	3	5
PVV	1	0.2	–	–	–	15
Local Parties	24	27	26	2	1	–
Other	3	1	–	–	–	17

Source: Derksen and Schaap, 2010.

time administrator as well as someone who can serve as an articulate ambassador for the town at the provincial and national level. In the more politicized larger cities, full-time aldermen have often stripped the mayors of all but their constitutionally prescribed functions, especially where the mayor belongs to a political party that has only a small power base in that community.

As left-wing parties are strong in the cities, it should come as no surprise that they would prefer the mayor to be elected, either directly by the voters or by the council, arguing that an appointed mayor is an anachronism in a mature democracy. Being better represented in the smaller communities, it is equally predictable that the Christian Democrats traditionally favoured the appointive system, suggesting that an appointed mayor brings continuity, impartiality and professionalism to local government. In true Dutch fashion, this debate has been going on for decades, while a pragmatic compromise has evolved in which mayors continue to be appointed, but in which local politicians are increasingly consulted in the nomination procedure. Since the 1970s, the local council submits a 'profile' of the ideal candidate to the King's Commissioner (that is, the provincial governor). This profile may include the kind of expertise that the council feels is most needed by their new mayor, but also his or her preferred political affiliation. The position is then advertised and the King's Commissioner sends the names of the applicants to the 'confidential committee' (*vertrouwenscommissie*), which is set up for this purpose by the local council and customarily includes all local party leaders. The 'confidential committee' usually interviews shortlisted candidates and makes its recommendation. Since the early 1980s these recommendations have become very influential: in the 1980s the candidate recommended by the 'confidential committee' was appointed in about 65 per cent of cases; and since the early 1990s this percentage had risen to around 80 per cent (Derksen and Schaap, 2010, p. 277). Effectively, Dutch mayors are now elected by the local council, despite still being appointed by the central government. This is not unlike the situation in neighbouring Belgium, but with an important difference: the Dutch mayor is still not a local politician from the local council.

This might have changed if the local electorate were involved in the selection of mayors. D66 used its bargaining power in the second Purple coalition and in the Balkenende II government to press for the popular election of mayors. First, the local council was allowed to consult the citizens by organizing a non-binding 'referendum' in which voters could express their preference for one of two candidates selected by the council. Between 2001 and 2008 only eight such 'referendums' were held, generally with low turnout figures; in two cases the local council nominated two candidates from the same party (Labour) from which to choose. In 2004, legislation was introduced to abolish the local council's involvement completely and have the mayor directly elected by absolute majority, with the first round coinciding with the council's elections. Together with the earlier move to make the offices of local alderman and councillor incompatible, giving the mayor his/her own electoral mandate would have reinforced the separation of power between local executive and council ('dualization' in Dutch constitutional parlance). However, in 2005, the constitutional amendment to abolish mayoral appointments by the central government was narrowly defeated during its second reading in the Senate (see Chapter 6). In 2008, the option for local councils to involve the voters in the selection of a new mayor was abolished.

There are also signs of decentralization in local policy-making. Constitutionally, two different regimes define the role of local government in policy-making: 'autonomy' and 'co-governance'. Autonomy refers to the policy domain in which the municipal government has independent authority, whereas co-governance refers to the tasks of local government in implementing national legislation. Autonomous policy-making is not without constraints, however. Municipal governments are 'autonomous' with regard to 'municipal affairs', but what is or is not a municipal affair is eventually determined by central government; historically, several tasks (care for the poor, provision of utilities and so on) have been taken away from local government. Moreover, even in regulating what is left to their autonomous responsibility, the local authorities need the approval of the provincial governments for their annual budget and most of their plans. The provinces, in turn, are also subject to supervision by the national government.

On the other hand, co-governance does not imply that local governments are without influence. In some cases, the implementation of national legislation or directives is indeed mechanical (for example, in the execution of municipal tasks in the organization of elections), but the Association of Dutch Municipalities (VNG) has normally been heavily involved in the drafting of the relevant passages in the law or decree. The VNG is generally considered to be among the most powerful organized interests in Dutch policy-making. In other cases, the central government lays down the general outlines of a policy, allowing local governments considerable leeway in their implementation. For example, a national law instructs local governments to regulate shopping hours, but merely provides a few parameters, such as a maximum of twelve shopping Sundays, to which the local regulation should conform. For smaller communities, such freedom in the context of co-governance is occasionally constrained by their lack of expertise, forcing them to rely on a 'model regulation' drawn up by VNG, but there is no denying that, despite supervision, new and more detailed central regulations and so on, co-governance nevertheless enables local governments sometimes to deviate substantially from the central government's intentions (Toonen, 1987).

The difference between autonomy and co-governance should therefore not be over-stated, but it is nevertheless important that, since the early 1980s, central government has been transferring policies from the regime of co-governance to that of autonomy. This is the case with library services, sports and recreation, public housing, social and cultural work, the preservation of monuments, and so on. The 2007 Social Support Act (*Wet Maatschappelijke Ondersteuning*) brought the provision of a wide array of care and welfare services under the control of the local authorities, with a further decentralization in this domain planned by the Rutte II government.

This ongoing process of decentralization can also be seen in the way that local authorities are financed. It used to be said that Dutch municipalities are tied to the central government by 'golden ropes'; that is, by their dependence on central-ly-controlled funds. Before the policy of decentralization came into effect in 1985, Dutch local governments raised only 7 per cent of their total revenues themselves, primarily through a real estate tax (this amount underestimates local income, as most local governments usually also make a profit from the buying and selling of land for building projects).

Another 24 per cent of municipal income was based on revenue sharing. Central government pays into a municipal fund, from which money is allocated to the municipalities on the basis of a complex formula in which the number of inhabitants is one of the most important criteria. There are no specific conditions attached to revenue sharing, so that, in 1985, the total proportion of municipal revenues that could freely be appropriated by the local council (albeit subject to overall provincial approval) amounted to less than a third. More than two-thirds of municipal revenues consisted of subsidies and grants from central government for specific purposes (schools, local transport and so on), thus curtailing local autonomy. Gradually, the number of such specific grants-in-aid has declined, from 514 in 1983 to 109 in 2009 (Derksen and Schaap, 2010, p. 186), and munic-ipal income from revenue sharing has increased. If we combine local taxes and revenue sharing, the proportion of local revenues that can be allocated without specific constraints from central government has risen from less than a third to more than half (see Table 8.2).

To a certain extent this financial decentralization has been a poisoned chalice, as central government has added less to the municipal fund than it saved by abolishing a specific grant, thus hiving off the responsibility for budget cutbacks at the central

Table 8.2   *Local Governments' Sources of Income, 1985–2009*

Year	Local taxes	Revenue-sharing	Grants-in-aid	Total	Total (€ billions)
1985	7.2	21.9	70.9	100.0	25.1
1991	10.8	27.2	62.0	100.0	23.9
1997	16.8	36.1	47.1	100.0	25.9
2003	18.3	39.2	42.4	99.9	34.4
2009	22.0	44.9	33.1	100.0	35.0

Source: Derksen and Schaap, 2010, p. 176.

level to local politicians. The total amount of local revenues has increased only in recent years, and many local governments had to raise local taxes substantially to finance the newly decentralized tasks. This led to increased criticism of local taxes, resulting in central government's decision to reduce local real estate taxes substantially in 2006 and to cap what remains of those taxes. Local governments received some compensation for the loss of tax revenue through revenue sharing, and other local taxes were also increased (sewage tax, garbage collection tax, fees for building permits, and so on). There should be no misunderstanding about the fact that the Netherlands is still a highly centralized country, and not only institutionally: the annual publication of local taxation levels always leads to a public outcry that such substantial differences between municipalities should not be allowed. At the same time there can be no doubt that, longitudinally, real decentralization has taken place in recent decades.

Europeanization

In 1985, the then President of the European Union (EU) Commission, Jacques Delors, famously claimed that after the introduction of the EU internal market, 80 per cent of national economic regulation would originate in Brussels. Dutch politicians have offered estimates of 30–70 per cent Europeanization of all new Dutch laws and regulations. The official website of the Second Chamber claims that 'More than half of the Dutch legislation is EU-initiated, including laws in the field of tackling crime, the environment, education, the free market and transport' (Second Chamber, 2013). Academic studies have also reported various estimates, but at a much lower level. Bovens and Yesilkagit estimate that 12.6 per cent of all Acts of Parliament, 19.7 per cent of all Orders in Council, and 10.1 per cent of all ministerial decrees were transpositions of EU directives (Bovens and Yesilkagit, 2010, p. 61). Breeman and Timmermans find much the same overall percentage of EU-initiated Acts of Parliament, but they do note an increase from less than 5 per cent in the early 1980s to between 15 per cent and 20 per cent in the late 2000s (Breeman and Timmermans, 2012, p. 160). It should be noted that such percentages refer to EU directives which call for national legislation. For a complete estimate of the impact of the EU on the Dutch legal system, we would also have to take into account EU regulations which take immediate effect without transposition into national law. Some of these regulations cover important fields, such as the Regulation on the Registration, Evaluation, Authorisation & Restriction of Chemical Substances (REACH), which came into force in 2007 (Haverland, 2009). If we add such EU regulations, and even decisions by the EU Court of Justice, Douma et al. (2007) estimate that 66 per cent of the legislation on environmental affairs that is in force in the Netherlands is influenced by the EU, but only 6 per cent of the legislation on education. An overall estimate covering all policy fields is not available. Whatever the exact percentage, it is clear that policies affecting Dutch citizens are no longer made in The Hague alone. This was brought home forcefully in 2011, when EU Commissioner for the Environment, Janez Potočnik, rejected the Dutch government's alternatives to giving the Hedwige polder back to the sea in the province of Zeeland. To compensate for the adverse ecological effects of deepening and restructuring the Westerscheldt access to the port of Antwerp, the Dutch and Belgian governments had agreed in 2005 to 'de-polder' the Dutch Hedwige and Flemish Prosper polders. The Hedwige polder covers less than 3 km^2, but after the flooding of most of the province of Zeeland in 1953, any piercing of dikes provokes emotional protests. Despite several studies concluding that there was no viable alternative to de-poldering, the Dutch government reconsidered its agreement with the Belgians in 2009 and decided to de-polder after all that same year, only to reject flooding the polder again in 2011. While the Flemish authorities threatened to take the Netherlands to court over its failure to meet its treaty obligations, a terse, two-page letter from Brussels, reminding the Dutch of their obligations under the EU Habitats directive, ended this embarrassing episode; in 2012 the Rutte II government gave up Dutch resistance to flooding the polder.

However, when gauging the amount of sovereignty (if such a thing can be measured) that has been transferred to the EU, it should be kept in mind that the Netherlands is one of the world's most open economies (see Chapter 9). Thus the argument that European integration provides a 'rescue of the nation-state' (Milward, 2000) from globalization by means of the pooling of resources does ring true in the Netherlands (see Hout and Sie, 1997). For example, the dependence of the Dutch economy on the German economy in particular has always limited Dutch monetary autonomy (see Chapter 9); since 1983, the exchange rate between the Dutch guilder and the German Mark had been fixed, and the Bundesbank effectively determined Dutch monetary policy without even consulting the Dutch central bank. The European Monetary Union (EMU) and the introduction of the euro still mean that Dutch monetary policy is made in Frankfurt, but now by the European Central Bank (ECB), and with the president of the Dutch central bank on the ECB's governing council (Berndsen, 1997). This example shows that Dutch influence over some policies has actually increased rather than decreased through European integration. Both the need to absorb EU policies and the desire to influence policy-making at the EU level are gradually resulting in changes in the Dutch political system. The remainder of this chapter focuses on these amendments; the Dutch government's and public's attitude to European integration as such is dealt with in Chapter 10.

Strengthening Coordination

Nowhere is the fragmentation of Dutch policy-making more obvious than in its confrontation with the more unified political systems of other member states in the process of EU policy-making, and in the implementation of EU policies. Originally, one of the attractions of European integration was that it provided an escape from what little coordination existed in the Netherlands. Sicco Mansholt, a former Dutch Minister of Agriculture and later EU Commissioner, explained to one of the authors why he pushed enthusiastically for a European agricultural policy in the early years of the EU:

> In the Dutch Council of Ministers I met the ministers from other departments, and I had to defend the farmers' interests against other interests, but in the European Council of Ministers I met only other ministers of Agriculture, and we all agreed on the importance of agriculture.

Thus European integration actually contributed to the weakness of policy coordination in the Netherlands, as an early example of a 'disaggregated state' (Slaughter, 2004). For a long time, departments coordinated their negotiating position in Brussels, not with other Dutch departments but with their 'clients'; that is, organized interests. In some policy fields, especially agriculture, it became standard practice to give temporary civil service status to representatives from interest groups or PBO boards to be able to include them in the official Dutch delegation (Robinson, 1961). Attempts to improve domestic coordination of the Dutch position in EU policy-making failed for at least 15 years because of unchecked rivalry between the Department of Economic Affairs and the Foreign Office, which had created competing directorates for the preparation of the Dutch position. When, in 1964, negotiations started over Nigeria's association with the 'EU', two Dutch delegations arrived, both claiming to represent the Netherlands. As Griffiths sums up the situation at the time:

> Valuable ministerial time has been wasted in resolving blistering interdepartmental rows over both policy content and departmental competence. Furthermore, in order to accommodate various departmental interests, the size of Dutch delegations at international negotiations has often proved large, unwieldy and cumbersome. Finally, and most importantly, the continuous squabbling has seriously weakened attempts to impart some unity to the overall direction of European policy. (Griffiths, 1980a, p. 286)

The situation with regard to the transposition of 'EU' directives into Dutch law was not much better. In the early 1980s, the Netherlands had implemented only 80 per cent of existing directives, at that time one of the worst records in the EU (Kooiman et al., 1988, p. 585). Many commentators have attributed the slow transposition of 'EU' directives into Dutch law to the time needed to consult all interested parties:

> It will be clear that the legislative process is hardly suitable for the implementation of EC directives. It is based on the wish to *achieve consensus* within Dutch society as a whole, within the various parts of the government and within the relationship of government and parliament. (Bekkers et al., 1995, p. 410)

Another potential explanation lies in the poorly organized preparation of the Dutch position in the negotiations in Brussels: not having realized the full potential of its influence in the drafting of the directives, the Dutch government had to make up for that omission at the implementation stage.

In general, the Dutch 'solution' to the coordination deficit has not been to centralize EU expertise and competence in a single department, or in the Prime Minister's office, but to put in place committees and procedures for timely consultation. The interdepartmental coordination mechanisms are different for each stage of EU policy-making (working group, Committee of Permanent Representatives (COREPER), Council) (Harmsen, 1999; Soetendorp and Andeweg, 2001). As soon as the Dutch Permanent Representative alerts the Foreign Office to a new proposal by the EU Commission, the proposal is put before the BNC (Assessment Committee for New Commission Proposals), a committee chaired by an official from the Foreign Office's European Directorate in which all departments are represented, set up in 1989 to assess new Commission proposals. Since 2001, the BNC also includes representatives of the associations of municipal and provincial governments. The main function of the BNC is to decide which department is most concerned and should take the lead in handling the dossier, and which departments are also immediately affected and should be consulted by the lead department. The lead department then produces a memo (known as *fiche)*, outlining the financial and legal implications for the Netherlands, the relation to subsidiarity, and a rough outline of the position to be taken in the Council working group. Once approved, the *fiche* is forwarded to the Coordination Committee for European Integration and Association Issues, known simply as CoCo. This committee consists of high-level civil servants from the various departments and is chaired by the Department of Foreign Affairs. CoCo reports to the Cabinet. For politically sensitive proposals, a higher level interdepartmental committee (HACEU) takes CoCo's place. Procedurally, coordination is centralized in this way, but substantive coordination takes place elsewhere, within the lead department or between the lead department and the few other departments involved in a policy area.

When a new proposal reaches the COREPER stage, domestic coordination takes place in the interdepartmental 'Instruction Meeting', convened each week on the day before COREPER meets, also chaired by a senior official from the Foreign Office European Directorate. A first draft of the instruction to the Permanent Representative is submitted by the lead department, and interdepartmental conflicts that have not been resolved bilaterally come to the surface occasionally at this stage. They can only be resolved by the Cabinet, but often there is no time to wait for a Cabinet decision. The Foreign Office will attempt to mediate, but it lacks the power to arbitrate. Such cases result in rather vague compromise instructions, effectively delegating a decision to the Permanent Representative. During Instruction Meetings, participants will also get their first opportunity to relate negotiations on a particular proposal to other dossiers, and to suggest linkages and package deals that fit in an overall strategy (Soetendorp and Hanf, 1998). During the COREPER stage, the positions of the other member states and the need to build coalitions, especially under qualified majority voting (QMV), may necessitate amendments to the instruction. The Permanent Representative enjoys easy access to all ministers and to the Prime Minister, and will often 'coordinate' a new position him/herself.

In the final stage, the proposal is discussed in one of the EU's Councils of Ministers. The negotiating position in any council meeting needs the seal of approval of the Dutch Cabinet. CoCo prepares such Cabinet decisions. Recommendations by CoCo are usually discussed first in the Cabinet Committee on the European Union (MCEU), before reaching the Cabinet itself. CoCo discusses a draft negotiating position prepared by the Foreign Office. The draft will usually propose a choice between the options listed by the Permanent Representative, based on the outcome of the relevant COREPER meeting. This will happen in close cooperation with the lead department on that particular dossier. Cabinet will usually endorse that choice without much discussion. If in the subsequent Council meetings a minister feels that his/her mandate is too restrictive, the minister will usually consult the Prime Minister or one or two of his/her Dutch colleagues if their departments are closely involved.

While this procedure has improved coordination, it still has two weak points: it starts late and still relies primarily on delegating responsibility to one of the departments. In 2004, one of the government's advisory councils criticized the coordination of the Dutch position in EU policy-making as 'primarily reactive in character. Coordination only commences once the European Commission issues a new proposal. Little attention is paid to the incubation processes that precede such a proposal. The emphasis is on the higher levels of the Council's hierarchy (the agendas of COREPER and Council). As a result, political involvement manifests itself only near the end of the decision-making process' (Council for Public Administration, 2004, p. 27). Another cause of the reactive nature of Dutch EU policy-making is that only 30 per cent of departmental civil servants feel their work is affected by the EU, and most of these spend less than a quarter of their working hours on EU-related activities (Mastenbroek and Princen, 2010). 'Doing the Dutch government's business in Brussels, with Brussels, or as a result of decisions made in Brussels, is a matter of pockets of specialists scattered around departments and agencies, not one of which involves a broad front of public servants' (Gueijen et al., 2008, p. 130). After a long period of being underrepresented, the Netherlands now has proportional representation within the EU Commission's bureaucracy (around 4 per cent), and is even overrepresented among the national experts seconded to the Commission (almost 6 per cent), but their expertise and advanced knowledge constitutes an 'under-utilised asset' of the Dutch government (Suvarierol and Van den Berg, 2008). For a case study of the considerable influence that a Dutch expert seconded to the Commission exercised in the field of chemical policy, see Haverland, 2009.

In addition, the procedure relies heavily on decentralizing coordination to one of the government departments. As the Council for Public Administration concluded: 'Up to and including the stage of the Council working groups, the lead departments are relatively autonomous. Other departments have to secure information from and influence on the lead department themselves.' In 2008, an internal report about the Dutch Presidency of the EU in 2004 criticized the lack of coordination and uniformity in the strategies pursued by the Dutch departments when presiding over EU Councils of Ministers (IOB, 2008).

Similarly, efforts to improve the implementation of EU Directives have also met with mixed results. The General Administrative Law Act of 1994 makes it possible to distinguish the implementation of European legislation from all other legislation. Implementation is put on a 'fast track', and exempted from normal consultation requirements. In 1997 an Interdepartmental Committee on European Law (ICER) was set up to provide, among other aims, the legal expertise needed for the implementation of directives, and to monitor the progress of implementation. Ellen Mastenbroek estimates that 99 per cent of existing EU directives have now been transposed into Dutch law (Mastenbroek, 2007, p. 49). As Beyers et al. conclude on the basis of interviews with officials in the three Benelux countries: 'It is unbearable for Dutch officials not to transpose European law' (Beyers et al., 2000, p. 77). However, Mastenbroek also points out that no less than 60 per cent of the directives have a delay in transposition, sometimes by several years: 'The problem with timeliness is structural, in that the Dutch record has not improved considerably since the late 1970s. Hence the Netherlands seems to suffer from a transposition deficit' (Mastenbroek, 2007, p. 57). Moreover, transposition does not always mean that the policy is actually carried out. In 1990, the Minister of Agriculture was forced to resign when it appeared that he had not acted on earlier warnings that widespread administrative fraud with EU fishing quotas was taking place. In 1997, in what became known as the Securitel affair, it came to light that Dutch ministers had neglected to comply with reporting requirements regarding technical specifications in Dutch legislation on a variety of topics (environmental protection, speed control, and so on). In 2001, the EU claimed back more than €200 million in European Social Fund (ESF) subsidies from the Dutch government because of alleged misuse. In all these cases, lack of coordination and central control contributed to the non-compliance.

A partial exception to the fact that the strengthening of coordination has not led to more hierarchy and arbitration is the position of the Dutch Prime Minister (see Chapter 5). For a long time, the EU was firmly within the province of the Minister of Foreign Affairs. Not only has this Minister lost ground as more and more policy areas were affected by European integration and other ministers became involved in EU policy-making, but the Prime Minister has also encroached on his terrain with the growing importance of the European Council and other forms of summitry. As late as the 1970s, the Dutch Prime Minister was the only head of government accompanied by the Minister of Foreign Affairs at such summits. The official position, outlined in a letter from Prime Minister Van Agt to Parliament, is still that the Prime Minister needs a mandate from the Minister of Foreign Affairs when he or she discusses matters with other EU heads of government that are formally within the portfolio of the Minister of Foreign Affairs. In practice, however, this is not always possible, and both Prime Minister Lubbers and Prime Minister Kok have clashed with their Ministers of Foreign Affairs about the exact demarcation of their responsibilities in EU affairs. There are regular calls to concentrate EU coordination in the Prime Minister's Office, under a junior minister or even with the Prime Minister directly in charge.

Strengthening the Core Executive

In Chapter 7 the rise of the judiciary as a political actor in the Netherlands was discussed, and the primacy of European over domestic legislation has been one of the main contributory factors to that ascendancy. In this respect, EU membership has weakened the position of the Dutch government, but in other respects Europeanization has had the opposite effect. The EU 'may enable the Dutch government to endorse policies against the wishes of the majority of the electorate' (Wolters, 1990, p. 221). While the Dutch may have lost some of their enthusiasm for further European integration, the impact of the EU on policy is still regarded as an inevitability; like the weather, sometimes it is fine and sometimes it is inclement, but little can be done to change it. This provides the Dutch government with an opportunity to hide behind 'Brussels'. Unpopular measures may be taken, deadlocks can be broken, because 'we shall otherwise be out of step with the rest of the EU'. The government has been able to defy even strong and well-integrated interest groups by pointing to EU policies as if they were forces of nature. It is, paradoxically, precisely in the field of agriculture (once 'Europeanized' to escape the grip of the Dutch core executive, as noted above) that 'Brussels' now serves as the scapegoat for measures ranging from quotas for cod and manure to the shift from price support to income support (Hennis, 1997). The EU's Stability and Growth Pact, and in particular its 3 per cent debt-to-GDP criterion for maximum financing deficits, has provided the government with a powerful 'weapon' against critics of its austerity measures in the wake of the economic crisis that began in 2008 (see Chapter 9). The EU may even design its policies for this purpose: 'One of the ancillary reasons for the ambitious targets of the common energy programme was to help member-states such as the Netherlands in overcoming their internal opposition [to nuclear energy]' (Van Der Doelen and De Jong, 1990, p. 66), or to liberalization and privatization (Correljé, 1997).

'Hiding behind Brussels' strengthens the position of the Dutch government not only *vis-à-vis* organized interests, but also against Parliament. The Dutch government's real position in EU policy-making is hidden from parliamentary scrutiny, even if the government's eventual vote in the EU Council of Ministers is not. For example, analysing the Dutch role in the shaping of the Biopatent directive (98/44/EC), Van Keulen observed

> notwithstanding domestic opposition, the government delegation explicitly did not want to impede the directive from being agreed. No doubt, this consideration can be explained by the fact that the lead ministry did not share parliamentary concerns. In the final Council meeting the Dutch government minister indeed cast the only no-vote. But, taking into account that no proof has been found for other influence attempts by the Dutch government to prevent the directive from being adopted, this vote seems primarily driven by the desire to make a symbolic gesture towards national parliament. (Van Keulen, 2006, p. 206)

The Dutch Parliament has long been criticized for not making adequate use of its powers to influence and control the activities of the government in the European arena. However, the Second Chamber has recently taken steps to recoup some of the lost ground. For example, in 1986 it set up a European Affairs Committee (EAC) (one of the last Houses of Parliament in the EU to do so – even the Dutch First Chamber had already created such a committee in 1970). Although lack of interest in matters European had been a major cause of the delay, the official reason was a fear that a separate European Affairs Committee would provide the other parliamentary committees with an alibi for neglecting the European dimension in their policy field. Still, the European Affairs Committee's main task is to coordinate the other parliamentary committees with regard to EU matters. Since 1991, the EAC receives all *fiches* about new Commission proposals that are approved by the Cabinet (see above), and distributes these to the parliamentary committees most concerned. The *fiches* should be sent to Parliament within six weeks of the publication of a new Commission proposal, and this deadline has not always been met, but recently there has been an improvement in this respect (Van Mourik, 2012, p. 42). Parliament also receives the agendas of EU council meetings in Brussels, together with details of the government's negotiating position. Since 2010, the agendas for European Council meetings are discussed in plenary meetings of the Second Chamber. Another sign of Europeanization in the working of the Second Chamber is that, since 1999, Dutch MEPs are allowed to participate in committee meetings and plenary sessions whenever an EU-related topic is being debated. They can take part in the deliberations, but they do not have the right to vote. With the 2007 Lisbon Treaty, the Dutch Parliament has also profited from the new opportunities for national parliaments to signal objections to legislation at the EU-level rather than only at the domestic level.

However, the same Lisbon Treaty also led to a weakening of the Dutch Parliament's involvement in Dutch EU policy-making: the transformation of its mandating power (*instemmingsrecht*) into a scrutiny reserve (*behandelvoorbehoud*). Parliament's mandating power began when the Second Chamber agreed to the ratification of the Schengen Agreement that abolished border controls between a number of, but not all, EU member states. Originally, the Schengen Agreement was not part of the *acquis communautaire* and thus outside even the weak democratic controls within the EU. For that reason, the bill for ratification of the treaty was amended by the Second Chamber to give the Dutch Parliament the right to discuss proposals before the meeting of Schengen's Executive Committee with the ministers concerned. The ministers were not allowed to take a position in the Executive Committee if no agreement with Parliament could be reached. The Treaty of Amsterdam later brought the Schengen Agreement under the EU umbrella. Even earlier, during the ratification procedure of the Maastricht Treaty, Parliament had claimed a similar mandating power for all Justice and Home Affairs matters. When ratification of the Lisbon Treaty was discussed in Parliament, the government argued that the treaty's strengthening of the legislative powers of the European Parliament obviated the original reason the Dutch Parliament gave for installing a mandating procedure. Parliament accepted this line of reasoning, with a few exceptions, but exchanged it for a scrutiny reserve for any proposal that one of the Chambers would deem politically significant. In that case, the Chamber has to notify the government within two months of receiving the proposal, and the government then has to make a scrutiny reserve in Brussels and engage in consultations with Parliament within four weeks. In 2010, the Second Chamber engaged this procedure for the first time with respect to a change in the EU budgetary procedure (Van Mourik, 2012, pp. 50–8). The transformation of the mandating power into a scrutiny reserve is seen as a weakening by many constitutional lawyers, but it should be noted that the scope of the Parliament's involvement is now much wider than under the mandating power, and that Parliament rarely used it in any case (Del Grosso, 2000). Perhaps a better indicator of Parliament's involvement is the decline in parliamentary attention to bills with EU links, as is evidenced by the decrease in the number of amendments per bill with a EU link compared with amendments to bills without such a link (Breeman and Timmermans, 2012, p. 67).

A Double Democratic Deficit

The processes of decentralization and Europeanization are not uniform across all policy areas in terms of their speed and scope, but they have common denominators. Both of these developments have strengthened the fragmentation of policy-making into policy-specific decision-making; at the subnational level through the proliferation of functional cooperative arrangements between municipalities, and at the European level through decision-making in councils for specific policy areas.

Both decentralization and Europeanization also contribute to depoliticization. Until recently, European integration and policies have largely escaped party politics. This may be one of the reasons why there is a broad consensus in Parliament about setting up better procedures and being informed in time, but why so little use is made of these powers and procedures. The preparation of the Dutch position in EU policy-making rarely involves politicians at all. Subnational government is also depoliticized government: the local executive is usually a broad coalition, the local issues rarely relate to party ideology, and the voters take their cues in local elections from national politics anyway. It is telling that, in Dutch, local politics is usually referred to as local *administration,* and is considered an appropriate object of study for students of public administration, rather than for political scientists.

Most important, both decentralization and Europeanization also appear to result in democratic deficits. The democratic deficit that results from the transfer of policy-making from The Hague to Brussels, in particular after the introduction of Qualified Majority Voting in EU Councils, is a phenomenon that is not peculiar to the Netherlands and has received sufficient attention elsewhere in the literature. We can only add that, as we have just seen, the Dutch Parliament has not been able to reduce that deficit substantially. What is less well-known is that, for very similar reasons, a democratic deficit is growing at the subnational level. To increase the economy of scale and to cope with newly decentralized tasks, local governments increasingly cooperate with their neighbours. The intermunicipal cooperation regions have formed a new layer of government between municipalities and provinces; they have their own apparatus and executive boards, but these are composed of representatives from the local executive boards. There are no regional councils that are elected, either directly or indirectly. Aldermen are held accountable for their role in the regional boards by their local council, but there they can easily escape responsibility by claiming to have reached the best possible compromise in the face of overwhelming opposition from the representatives of the neighbouring towns. The *landsdelen* have yet to reach the same level of development as the intermunicipal regions, but here too democratic legitimation and control are lacking. Dutch governance is increasingly multi-level governance, but it is also increasingly technocratic and fragmented governance, rather than democratic and cohesive governance.

9

Economic and Welfare Policy

Open Economy

The Netherlands is a highly prosperous country. With a size ranking only 133rd in the world in terms of surface area and only 61st in terms of population size, the economy ranks 16th in gross domestic product (GDP). It is the sixth-largest economy in the European Union, ranking only behind Germany, France, the UK, Italy and Spain. In GDP per capita (corrected for purchasing power parity), in 2010 it followed only Luxembourg (whose figures are inflated by the many people who work there but live outside the country). The Dutch figure of US$42,475 compared favourably with the US$46,588 figure for the USA.

Dutch wealth was originally founded on its commercial success in the Golden Age of the seventeenth century. At that time, Amsterdam was the commercial centre and richest city in Europe. The Dutch East India Company (VOC) was founded in 1602 and was the first company to issue stock. It dominated trade with Asia and at its peak owned 40 warships and 150 merchant ships and employed more than 10,000 soldiers. Because of its financial importance, it was to Amsterdam that John Adams came in 1782 to negotiate a loan of 5 million guilders that was of crucial importance to his fledgling nation, the USA.

With its position declining in the nineteenth century (the Dutch East India Company became bankrupt and was dissolved in 1800), the wealth of the country is again based on trade and finance. Despite its size, the Netherlands is the fifth-largest exporter of goods in the world, behind China, the USA, Germany, and Japan. It is the second-largest exporter of agricultural products, ranking only behind the USA, and is in the top three in terms of exports of vegetables. The value of exports of goods and services amounted to 84.2 per cent of GDP in 2011. About 30 per cent of the income of the country is earned from exports. The country also ranked eighth in the world in terms of the import of goods and services (Hollandtrade, 2012). For 2012, using a series of indicators, including trade-to-GDP ratios, the International Chamber of Commerce rated the Netherlands as the sixth most open economy among the 75 nations studied, behind only Hong Kong, Singapore, Luxembourg, Belgium, and Malta (International Chamber of Commerce, 2013).

Many of the exports are the result of redistribution, with goods coming into the country and being transported throughout Europe. For example, approximately 40 per cent of all Japanese goods imported into Europe pass through the Netherlands, and imports from China are becoming increasingly important. More than 80 per cent of Dutch exports therefore remain in Europe. According to the World Bank, in 2010 the Netherlands ranked fourth on the bank's Logistics Performance Index (behind Germany, Singapore, and Sweden). The Port of Rotterdam may lay claim to being the largest port in Europe and is in the process of a land reclamation project that will expand its capacity by 20 per cent in 2014. Schiphol Airport is the fourth-largest airport in Europe in terms of both cargo and numbers of passengers carried. The Netherlands has the world's largest inland fleet and barges move up and down the Rhine and other inland waterways. The transportation network can easily reach the nearly 160 million inhabitants of most of Europe's industrial areas that lie within a 300-mile (483 km) radius of Amsterdam. Even before the opening of a new rail link in 2007, Germany was the most important trading partner, followed by Belgium, the UK, and France.

All sectors of the economy contribute to trade, but they vary in size and in their contribution to the value of exports. During the twentieth century, the economy of the Netherlands underwent major restructuring, as can be seen in Table 9.1. If the well-known trichotomy of primary, secondary and tertiary sectors of the economy (that is, agriculture, industry and services) is examined, we can see that, at the end of the nineteenth century, agriculture was the largest sector, and industry was barely larger than services. The changes in relative size during the century, however, were substantial.

Of the three, the greatest change occurred in the agricultural sector. From being the largest at the beginning of the twentieth century, it was by far the smallest at the end, falling by 90 per cent to only 3 per cent of employment in the twenty-first century. Agriculture now accounts for only 2–3 per cent of GDP. Nevertheless, it remains important to the Netherlands, as agricultural and food products make up about 15 per cent of the export package. The Dutch food, drink and tobacco industry is one of the largest in the world, providing a home base for multinationals such as Unilever and Heineken. The Netherlands is also one of the world's leading dairy producers, but the export of meat products, in particular poultry and pork, accounts for almost an equal volume of exports as do dairy products (Economic

Table 9.1 *Employment by Economic Sector, 1899–2008 (Percentage of Persons Employed)*

Year	Agriculture/fishing	Industry	Services	Other	Total
1899	36	31	30	3	100
1930	20	40	39	2	101*
1960	12	45	41	4	102*
2008	3	21	76	1	101*

Note: * Due to rounding errors.
Sources: Based on data published in CBS (2001) and Statistics Netherland.

Affairs, 2001, 2004). In addition to the famous bulb fields, greenhouses produce flowers, potted plants, cucumbers, tomatoes, lettuces, onions, and mushrooms.

The Industrial Revolution was relatively late in coming to the Netherlands. For example, in 1853, there were only 364 steam machines in the country, compared with 2,040 in Belgium three years earlier, and 5,322 in France, all of which lagged behind the UK (Buunk, 1999, p. 16). Rapid industrialization began only in the last decade of the nineteenth century, after the government had made improvements to the infrastructure, particularly in the form of railways and canals. After the Second World War, the need for reconstruction to improve industrial output was a high priority, and employment in that sector reached a high of 45 per cent in 1960. Yet the Netherlands has never been a classical industrial nation, as this percentage still lagged behind that of neighbouring countries such as Germany, France, the UK, and Belgium. Nevertheless, after 1960, the closure of the mining industry, the virtual disappearance of the textile industry and other restructuring led to loss of employment in this sector. At the beginning of the twenty-first century, the percentage of the labour force working in the industrial sector was lower than it had been at the beginning of the previous century.

Despite this sector diminishing in its percentage of the labour force employed, it remains highly important in terms of trade. The huge petrochemical industry is indicative of how raw materials are imported and turned into other products to be exported. Royal Dutch Shell is among the top three oil companies in the world, and one of the largest companies in terms of volume in the world (Buunk, 1999, p. 33). In addition, other major producers such as BP, Exxon and Texaco have refineries and petrochemical operations in the Netherlands. Rotterdam has become the major storage depot for petroleum products for north-western Europe and is the home of the oil spot market. In addition to Shell Chemical, AKZONobel and DSM have become major international chemical producers, the latter having made the conversion to chemicals after the state mines were closed in the 1960s. The chemical sector has also been the most expansive industrial sector in recent years. Another Dutch multinational, Philips, is a major producer of electronic products (Economic Affairs, 2001). As industrial employment began to decline from 1960, much of the slack was taken up by governmental, social, and community services, including education. However, such employment has declined since 1987. At the end of the century, the strongest gains were made in commercial services, such as retailing, hotels and restaurants, financial and business services, and communication (Visser and Hemerijck, 1997, p. 29). In 2008, 76 per cent of employment was in the service sector. With so much of the population employed in this sector it too contributes to exports. Harbour dredging and ocean salvage are Dutch specialities, and the companies involved operate almost exclusively outside the country. Another important area is transportation. During the last decade of the twentieth century, the Netherlands increased its share of total world exports of transport services and just edged out France and Germany to be the largest exporter of transport services in Europe and third in the world.

The Netherlands has also been important in terms of investment and financial services. The ABN-AMRO bank has offices in 50 countries across the world, and the RABO bank is represented in 48 countries. The ING group is one of the world's largest providers of insurance and financial services (Relbanks, 2013). In 2010, the country was ranked as the seventh-largest foreign investor in the world behind the USA, the UK, France, Germany, Hong Kong, and Switzerland (but ahead of Japan). The open economy is again emphasised, as the Netherlands is the eighth-largest recipient of foreign investment (following the USA, Hong Kong, the UK, France, Germany, Belgium, and Spain). A report compiled by Bloomberg ranked it as the second-best place (among 160 markets) to do business. It was ranked fifth on the Global competitiveness Index by the World Economic Forum, and fourth on the Global Innovation Index published by INSEAD (Hollandtrade, 2013).

Macro-economic Policy

The rosy picture of a rich and prosperous country is something that older inhabitants might have doubted at the end of the Second World War. Although the country had capitulated after only a few days, 250,000 citizens lost their lives through war, deportation, and hunger. During the last years of occupation, the Germans exploited the Netherlands in their final efforts to wage total war. By 1948, after years of depression and occupation, the average income per household had fallen to the same level as it was in 1929. The time was ripe for a greater role for the government in the management of the economy (Prak and Luiten van Zanden, 2013).

In Chapter 2 it was noted that the first 'rule' of Dutch politics formulated by Lijphart concerned the 'business of politics'. Lijphart was referring to the fact that politics in the Netherlands is seen not so much as a game but as serious business, and that participants are expected to act accordingly. However, this rule could be slightly extended to imply that the country should be run as a business, and observers occasionally refer to the country as 'Netherlands Inc.' Of course, a government is not a profit-making company, but it does seek to maximize the economic benefits of its 'shareholders' – the inhabitants of the Netherlands. The major challenge for Dutch economic policy-making is that it has to do so in such an open economy.

To manage an open economy and keep that economy competitive, a number of macro-economic goals are of importance. The price of export articles must remain competitive, which means that labour costs must not be allowed to rise so high as to price products out of the market. Similarly, inflation must be kept low. To make the country attractive to foreign investment, the currency exchange rate must be reliable and stable, and government finances must be in order. These have been major priorities for governments in the post-war period. In addition, the government has taken on increasing responsibility for providing for the welfare of the citizens, and in particular to protect them from a repeat of the experience of depression in the 1930s. A major priority, has been to provide full employment for the citizenry.

To discuss all aspects of macro-economic policy would go far beyond the scope of this book. One would have to discuss the policy of industrialization following the war and the reaction to globalization more recently. It would need to discuss housing policy, as the need for adequate housing was one of the major problems facing the country in the post-war period. It would need to discuss how investment in and the expansion of education is related to changes in the structure of the workforce and maintaining prosperity in the face of challenges from emerging economies. It would have to address the provision of healthcare for the population, and how to keep rising costs under control. Because it is not possible to discuss all such topics in this book, the discussion here will focus on two aspects that have attracted national and international attention and are specifically related to the country – the 'Dutch disease' and the 'Dutch miracle'. Following these discussions, attention will be given to the reaction of the government to the crises arising from the financial problems that have emerged since 2008.

The Creation of the Welfare State and the 'Dutch Disease'

The emergency law providing a state pension for all citizens over the age of 65, which was introduced by the Minister of Social Affairs, Willem Drees, in 1947, can be seen as the first step in the creation of the modern welfare state in the Netherlands. A grateful citizenry long referred to him as 'Father Drees'. The emergency law was made permanent in the Old-Age Pension Act (AOW) of 1956. This was followed by a widows and orphans law (1959); child benefits (1962; such benefits for employees had been introduced in 1939); and major medical insurance (1967). A general programme for disabled citizens was added in 1976. In addition to those covering all citizens, programmes were introduced specifically for the employed. In 1949, unemployment compensation insurance was instigated, and compulsory medical insurance was introduced in 1964. A law providing disability compensation was passed in 1967, and in the same year a new law replaced pre-war legislation for sick leave.

Provisions for social security in the Netherlands can be divided into three categories. The first are programmes for all citizens (*volksverzekeringen*). These are financed by premiums paid by those employed and come out of general funds. The oldest of these, the old-age pension scheme (AOW) is a general insurance programme; other examples include insurance for exceptional medical costs (AWBZ) and child payments (*kinderbijslag*). The second are insurance programmes for those who are employed (*werknemersverzekeringen*). The most important is perhaps unemployment benefits, but these also include disability insurance (WIA) and sickness insurance. The third form consists of welfare programmes that provide for citizens who need basic assistance. These are financed out of general funds.

Many of the benefits for these programmes have often been quite generous, at least by international standards. For example, unemployment benefits and disability payments were set originally at 80 per cent of the previously earned wage. Since disability benefits continued at this level until the age of retirement (and were indexed to cover inflation), 'disability' became, in some cases, an attractive alternative to unemployment.

An exception has been old-age benefits. However, most households will have supplemental benefits from pensions directly related to their previous employment. Both employers and employees pay into a pension fund that is related to the sector of employment and not the individual firm. As a result, the Netherlands has the largest pension reserve in the world. The aim has been to provide a total pension (that is, government and private) equal to 70 per cent of the final salary. Pension funds have suffered during the recent financial crisis and some pensions have been cut by a few per cent.

In addition, besides providing coverage against economic difficulties, the Dutch welfare state attempted to ensure that all citizens shared in the increased wealth of the nation and that a 'just' distribution of the national income was realized. One of the most controversial measures taken in this regard was the linking of minimum wage levels and levels of benefits from most of the above-mentioned insurance programmes to the rise in wages of those employed in the private sector. This idea was in a sense a logical extension of the automatic price compensation clauses that were introduced into labour contracts in the 1970s. If employees received additional wages, at least in part because of a rise in prices, then those receiving benefits were similarly in need of an increase. Thus the principle of 'coupling' was introduced, whereby rises in benefits were 'coupled' to rises in wages. This principle was also extended to the salaries of government employees.

The result of 'coupling' was that, when new contracts were negotiated between the employers and the unions in the private sector, government costs for salaries of civil servants and for beneficiaries of insurance programmes rose automatically. More revenue was needed to pay for such increases, often necessitating an increase in the rates of insurance premiums and in taxes, which in turn produced higher wage costs. As a result, an automatic wage spiral was introduced, pushing up wage costs and increasing the size of the public sector.

In the space of a few decades the welfare system in the Netherlands went from one of the smallest in Western Europe to one of the largest (Cox, 1993, pp. 3–4). In 1953, social insurance premiums amounted to only about 5 per cent of the net national income. During the ensuing decade, this figure more than doubled, to almost 11 per cent. As a result of new programmes introduced in the 1960s and early 1970s, the amount for insurance premiums continued to rise throughout the 1970s. Beginning at 15 per cent in 1970, the percentage of net national income rose to 24 per cent at its peak in 1983.

Virtually all of these programmes were introduced in a period in which the economy was expanding and employment rates were high, and relatively few people were in need of the benefits. However, following the oil crisis of 1973, as the economic boom slowed and unemployment increased, more and more people laid claims to benefits. In almost all cases, the numbers skyrocketed above the predictions that had been made at the time of the system's introduction. More and more revenue was required to provide the benefits that had been promised. Tax revenues in this period remained surprisingly steady. In fact, even if one goes back to an earlier date, these figures do not change as substantially as the figures for the social insurance premiums. After the Second World War, total tax revenues as a percentage of net national income amounted to about 30 per cent, but as a result of tariff reductions, this fell to 23 per cent in 1955 (De Wolff and Driehuis, 1980, p. 28). After this low point, however, as the government began to take on new responsibilities taxes were gradually increased. The official government figures are slightly lower than those reported by De Wolff and Driehuis, who claim a level of 26 per cent for 1970.

If the Dutch state was 'large' in fiscal terms, it was not so much because of government outlays but rather to transfer payments, and it was the rise in social insurance premiums that contributed most to the increase in the size of the public sector. Total public expenditure was thus increasing more rapidly than government income via taxation and insurance premiums, and much of the increase resulted from the unexpectedly high levels of expenditure on the social insurance programmes, as noted above. The difference between government tax and premium revenues and government expenditures had to be made up through non-tax revenues or borrowing. Both of these sources were employed, particularly in the 1970s and into the early 1980s, and the result became known as the 'Dutch disease'.

One source of income was revenue from the sale of natural gas. Natural gas had been discovered in the north of the country and after the oil crisis of 1973 this began to provide a substantial income to the government (Lubbers and Lemckert, 1980). Income from the sale of natural gas was used to fund the social welfare programmes. This meant that an income source that would eventually dry up was being used not to improve economic infrastructure but for welfare benefits. This is one indication of the 'Dutch disease'.

The second source of income was borrowing. Because revenues, even including gas receipts, did not always match expenditure, the government was forced to borrow money not only for long-term investments but also for current outlays. In only a decade, the national debt rose from something over €68 billion in 1982 to almost €154 billion in 1991. These figures amounted to 43.8 per cent and 71.0 per cent of the national income, respectively. In the same period, interest payments on debt rose from about 2 per cent to almost 6 per cent of GNP, a figure considerably higher than the average of the then five larger EC countries.

These figures became a major political concern. The term 'financing deficit' (*financieringstekort*) became a common term in political debate and is still easily recognized by large segments of the population. This term refers not to the actual deficit in the current budget, but to the difference between revenues and expenditure minus the amount paid on long-term loans. The assumption is that as such loans are paid off, the amounts become available for new loans. When a gap still exists between income and outlay, it can be plugged either by additional loans or by monetary measures, such as simply printing new money. Most Dutch economists viewed a financing deficit of 4–5 per cent of net national income as being tolerable. Before 1979, the financing deficit figure had never exceeded 4.4 per cent, but thereafter it began to rise dramatically, to a peak of 10.7 per cent in 1982. Since it would not be possible to continue to borrow endlessly for social welfare benefits that would be continuing, this was a second sign of the 'Dutch disease'.

In summary, the Dutch welfare state was constructed to protect citizens from economic hardships and uncertainties, such as those that had been felt during the years of economic crisis in the 1930s. It was founded on the principle of solidarity among the citizenry in attempts to bring about an equitable distribution of the wealth of the country. However, claims for benefits from welfare state programmes almost always exceeded initial estimates and it became difficult to raise the funds to provide these benefits. Insurance premiums added about 45 per cent to the labour costs, which made it difficult for Dutch companies to compete in the international market. Revenues from natural gas could not provide a long-term solution. Government borrowing also had its limits. Though begun with the most noble of intentions, by the end of the 1970s the country was suffering from 'the Dutch disease'. It became clear that the financing deficit had reached intolerable levels. Borrowing by the government took funds away from other areas of investment and burdened future budgets with higher interest payments. Discussion of the desirable level, or an agreed maximum level of the financing deficit, became a major focus in negotiations surrounding the formation of new Cabinets. Moreover, the country entered a period of 'immobile corporatism' (see Table 7.1 on page 193) and the style of negotiation between the trade unions and employers became 'confrontational' (Woldendorp, 2005). By the 1980s it had become clear that the time had come to search for a cure.

Restructuring the Welfare State and the 'Dutch Miracle'

Job Creation

After the end of the Second World War, with no wish to return to the high levels of unemployment in the 1930s, the government set full employment as one of the primary goals of its macro-economic policy. To achieve this and to provide for economic recovery, it was necessary to restore the trade position of the country. In an open economy such as the Netherlands, it is important that the prices of goods and services to be exported must be competitive in the international markets. To achieve this, the government worked to gain the cooperation of both trade unions and employers. By means of a 'guided wage policy' (*geleide loonpolitiek*), wages in the Netherlands were kept artificially low. It was during this period that corporatist structures described in Chapter 7 (the most important being the Foundation of Labour and the Social and Economic Council – SER) were set up.

This policy contributed to the spectacular post-war economic recovery in the 1950s and 1960s, and the government's goal was essentially achieved. Unemployment levels were generally no higher than 1–2 per cent (about 70,000 people), the result of individuals being in the process of changing jobs. The demands of economic growth were in fact so great that labourers from Mediterranean countries, primarily Morocco and Turkey, were recruited as 'guest workers', often to perform the most menial tasks. Many thought that the problem of unemployment that had been so evident during the years of the Great Depression had been solved.

Although, by the definition that was used, employment appeared to be at its full level, in fact the participation rate, that is the percentage of the working-age population employed, was not particularly high. This was in large measure a result of the low rate of participation of women, one of the lowest in Europe. Until 1960, no more than 20 per cent of women had ever been employed at any given time. Because of the Nazi occupation during the Second World War, women had not been brought out of the kitchens into the factory to support wartime production, as they had in the USA and the UK. As Visser and Hemerijck (1997, p. 33) stated, 'Women's work, for wages, was girl's work.' Marriage meant the termination of an employment contract in services and public employment. Only as late as 1973 was a law passed forbidding employers to dismiss women for reasons of marriage or pregnancy (ibid.). Roughly speaking, at the end of the 1960s one could say that in the Netherlands, in terms of paid employment, most men were employed and most women were not.

At the beginning of the 1970s, the number of unemployed people began to rise slightly, and political leaders spoke of the unacceptability of having more than 100,000 unemployed. Nevertheless, by 1971, this figure had been surpassed and numbers continued to creep up slowly to approximately 300,000 at the end of the decade. As the 1980s began, unemployment rose dramatically, with the annual increases equal to the total figure for 1973. At the peak in 1983 and 1984 the number unemployed exceeded 800,000. According to the definition used by the Netherlands Bureau for Economic Policy Analysis (*Centraal Planbureau*), these 800,000 unemployed represented an unemployment rate of 9.7 per cent. However, other definitions viewed the rate as being considerably higher, as much as 14–17 per cent. Whatever definition is used, the rise was dramatic and no one could deny the extent of the problem. As the high unemployment rate also affected the balance between unemployment premiums and unemployment benefits, this was yet another aspect of the 'Dutch disease'.

Finding a cure for the disease thus needed to include finding a solution to unemployment. Creating jobs required making Dutch exports more competitive on international markets. The rise in wages after the 'wages explosion' of the 1960s had put pressure on such competition. A reduction in wage costs was thus needed, not only to improve the position of Dutch goods and services on the international market, but to create jobs. Moreover, job creation would help to lower the budget deficit. If people are employed, they not only do not need to receive unemployment (and possibly other) benefits, but they themselves pay taxes. Thus, beginning in the early 1980s, the theme of successive governments became 'Jobs, jobs, jobs' (Lubbers, 1997). To achieve a reduction of wage costs, traditions based on the guided wage policy after the Second World War were revived.

In 1982, to force such an agreement, the government put pressure on the trade unions and employers by threatening a wage freeze 'unless they agreed to find a way to moderate wage growth and devise a programme of new employment through work sharing, or the so-called "spreading of jobs"' (Lubbers, 1997). Surprisingly, the ploy was successful in bringing the trade unions and employers together, and that same year they reached an agreement that has become known as the Wassenaar

Accord, named after the municipality in which it was negotiated. The trade unions agreed to a voluntary wage restraint over the coming years, resulting in losses of real income. These losses were softened by the agreement of the employers to drop their opposition to a reduction of the 40-hour working week.

The importance to be accorded to the Wassenaar Accord is debatable. More importance was attached to it later than at the time of the agreement. Woldendorp (2005) has even argued that it was not a 'watershed' at all. In any case, the negotiating style of the unions and employers did change from 'confrontational' to 'bargaining' and the period of 'immobile' corporatism gave way to 'innovative' corporatism (Visser and Hemerijck, 1997; see also Chapter 7). The unions returned to voluntary wage moderation and held to this strategy over the ensuing years. More collective wage agreements were reached than in the previous period (Woldendorp, 2005). The Wassenaar Accord marked the beginning of what has become known as the 'polder model', in which the trade unions and employers are consulted by the government and involved in the economic decisions that must be made. In fact this was a return to older traditions, but the revival made it possible to reach numerous new agreements that led to lower labour costs and job-sharing, and thus to more persons employed.

The measures taken in this period to combat the Dutch disease were successful in creating new jobs. Whereas the number of jobs fell by between one per cent and over two per cent in each of the years 1981 through 1983, beginning in 1985 the number increased annually by between just over one per cent to three per cent in each of the following years until 2003 (with dips in 1993 and 1994 (Salverda, 2005; Langenberg and Nauta, 2007). After a slowdown between 2003 and 2005, the number of jobs increased again in 2006. In its 2007 Progress Report, in the context of the Lisbon Strategy, the government was able to claim 'as of May 2007, the Netherlands boasts the lowest unemployment rate in the entire EU' (Progress Report, 2007, p. 43). For 2008, on the eve of the global financial crisis, the OECD projected that the unemployment rate in the Netherlands would fall below its estimate of the structural unemployment rate of 3.5 per cent (OECD, 2008, p. 10). The job creation machine of the Netherlands in this period is referred to as the 'Dutch miracle'.

Reducing the Public Sector
Curing the Dutch disease was not easy; strong medicine was needed. Wage moderation was only one of the bitter pills that many thought would never be swallowed by the Dutch workers and the public. Hoogenboom and Van Vliet (2000) argue that the cure consisted of five such pills:

- reducing wage costs;
- reforming the system of social welfare;
- restructuring governmental finances;
- improving the functioning of markets; and
- providing a stable monetary climate.

The acceptance of wage moderation in the Wassenaar Accord meant that the 'no-nonsense' Cabinet under Prime Minister Ruud Lubbers (1982–86) was freed to turn its attention to other measures. One of the 'pills' to help cure the Dutch disease involved restructuring governmental finances, in particular a reduction in the size and costs of the state. Whereas wage moderation in the private sector had indirect benefits for government finances, the reduction of wage costs of government employees had direct effects. This challenge was tackled by the Cabinet, which proposed a reduction in governmental salaries of 3.5 per cent, effective from January 1984. The proposal, not surprisingly, was opposed by the public-sector unions, which organized one of the largest post-war strikes in the Netherlands. However, the unions quickly found that they had become isolated after the acceptance of wage moderation by the private-sector unions. Eventually, wages were cut by 3 per cent, taking effect in 1986. To secure acceptance of the cut, the working week was shortened from 40 to 38 hours, in most cases resulting in 12 extra 'vacation' days per year (Visser and Hemerijck, 1997, p. 101). In a related measure, the level of the minimum wage was also reduced by 3 per cent. Moreover, both government salaries and the minimum wage were uncoupled from the trends in the private sector. The minimum wage was frozen for the rest of the decade and for part of the 1990s (Hoogenboom and Van Vliet, 2000, p. 6).

These steps having been taken, Prime Minister Lubbers (1997) later wrote, 'the government took the next step and re-engineered the incentive system of the welfare state, placing more risk on companies and individuals and less on the government'. The change in incentives involved altering the cost–benefit ratio between work and welfare, making work more attractive. Lowering the minimum wage had the side-effect of lowering the welfare payments that are the final support in the welfare system, since these benefits are tied to the level of the minimum wage.

As mentioned above, the generous benefit provisions of the welfare state had influenced this cost–benefit ratio and had in some cases made benefits preferable to work. The 1976 law providing coverage for those disabled and unable to work had been the final jewel in the crown of the Dutch welfare state (Visser and Hemerijck, 1997, p. 126). Legislation in 1967 had removed the distinction in earlier legislation between disability that occurred on the job and other sources of disability (the so-called *risque professionnel* versus *risque social*) for those employed in the private sector. The 1976 law extended this to the self-employed, civil servants and even those who were disabled from birth. The benefits were generous: 80 per cent of the last-earned wage. At the time that the 1967 legislation was enacted, it was predicted that the numbers receiving disability benefits would eventually rise to between 150,000 and 200,000, yet by 1988 the number receiving benefits had exceeded 800,000, and it became conceivable that the 1,000,000 figure might be reached.

Several factors help to account for the increase above expectations. First, the definition of disability was gradually extended beyond physical disabilities to include stress-related illnesses. In 1988, 31 per cent of new cases were based on stress-related sickness. Second, disability became, under some circumstances, an attractive alternative to unemployment. A person was considered disabled if he or she was unable to perform a new job similar to the one previously held. If no such job was available, the person continued to receive benefits. Most would never find a similar job and thus received benefits until the age of 65, whereas unemployment benefits would have stopped after six months to two years. As unemployment rose in the 1980s, employers attempted to get as many workers as possible, often older workers, classified as disabled.

The first attempt at reform came in 1987, when benefits were cut from 80 per cent to 70 per cent of previous wages. However, most collective wage agreements restored the higher level through private insurance arrangements. A proposal in 1991 to make the length of time that benefits could be paid contingent on the number of years of employment led to a 250,000-strong demonstration in The Hague. Both coalition partners at the time (PvdA and CDA) lost considerable support at the subsequent elections in 1994. In 1992, financial incentives were introduced for companies, to provide a 'bonus' for hiring disabled workers and a 'malus' if they were dismissed. Making employers responsible for integrating the disabled into the workforce is a characteristic feature of the Dutch system (Høgelund, 2003). New legislation in 1993 widened the type of work that a beneficiary was required to accept, and benefits became subject to review after five years.

In 1994, for the first time, the numbers receiving benefits declined, but between 1996 and 2002 they began to rise again, reaching 988,000 in 2003 (Statistics Netherlands). These figures were roughly three times those of Germany and the USA, and twice that of Sweden. The average age of applicants was less than 45, and nowhere was the difference between younger and older workers as small. Part of this was accounted for by the relatively high percentages among young women under 35. A major overhaul took place in 2005, when the Law on Work and Income according to Working Ability (WIA) replaced the Law on Disability (WAO). Under this new law, three categories were introduced: less than 35 per cent disabled; between 35 and 80 per cent; and greater than 80 per cent inability to work because of sickness or disability. Those in the 'less than 35 per cent' category receive no government benefit and, at least in principle, remain in the service of their employer. The fully disabled (that is, greater than 80 per cent) receive a benefit equal to 75 per cent of their last salary. Those in the middle category receive benefits to supplement their earnings. The various measures have had modest success, stopping the rise in numbers of claimants and bringing about a decline in the numbers receiving benefits to 816,000 in 2012.

The restructuring of the welfare state continued into the twenty-first century. Measures were taken not only to reduce the amount of money that had to be paid out for various programmes, but also to reduce the numbers of people receiving benefits. In 2004, the new Work and Social Assistance Act transferred both budgetary and policy responsibilities for social assistance to the municipalities. These were allowed to retain any surpluses, which provided an incentive to promote the re-entry of recipients into the labour market (OECD, 2008, p. 20). In 2006, unemployment benefits were raised to 75 per cent, but their maximum duration was reduced from five years to three years and two months, and entitlement conditions were made stricter.

Fiscal Responsibility

As noted above, 'the Dutch disease' involved both excessive deficit spending and the use of the income from natural gas sales, which would eventually end, for structural expenditure. The attempts to reduce expenditure have been discussed, but additional measures were needed to get governmental finances in order. Successive Cabinets have made serious attempts to restructure governmental finances and introduce better financial discipline. This was begun during the Cabinets led by Prime Minister Lubbers and continued under the Purple Cabinets (1994–2002). In the latter, Minister of Finance Gerrit Zalm introduced new budgetary procedures. During the formation of these Cabinets, agreements were reached on a ceiling for government expenditure during the coming period; income and expenditure were to be kept separate, and expenditure would not rise as a result of an increase in income. These measures became known as the 'Zalm norm'. The Cabinet also agreed to use conservative economic predictions to increase the probability that unexpected developments would more often be pleasant rather than unpleasant surprises.

An important requirement for a successful open economy is a stable monetary climate. To create trust among foreign investors and stability for Dutch exporters, in 1983 the Dutch guilder was tied to the German Mark. In connection with the move towards integration in Europe, the Dutch cooperated to move towards the establishment of a European Monetary Union (EMU). To join the EMU, five conditions had to be met, the most important of which were a budget deficit of no more than 3 per cent of GDP and a total governmental debt of not more than 60 per cent of GDP. Though in 1997 the Netherlands still had a debt that was equal to 72 per cent of GDP, exceptions were allowed and the country had fewer difficulties in satisfying the criteria than many of the other participating nations. The value of the guilder was pegged at 2.20371 to the new euro, which went into effect on 1 January 1999. On 1 January 2002 the new currency was introduced to the public (Buunk, 1999, pp. 75–9).

Once the euro was in place, it was the intention that the participating countries worked within the above-mentioned monetary and fiscal rules. However, not all countries were able to do so and, over the objections of the Dutch, the requirements listed above were to some degree eased. Even the Dutch government was not able to hold the deficit below the 3 per cent level, however, because of economic downturns in 2003. New, tighter measures were introduced to bring the deficit back into line. In the years 2006 through 2008, the budget showed a small surplus and governmental debt was reduced to below the 60 per cent norm to almost 50 per cent (OECD, 2013). This, plus low levels of unemployment, seemed to indicate that there had indeed been a 'Dutch miracle', and the future was looking good.

New Challenges and Crises

Labour Market Participation

Miracles are not necessarily everlasting, however, and may produce side-effects, and this was the case with the job creation machine of 'the Dutch miracle'.

An assumption of the Lubbers government in the early 1980s was that even if the measures were successful, there would not be enough jobs to go round. Thus part of government policy was to spread out available jobs. Part-time employment was stimulated, so that a larger number of citizens could participate in the labour market. Early retirement was stimulated so that younger people could become employed. And, as part of the Wassenaar Accord and related measures, wage cuts were compensated by a reduction in working hours. While such measures contributed to 'the Dutch miracle', they also contributed directly to new challenges that were to face the government in subsequent years (OECD, 2008).

At the beginning of the new millennium, the challenge was very different. Rather than there being a fear that there would not be enough work for all, the concern was that there would not be enough workers. In its *Economic Survey 2008,* the OECD concluded that:

> the economy is now facing labour shortages, related to the greying of the population and the continued weak labour market-participation of several groups. In addition, part-time work remains widespread and net migration flows have turned negative in recent years. If the policy setting remains unchanged, medium-term growth is likely to be impaired by insufficient labour resources and demographic ageing will be a burden for the public finances. (p. 8)

This was a concern across Europe in general, and in 2000 the European Union formulated the so-called Lisbon Strategy. In this strategy, in terms of labour participation, goals were set to have a by 2010 total labour participation rate of 70 per cent, 60 per cent for women and 50 per cent for older workers. These goals were met in the Netherlands by 2007, with percentages of 76.0, 69.6, and 50.9, respectively. However, the Dutch government set higher goals for the Netherlands. The European definition of participation included work for at least 12 hours a week. As a result of the measures begun in the 1980s, the Netherlands has the highest rate of part-time employment in Europe: as a percentage of employment as a whole, 37.1 per cent was part-time employment in 2010; the second highest figure was for Ireland, with 24.8 per cent. Nearly 75 per cent of part-time workers are women (Hollandtrade, 2012). This means that there is a substantial labour potential among women. Additionally, many working hours are potentially available among workers aged over 55; the government has therefore set a target of 80 per cent participation for this sector by 2016.

Various measures have been taken to increase the working hours of women. The government has proposed tax measures that would make working outside the home more attractive for women, and in particular for married women. In addition, in 2007, a new Childcare Act made an employer contribution mandatory to assist parents with health insurance payments, and the government makes an income-based contribution towards the cost of childcare. Beginning with the school year 2007–8, school boards were required to ensure that approved childcare was available after school hours. In April 2008, a Part-time Plus Task Force was begun, in an to attempt to identify and eliminate barriers to labour participation by women (Ministry of Economic Affairs, 2008). The government has also made attempts to reduce the pay disparity between men and women, and to encourage employers to promote more women to senior positions (Progress Report, 2007, pp. 44–6).

In addition to part-time employment, the measures of the 1980s stimulated early retirement. Largely because of these retirement schemes, the participation of older people in the labour market fell, so that in 1995 only 13 per cent of women and 39 per cent of men between the ages of 55 and 64 were employed. Participation had risen to 29.5 per cent and 53.8 per cent, respectively, by 2006, but the figures were still low in comparison internationally (OECD, 2008, p. 78). In that year, new legislation came into effect, with the express objective of encouraging people to continue working at older ages, and to discourage early retirement; the government aimed to motivate all workers to continue in employment to at least the age of 65. For 2012, the OECD reported an employment rate for those between the ages of 55 and 64 of 58.6 per cent, compared with the OECD average of 55.6 per cent, but this was still far behind nations such as Iceland, Norway, Sweden, Switzerland, and New Zealand (OECD, 2014). Various measures have been considered, but the most controversial step was taken in July 2012 with the historic decision to raise the age of retirement in steps of one to three months each year until 2023, when retirement will start at the age of 67. Age 65 had remained unchanged as the retirement age since 1957, when government pensions (AOW) were permanently introduced. This new measure will not only help to prevent a shortage of labour, but will also ease problems with Dutch pension schemes. Increasing life expectancy puts greater demands on both the state pension scheme and on private pension funds, but the global financial crisis (see below) has lowered the value of pension funds' investments, and the 'greying' of society results in relatively fewer workers paying AOW premiums for increasing numbers of retired citizens. Raising the age of retirement means that people will pay such premiums for longer and receive pensions for a shorter period.

In addition to the legislation relating to women and older workers, the government has introduced measures to increase employment among what it refers to as 'vulnerable groups', in which it includes 'minorities [and] people who are partially able to work and recipients of social assistance benefit'. In 2009, an earned income tax credit was introduced, which gave those at the lower end of the labour market a greater incentive to accept employment. Employers were also offered a financial incentive for providing employment to those who had not worked for some time. Since 2008, municipalities have been given more possibilities to assist workers to gain experience while retaining their social benefits (Ministry of Economic Affairs, 2008, p. 63).

With the ageing of the population, all measures to increase employment among older citizens and women, as well as those to stimulate full-time rather than part-time employment and to return those with disabilities to the work force, are not seen as being sufficient to compensate for the shrinking labour force. To make up for such losses and to provide for growth, it will be necessary to import workers from other countries. However, as was discussed in Chapter 2, immigration has become a sensitive issue in the Netherlands. The Aliens Act 2000 changed asylum policy and has reduced the influx of asylum seekers. Family-related migration has been reduced by tightening age and income requirements, and by the introduction of language and cultural tests. As a result, in recent years the net flow of migration has dropped and even became negative for 2003 through 2006, before again becoming positive (that is, more immigrants than emigrants) in subsequent years. Although the government now seems to be concentrating more on the problems of integration, which should assist first- and second-generation immigrants to become less dependent on social benefits and improve their position in the labour market, it will probably also have to consider opening its borders, especially to skilled workers.

Global Financial Crisis

Still basking in the glow of 'the Dutch miracle', no one really saw the financial crisis coming, certainly not in the Netherlands. When the new Balkenende IV Cabinet presented its first Budget message in September 2007, it was highly optimistic. It predicted growth rates for 2007 and 2008 of 2.5 per cent or more. The governmental budget was expected to show a surplus in 2008 of 0.5 per cent, rising to 1.0 per cent in 2011. The level of debt would be reduced to 45 per cent of GDP in 2008, and fall to less than 40 per cent in 2011, 'the lowest level in more than thirty years' (State Budget, 2008).

A year later, the Cabinet was still cautiously optimistic that the country was 'well-prepared' for the economic downturn. The international economic unrest would not leave the Netherlands untouched, but

> the Netherlands is nevertheless in a good position. Unemployment in 2008 is very low at 4 per cent and the expectation at the moment is that it will remain stable. Government finances are healthy and revenues and expenditures are developing in line with the goals set down in the Coalition Agreement ... The plans of the Cabinet in the Coalition Agreement can be carried out without alterations. (State Budget, 2009)

Reality hit a year later, however:

> The worldwide crisis has hit the Netherlands hard. The good starting position of the economy has absorbed many blows, but the consequences of the crisis are visible everywhere. 2010 will continue to be a crisis year. (State Budget, 2010)

The crisis began in the USA. High levels of savings in China, Japan and the oil-producing countries led to investment in the USA, lowering interest rates there. Easy credit led US banks to extend mortgage credit to home buyers who would not previously have been able to obtain a mortgage (the 'subprime' mortgages). These mortgages were bundled and 'securitized' and sold around the world. When interest levels increased in 2007, many home owners could no longer afford their payments and were forced to sell or forfeit their property. Banks were forced to write off millions of dollars of loans. Not knowing how much these write-offs would be, banks lost trust in one another, interbank lending declined almost completely, and interest rates rose.

With credit so tight, many companies were unable to obtain loans and world trade fell dramatically. Thus what had begun as an American problem that many Dutch authorities had thought could be contained there, became a world problem. The financial crisis entered the Dutch economy via three channels: 'plummeting global demand, problems with bank balance sheets, and the decline in producer and consumer confidence' (Masselink and van den Noord, 2009, p. 2). As was stressed earlier, the Netherlands has a very open economy, so a decline in international trade had immediate effects on the country. Related to this, Dutch banks were also heavily dependent on external developments. Stock prices fell, and while Dutch households hold relatively modest levels of stocks, pension funds, which are important savings for most households, lost value. Decreases in household wealth and pension fund savings led to lower levels of consumption and the economy went into recession. Because of the crisis of confidence, 'both private consumption and investment suffered more in the Netherlands than in other European countries' (ibid., p. 6).

Although taken by surprise, the government attempted to react, both alone and in cooperation with the European Union. After its cautious optimism in the Budget message of September 2008, in the following month the full effects of the crisis on the Netherlands became clear. In the hectic month of October, a number of drastic measures were taken. After first cooperating with the governments of Belgium and Luxembourg to support the Fortis Bank, the Dutch portion, ABN-AMRO, was nationalized by the Dutch government at a cost of €16.8 billion. It also extended capital of €10 billion to the ING bank and €3 billion to the largest insurer in the country, AEGON. The following month, €750 million was extended to a smaller bank, SNS REAAL, which was eventually nationalized outright in 2013. In October, the government had also attempted to restore confidence in the financial system by raising the guarantee on bank deposits to €100,000, and subsequently extended this guarantee to the 120,000 Dutch investors who had placed their savings in the Icelandic Icesave bank. Those who had lost their savings with this bank were to be reimbursed up to the €100,000 amount.

The illusion of a lasting 'miracle' was dashed in October 2008. Since then, the government has constantly been dealing with this crisis and the crisis of the euro (described below). Rather than the 1 per cent surplus in 2011 that the Cabinet had predicted in 2007, the Budget showed a deficit of 4.7 per cent for that year. Even this was better than the figures for 2009 and 2010, which had deficits exceeding 5 per cent. Rather than paying down the government debt to below 40 per cent, as predicted, the level in 2011 was 65.2 per cent. Thus, for three years in a row, the Netherlands had exceeded European norms (Statistics Netherlands). GDP shrank by 3.5 per cent in 2009, and only by the end of 2011 had it climbed back to pre-crisis levels, meaning it had been at a standstill of four years (CPB, 2012). From the fourth quarter of 2010 through the first quarter of 2013, the economy again shrank (Statistics Netherlands, June 2013). Figures for May 2013 showed that 659,000 people were unemployed – 6.6 per cent of the working population. Even these figures may have underestimated the downturn, however, as many self-employed workers had their hours reduced, but did not register as unemployed (OECD , 2012, p. 4).

The Euro Crisis
To enter the eurozone, countries had to comply with the provisions of the Stability and Growth Pact. However, meeting the deficit requirement of at most 3 per cent, and particularly the debt requirement of no more than 60 per cent of GDP, was difficult, and exceptions were made, including for the Netherlands. Later it was learned that, with the help of American banks, Greece and Italy were able to conceal their true levels of debt to enable them to obtain entry to the eurozone.

The introduction of the euro was done with certain liabilities. The Euro was a monetary union (that is, with a single currency), but not a fiscal union (that is, countries had different tax and pension policies). The fiscal policies of the member countries were expected to converge, but there was no common treasury to ensure this. Moreover, there was no European-wide approach to bank deposit insurance, oversight, or recapitalization of failing banks, that a banking union would have provided. Finally, there were no strong means for enforcement of the provisions of the Stability and Growth Pact.

This weakness quickly became evident when, with some economic downturns in the early years of the twenty-first century, even France and Germany, who had been instrumental in devising the goals, were unable to meet them. Rather than being enforced, the rules were weakened (see Chapter 10). Thus the monetary union was not as strong as it might have been when the major crisis began. When faced with a choice between abandoning the rules or facing economic and financial chaos, countries not surprisingly chose the former. The major industries of Greece – shipping and tourism – were hit hard by the crisis, and the country incurred large deficits and a high debt to GDP ratio. The Irish government was forced to provide guarantees to banks that had over-extended themselves in financing property developers. The Portuguese government had overspent and had a bloated civil service. Spain was hit by high unemployment and problems with the banking industry, as was Cyprus with the latter.

By 2011, 17 EU countries failed to comply with the 3 per cent deficit rule, and 12 had debt ratios greater than 60 per cent, leaving only six in compliance with the Stability and Growth Pact norm (European Commission, 2012). Ireland, Portugal, Spain, and Cyprus were given assistance, but it was Greece that caused the greatest difficulties for the euro countries and posed the greatest threat to the euro itself. There was talk of a 'Grexit' (that is, Greece leaving the euro), but the consequences could have been disastrous for the entire zone. To prevent this from happening, cooperative efforts by the European Commission, the European Central Bank and the International Monetary Fund negotiated a series of bailout operations for Greece. These were made under very serious restrictions that led to considerable social unrest in the country.

To provide financial assistance to the countries in difficulties, the other members of the eurozone had to provide guarantees. If Greece were to default on its financial obligations, the taxpayers of the other countries would have to pay for it. Obviously, the Netherlands had to accept its share of the guarantee obligations, amounting to billions of euros. The Dutch Minister of Finance tried to assure the voters that the loans would be repaid, but this was met with scepticism by the Socialist Party, and in particular by Geert Wilders of the Freedom Party. He stated firmly that he would not provide one cent of assistance to the Greeks.

Meanwhile, the Netherlands itself was faced with a deadline from the European Commission to provide indications of how the country intended to bring its finances within the 3 per cent and 60 per cent guidelines. In the spring of 2012, the government parties (that is, the two coalition partners and the Freedom Party, which had committed itself to supporting them) went into conclave in an attempt to produce a budget for 2013. They met in secret, and though at times it was rumoured that an agreement was close, in the end Geert Wilders backed out, and on 23 April 2013, Prime Minister Rutte submitted the resignation of the Cabinet. As the Netherlands has always been one of the strongest supporters of fiscal responsibility and the imposition of strict regulations on other countries (including, and especially, Greece), this was a potential source of considerable embarrassment. It also threatened to weaken the euro even more, since if the Netherlands could not manage to meet the requirements, how could it expect other countries do so? Almost amazingly, and in the spirit of cooperation that has long typified Dutch politics, three smaller parties (D66, Green Left and the Christian Union) stepped up and within two days had hammered out a package that could be submitted to the European Commission. This, however, was only a temporary measure, since new elections would determine how much of the package would survive.

Consensus and Conflict on Macro-economic Policy

Throughout this book, and especially in Chapter 7, the focus has been on compromise and consensus building in the Netherlands. Without contradicting this basic premise, it should be noted here that this does not mean that there is no disagreement on the macro-economic policies to be followed. Not even all economists are agreed that the strict austerity policies followed by the European Union and the strict limits imposed by the Stability and Growth Pact (now the Fiscal Pact) are the proper response to the financial crisis. The Dutch economy may be a very open one, but it also has a domestic market, and what is good for strengthening the competitiveness of Dutch exports may not be good for domestic consumers and firms dependent on them. Some economists and political parties would argue for a Keynesian approach that would increase investment and cut taxes in order to stimulate the economy. In the Netherlands, this also became an issue in the campaign prior to the election of September 2012. The Liberal Party presented itself as the champion of budget cutting and fiscal responsibility, whereas parties on the left called for more flexibility and greater investment to stimulate economic recovery. As the campaign developed, the race was between the Liberal Party and the Labour

Party to become the largest in Parliament. The Liberal Party won, but the two opponents joined to form the new Cabinet – Rutte II.

The rather unusual formation process, in which exchange was dominant over compromise, has already been mentioned in Chapter 5. In dealing with the economic crisis, the Liberal Party prevailed on the question of budgetary discipline, and the Labour Party agreed to accept the 3 per cent limit on the budget deficit. The Labour Party, in turn, received guarantees that purchasing power, especially of those with lower incomes, would be protected. A new package of budget cuts was agreed, totalling €16 billion. The major provisions in the package included €3.3 billion in raised taxes and premiums, cuts of €5.4 billion in healthcare, €3.2 billion in social welfare, €2.6 billion from public administration, and somewhat surprisingly, €1 billion in development aid.

In attempting to implement these and subsequent cuts, the Cabinet reverted to the time-honoured procedures described in Chapter 7 and in the text above. These followed on from the steps the previous government had taken to reach an accord on pensions and the raising of the age of retirement to 67. This agreement was negotiated in June 2011 by the employers and the trade unions under the auspices of the Foundation of Labour. The new Cabinet Rutte II moved to attempt to reach further agreements, using both the Foundation of Labour and the Social and Economic Council as bases. The most prominent of these has been the Social Accord reached in April 2013. This agreement has been compared by some to the Wassenaar Accord of 1982. Employers and trade unions agreed to a package of measures to prevent unemployment levels from rising further. In that same month, a healthcare accord was reached, though in this case the trade union for public employees did not agree. In July 2013, an energy accord was reached between the government, employers, unions, and environmental organizations that included measures that would allow the Netherlands to reach the level of 14 per cent renewable energy, as required by the European Union.

In negotiating these agreements, the government has attempted to follow the Dutch pattern of consensus building. This is obviously done in order to create as broad a support base as possible, thereby reducing potential social unrest resulting from unpopular measures. The situation was made even more difficult for the Cabinet when, in May 2013, the European Commission demanded additional cuts in order to reach the 3 per cent level for 2014. Lacking a majority in the First Chamber, the Cabinet negotiated with the opposition parties D66, Christian Union, and SGP to provide a package of cuts that could achieve support in both Chambers of Parliament. In November 2013, European Commissioner Olli Rehn announced his approval of the package, even though it was likely that the Netherlands would still not get its deficit below 3 per cent in 2014. The attempt to comply with European norms, avoid social unrest, and develop policies that will not affect the electoral position of the partners in the Cabinet adversely is the challenge facing the government.

In its 2012 Economic Survey of the Netherlands, the OECD formulated a number of specific challenges that the government must face. Government finances should be brought under control to give confidence and comply with the rules of the Stability and Growth Pact. The government should provide conditions that will allow companies to be innovative in order to continue to profit from the globalization of the economy. Steps should be taken to reform employment protection, so that the labour market can become more flexible and resources can be made as productive as possible. The labour reserves (women, older workers, and those with disabilities) should be mobilized further. The government must also act to bring the rising expenditure on healthcare under control (OECD , 2012).

10

Foreign Policy

'Constants' in Dutch Foreign Policy

Peace, Profits and Principles is the catchy, alliterative title of a book on Dutch foreign policy by Joris Voorhoeve (1979), scholar-politician and one-time Minister of Defence (1994–8). Under these three headings he sought to analyse the major traditions of Dutch foreign policy, which he described as 'maritime commercialism', 'neutralist abstentionism' and 'internationalist idealism'. Others have objected to the concept of traditions in this respect, even arguing that the Dutch have insufficient historic sense for traditions. Such authors prefer to speak of tendencies, themes or constants, and some of them have amended or enlarged Voorhoeve's list. On closer inspection, however, the themes mentioned by other authors remain closely related to the clusters of attitudes mentioned by Voorhoeve (Heldring, 1978; Scheffer, 1988; Hellema, 2010; Hellema et al., 2011; Knapen et al., 2011). There is also very little disagreement concerning the origins of such tendencies or traditions.

Both the size and geographical location of the country have left their imprint on its external relations. The Dutch domestic market being quite small, but located ideally to serve as a gateway to the European hinterland, the Netherlands came to rely on maritime trade (see Chapter 9). This brought an Atlantic perspective to its foreign policy, sometimes bordering on anti-continentalism. In the seventeenth century, Pieter de la Court, a Leiden merchant and political scientist, even advocated cutting a wide swath of water to the east of the province of Holland to separate it from the European continent. As late as the 1950s, the Dutch Foreign Office proclaimed: 'The Netherlands cannot exist without Europe, but it is a continental European nation neither in its history, nor in its character.' This attitude was also recognized abroad, as when French Foreign Minister Maurice Couve de Murville was reported to have explained to his US counterpart that:

> The Netherlands was an island in the same sense that the United Kingdom was an island. The Dutch had never really been interested in Europe, always looking out over the waters at other areas of the world … [T]hey were not Europeans – at least they were not continental Europeans – as were the French and the Germans. (Quoted in Reyn, 2009, p. 414)

Despite early altercations with the British, and later irritation over American pressure to decolonize and restructure its armed forces, the Netherlands continued to rely on these two powers outside the European continent. This reliance is a result partly of the importance of maritime trade, but also of the desire to have a countervailing power to the dominant state on the continent, be it Germany or France.

The significance of trade for the Dutch economy has also led to Voorhoeve's second tradition, 'neutralist abstentionism'. The Dutch colonial empire could not be defended adequately, and was therefore best protected by a neutralist policy. The flow of commerce was best served by an opportunistic abstention from European power politics. Any disturbance of the balance of power could be detrimental to trade, and was therefore deplored. After the Second World War, the failure of neutralism as a security strategy was recognized by Dutch politicians and the public alike, and joining the Atlantic Alliance has been interpreted as an unequivocal abandonment of the neutralist tradition. Other observers, however, maintain that NATO membership constitutes less of a break with tradition than it might seem at first sight. When the international status quo was no longer guaranteed by a Pax Britannica, the Dutch supported a Pax Americana. Both the old and the new situations in which the Dutch found themselves allowed them an '*afzijdigheid in afhankelijkheid*' [aloofness in dependence] (Scheffer, 1988):

> membership in a Western bloc, dominated by one superpower has permitted a continuation of traditional Dutch neutrality within a new framework and has relieved them of the need to develop an ambitious foreign policy of their own. (Bodenheimer, 1978, p. 251)

The third of Voorhoeve's constants in Dutch foreign policy, 'internationalist idealism' in the words of Voorhoeve, is attributed to the Calvinist church minister in every Dutchman, rather than to the merchant in him. Especially when this idealism transforms the Dutch government into a Dutch uncle, wagging an admonishing finger at other nations, the relation with Calvinist moralism is too obvious to miss. The same can be said of another manifestation of internationalist idealism, the emphasis on international law. Article 90 of the Constitution even charges the government with the promotion of 'the development of the international rule of law'. Such legalism is not entirely alien to Calvinist culture, but often, however, minister and merchant have gone hand in hand. Ever since Hugo Grotius, the content of international law has rarely failed to serve the Dutch interest in free trade and open sea passages. The Dutch interest in neutralist abstention from power politics is easily disguised as moralism.

In this chapter we shall take a closer look at these three clusters of supposedly constant foreign policy preferences, by examining the Dutch role in three international organizations. Dutch politicians and pundits never seem to tire of debating whether the Netherlands is the largest of Europe's small countries, or the smallest of the large countries. When discussing at the beginning of this book how small a country the Netherlands is, we could have noted that it is large in terms of membership of international organizations: '[T]here was hardly a combination of capital letters of which the Netherlands did not eagerly become a member' (Van Der Beugel, 1995, p. 120). The three most important of these acronyms are also most suited to a discussion of the three 'constants' in the foreign policy of the country: NATO ('peace'), the EU ('profits') and the UN ('principles').

Farewell to Atlanticism?

The Dutch decision to join the Atlantic Alliance was opposed only by the Communist Party, and has never been seriously questioned. The original support for NATO should be understood against the backdrop of anxiety over Soviet imperialism, fuelled in particular by the Communist takeover in Czechoslovakia in 1948. Gratitude for the American effort to liberate the Netherlands in 1945 and for Marshall Plan aid for rebuilding the ruined Dutch economy also played a part, tempered only marginally by anger over American pressure to end the successful military actions against Indonesian insurgents or to rebuild and restructure the armed forces (Mallinson, 2010).

Despite later criticisms of NATO membership of the then dictatorial regimes of Portugal and Greece, despite opposition to American involvement in Indo-China and Latin America, and even despite misgivings over NATO's nuclear strategy, public support for NATO membership has never wavered – at the height of the controversy over NATO's nuclear weapons, the percentage in favour of leaving the Alliance did not exceed 20 per cent (Everts, 1983, p. 30), and no major party has ever advocated withdrawal from NATO, not even a partial, 'French', one. During the first decades of the Alliance, the Netherlands acted as a particularly staunch ally and a loyal supporter of US leadership in the Alliance.

The Dutch share in NATO's defence expenditure has been relatively high compared with that of other smaller member states (Voorhoeve, 1979, pp. 130–1; Honig, 1993). The Dutch were among the 15 countries that joined the USA in the Korean War (a UN mission *de jure,* but *de facto* a US mission). In 1957, the Netherlands wasted no time in becoming the first European ally to accept American nuclear missiles on its territory. While other member states demanded a say in the engagement of such weaponry ('dual key'), the Dutch were happy to leave this responsibility entirely to the US government. A new quarrel with the Americans over Dutch colonialism, this time about the Dutch–Indonesian conflict over New Guinea in 1961–2, did little to weaken Dutch enthusiasm for the Atlantic Alliance. This is evidenced, for example, in the steadfast refusal of long-time Foreign Minister Joseph Luns (1956–71) to convey to Washington the protests of the Dutch Parliament over American intervention in Vietnam. As will be seen in the next section, the Dutch government long objected to plans for European rather than Atlantic defence arrangements, and served almost as an American proxy in the European Union. One author even struggled to find a distinction between the Dutch role of faithful ally and that of a vassal or satellite state: the submission of the Dutch to American leadership, he suggested, was not imposed, but voluntary! (Van Staden, 1978, p. 153).

The Atlantic orientation of Dutch foreign policy apparently weakened between 1970 and 1985. After the retirement of Luns as Minister of Foreign Affairs in 1971, the Dutch government had fewer misgivings about decrying US overt and covert involvement in Latin America, and in Vietnam in particular. Over strong US objections, the Netherlands supported the acceptance of the People's Republic of China as a member of the UN in 1971. In 1975, the Dutch even targeted Cuba as one of the countries on which to concentrate its development aid. However, the most important purported example of a change in Dutch foreign policy in this period was an increased emphasis on arms control, and in particular on a reduction of nuclear weapons. The proposal by the US Carter administration in 1977–8 to introduce the 'neutron bomb' (or the 'enhanced radiation, reduced blast' weapon as it was officially called) served to mobilize a large portion of the population into what became known as the 'peace movement', a loose coalition of left-wing political parties, trade unions, fringe groups and individuals, dominated by two organizations linked to the churches in the Netherlands, the Catholic Pax Christi and the Interchurch Peace Council (IKV). The fact that President Carter decided to shelve the plans for the neutron bomb was interpreted by the peace movement as a victory, and reinforced its resolve when, only a year later, in 1979, NATO decided on the modernization of the alliance's intermediate-range theatre nuclear weapons. As part of those plans, the Netherlands was to accept the stationing of 48 cruise and Pershing II missiles on Dutch territory.

That proposal sparked what became probably the greatest political controversy over foreign policy since decolonization. Unprecedentedly large demonstrations (each of around half a million participants) against the missiles took place, in Amsterdam in 1981 and in The Hague in 1983. The following year, 3.2 million Dutch citizens petitioned the government to reject NATO's nuclear modernization. Surveys consistently showed that the majority of the population were opposed to the missiles. The main political parties were divided internally, though officially the VVD welcomed NATO's plans, and the PvdA opposed them. For the newly formed CDA, however, the situation was most threatening because of the involvement of the churches in the peace movement. In the absence of consensus, immobilism is often the result, and this case proved no exception. The Dutch government announced formal reservations to the NATO plans in what became known as 'the Dutch footnote' to the protocol of the NATO meeting (on the government's internal decision-making, see Kaarbo, 2012, pp. 92–100). The Dutch were granted a two-year delay to determine their position, but this proved insufficient and further postponements were necessary. Eventually, the Dutch position within NATO became untenable, and in 1984 Prime Minister Lubbers presented a compromise that must be one of the most ingenuous depoliticization ploys in the history of consociationalism. A final decision to accept or refuse the American missiles was to be postponed by one more year. If by 1 November 1985 the Soviets had not increased the number of their SS-20 missiles, the Dutch would refuse to accept the cruise missiles, whereas any increase in the number of SS-20s would lead to automatic acceptance of the US missiles. In practice, this clever manoeuvre shifted responsibility for Dutch foreign policy to the Kremlin. After a year, the Soviets appeared to have added to their number of missiles, and without any significant protest it was decided to accept the American weapons. Shortly afterwards, however, Mikhail Gorbachev and Ronald Reagan reached an arms reduction agreement, making the Netherlands the only NATO country to accept the cruise missiles, but where they were never deployed.

It was this episode in particular that led to the diagnosis of 'Hollanditis', a supposedly contagious Dutch disease (Laqueur, 1981). Laqueur and others speculated about a re-emergence of neutralism in Dutch foreign policy, now that both gratitude for American aid and fear of Soviet expansionism had waned. Such a diagnosis is valid only if it is accepted that the penchant for neutralist abstentionism disappeared when the Netherlands joined the Atlantic Alliance. If, on the other hand, we agree with the view that NATO only provided the security umbrella under which the Dutch could continue to foster their aloofness from power politics, the Dutch misgivings about nuclear weapons and American foreign policy cannot be interpreted in this way.

We need not go deeply into the merits of the Hollanditis diagnosis, however, because the end of the cruise missiles controversy also signalled the end of this period: the peace movement all but disappeared and the foreign policy consensus was restored. The continuation of the Atlantic orientation showed itself in such decisions as the removal of Cuba from the list of recipients of Dutch development aid; the unquestioned participation in the US-led coalition in the Gulf War in 1990–1 (when the near-unanimity in the Dutch Parliament contrasted starkly with the divisions in the US Senate); the commitment of Dutch F-16 planes during NATO's bombing campaign in the Kosovo crisis in 1999 and so on.

In all likelihood there has hardly been a deviation from Atlanticism in the intervening years. Yet it should be remembered that, to the extent that there are foreign policy traditions, they are traditions of the Dutch foreign policy elite, not of the general public. More than other policy areas, foreign policy has always been in the hands of a small, close-knit establishment. In general, foreign policy has not been the subject of conflicts between the political parties, with a few notable exceptions (such as rows over a Dutch embassy to the Holy See in the 1920s, for example). Foreign policy-making was also never embedded in a neo-corporatist network of interest groups and advisory councils; in many respects it was the last remnant of a nineteenth-century style of politics: elitist and non-partisan. This changed abruptly in the late 1960s and early 1970s, however. In Chapter 2 we saw how depillarization at first seemed to change the policy-making style, with politicization, polarization, and a call for more citizen involvement. In the field of foreign policy this resulted in more partisan proposals for the Netherlands' external relations, especially by the Labour Party, and by more vocal and visible 'action groups' seeking to change the country's foreign policy. The Dutch foreign-policy elite was not used to domestic critique, and may have reacted at first with uncertainty, but while the official rhetoric became more neutralist, the reality was not affected very much. After all, the cuts in the Dutch defence budget in the mid-1970s, which have often been used as evidence of Hollanditis, were no greater than in many other NATO countries. On the contrary, in fact, the relative contribution of the Netherlands to NATO defence expenditure increased slightly during the 1970s, whereas that of countries such as the USA or the UK decreased during that period (Voorhoeve, 1979, p. 130).

The end of the Cold War has probably weakened Dutch Atlanticism, even though the effect is only slowly being felt. The collapse of the Soviet threat has eroded NATO's *raison d'être*, and while the Netherlands remains committed to NATO and its eastward enlargement, it, like other countries in the Alliance, has been forced to rethink its foreign and defence policies. The most important change has been a shift from the defence of Western Europe (and the north German plains in particular) to participation in peacekeeping missions around the globe. This change allows for both a reduction in the size of the armed forces, especially of the army (all battle tank regiments have been abolished, for example), and the development of small, self-contained units that can be deployed rapidly. One of the immediate consequences of this reorientation has been the abolition of conscription and an abrupt transition to a purely professional military. The traditional boundaries between army, navy, and air force are also blurred because of this development, as all were brought under the direct control of a single chief of staff. The shift to an expeditionary force fits with NATO's new strategy also to play a role 'out-of-area', but the emphasis on peacekeeping and promoting the international legal order also increased the salience of the UN in Dutch security policy.

In addition, Dutch Atlanticism was no longer promoted as strongly by the USA. The end of the Cold War has led to a declining interest of the USA in Europe as the most likely theatre for a conflict with the former Soviet Union. As a result, the USA has become less jealous of other forms of defence cooperation in Europe. European defence cooperation became a more viable option with the 1998 St Malo agreement between France and the UK to give the EU a military capacity. If the UK, America's staunchest ally, was giving up NATO's monopoly over security policy, the Netherlands had no choice but to follow (Van Staden 2011, p. 18). Today, the Atlantic Alliance is no longer mentioned as *the* cornerstone of Dutch security policy; it has to share this role with the EU.

Yet these shifts to the UN and the EU should not be overestimated. As we shall see below, the Dutch experience in Srebrenica, Bosnia and Herzegovina, has made Dutch policy-makers wary of UN peacekeeping missions with their vague terms of engagement and poor command structures. From that perspective, the ideal situation for the Dutch is a UN mission carried out by NATO, such as the ISAF (International Security Assistance Force) mission in Afghanistan (see Box 10.1). The EU's common security and defence policy has been slow to develop. There have been a limited number of EU peacekeeping missions (the largest being in Chad and the Central African Republic in 2008–09), mostly under UN auspices, and the number of battle-groups that can be deployed readily is still small.

As a result, 'Atlanticism' may have lost its geo-political anchoring, but it has not yet disappeared (Van Staden, 2011). Even the adoption by the US Congress in 2002 of the 'The Hague Invasion Act' (officially titled the American Service-Members'

Protection Act), allowing for the use of force to liberate US citizens from Dutch prisons if they were detained to stand trial before the International Criminal Court, has hardly caused a stir. The choice for the American Joint Strike Fighter over European competitors to replace the F-16 fighter planes also shows a continued Atlantic orientation. Gradually, however, 'Atlanticism' is no longer a part of a foreign policy consensus, but is contested between the VVD, the small Protestant parties and part of the CDA on the one hand, and Labour, D66, and GreenLeft on the other (not counting the largely isolationist populist parties of the left and right). The fact that, prior to the invasion of Iraq, the outgoing Dutch government limited itself to political and not military support was a result of the formation of a new government of CDA and Labour. When this coalition did not come about, Dutch ground forces were deployed in the Iraqi province of al Mutanna (Kaarbo, 2012, pp.100–08). In 2010, an inquiry into the decision-making surrounding the Dutch involvement in Iraq concluded that the Dutch government's 'Atlantic reflexes' (Davids Committee, 2010, p. 426) had prematurely precluded a search for a European response and had led to ignoring both aspects of international law and doubts of the Dutch intelligence services about the existence of Iraqi weapons of mass destruction. That 'Atlanticism' has become contested is also illustrated Dutch decision-making over deploying troops in Afghanistan (see Box 10.1)

BOX 10.1

Dutch Domestic Politics and Afghanistan

The domestication of Dutch foreign policy is amply illustrated by the decision-making over Dutch involvement in Afghanistan in the aftermath of the US-led invasion of that country in 2001, after 9/11. At first, the Dutch role was limited: a few F-16 fighter planes and navy frigates, and later also special forces. In 2005, a large contingent of ground troops was asked to take the lead in the UN-initiated NATO mission in the province of Uruzgan, a Taliban stronghold, for two years (2006–08). It was the first time that public opinion research had found no majority support in the population for a military mission (Everts, 2008, pp. 164–81). The Dutch military intelligence service reported that Uruzgan was too dangerous a region for a mission that was to concentrate on nation-building (Kaarbo 2012, p. 110). Nevertheless, within the ruling Balkenende II government, CDA and VVD – the two most Atlanticist of the major parties, were in favour of deployment. This was different for the third party in the coalition, D66, at least for that party's parliamentary party. For that more Europeanist than Atlanticist party, the intelligence reports were too much of a reminder of the 'mission impossible' on which Dutch troops had been sent to Bosnia, leading to the Srebrenica debacle in 1995. The party's spokesperson, MP Bert Bakker, had previously chaired the parliamentary inquiry into Srebrenica. But strategic considerations also played a role. D66 had alienated many of its moderate supporters by joining a right-wing coalition of the CDA and VVD. In defence of its participation in that government, it could

→

→

point to two major constitutional reforms (regarded as the 'crown jewels' for D66) that CDA and VVD had reluctantly agreed to support in return: popularly elected mayors and an electoral reform introducing districts. But earlier in 2005, the constitutional amendment allowing the popular election of mayors failed to achieve the required two-thirds majority in the Senate when the opposition Labour Party voted against. When subsequent discussions within the coalition showed that support for the electoral reform proposal was crumbling, the cabinet minister responsible, D66 leader Thom De Graaf, resigned. D66 stayed in the coalition, but it was now in search of an issue with which to raise its own profile. Taking the lead in the opposition against the unpopular Uruzgan mission provided a timely opportunity, and D66 threatened to bring down the cabinet unless the request for troops was denied. It proved to be a costly miscalculation: the threat of a cabinet crisis led to a conflict between D66's ministers and its parliamentary party. Moreover, the opposition Labour Party became convinced by NATO's contingency plans that fears of another Srebrenica were unfounded. Previously, Labour had not supported the more limited deployment of Dutch forces in Afghanistan, and its leader, Wouter Bos, explained his party's position in a 2006 interview: 'I believe that the future of Dutch foreign policy is very much within European foreign policy, and that's where we should go first to find our partners. We shouldn't, almost without any type of criticism, follow the Americans whenever they ask us something – which I am sad to say has been the pattern of the last few years in the Netherlands' (cited in Kaarbo, 2012, p.111; see also Kaarbo and Cantir, 2013). Labour motivated its change of heart with Dutch commitment to 'international solidarity', but it was also rumoured that the desire to be regarded as a reliable future coalition partner may have played a role (Kaarbo, 2012, p. 117). Labour's support secured a parliamentary majority for the mission. D66 then reneged on its promise to pull out of the coalition and its parliamentary leader, Boris Dittrich, resigned, plunging the party into a crisis. A few months later, D66 brought down the government, but on an unrelated issue.

One lesson of Srebrenica had not been learned in the decision-making over Uruzgan: to have guarantees about succession at the end of the mission's agreed duration. Labour had limited its support to one two-year mission, but no NATO country volunteered to take over the role of the Dutch forces as 'lead nation'. In 2007, pressure mounted to stay for another two years. While Dutch public opinion had never rallied around the flag once it was planted in Uruzgan, the government – now of CDA, Labour, and Christian Union – decided to continue Task Force Uruzgan until 2008, albeit with a slightly larger contribution from other countries. For the Labour Party this was a difficult decision, and at its insistence, the decision explicitly mentioned that the mission would definitely end in 2010.

In 2009, however, Foreign Affairs Minister Verhagen (CDA) made public statements to the effect that there was room to discuss another extension. Labour and Christian Union tried to put a stop to any speculation about a third mandate by introducing a parliamentary motion reminding the government of the agreement to pull out in 2010. The motion received broad support in Parliament, except from CDA, the small, orthodox SGP, and D66(!). Diplomatic cables later made public by WikiLeaks show

→

→

that intense pressure was put on the Labour leader, Finance Minister Wouter Bos, to agree to yet another extension. High-ranking civil servants working for minister Verhagen and Prime Minister Balkenende even asked American diplomats to help them turn their Cabinet colleague Bos – for example, by suggesting that the US Secretary to the Treasury should tell Bos that the Netherlands would no longer be invited to G20 meetings if it did not renew the Uruzgan mission (Gijswijt, 2011, p. 44), but ultimately such efforts had no effect. To agree to stay in Uruzgan after originally limiting the mission to two years, and after reluctantly extending it for a final period of two years, would be too much of a loss of face for Labour domestically, and for the Netherlands internationally. The fact that its refusal to change its mind would put the coalition at risk was no longer a major concern for Labour: cooperation within the coalition was difficult, and the government was unpopular. On 19–20 February 2010, the government fell and the Netherlands announced its withdrawal from Uruzgan.

That was not the end of the Dutch involvement in Afghanistan, however. In 2010, the Rutte I government proposed a police-training mission in the Northern province of Kunduz. Together with armed forces to protect the trainers, its 500-odd personnel were about a third of the number involved in Task Force Uruzgan. The Freedom Party, which was part of the parliamentary majority supporting the government (see Chapter 5), was opposed to the mission, as was the opposition Labour Party. CDA and VVD received support from D66, Green Left and Christian Union, which became known as 'the Kunduz coalition'. For CDA and VVD, the mission was to show NATO that the Netherlands continued to contribute to the alliance's 'out-of-area' operations, but for the three support parties it was important that 'Kunduz' was a contribution to building a *Rechtsstaat* in Afghanistan. This proved to be a difficult combination, with the Afghan government being forced to promise that policemen trained by the Dutch would not be involved in military operations, etc. Green Left may have hoped that joining the Kunduz coalition would be a prelude to joining a governing coalition, but it merely led to internal unrest, a disastrous result in the 2012 elections, and the dismissal of the party leader. The Kunduz mission started in 2011 and was supposed to last until 2014, but in July 2013 it was quietly terminated when Germany, the 'lead nation' in Kunduz, decided to leave.

The more than ten years of Dutch involvement in Afghanistan have come at a heavy cost in terms of casualties (25), in terms of impact on the Dutch armed forces, and financially. It is too early to assess its lasting accomplishments, if any. But the decision making surrounding the Uruzgan and Kunduz missions show how interrelated domestic coalition politics and foreign policy have become.

A European Turnaround?

Until the 2005 referendum on the EU Constitutional Treaty (see Box 10.2), the Dutch had a reputation for being enthusiastic subscribers to the ideal of an integrated Europe. In a Europe of multiple speeds, the Netherlands always chose the highest gear, whether it was with regard to the abolition of border controls (Schengen) or to monetary policy (the euro). The differences between the major political parties in terms of their support for European integration and EU enlargement were negligible. Public opinion in the Netherlands always seemed to be consistently among the most pro-integration in the Union (Everts, 2008). To the surprise of political leaders both at home and abroad, Dutch voters clearly rejected the EU constitutional treaty in 2005. It would be too easy to dismiss this referendum result as having to do more with either the unpopularity of the incumbent government, or with the post-Fortuyn populist mood of the voters than with the EU, but studies have shown that, while the details of the constitution may not have been the primary bone of contention, voting 'no' was clearly associated with concerns about the EU rather than with domestic criticism. If a

---

BOX 10.2

The Dutch 'No' to the EU Constitution

After first jolting the political establishment in The Hague by giving the List Pim For-tuyn (LPF) 26 seats in Parliament in 2002, the electorate created a second shockwave by turning out in high numbers (63.3 per cent) to soundly defeat the 'Treaty Establish-ing a Constitution for the European Union' on 1 June 2005.

In some ways this second shockwave was a result of the first. Various attempts to write the referendum instrument into the Constitution had failed, and a temporary ref-erendum act expired in January 2005 (see Chapter 4). It was thus rather surprising that the VVD joined the traditionally pro-referendum parties PvdA, Green Left, D66, SP and the populist Right to form a parliamentary majority that passed special legislation calling for an advisory referendum on the EU Constitutional treaty, leaving only the Christian parties CDA, CU, and SGP opposed. It is hard to avoid the conclusion that the uncer-tainty and insecurity that overcame the political elite after the 2002 election contributed to their willingness to seek the advice of the voters on the European Constitution.

The hope was, apparently, that by calling a referendum they could give the impres-sion of listening to the voters, who would in turn validate their intentions: one of the explicit aims of the referendum was to 'increase societal support for the parliamentary ratification of the EU Constitutional Treaty' (Crum, 2007, p. 18). This hope was based on the fact that an overwhelming majority of MPs (128 out of 150) favoured ratifica-tion, and that early opinion polls showed that more than 70 per cent of Dutch citizens supported a constitution for Europe (Aarts and Van Der Kolk, 2006, p. 243). No one seemed fully prepared for the direction that the referendum took.

With no experience in holding referendums, no one took the lead in rallying support for the treaty, and the initiative went to the opposition. The Socialist Party was the earliest to begin its campaign, and was in the forefront of opposition until the day of the vote. The Christian Union achieved some of its first prominence when joining the opposition. On the Right, the various heirs to Pim Fortuyn also opposed the treaty, but they were in too much disarray to play a leading role. When the constitution's support-ers were finally aware of the situation, they resorted to scare tactics (the lights would

→

more general malaise in Dutch democracy also played a part, it is because the preparation, content and selling of the treaty epitomized for many the elitist character of Dutch politics: 'this reinforced existing sentiments of estrangement between the electorate and the political establishment' (Crum, 2007, p. 24).

Since the referendum, the Dutch government has felt forced by public sentiment to assume a Eurosceptic position. It now emphasizes subsidiarity, opposes further enlargement in practice, never ceases to complain about its net contribution to the EU budget, seeks to postpone giving citizens of new Eastern European member states access to the Dutch labour market, and is most hard-hearted in the conditions it wants to have attached to rescue packages for the Greek economy.

→

go out in The Netherlands after a 'no' vote, warned one cabinet minister; peace in Europe would be at risk, added another) that proved to be counterproductive (Nijeboer, 2005). Moreover, as the voters learned more about the content of the proposed constitution, they also became more opposed to it. Disaster could no longer be averted. The only thing saving the major parties from total humiliation was the rejection of the treaty by French voters three days prior to the Dutch vote.

Studies showed a variety of motivations associated with the 'no' vote. One complaint was about lack of information, not so surprising since the electorate had hardly been informed about European developments over the previous half century, and merely sending each voter a summary of the proposed constitution hardly filled the need. It was also clear that the referendum had come too soon after the introduction of the euro currency in 2002, which voters felt had led to price increases and in general had not been favourable to the Dutch economy. Likewise, it came too soon after the largest expansion of the EU, when ten new countries joined in 2004. Many voters were concerned that small member states would lose influence, and that jobs would be relocated to countries where labour was cheaper. Some even feared a loss of language, culture, and identity. Finally, there was a feeling that the Netherlands was paying too much to the EU, and that the Constitution would not increase prosperity (Aarts and Van Der Kolk, 2006; Nijeboer, 2005). Not surprisingly, voters for the parties that opposed the treaty overwhelmingly rejected the Constitution, but Labour voters also voted strongly against, while Liberal and CDA voters were fairly evenly split. Only supporters of D66 turned out a clear majority favouring ratification (Aarts and Van Der Kolk, 2006, p. 246).

Though the referendum had been advisory, most parties had committed themselves to accepting the result, and with such a clear message, the ratification was not even put to a vote in Parliament. The government used the referendum result to obtain a reduction in the Dutch contribution to the EU, and it pushed for the new Treaty of Lisbon, from which every reference to a constitution was removed and in which subsidiarity was given more prominence. This was sufficient for the Labour Party, now in government, to drop its earlier insistence on a new referendum. Somewhat surprisingly, forgoing a new referendum has not led to an outcry among the electorate. Just as the first shock of 2002, the second shock does not seem to have led to any long-lasting change of the political system.

This diagnosis of a dramatic Dutch turnaround with regard to European integration is an exaggeration, however. Actually, the reputation for being among the most enthusiastic proponents of integration is based on only a relatively short period: from 1973 to 1991. After the Second World War, the importance of Germany, with its spectacular recovery, for the Dutch economy constituted a new reality that the Netherlands was reluctant to accept (Segers, 2013). When the European Coal and Steel Community (ECSC) was set up, the Dutch were taken by surprise and strongly objected to a supranational authority, whereas supranationality was later to become one of the characteristic Dutch desires in Brussels. Another source of hesitation was even more curious – fear by all major parties except the Catholic KVP of a papist Europe. This fear even had an impact on the composition of the 1952–56 cabinet. In Chapter 2 we noted that in 1952 the portfolio of Foreign Affairs fell to the KVP, but that the other parties balked at the prospect of all the Foreign Ministers in the European Community being Catholic. As a compromise, a non-partisan Minister of Foreign Affairs, the banker Johan Willem Beyen, was appointed, and the Catholic diplomat Joseph Luns became Minister without Portfolio, with the right to call himself Foreign Minister when abroad. Ironically, it was the Catholic Luns who turned out to be a staunch Atlanticist, and Beyen who became one of the founding fathers of the European Community (Mallinson, 2010, pp. 205–7). The latter succeeded, together with Belgium's Minister of Foreign Affairs, Paul-Henri Spaak, in laying the foundation of the EC Treaty after attempts at a European Defence Community and a European Political Community had foundered in 1954.

Beyen was more enthusiastic about European integration than most of his colleagues in the Dutch government. Once initial hesitations about a Vatican conspiracy had been overcome, two important reservations about European integration remained: a rejection of domination by one or more of the larger member states, and a continued emphasis on Atlantic cooperation in the areas of defence and foreign policy. The fear of a directorate of larger countries – Germany, or a Franco-German coalition – made the Dutch into proponents of widening the Community by including more countries, but it was translated primarily into proposals to strengthen the supranational institutions of the Community: the Commission, the Court, and the European Parliament.

This emphasis on supranationalism is sometimes mistaken for a sign of enthusiastic support for European integration. Paradoxically, it was actually a form of protection of national interests. Because of his supranationalist attitude, a Dutch Minister of Foreign Affairs was once criticized by the opposition as 'a covert apostle of national sovereignty' (quoted in Hellema, 1995, p. 321). Countries such as the Netherlands, it was felt, are too small to exert influence in an intergovernmental power game. Supranational bodies, on the other hand, are likely to pursue pan-European interests, and such interests are deemed to be more compatible with Dutch interests than are specific German, French, or even British, interests. Thus supranationalism became a preoccupation of the Dutch within Europe, from the near-unanimous motion in the Second Chamber to transfer powers to supranationalist institutions in 1948, to the conflict in 1991 between the Netherlands as

temporary chair of the EU and most other member states regarding supranationalist tendencies in a Dutch draft for the Maastricht Treaty. The Dutch support for
a directly elected European Parliament with real powers is another example of the
supranationalist preference.

Officially, the Dutch have always worried about the 'European democratic
deficit': decision-making increasingly shifts to Brussels, where it is outside the
purview of national Parliaments without similar scrutiny by the European Parliament. This gap in democratic accountability should be filled by a competent European Parliament. The introduction of direct elections to the European Parliament,
first held in 1979, was celebrated as a Dutch victory for democracy. Turnout for
these elections was low everywhere, but it was particularly low in the Netherlands
(see Chapter 4). This has not helped much in giving the supranational Parliament
democratic legitimacy, but the low turnout has only strengthened the resolve of the
Dutch government to push for more powers for the European Parliament, claiming
that the low turnout was caused by a reluctance to vote for a third-rate legislature. It
is difficult to ascertain to what degree this concern for European democracy is real,
or whether it has merely served as a flag of convenience under which to strengthen
the supranational character of the Community.

Whichever explanation is the correct one, it should be emphasized that the
campaign for supranationalism has generally taken second place to the Atlantic
orientation in Dutch European policy. The Dutch attitude is epitomized by Foreign
Minister Joseph Luns' finest hour: his 'no' to Charles de Gaulle's aspirations in
1961–2. In 1960, the French President announced his proposals for a European political union, which included taking over some of NATO's military responsibilities,
and in which European institutions would be controlled firmly by intergovernmental
bodies. Because France was the only nuclear power within the Europe of the original
six member states, and De Gaulle's suggestion that the new political union's secretariat would be located in Paris, provided sufficient fuel for concerns of a Gaullist
Europe. This anxiety, the lack of supranational elements in the proposal, and the challenge to America's leadership of the alliance by the formation of a French-led European defence bloc within NATO, all ran counter to established Dutch foreign policy
precepts. All other member states apart from the Netherlands agreed to underwrite the
French plans. Luns demanded that the political union should not affect NATO, and
that it should develop supranational institutions. He was willing to drop these conditions, however, provided that the United Kingdom be included.

This last element, which became known as the Dutch *Préalable Anglais*, is
interesting, since it shows that, for the Netherlands, Atlanticism took priority over
supranationalism. Because of its special relationship with the USA, British accession to the Community would provide the Dutch with a powerful ally in promoting
an Atlantic orientation within the EU. At the same time, it was well-known
that the British were (and still are) exceedingly wary of transferring any of their
national sovereignty to a supranational organization. The Dutch could not hope to
find support for their plans from British membership of the community. After the
inconclusive 1961 summit, the Dutch were gradually forced to accept compromise

proposals, and they might have lost their struggle had not De Gaulle 'snatched defeat from the jaws of victory' by rejecting the compromises, reverting to his original plan and vetoing British membership. In 1962, the Netherlands (now joined by Belgium) once again, and this time definitely, vetoed the proposals.

It was only after the UK eventually joined the Community in 1973 that the Netherlands wholeheartedly embraced European integration. The Dutch also became less opposed to a common 'EU' foreign policy because they learnt from the 1973 Arab oil embargo that it can be risky to stand alone. Before 1973, the Netherlands had a strongly pro-Israel reputation, perhaps not always warranted by its actual policies (Soetendorp, 1989). The Arab countries took particular offence at the Dutch adherence to the English version of resolution 242 of the UN Security Council, calling for Israeli withdrawal from 'occupied territories', rather than 'the occupied territories' mentioned in some other versions. When war broke out in the Middle East in 1973, the Dutch government unequivocally condemned the Arab countries, just as it had done in 1967. It refused to join the other 'EU' member states in a common reaction, because of the more pro-Arab attitude of the French in particular, and it secretly supplied considerable quantities of ammunition, spare parts and weapons to Israel (Hellema, 2010, p. 273). In retaliation, in October 1973 the Arab countries imposed an oil embargo not only on the USA, but also on the Netherlands, and the embargo on the Netherlands was kept in place four months longer than that on the USA. Despite panicky reactions at first – to save oil, 'car-free Sundays' were declared! – the economic effect of the embargo was insignificant because oil was diverted from other 'EU' countries to the Netherlands, despite irritations over the wayward position of the Dutch in this conflict. The political effect has been more important. Not only has the Dutch policy towards Israel been brought into line with that of other 'EU' countries, but the Netherlands has also come to see the advantages of a common European foreign policy.

The limits of the strategy of supranationalism became evident when the Netherlands took over the 'EU' presidency in July 1991. It immediately redrafted the existing Luxembourg proposal for the Maastricht Treaty, to include more supranationalist elements. Instead of different mixtures of supranationalism and intergovernmentalism for different 'pillars', all policies, including foreign policy, were to be brought under a single structure with a strong Commission and a strengthened European Parliament. This was rejected in no uncertain terms by all other member states apart from Belgium. Because of this humiliating defeat, 30 September 1991 is still known as 'Black Monday' among Dutch policy-makers (Hellema, 2010, pp. 355–63).

The episode marked the end of nearly two decades of almost unmitigated Dutch enthusiasm for European integration. From Maastricht onwards, intergovernmentalism increasingly dominated EU decision-making. For example, attempts to confine the European Monetary Union to a small group of Northern European countries and to give it a supranational structure failed. To the horror of the Dutch, economic growth also allowed countries such as Italy and Spain to meet the convergence criteria in 1999, and although a supranational European Central Bank came into being, it had to share power with the intergovernmental council of finance ministers (ECOFIN). Dutch policy-makers had their worst fears confirmed in 2003, when both France and Germany were granted exemptions under the Stability and Growth Pact when their budget deficits exceeded 3 per cent of GDP. That Germany, the most important ally of the Netherlands in demanding strict rules within the EMU, had violated the rule was seen as a betrayal. It is ironic that, some 10 years later, the Netherlands itself was allowed extra time to reduce its budget deficit. As a result of the waning of supranationalism, the Dutch themselves have become more intergovernmentalist: for example by insisting on keeping 'their own' Commissioner, demanding a stricter application of the subsidiarity principle, fighting hard to get a heavier voting weight in the Council than Belgium's, and embracing the intergovernmental Open Method of Coordination for new common policy-making (Verbeek and Van Der Vleuten, 2008, p. 369).

The intergovernmental turn of the European Union was not the only cause of reduced Dutch enthusiasm (Van Der Harst, 2011). Until 1990, the Netherlands had been a net earner from the 'EU', receiving more in subsidies (particularly under the Common Agricultural Policy) than it contributed. Because of enlargements and the growing importance of the Structural Funds at the expense of the Common Agricultural Policy, the Netherlands became one of the largest net contributors in relative terms. Fears arose that further enlargement with Central and Eastern European countries could only increase the discrepancy. When British Prime Minister Margaret Thatcher had 'wanted her money back', the Dutch had been among the first to point out that a cost–benefit analysis of a country's 'EU' membership involves many more factors than merely subsidies and contributions, but now the Dutch government threatened to block EU enlargement if the problem of the Dutch contribution was not addressed. In an unprecedented feat of ministerial coordination, Dutch ministers resisted even the smallest increases in the Union's budget in all ministerial councils. This strategy of obstruction worked, and at the Berlin summit of 1999 the Dutch received an even greater reduction (€1.5 billion per year) than they had hoped for. However, the Netherlands remained one of the largest net contributor per capita, even according to the EU Commission's own calculations. The Dutch government perceived this as one of the causes of the 2005 referendum outcome, or at any rate used it to demand a further reduction. Before the end of 2005, the member states indeed lowered the Dutch annual contribution by another €1 billion. Still, Dutch contributions to, and subsidies from, the EU do not balance, and the Dutch government continues to press for a smaller EU budget.

In a sense, the Netherlands has returned to the more cautious attitude towards European integration that it espoused before 1973. There are important changes, however. Atlanticism is no longer the reason for Dutch reservations, but rather the realization that supranationalism is impracticable as a prophylactic against power play by Germany and France. One observer has argued that the Dutch journey into the European continent has merely been delayed by the temptations of Atlantis and supranationalism, just as Ulysses' homecoming was delayed by the spell cast by the nymph Calypso (Segers, 2013, pp. 280–2).

If the 2005 referendum marks a change, it is that European integration has become part of the agenda of Dutch domestic politics. Public opinion itself has not changed very much (Everts, 2008): support for European integration fluctuates but shows no clear trend and remains well above the EU average (see Figure 10.1).

The proportion thinking that Dutch EU membership is a good thing, or who disagree that the Netherlands would be better off outside the EU is generally between two-thirds and three-quarters. Answers to similar questions, such as whether, on balance, the Netherlands has benefited from being a member state, show similar patterns. At the same time, however, the percentage of Dutch people who regard themselves as European citizens (in addition to being a Dutch citizen) is lower than the EU average; according to the 2004 European Election Study it is less than half of the average of the other five founding members (Thomassen, 2007). Whereas the people in most other member states are more satisfied with democracy at the EU level than at the national level, and have more trust in the European Parliament than in their national parliaments, in most years this is the reverse in The Netherlands (Thomassen, 2007). Dutch support for the European Union clearly takes the form of 'output legitimacy' rather than 'input legitimacy'.

The 2005 referendum may not have affected attitudes to European integration, but it has shown that there are differences of opinion, and through the referendum political parties have learned that voters can be mobilized on these issues. The small orthodox Protestant parties had always been concerned about the erosive effects of European integration on the country's national, and religious, identity. The Socialist Party sees Europe primarily as a neo-liberal project that threatens the Dutch welfare state. The Freedom Party was founded after the referendum and focuses primarily on

Figure 10.1　*Attitude towards EU Membership, 2000–2012 (% seeing EU membership 'as a good thing')*

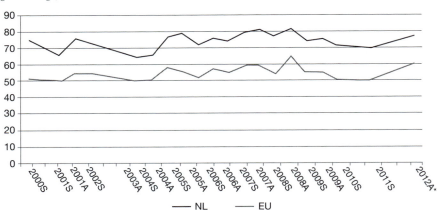

Notes: * Autumn 2012 % reporting that the country 'is better outside the EU'; S = Spring and A = Autumn; for most years the relevant questions were not included, so the data are interpolated.
Source: Eurobarometer.

its opposition to Islam, but the party quickly established itself also as the most Eurosceptic party, advocating withdrawal from the euro. Among the more centrist parties, CDA and PvdA remain by and large pro-European, but the VVD has clearly moved to a more critical position, still strongly supportive of the liberalization of the internal market ('negative integration'), but critical of EU regulation ('positive integration'). The membership of the VVD and D66 (the latter being the most pro-European of the Dutch parties) of the same Liberal Party group in the European Parliament is more and more difficult to explain. The positioning of the parties thus conforms to the new cultural dimension that is increasingly visible in Dutch politics (see Chapter 3).

Interests versus Idealism?

In the past, the third constant of Dutch foreign policy, 'internationalist idealism' or moralism, primarily took the form of the promotion of international law. As a result, The Hague has become the seat of international judicial institutions – from the International Court of Justice and the Permanent Court of Arbitration to the Iranian Claims Tribunal, the International Criminal Tribunal for the Former Yugoslavia and the International Criminal Court. Commitment to international justice is also evidenced by the decision, in 1999, to allow a defunct Dutch airbase to be placed under Scottish jurisdiction for the trial and imprisonment of Libyan suspects in the Lockerbie case.

The moral dimension of Dutch foreign policy has also resulted in a concern for human rights abroad, in participation in peacekeeping and peace-enforcing missions, and in particular, in providing aid to developing countries. Whether out of a sense of guilt for its colonial past, or as a modern extension of the churches' missionary work, the Dutch attitude towards developing countries long bordered on Third-Worldism. As chairman of a UN commission, the Dutch Nobel Prize-winning economist, Jan Tinbergen, was instrumental in setting as a target for the 1970s, that all rich countries spend at least 0.7 per cent of their national income on development aid. Only Sweden and the Netherlands met this target before the 1975 deadline. In 2008 and 2009, the Dutch budget for development aid equalled 0.8 per cent of the national income. Even in absolute terms, the Netherlands is one of the world's largest donors. Multilateral aid (through the UN and the World Bank, and increasingly through the EU) constitutes about one-third of the total outlays for development assistance and, officially, is preferred to bilateral aid. The Dutch Minister without Portfolio in charge of these matters is therefore called the Minister for Development Cooperation, rather than Development Aid.

If there were controversies in the past, it was about the criteria for the selection of countries receiving bilateral aid. The degree of poverty, a modicum of 'good governance' by the government of the receiving country, and the existence of an historic responsibility (that is, to former colonies such as Indonesia and Surinam), have always been applied. More controversial has been the degree to which Dutch companies can profit from the aid. In 2012, the Rutte II government, for example, announced that the Minister for Development Cooperation would also be the Minister for International Trade, to emphasize that the two should be interrelated. In recent decades, bilateral aid has been concentrated, both in terms of the number of receiving countries (36, primarily in Africa) and in terms of the types of projects (water management, food, security and the rule of law, and public health and rights regarding sexuality).

Since the 1990s, however, development aid itself has become controversial (Malcontent, 2011). Economic growth has made some recipients of Dutch aid, such as Indonesia, so rich that continued aid seems unnecessary. The effectiveness of the aid given is increasingly called into question, and potentially negative side effects such as increasing corruption are mentioned. Others wonder whether the budget for development aid should remain untouched in the government's budget cutbacks to reduce the size of the collective sector (Chapter 9). The Freedom Party opposes all development aid with the exception of emergency relief, and the Liberals seek to reduce the percentage of GDP devoted to development aid to the average of the 15 richest countries in the eurozone (currently 0.44 per cent). On the other side of the political spectrum, Labour and other parties on the left defend the current 0.8 per cent benchmark. The first result of the fight over the budget for development aid has been that it has become 'diluted' – for example, by using it to support Central and Eastern European countries, or to help finance peace-keeping operations. Recently, the aid budget has been reduced to 0.7 per cent of GDP. From 2005 to 2008, the Netherlands ranked highest on the Commitment to Development Index of the independent Center for Global Development (CGD), primarily because of the Dutch budget for development aid. Since then it has slipped (in small part also because of a different method for calculating the index) to sixth place in 2012 (Center for Global Development, 2013). Some recent governments have given the portfolio of Development Cooperation to a junior minister (Balkenende I; Rutte I).

The protection of human rights is an official goal of Dutch foreign policy, and since 1999 the Netherlands has been one of the few countries with a special roving Ambassador for Human Rights. Prominent Dutch politicians have been appointed as the UN's High Commissioner for Refugees (former journalist and minister Gerrit Jan Van Heuven Goedhart in 1951, and former Prime Minister Ruud Lubbers in 2000) and as The Organization for Security and Co-operation in Europe (OSCE) High Commissioner for Minorities (former Minister of Foreign Affairs, Max Van Der Stoel in 1994). A prominent example of Dutch concern over human rights is its relationship with South Africa during apartheid. Because of its historical links to the Boers in South Africa, the Netherlands voted in 1961 against expelling the country from the UN for its policy of apartheid, but subsequently the Dutch became rather more critical of the apartheid regime. After 1963, the Netherlands complied with a non-mandatory embargo on military supplies to South Africa. The issue became politicized during the Van Agt I government (1977–81). In 1979, a left-wing faction of the CDA twice introduced a parliamentary motion demanding a unilateral oil embargo of South Africa if a European-wide embargo could not be achieved. Both motions received majority support, but the government ignored the first and refused to carry out the second (Kaarbo, 2012, pp. 83–92). However, the episode made it clear that opposition to the apartheid regime was strengthening. As a temporary member of the Security Council in 1983-84, the Lubbers I government, composed of the same parties as the Van Agt I government, took the initiative to introduce a resolution boycotting weapons made in South Africa. The Dutch government also offered financial assistance to victims of apartheid.

It is not only in South Africa that the Netherlands has supported the cause of human rights – support to a degree symbolized in the person of Foreign Minister Max Van Der Stoel (1973–77, 1981–82). Streets have been named after him in Greece and Eastern Europe because of his support for democrats and dissidents when these countries were still ruled autocratically. Respect for human rights is also a criterion for receiving Dutch development aid. When a military dictatorship took over the former Dutch colony of Surinam, hesitations about continuing the country's aid package grew, and when, in 1982, 15 prominent opponents of the dictatorship were imprisoned and executed in a single night, all development aid was immediately suspended. In 1992, another former Dutch colony, Indonesia, did not wait for this to happen. Angered by what it called 'the reckless use of development assistance as an instrument of intimidating or as a tool of threatening Indonesia' (quoted in Baehr, 1996, p. 128) because of human rights violations, the Suharto regime announced that it would no longer accept Dutch development aid. If the dilemma between protection of human rights and providing development aid can still be solved, it is not so easy to give priority to human rights when more vital national interests are at stake. Because of China's enormous potential as a trading partner, the gradual opening of the Chinese economy to Dutch companies has clearly made the government more circumspect in criticizing human rights violations in China. In 2009, for example, Prime Minister Balkenende refused to meet the Dalai Lama after pressure from the Chinese government.

Concern over human rights violations also plays a role in the Dutch readiness to supply personnel for peacekeeping operations. In addition to the protection of the Kingdom's interests, article 97 of the Constitution charges the Dutch armed forces with the maintenance and promotion of 'the international legal order'. As a result, the Dutch armed forces have been actively involved in a large number of international operations to enforce or keep the peace. While some of these missions have been in the context of *ad hoc* coalitions (such as the US-led operation 'Enduring Freedom' in Afghanistan), or under the umbrella of NATO (Kosovo), the EU or the OSCE, the deployment of Dutch troops has primarily taken place under the flag of the UN. The largest missions as 'blue helmets' have been to Korea (1950–5), the Lebanon (1979–85), Bosnia-Herzegovina (1992–5), Ethiopia-Eritrea (2000–01), and Mali (2013–15). The deployment of 'Dutchbat', a battalion of some 800 Dutch soldiers, to protect the Muslim-held enclave of Srebrenica against the surrounding Bosnian-Serb forces became a traumatic experience. The lightly armed Dutch blue helmets, left without air support, were unable to prevent the capture of Srebrenica by the Bosnian-Serbs. When it became known that thousands of Muslim men were not only disarmed, but were killed in nearby fields, it dawned on the Dutch that 'the biggest single mass murder in Europe since World War II' (Holbrooke, 1998, p. 69) had occurred on their watch. A later study by the Netherlands Institute for War Documentation and a Parliamentary Inquiry were highly critical of the Dutch government's decision to send Dutchbat to Srebrenica without a clear mandate, without adequate armaments, without guarantees of air support, and without another country taking over after the agreed period of Dutch engagement had ended. The experience of Srebrenica has made the Dutch government reluctant to join UN operations whenever there is a high risk of getting involved in actual hostilities. In such situations, the preferred arrangement is now a UN mandate implemented by NATO or the EU, such as NATO's ISAF (International Security Assistance Force) in Afghanistan and the EU's mission in Chad and the Central African Republic. Since 'Srebrenica', the protocol for government decision-making about joining international operations has been tightened, and a new article in the Constitution now demands that Parliament should be involved (without a formal parliamentary veto). This has had the unintended consequence of politicizing decisions to deploy Dutch troops abroad (see Box 10.1).

The Domestication of Dutch Foreign Policy

Staunch Atlanticism in security matters, cautious Europeanization to profit from Germany's economic growth, and an active role in the UN and in development cooperation to satisfy its moral ambitions: if Dutch foreign policy could ever have been characterized so simply, it is no longer the case. The international environment has changed since the end of the Cold War, and the Netherlands is slowly adapting to these changes, as are other countries. For the Netherlands, an additional adaptation may be to its own size. In his overview of the international position of the Netherlands, Thomas R. Rochon argues that its proud legacy of once having been one of the world's great powers, overseeing a global trading empire, 'accounts at least in part for the Dutch tendency to take a more active stance in the international system than is typical of other small nations' (Rochon, 1999, p. 266). Between the end of the Second World War and the end of the Cold War, the international situation compensated for the decrease in influence of the Netherlands because of the loss of its colonies. For a long time the UK remained outside the EU, and France militarily outside NATO, giving the Netherlands a crucial role representing Atlantic (and US) interests within the EU when the latter still consisted of only six countries. Now, strictly numerically speaking, the Netherlands sees its influence diluted by the enlargements of both EU and NATO. More important, the UK has become a member of the EU and, after De Gaulle, French foreign policy is less 'exceptionalist' even with respect to NATO. More than half a century after the end of the Second World War, a reunified Germany is no longer shy about using its influence or about sending its troops abroad. Adjusting Dutch foreign policy ambitions to the real size of its influence is not yet complete. A recent overview concludes that the country is still 'punching above its weight', assuming the role of a moral-guide in human rights, spending above-average development aid budgets, and insisting on maintaining a defence force 'that could be deployed at all levels of the violence spectrum in any place in the world' (Knapen et al., 2011, p. 37).

Adjustment to a changing world and a smaller role is complicated further by the politicization of Dutch foreign policy, which is no longer the domain of a non-partisan elite, insulated from party-political competition and largely unnoticed by public opinion. We noted this development in the struggle over the stationing of cruise missiles, in the various decisions about the Dutch involvement in Afghanistan, in the referendum on the EU constitution, and in the erosion of the budget for development cooperation. Sometimes public opinion is mobilized (as in the cases of the cruise missiles and the EU referendum), but the polarization of political parties over foreign policy is most notable. In recent years, two governments resigned prematurely over foreign policy questions (Kok II and Balkenende IV). This politicization of foreign policy is partly the result of domestic factors (Vollaard and Van Willigen, 2011) as increasing electoral volatility forces political parties to campaign more actively and on more policy areas to attract voters. The same volatility complicates the formation of government coalitions and sometimes necessitates the inclusion of parties with divergent foreign policy preferences (LPF, Freedom Party, Christian Union). International developments have also contributed to the politicization of Dutch foreign policy. Globalization implies that international developments often directly influence domestic affairs, and the Europeanization of more and more policy areas makes it increasingly difficult to make a clear distinction between foreign and domestic policy. As a result, more actors (government departments, interest groups, citizens) are involved in foreign-policy-making. The very fact that the traditional anchors of Dutch foreign policy (Atlanticism, EU supranationalism, international moralism) are dragging has given domestic actors more room for manoeuvre and has turned foreign-policy-making into a two-level game (Verbeek and Van Der Vleuten, 2008).

11

Evaluating Consensus Government

Fragmentation and Horizontal Coordination

Only in the Dutch language itself is the country known by the singular label *Neder-land*; elsewhere it is the plural the Netherlands, *Pays Bas,* or *Niederlande*. Despite Napoleon Bonaparte's successful territorial centralization, the overwhelming first impression foreign students of Dutch politics are bound to develop is still one of remarkable fragmentation, if not territorial, at least in terms of decision-making. Indeed, this book has no doubt contributed to that impression.

We began our exploration of governance in the Netherlands with the source of fragmentation that has put the Dutch polity on the map of comparative politics: *'verzuiling'* – in English, pillarization (see Chapter 2). According to authors on pillarization, Dutch society was 'deeply divided' and 'highly segmented' by the social cleavages of religion and class. Since the late 1960s, however, the pillars have crumbled in a process referred to as depillarization. In Lijphart's classification, societies are either segmented (pillarized) or homogeneous, so that theoretically it would be expected that depillarization had rendered Dutch political culture more homogeneous. In reality, the result has probably been even greater fragmentation. The pillars of the past at least divided society into only three to five (depending on the definition used), easily recognizable, homogeneous segments. Within these segments political and social activities were highly integrated. Depillarization has broken up these social segments into numerous smaller parts, without replacing the former intrapillar mechanisms of integration with some functional equivalent. Political parties are criticized for having lost their function of interest aggregation (see Chapter 3); single-issue groups now play a more prominent role; and no realignment along new cleavages structures electoral behaviour. The weakening of the religious dimension has not simplified the ideological space of Dutch politics, as a new cultural dimension is growing in importance.

Depillarization has done little to simplify the Dutch party system. The number of parties that contest parliamentary elections has fluctuated, but the trend has certainly not been downwards. We have argued that the Dutch electoral system of

272

extreme proportional representation cannot be held responsible for the development of the multi-party system, but it certainly has done nothing to deter smaller parties or to reduce artificially the number of parties that achieve representation in Parliament (see Chapters 3 and 4). Even the mergers of three parties into the CDA, of four parties into Green Left, and of two parties into the Christian Union have not affected the characterization of the Dutch political landscape as a multi-party system. Most important, all the parties remain minorities, both in the electorate and in Parliament. To secure parliamentary majorities for the government, the Cabinet is based on a coalition of several political parties, usually arching over at least one of the two social cleavages. The cultural and political fragmentation is thus carried over into the heart of decision-making (see Chapter 5).

In addition to cultural and political fragmentation, our exploration has identified legal–administrative fragmentation. The incorporation of relatively strong, cohesive interest groups into the decision-making process has resulted in the 'sectorization' of policy-making into various formal and informal policy communities. The bureaucracy contributes to such functional fragmentation through its high degree of departmental specialization and autonomy (see Chapter 7). The recruitment pattern of Cabinet ministers also favours specialized expertise (see Chapter 5), and Parliament does little to counterbalance the fragmentation because its committee system (mirrored by committees within the major parliamentary party groups) is also based on policy sectors (see Chapter 6).

It is only in the Cabinet and in Parliament that political and legal–administrative fragmentation both have a role: the Cabinet is both a coalition of parties and a board of departmental chiefs, and Parliament has been described as both a political arena and a marketplace for trading social interests (see Chapters 5 and 6). Sometimes the two sources of fragmentation may counterbalance each other, but it is rare to see them reconciled into one integrated policy. The growing roles of the EU and (partly because of European integration) of the judiciary as policy-makers only add to the fragmentation.

Observers accustomed to more homogeneous societies and political systems may well wonder how the Dutch system can work at all. In Chapter 2 we referred to Dahl's bewilderment ('theoretically, your country cannot exist'), and he was reacting only to the fragmentation caused by pillarization. One might feel that only strong hierarchical leadership could prevent such a fragmented system from collapsing, but the very sources of fragmentation we have described extend into the core executive; there is no centre that has the power and authority to coordinate the various components that make up the Dutch polity.

Instead, in this fragmented political system decisions are not taken, but negotiated, or as Prime Minister Drees put it to Parliament in 1957, coordination is through consultation. Indeed, whatever criterion is used, or whatever aspect of the political system is analysed, the Netherlands always has high scores for power-sharing and cooperation, and low scores for 'power-hoarding' (see King, 2001) and competition. Together with Austria, Belgium and Switzerland, the Netherlands is regarded as one of the classic cases of consociational democracy, in which the destabilizing effects of deep social divisions are neutralized by cooperation among the leaders of the social segments (see Chapter 2). Corporatism – a combination of non-competitive relations among interest associations, with bargaining between interest associations and government – is also characteristic of the Dutch political system: again, the Netherlands always has a high score, regardless of the operationalization of corporatism that is used (Chapter 7). In the absence of a single party gaining a majority, the Netherlands has never been governed by a single-party minority government, but instead by coalitions, and the extent to which coalitions include parties that are not needed to secure a parliamentary majority is higher only in Finland (Mitchell and Nyblade, 2008, p. 207). On a dimension from monocratic to collegial leadership (that is, shared face-to-face decision-making by a body of more or less equals) only the Swiss government scores higher than the Dutch government on collegiality (Baylis, 1989, p. 147). Aspects of consociationalism, corporatism, broadly-based coalition government and collegial leadership are included in Lijphart's recent classification of countries as either consensus democracies (defined by institutional features that facilitate the involvement of as many different parties and groups as possible) or majoritarian democracies (defined by institutional features that concentrate power in the hands of the majority). Lijphart distinguishes a 'federal–unitary' and an 'executives–parties' dimension of consensus democracy. On the latter dimension, the Netherlands is among those countries that conform most closely to the ideal type of consensus government (Lijphart, 2012, pp. 305–06). Fragmentation and horizontal coordination are less and less exceptional to the Dutch case. In most countries in the Western world, civil society has been affected by individualization, as captured in Putnam's 'Bowling Alone' metaphor (Putnam, 2000). Stable, organized collective groups are giving way to *ad hoc* single-issue groups, which individuals join temporarily, if at all. Similarly, everywhere centralization and hierarchical control are giving way to networks and bargaining. The other member states of the EU also feel the impact of an additional centre of decision-making, of the growing importance of the judiciary and so on. As Mair (1994) has argued, the Netherlands is no less consensus-oriented than in the past, but other countries are becoming more consensus-oriented (but see also Hendriks and Michels, 2011). The difference with the Netherlands is that fragmentation and horizontal coordination are not new but are long-established features of Dutch politics, and that they are further advanced. It is now fashionable to describe the development of fragmentation and horizontal coordination as a trend 'from *government* to *governance*', but as we concluded in Chapter 7, the Netherlands has always been an example of governance rather than of government. In that respect, the Dutch political system forms a natural laboratory to study the advantages and disadvantages of consensus government.

The Consequences of Consensus

One of the obvious advantages of consensus politics is the high legitimacy accorded to the decisions that emerge from all this negotiation and consultation, even if the decisions themselves are unpopular. Lijphart has drawn attention to the fact that, in the Netherlands, protest tends to evaporate once a decision is made. In 1949, before a two-thirds majority of Parliament had approved decolonization, only a small minority of the population agreed with the proposal to grant independence to Indonesia, but after the vote there were no protests or demonstrations (Lijphart, 1966, pp. 111–24, 247–9, 283–4). In 1964, a pirate commercial television station started broadcasting from a converted oil rig just outside territorial waters. Although a special antenna was needed to receive the broadcasts, they became very popular, and surveys showed that 70 per cent of the population felt that the government should do nothing to hinder the broadcasts. However, when the government never-theless silenced the television station, only 33 per cent of the population disagreed with the measures taken (Lijphart, 1975, pp. 159–61). Lijphart believes that this passive acceptance of elite measures has decreased since the late 1960s; yet addi-tional recent examples are not difficult to find. In the 1980s, the long and emotional conflict over the liberalization of abortion ended in a compromise, effectively legal-izing abortion: the anti-abortion lobby was then all but reduced to one Catholic priest's lonely vigil in front of Parliament. The population, as well as some polit-ical parties, were bitterly divided about NATO's plans to station American cruise missiles in the Netherlands: a compromise was reached in 1984 and the peace movement has hardly been heard from since. Apparently, the efforts to find solu-tions that are palatable to as many people as possible give satisfaction even to those with opposing views or interests, just as the opportunities to influence legislation apparently allow opposition parties to vote with the government (see Chapter 6). In the field of industrial relations, the cooperation between government, trade unions and employers' associations has also produced high legitimacy: between 1960 and 1995, on average only 20 working days were lost per 1,000 employees per annum through strikes, compared with 104 days in France, 196 days in the USA, or 268 days in the UK (Visser and Hemerijck, 1997, p. 95). Since then, the strike figures in the Netherlands remain among the lowest of OECD countries, together with Germany, Japan, and Switzerland (OECD, 2006, p. 110).

A second advantage of consensus politics is continuity in government policy. The fragmentation of the party system has meant that there has always been an overlap between a new government and its predecessor. Even after the landslide 2002 elec-tions, the Balkenende coalitions included 'Purple' parties. Moreover, the involvement of both opposition parties and organized interests in policy-making further reduces the space for radical departures from existing policies. As a result, the Dutch have been spared swings between, for example, nationalization and privatization. When, in 1994, the Christian Democrats were sent into opposition for the first time since the intro-duction of universal suffrage, new policy departures were confined to the domain of ethics and public morality; and when the Christian Democrats returned to power in 2002 they made no attempt to undo these changes (see Chapter 5).

Internationally, the advantages of consensus politics have attracted the most attention, even admiration. Domestically, however, the discourse focuses more on the disadvantages. As we re-emphasized at the outset of this chapter, consensus politics is not caused by social or political homogeneity, but is a consequence of fragmentation: 'The Dutch have a consensual system not because they always agree about everything, but rather because they often disagree' (Hendriks 2001, p. 38). Because of heterogeneity and fragmentation, the number of veto points is considerable: policy-making moves slowly, if at all. In the Netherlands this is known as the 'viscosity' ('*stroperigheid*' in Dutch; literally: syrupiness) of policy-making. Occasionally, those opposing a new proposal may signal a willingness to be overruled as part of a package deal or in an agreement to disagree. But if a minority party or one of the social partners is vehemently opposed to some new policy, the majority will often prefer not to force the issue by bringing it to a vote, as that might mortgage future cooperation. For example, it took 20 years before the abortion issue was 'resolved'; it took six years from NATO's 1979 dual-track decision until 1985 to make a decision on the cruise missiles; it has proven impossible to agree on legislation of strike activity; no one dares to break the deadlock on child benefits; until 'the long year of 2002' (see Box 1.3) a tacit agreement among the main political parties prevented discussion of the problems of an increasingly multi-cultural society, and so on. This is not always detrimental: by the time the Dutch agreed to accept the cruise missiles, an arms reduction agreement had made them redundant; in the absence of a strike law, the courts have developed their own criteria for judging the legality of strikes, and these criteria appear to be acceptable to both trade unions and employers. Moreover, deadlocks are sometimes broken: by the judiciary in the case of euthanasia (see Box 7.1), or by the government itself in the episode leading to the Wassenaar Accord (see Chapter 9). However, despite such qualifications, 'viscosity' is a real disadvantage of consensus politics (Hendriks and Toonen, 2001).

In addition, even when agreement on a new policy departure is finally reached, the involvement of so many agents in policy-making may result in convoluted compromises that are sometimes deliberately vague in order to keep everyone on board. An extreme form of compromise is known to the Dutch as '*gedogen*' (usually translated, somewhat awkwardly, as 'to tolerate'), which means that the law is strict enough to satisfy opponents of a particular practice, but is not always strictly applied in order to satisfy proponents of that practice. For example, the law allows abortion only if the pregnancy is defined as an emergency by both the pregnant woman and a doctor, and after a 5-day delay for reconsideration, whereas in practice 'abortion on demand' during the first 24 weeks of a pregnancy is tolerated. The law strictly forbids the sale of any drugs, but 'coffee shops' selling soft drugs are officially tolerated. The law sets clear limits on air traffic for the purpose of noise control, but on several occasions the Minister of Transport has decided to tolerate Schiphol Airport exceeding these limits. And more examples could be given.

The examples of '*gedogen*' and 'viscosity' make clear that zero-sum, black-and-white issues that do not lend themselves to a substantive compromise in fact expose the Achilles' heel of Dutch governance: in a democracy, such decisions need to be taken by a majority, but in the absence of a majority there is nothing to fall back on if no consensus can be reached.

Public Confidence in the Political System

No discussion of the strengths and weaknesses of the political system would be complete without an examination of the confidence that the public has in that system. While a decline of public confidence in the political system is perceived in most Western democracies, in the Netherlands the disadvantages of consensus democracy are believed by political pundits and politicians themselves to contribute to a widening confidence gap between citizens and the politicians who represent them. In the 2006 Dutch Parliamentary Study, 66 per cent of MPs affirmed that such a gap does indeed exist.

To attempt to understand better whether a confidence gap is emerging, researchers have examined a range of attitudinal concepts; legitimacy, trust, satisfaction, acceptance, support, and confidence are, for example, positive concepts, whereas cynicism, disaffection, discontent, distrust, alienation or related concepts are negative. Besides the concepts themselves, one must also consider the object of these attitudes, which can vary from the society itself, to the regime and its institutions, and the political actors who hold positions of power. To examine all of these here would go far beyond the scope of the discussion here (see for example, Hendriks et al., 2011, 2013). Some indicators of how the public evaluates the system of governance in the Netherlands can nevertheless be presented here.

In 2012, several questions were posed in the Dutch Parliamentary Election Study to uncover how the Dutch public felt about the political system. A broad question asked whether the respondent was satisfied with democracy in the Netherlands; 15 per cent said they were very satisfied and 66 per cent said they were fairly satisfied, therefore only 19 per cent said they were not satisfied. Fewer, but still a solid majority (62 per cent) indicated satisfaction with decision-making in the country. Two-thirds felt that the opinions of MPs reflected those of the electorate, and 87 per cent said they were satisfied with the way those MPs were elected. When asked about the politicians in the country, the respondents seemed to have mixed feelings. Almost half neither agreed nor disagreed that politicians were honest (15 per cent agreed; 36 per cent disagreed), and the majority felt that politicians did not keep their promises (another 41 per cent neither agreed nor disagreed on this point). On the other hand, only 24 per cent agreed that politicians were profiteers (46 per cent disagreed) and only 6 per cent felt they were corrupt.

A problem with such figures is similar to that of the glass that is either half-full or half-empty. Clearly it would be unlikely that the glass could ever be filled to the rim – that is, that everyone was satisfied with everything to do with the government, but it is impossible to know what absolute levels for such indicators should be. To put them into at least some perspective, two questions can be posed: (i) How do the levels of confidence, satisfaction, trust and so on compare with comparable countries; and (ii) Are these levels changing; in particular, is disaffection increasing? Both of these questions can be examined using data from the Dutch Parliamentary Election studies and from other sources.

The *Eurobarometer* survey, conducted by the European Union, has asked the broad general question "On the whole, are you very satisfied, fairly satisfied, not

Figure 11.1   *Satisfaction with the Functioning of National Democracy in EU Member States, Spring 2013 (percentage very/fairly satisfied)*

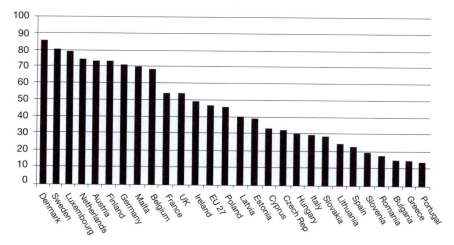

Source: Eurobarometer 79 ©European Union, 2013.

very satisfied, or not at all satisfied with the way democracy works in [your country]?" in all member states. In the Spring 2013 survey, the citizens of Denmark (86 per cent), Sweden (81 per cent), and Luxembourg (80 per cent) were the most satisfied (Figure 11.1). The Netherlands ranked fourth (75 per cent), well above average for the 27 countries of the EU (48 per cent).

These results do not provide any immediate cause for concern, or at least indicate that concern should be greater in a number of other countries, but, as mentioned above, satisfaction is only one of the concepts that can be examined. The *Eurobarometer* surveys regularly include one set of questions that is particularly useful here. These refer to whether the citizens of the various European countries tend to trust a range of institutions in the country. Among these are the government, Parliament, regional authorities, and the political parties in the country (see Figure 11.2).

These *Eurobarometer* figures could possibly give greater reason for concern, as only for regional authorities do they show a majority trusting the institution. At 49 per cent, the percentage trusting Parliament is about as high as the percentage not trusting that institution (48 per cent). For the government and for the political parties, there is more distrust than trust among Dutch citizens. However, for all four institutions, trust is considerably higher in the Netherlands than the EU average (see Figure 11.2). Note that, as the Netherlands is also included in the EU average, the contrast with the remaining 26 countries would be even greater. Only five of the 27 member states show more trust in Parliament (Sweden leading with 70 per cent and Slovenia trailing with 6 per cent) and in political parties (Malta was highest with 46 per cent; Greece lowest with 4 per cent). For trust in the government, only six EU

Figure 11.2 *Trust in Political Institutions, Spring 2013 (percentages)*

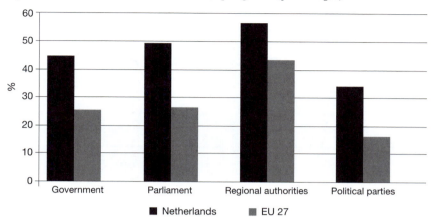

Source: Eurobarometer 79 ©European Union, 2013.

countries show higher figures (Luxembourg was highest with 62 per cent and Spain lowest with 8 per cent). And eight countries report more trust in regional authorities (Denmark the most with 73 per cent, and Italy least with 15 per cent).

Our second benchmark is to see whether such indicators of public confidence in the system show a decrease over the years. This is particularly relevant, as various observers have been concerned with a legitimacy crisis or confidence gap that may have arisen in recent decades. To gain some insight along these lines, it is possible to examine these data over time. The question concerning satisfaction with how democracy works has been asked at regular intervals in the *Eurobarometer* surveys since 1973. Figure 11.3 presents the trend over a 40-year period. In contrast to those who are concerned with a legitimacy crisis, these figures show not a decreasing but an increasing trend, as indicated by the regression line in the figure.

In the 1970s and 1980s the percentages fluctuated in the 50–60 per cent range, with an all-time low of 50 per cent in 1982. The late 1980s saw the beginning of a rising trend, eventually peaking at 78 per cent in 2000. The early 2000s show a precipitous drop to 59 per cent in 2003, but satisfaction recovered quickly, reaching a record 80 per cent in 2007 (Bovens and Wille, 2008).

There have been many fluctuations, as is to be expected in sample surveys, but the low levels in 2002 and 2003 may be related to the emergence of Pim Fortuyn in the spring of 2002 (see Box 2.1 on page 28). The emergence of Fortuyn has at times been seen as one of the indicators of a crisis of confidence among the Dutch public. If so, then these figures give no indication of a 'writing on the wall' that would lead one to have predicted the events of that turbulent period. True, well before Fortuyn announced his candidacy, the rise of a populist right-wing party had been predicted as an anti-system reaction to the disappearance of opposition

Figure 11.3   *Satisfaction with the Functioning of Democracy in the Netherlands, 1974–2013 (% very/fairly satisfied)*

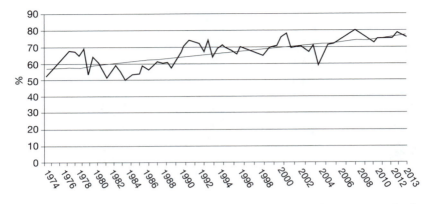

Note: For most years, the relevant questions were included in both the Spring and Autumn *Eurobarometer* surveys. For the few surveys in which the relevant questions were not included, the data are interpolated.

Source: *Eurobarometer*, various years ©European Union, 1974–2013.

within the system during the Purple coalition (Andeweg, 2000; Thomassen, 2000), or as the result of ignoring anxiety over the development of a multi-cultural society (Pellikaan and De Keijser, 1998), but no one had foreseen an electoral landslide of such a magnitude. Even retrospectively, examination of these figures would not have led to such a prediction. These figures lend more support to the argument of Van Der Brug that the discontent among the Dutch electorate in 2002 was not the cause of the success of Pim Fortuyn, but the result (Van Der Brug, 2003, 2004; see also Van Der Zwan, 2004): Fortuyn was a catalyst to bring to the surface latent feelings that the electorate themselves might not previously have acknowledged.

Since 1997, the questions concerning trust in political institutions have also been asked frequently in the *Eurobarometer* surveys. Figure 11.4 presents graphs of the trend in trust in government, Parliament and parties (data on trust in regional authorities is not available for the entire period) found in these surveys. All three graphs present rather similar patterns. Trust in these institutions was at comparatively high levels between the autumn of 1997, when the questions were first asked, until the autumn of 2001. It then drops significantly in 2002 and reaches its lowest levels in the graphs for the autumn of 2003. They begin to rise again almost to the earlier levels before falling off after the beginning of the fiscal crisis in 2008. Once again, there is no evidence of declining trust that would have led to the success of Pim Fortuyn in the spring of 2002, but clear evidence of a fall in trust after the events of that election and the difficulties of the Cabinet that followed.

Figure 11.4 *Trust in Political Institutions, 1997–2013*

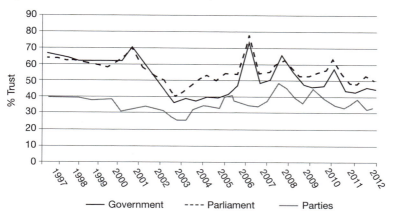

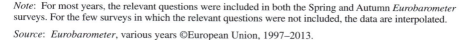

Note: For most years, the relevant questions were included in both the Spring and Autumn *Eurobarometer* surveys. For the few surveys in which the relevant questions were not included, the data are interpolated.

Source: *Eurobarometer*, various years ©European Union, 1997–2013.

Having looked at satisfaction with the workings of democracy as a whole and at trust in individual political institutions, we now turn to the trend in trust in politicians. Since 1971, the Dutch Parliamentary Election Studies have included a set of four statements to measure attitudes about politicians: 'MPs don't care about the opinions of people like me', 'One gets to be an MP because of political friends rather than ability', 'Ministers are working primarily for their own interests', and 'Politicians consciously promise more than they can deliver' (the latter three statements were used only between 1977 and 2010).

In general, these trends do not provide strong evidence for a growing confidence gap. Only one of the statements shown in Figure 11.5 shows a strong upward trend over a third of a century. The percentage agreeing that 'politicians consciously promise more than they can deliver' has risen from 75 per cent in 1977 to 91 per cent in 2010. However, one can question whether this is a good measure of political cynicism or a statement of fact. Especially in a political system with coalition governments, politicians make statements (promises?) at an election that often must be watered down during coalition negotiations. For other statements, the percentage agreeing that the 'Cabinet ministers and junior ministers are primarily working for their own interests' has jumped about 10 points (to 38 per cent) in the two most recent surveys in which the question was asked. On the other hand, the trend for the statement 'MPs do not care about the opinions of people like me' indicates somewhat fewer people in agreement. In general, the percentages show a surprising stability over four decades.

Interestingly, and in line with the trends in democratic satisfaction and institutional trust, the 2002 election study shows no rise in cynicism. That came later, in the 2003 study, and here too we see a return to previous levels in subsequent years.

At the same time, there is undeniably a strong relationship between the responses to these statements and the vote for the LPF in 2002. Those who provided the negative response were considerably more likely to vote for the LPF than those providing the positive response. As stated above, apparently the spectacular rise of the LPF is accounted for more by successful mobilization of pre-existing latent discontent than by a sudden increase in discontent. To the extent that there have been increases in dissatisfaction, distrust, or cynicism, we have already referred to Van Der Brug's argument that some voters at least seem to have realized their own disgruntlement only after it was formulated by Pim Fortuyn, and to some extent at least the decline of public confidence in political institutions has been a consequence rather than a cause of the events in 2002. Yet the effects do not seem to have been long-lasting.

In conclusion, it seems clear that the Dutch public has comparatively high levels of satisfaction with the system of government and confidence in their political leaders. This conclusion is in agreement with that found in a study of 'disaffected democracies', in which Putnam et al. concluded: 'Overall, there is evidence of some decline in confidence in politicians in 12 out of 13 countries for which systematic data are available'; that one exception in their data was the Netherlands (2000, p. 14).

There is, however, a caveat to such an optimistic conclusion. None of the longitudinal analyses here provided indications of discontent that led to the political upheavals of 2002. This is a disturbing conclusion. It is possible that researchers have not been able to develop measures that adequately measure the political feelings in the electorate. Or, the electorate itself may not be aware of its own latent

Figure 11.5   *Cynicism about Politicians, 1971–2012 (percentages)*

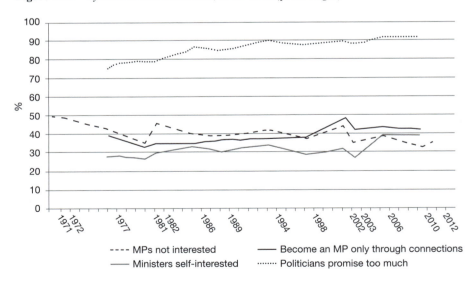

Source: Dutch Parliamentary Election Studies.

feelings of discontent and do so only when someone or something emerges to trigger them. Even, in this case, one can conclude for the Netherlands that such feelings, if they exist, are latent and by far not as manifest as in many other countries.

Attempts at Reform

Nevertheless, the 'blip' in political trust and the 2002 shock wave that produced it opened a window of opportunity for critics of consensus politics and advocates of constitutional reform. Both political and administrative reforms have featured on the political agenda at least since the turbulent 1960s. In true Dutch tradition, several commissions have been set up to study the problems and to recommend remedies; their reports provide valuable insights into the evolution of thinking about these issues by Dutch political elites (also see Andeweg, 1989; Andeweg, 1997a; Hendriks, 2009; Jacobs, 2011, pp. 167–203).

With regard to administrative reform, the emphasis originally lay in strengthening coordination, as can be seen when comparing the reports of successive commissions set up to advise on reform. The 1971 Van Veen Commission, for example, recommended a reduction in the number of departments and better procedures to improve coordination. The 1981 Vonhoff Commission contrasted a powerful world of advocates of 'partial interests' and a weak world of advocates of the 'general interest' and suggested redressing this imbalance by grouping together government departments into five main policy areas, each with its own coordinating minister, replacing specialized advisory councils by more general ones and so on. In 1982, a Government Commissioner for Administrative Reorganization was appointed to develop these ideas further. In 1990, the Deetman Commission, composed of the leaders of the parliamentary parties in the Second Chamber, issued no fewer than 98 suggestions for reform, some of which were followed up on by subcommittees. Improving coordination and strengthening the position of generalists still featured prominently, with recommendations similar to the ones mentioned by previous commissions, but also by new ones, such as setting up a general civil service, strengthening the Prime Minister's position, having fewer parliamentary committees but with a broader scope, and the introduction of some form of districts into the electoral system in the expectation that this would result in more generalist MPs. However, the emphasis has shifted to a concern with the size of the administration: decentralization, fewer and smaller 'core' government departments and so on. In later years, with the New Public Management becoming fashionable, downsizing (privatization, outsourcing, and so on) was also advocated for other reasons than improving coordination. The 2012 Rutte I government included a Minister without portfolio for Government Administration (combined with Public Housing); coordination is no longer mentioned and budgetary motives seem to dominate.

With regard to political reforms, we can also see a gradual shift in the diagnosis that is implicit in the Commissions' reports. The 1967 Cals–Donner Commission's main concern was the weak link between the election outcome and the composition of the new government, which was not surprising as the Commission was set up in reaction to the emergence of D66 with its agenda of democratic reform (see Chapter 5). The Commission eventually advised against a directly elected Prime Minister, but a narrow majority did recommend a separate election for the office of *formateur,* to be elected concurrently with Parliamentary elections. In 1982, the Biesheuvel Commission returned to this question and suggested that the newly elected Second Chamber should select the *formateur.* The Biesheuvel Commission (officially named 'Commission on the relation between voter and policy-making') also recommended the introduction of a form of referendum: a popular veto over bills approved by Parliament (see Chapter 4). The 1990 Deetman Commission, which discussed both administrative and political reforms, also advocated this form of referendum, but viewed it as a way of combating a 'legitimacy crisis' in Dutch politics. This marked a shift in emphasis in the discussion, from a concern about government formation to a more general concern over the perceived confidence gap between citizens and politics. This can be seen most clearly in the discussion around electoral reform (see Chapter 4). The Cals–Donner Commission had rejected the introduction of the 'German electoral system' (mixed member proportional – MMP) in which part of the Second Chamber would be elected in single-member districts, because this would not strengthen the relationship between election outcome and government formation. The Deetman Commission, however, embraced this electoral system, because election in a district would bring MPs into closer contact with the voters, and thus help to narrow 'the gap' (as well as turn to MPs into generalists, as noted above). Later variations on MMP, such as Minister De Graaf's ill-fated proposal, were advocated for the same reason. In 2006, yet another commission, the National Convention, also mentioned the referendum and a frequent involvement of 'citizens' assemblies' as a means of narrowing the gap.

Thus reforms were originally proposed to move the Dutch political system in a more majoritarian direction: reducing fragmentation, strengthening coordination, and making the formation of governments more dependent on the election outcome. Later, the reforms came to reflect a populist agenda, even before the emergence of populist parties: reducing the size of the government and making the system less elitist (the referendum, MPs in close contact with voters and so on). Whatever the proposals and the reasons for making them have been, their most striking characteristic is that they have largely failed. Thus, even in the aftermath of Fortuyn and the 2002 landslide election, there has been no rush to adopt reforms. Looking back at nearly half a century of attempts at reform of the national political system, the harvest is decidedly meagre: fewer advisory councils and parliamentary committees, a central civil service for the highest ranks, the abolition of compulsory voting, the lowering of the threshold for preference votes to take effect, one national referendum, conditionally allowing citizens to put issues on the parliamentary agenda, and the decision to let Parliament rather than the monarch appoint *(in) formateurs.* Almost typically for a consensus democracy, there are calls for a delay or for new studies.

Ironically, the failure of most reform proposals is itself indicative of at least some sort of gap between citizens and elites in the Netherlands. The political elites worry about a confidence gap but are unable to agree on reforms (Ziemann, 2009), whereas a majority of the citizens do support a number of reforms. The 1967 Election Study showed that only one year after D66 had been founded with the directly elected Prime Minister as the main plank of its platform, 50 per cent of the electorate (strongly) agreed, and only 37 per cent disagreed that 'From now on, the voters should elect not only the members of Parliament, but also the Prime Minister'. In more recent Dutch Parliamentary Election Studies, similar percentages (53 per cent in 2003, 46 per cent in 2010, and 44 per cent in 2012) were in support of the statement that 'The Prime Minister should be directly elected by the voters'. Support for direct election of local mayors actually rose, from 53 per cent in 1967 to 68 per cent in 2003, dropping only slightly to 66 per cent in 2010 and 65 per cent in 2012. In the 1967 Election Study, 61 per cent of the electorate (strongly) agreed, and only 28 per cent disagreed, that 'On some issues the people have to vote themselves (a so-called referendum)'. This has risen in recent surveys to between 70 per cent (2010) and 80 per cent (2012). Longitudinal data about public support for reform of the electoral system is lacking, but it is not clear that the voters are demanding regional representation. Voter opinion seems to be split fairly evenly on this issue, with 56 per cent agreeing in 2003 that 'The Second Chamber pays too little attention to regional interests', and 55 per cent feeling that 'Every region and big city should be represented by at least one MP', but only 47 per cent agreeing that 'MPs should be elected in districts'. Since support for such reforms was as high before 2002 as afterwards, and unrelated to the blip in political trust, this cannot be read as criticism of the system, but more as a desire to further improve it (Irwin and Van Holsteyn, 2002). If there is a 'gap' between citizens and elites in the Netherlands, it is visible most clearly with regard to political reform.

The Future of Consensus Government

At first sight, it would seem that consensus government has been successful in dealing with the populist challenge of 2002 and later years. The hallmark of consensus government is inclusion and collaboration, and this was also applied first to the LPF and later to the Freedom Party. The Christian Democrats and the Liberals decided not to treat the populists with a *cordon sanitaire*; that is, cordon them off and to isolate them in Parliament. Instead, the LPF was immediately invited to join the Cabinet formed in 2002 and accept governmental responsibility. In 2010, the Freedom Party was accepted as part of the governing coalition if not of the government itself. In both cases the strategy was costly in terms of Cabinet stability, but effective in defusing the populist challenge. The LPF was eliminated and the Freedom Party lost nine seats in Parliament after bringing down the Rutte I coalition prematurely. Together with the recovery of political trust, this has given the impression of a return to 'normalcy' – to consensus politics as usual. The political establishment felt confident enough to close the window of opportunity for political reform by rejecting all proposals made by the National Convention and by the Citizens' Assembly. The citizens were denied a second referendum to pass judgement on the Lisbon Treaty replacing the EU Constitutional Treaty. From being slightly suspect, the 'polder model' was once again embraced as the answer to the economic downturn after 2008.

Radically opposed to this reading of recent developments as a return to normalcy is a more alarming diagnosis in which the current state of calm is deceptive. From this perspective, consensus government itself breeds populism. Writing in 1968, Lijphart warned that the absence of competition in a depillarized society would result in opposition to the system from neo-democrats seeking radical reform. Today, that anti-cartel opposition seems to come primarily from both right-wing and left-wing populists, but otherwise Lijphart's prediction appears to have come true (Andeweg, 2001) even though Lijphart himself is now much more optimistic about consensus government regardless of the existence of deep social divisions (Lijphart, 2012). In Chapter 4 we noted that Dutch voters increasingly seem to be holding governing coalitions accountable – at least, governing coalitions suffer more frequent and more dramatic losses in the elections following their term of office. This phenomenon is not specific to the Netherlands: Mair has noted a tendency towards 'bipolarity' in European party systems; that is, an alternation between different parties or coalitions of parties in government. Yet the Netherlands is one of the few countries in which there are no signs of a bipolar party system. Back in 1967, Labour politician Van Thijn warned against a situation in which the pendulum of power cannot swing freely from one block of parties to another, set in motion by the electorate holding the incumbent government accountable. Voters' discontent will then be fanning out in all political directions without giving a mandate to an alternative government. Van Thijn feared that this could only increase discontent, causing voters increasingly to opt for radical parties. The result would be a pincer movement in which ever-stronger anti-establishment parties on both left and right would eventually crush the weakened centre, leading to a Weimarian showdown (Van Thijn, 1967). At the time, Van Thijn's diagnosis was dismissed as an alarmist ploy to sell his own proposals for political reform, but almost half a century later the first signs can be detected.

The three established parties most committed to consensus government – CDA, PvdA and VVD – have seen their share of seats erode in recent elections. They once dominated Parliament, with more than 80 per cent or even 90 per cent of the seats in their possession. In 2010 these three parties together controlled barely half of the seats in the Second Chamber. At the same time, the anti-establishment parties have grown stronger. In this category we grouped parties of the left, such as the Communist Party in the past, and in more recent years the Socialist Party, which has at times presented itself as the *'tegen-partij'* (the 'against' party), and parties of the right such as the Poujadist Farmers' Party of the 1960s and 1970s, the extreme-right Centre Democrats in the 1980s, and more recently the LPF and the Freedom Party. Between 1945 and 2000 the anti-establishment share of seats never exceeded 10 per cent (averaging 4.5 per cent), but in the first five Parliaments of the twenty-first century their support never fell below 10 per cent (averaging 21 per cent).

Figure 11.6   *Relative Strength of Old Established Parties and Anti-Establishment Parties, 1946–2012 (% of seats in the Second Chamber)*

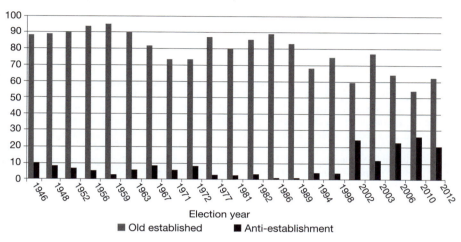

Note: 'Old established parties' include PvdA, VVD, CDA (ARP, CHU, KVP); 'Anti-Establishment parties' include the Communist Party, Farmers' Party, Centre Democrats (Extreme Right), Socialist Party, List Pim Fortuyn, Freedom Party.

Of course, there are other parties besides 'old established parties' and 'anti-establishment parties', but it is clear that this development makes the formation of coalition governments more difficult. It has resulted in new combinations of parties: Purple (Kok I, Kok II, Rutte II); a coalition of Christian Democrats, Labour and the small orthodox Christian Union (Balkenende IV); the inclusion of the populist parties in coalitions (Balkenende I and Rutte I); and, formally at least, to a minority government (Rutte I). Electoral volatility increases the probability of incongruent majorities in the two houses of Parliament (see Chapter 6), which further complicates the formation of stable majority governments. There is a risk that Dutch politics is entering a vicious cycle in which the decline in support for the established parties leads to more heterogeneous and unstable coalitions, which in turn leads to further erosion of their support and so on.

Thus a great deal rides on which diagnosis is correct. Those who believe that the long year of 2002 was an anomaly, and that the return to normalcy is real, are reluctant to give up the elitist style of consensus politics that has served Dutch society so well for so long. Those who fear that the social conditions for consensus politics to work have largely disappeared warn that '2002' was an event most likely to repeat itself unless the style and structure of Dutch politics is changed to allow for more effective popular accountability. This is the choice facing the governance and politics of the Netherlands.

Further Reading

Below are our suggestions for a selection of English-language books and articles. The reader should be aware that increasingly information on and analyses of Dutch politics are published in comparative studies. Here we confine our suggestions largely to publications devoted exclusively to Dutch politics. Those searching for more extensive reading lists in English are referred to Andeweg and Cohen de Lara (1999a, 1999b) for publications before 1998, and to Woldendorp (2008) for publications in the years 1998–2008. For English language updates on elections, coalition formations and so on, see the chapter on the Netherlands in the *European Journal of Political Research*'s annual *Political Data Yearbook* (for example, Voerman and Lucardie, 2012; see also www.politicaldatayearbook.com). We also include English-language websites where interested readers may find further information, but we assume no responsibility for the continuity and maintenance of the sites mentioned.

1 The Country, the Nation and the State

There is no shortage of material on Dutch history; an excellent short overview of Dutch and Belgian history is Kossmann-Putto and Kossmann (1994). The more extensive Blom and Lamberts (2006) also takes a combined look at the Netherlands and Belgium, as does Arblaster (2006). The period of the Dutch Republic has attracted considerable interest from historians; see Israel (1995), Pollmann (2011) and the interesting, if somewhat controversial, accounts of the beginning and the end of the Republic by Schama (1987, 1977). Lechner (2008) discusses the national identity. Roes (2008) supplies data on social and cultural trends. Alkema (2006) provides a brief introduction to the Dutch Constitution; for a more extensive discussion, see Besselink (2004). An authorized translation of the Constitution of the Netherlands may be found on the website of the Ministry of the Interior and Kingdom Relations (http://www.rijksoverheid.nl/documenten-en-publicaties/brochures/2008/10/20/the-constitution-of-the-kingdom-of-the-netherlands-2008.html). The English-language website for the Dutch Royal House is http://www.koninklijkhuis.nl/globale-paginas/taalrubrieken/english/members-of-the-royal-house; it contains both historical and contemporary material related to the monarchy. The website of the Ministry of Foreign Affairs (http://www.government.nl/ministries/bz) contains general information about the Netherlands. An English-language website for Dutch people living abroad, with information about the country's history, culture, food and so on can be found at www.thehollandring.com. Both of these websites provide numerous links to other sites having information about various aspects of the country. The World Factbook (http://www.cia.gov/library/publications/the-world-factbook/index.html), published by the US Central Intelligence Agency (CIA), presents general information on most of the countries of the world, including the Netherlands.

2 A Country of Minorities

Lijphart's classic book remains required reading for anyone studying Dutch pillarization and consociational democracy. In English, the latest (second) edition is Lijphart (1975), but in Dutch there is a ninth edition (Lijphart, 1992), reissued by Amsterdam University Press in 2008; and in 2011 also as an ebook. For reviews of the literature on pillarization, see Bax

(1990) and De Rooy (1997). For the impact of depillarization on Dutch consociationalism, see Andeweg (1999) and Koole and Daalder (2002). Lijphart (1989), Mair (1994), and Pennings and Keman (2008) discuss changes in Dutch politics using the criteria of consensus democracy.

On religious change and secularization, see Sengers (2005). The multi-cultural NGO Forum makes a useful factbook on Muslims in the Netherlands available on its website www.forum.nl/Portals/International/english-pdf/Muslims-in-the-Netherlands-2010.pdf. See also Duyvendak et al. (2010).

3   Political Parties and the Party System

Because of the origins of the major parties in one of the pillars, the reading suggested for Chapter 2 is also relevant here. For individual parties or party families, we suggest Ten Napel (1997) for the Christian Democrats; Van Praag (1994), and Wolinetz (1996) for the Social Democrats; Daalder and Koole (1988) for the Liberals; Voerman (1995) for the Green Left; and Mudde and Van Holsteyn (2000) and Vossen (2010) for the populist right. On the fate and impact of new parties, see Krouwel and Lucardie (2008) and Otjes (2012). Longitudinal data on party organization are collected by Koole and Van De Velde (1992) and analysed in Koole (1994). On party membership, see Tan (1998). Some of the suggestions listed for Chapter 4 also give information on developments in the Dutch party system. The Documentation Centre for Dutch Political Parties at Groningen University maintains a website with English-language information (www.rug.nl/dnpp). The websites of the main political parties in the Netherlands are listed in Box 3.1.

4   Elections

Electoral turnout is analysed by Van Egmond et al. (1998) and Howe (2006). For the electoral system and its reform, see Andeweg (2005) and Van der Kolk (2007). Van Praag and Brants (1999) analyse Dutch election campaigns. See Scheepers et al. (1994) for sociological explanations of electoral behaviour. Policy voting is analysed by Van Der Brug (1998), Van Wijnen (2001) and, in the form of 'directional voting', by Aarts et al. (1999). Changes in electoral behaviour are discussed by Irwin and Van Holsteyn (2008), and by Aarts and Thomassen (2008). More specifically for the two elections in 'the long year of 2002', see the special issue of *Acta Politica* (vol. 38, 2003, p. 1).

5   The Core Executive

For studies of both coalition formation and coalition government in the Netherlands, see Andeweg (2008). The outcome of coalition formations is analysed by Van Deemen (1990), Van Roozendaal (1993) and De Vries (1999). The recruitment of Dutch ministers is discussed by Bakema and Secker (1988) and Secker (1994). For decision-making in the Dutch Cabinet, see Andeweg and Bakema (1994) and Timmermans (2003). On the position of the Dutch Prime Minister, see Andeweg (1991) and Fiers and Krouwel (2005). The Council of State includes an English summary of its history and activities on its website at www.raadvanstate.nl/the-council-of-state.html. Information on the composition of the Cabinet and how it works can be found on the website of the Department of General Affairs (www.government.nl/ministries/az).

6   Parliament

For the position of Parliament in the Dutch parliamentary system, see Timmermans and Andeweg (2003). Unfortunately, the English-language version of the standard text on the

Dutch Parliament, Van Raalte (1959), has never been updated. The origins of bicameralism in the Netherlands are discussed in Beekelaar and De Schepper (1992). On the recruitment of MPs, see Leijenaar and Niemöller (1997) and Secker (2000). On political representation, see Andeweg and Thomassen (2005) and Louwerse (2011). Party discipline in Parliament is analysed in Andeweg and Thomassen (2011). The First Chamber of Parliament's website (www.eerstekamer.nl) contains English-language information, and the Second Chamber maintains an English-language website at www.houseofrepresentatives.nl.

7   The Policy-Making Process

Dutch corporatism is discussed by Visser and Hemerijck (1997), Hendriks and Toonen (2001), Van Waarden (2002), Woldendorp (2005) and Woldendorp and Delsen (2008). On quangos, see Van Thiel (2004). The SER website can be found at www.ser.nl, and includes information in English. On the Dutch bureaucracy, see Van Der Meer and Dijkstra (2011). For the political role of the judiciary, see Van Geffen (2001). Van Der Schyff (2010) discusses the proposed introduction of judicial review. Information concerning the judiciary can be found on the website of the Ministry of Justice at www.government.nl/issues/administra-tion-of-justice-and-dispute-settlement, and regarding the Public Prosecution Service on www.om.nl/vast_menu_blok/english. For the extent of political patronage in quangos, the civil service, and the judiciary, see Van Thiel (2012).

8   Multi-Level Governance

Dutch subnational government in general is discussed in Toonen (1990). On provincial government, see Toonen (1992) and De Vries (2004); on local government, see Raadschelders (1994), Denters et al. (2005),and Hulst and Van Montfort (2007). Schaap (2009) discusses the role of appointed mayors in the Netherlands. The website http://www.overheid.nl/english/sites has links to the sites of various Dutch municipalities and provinces; however, many of the sites will be in Dutch only, such as the site of the Organization of Dutch Municipalities (www.vng.nl). Studies of the preparation of the Dutch position in EU policy-making include Harmsen (1999), Van Keulen (2006) and Geuijen et al. (2008).

9   Economic and Welfare Policy

The suggestions with regard to corporatism (in Chapter 7) are also relevant for this chapter. Visser and Hemerijck (1997) is a particularly useful source. The development of the Dutch welfare state is analysed in Cox (1993). For the reforms of the welfare system, see Aarts et al. (1996), Van Der Veen and Trommel (1999),Green-Pedersen (2001, 2002), Delsen (2002), Høgelund (2003), Woldendorp and Keman (2007), and Vis et al. (2008). Kickert (2012) discusses the Dutch government's response to the financial crisis.

10   Foreign Policy

Although outdated by now, Voorhoeve (1979) is recommended for those interested in the development of Dutch foreign policy up to the late 1970s. For a more recent analysis, see Verbeek and Van Der Vleuten (2008) and Knapen et al. (2011). The website of the Ministry of Foreign Affairs has extensive information about various aspects of the foreign policy of the Netherlands, including development aid (www.government.nl/ministries/bz). The Department of Defence (www.government.nl/ministries/def) provides information concerning the Dutch armed forces, international missions, and the current defence budget.

Bibliography

Aalberts, C. and M. Kreijveld (2011) *Veel gekwetter, weinig wol: De inzet van sociale media door overhead, politiek en burgers* (Den Haag: SDU Uitgevers).

Aardema, H., A. Korsten, K. Riezebos and M. Van Dam (2011) *De Vallende Wethouder; een onderzoek naar de vertrekredenen van onvrijwillig teruggetreden wethouders in de bestuursperiode 2006–2010* (The Hague: Ministry of the Interior and Kingdom Relations).

Aarts, C. W. A. M., S. E. Macdonald and G. Rabinowitz (1999) 'Issue Competition and Party Support in the Netherlands', *Comparative Political Studies,* vol. 32, pp. 63–99.

Aarts, K. (2001) 'The Impact of Leaders on Electoral Choice in the Netherlands – Revisited', *Acta Politica,* vol. 36, pp. 380–401.

Aarts, K. and H. Van Der Kolk (2006) 'Understanding the Dutch "No": The Euro, the East, and the Elite', *PS: Political Science and Politics,* vol. 39, pp. 243–6.

Aarts, K. and J. Thomassen (2008) 'Dutch Voters and the Changing Party Space 1989–2006', *Acta Politica,* vol. 43, pp. 203–34.

Aarts, K., H. Van Der Kolk and M. Kamp (1998) *Dutch Parliamentary Election Study 1998: An Enterprise of the Dutch Political Science Community* (Enschede: Dutch Electoral Research Foundation. NIWI (Nederlands Instituut voor Wetenschappelijke Informatiediensten)/ Steinmetz Archive), Codebook P1415 and P1416.

Aarts, L. J. M., R. V. Burkhauser and P. R. De Jong (eds) (1996) *Curing the Dutch Disease* (Aldershot: Avebury).

Adams, M. and G. Van er Schyff (2006) 'Constitutional Review by the Judiciary in the Netherlands', *Zeitschrift für Ausländisches Öffentliches Recht und Völkerrecht,* vol. 66, pp. 399–413.

Akse, D. et al. (2010) 'Invloed Politiek op Stemwijzers te Groot', *De Volkskrant,* 3 February 2010.

Alberda, W. (1990) 'Werkloosheid', in J. W. Van Deth and S. C. P. M. Vis (eds), *Politieke Problemen* (Leyden: Stenfert Kroese), pp. 73–90.

Algemeen Rekenkamer (2011) *Financiering politieke partijen. Available at: www.rekenkamer. nl/Publicaties/Onderzoeksrapporten/Introducties/2011/02/Financiering_politieke_ partijen; accessed 21 December 2013.*

Alkema, E. A. (2006) 'Constitutional Law', in J. Chorus, P. H. Gerver and E. Hondius (eds), *Introduction to Dutch Law,* 4th edn (Alphen: Kluwer), pp. 301–42.

Allison, G. and P. Zelikov (1999) *Essence of Decision: Explaining the Cuban Missile Crisis,* 2nd edn (New York: Longman).

Andeweg, R. B. (1982) 'Dutch Voters Adrift: On Explanations of Electoral Change (1963–1979)', Doctoral dissertation, Leyden University.

Andeweg, R. B. (1989) 'Institutional Conservatism in the Netherlands: Proposals For a Resistance to Change', *West European Politics,* vol. 42, no. 1, pp. 42–60.

Andeweg, R.B. (1990) 'Tweeërlei Ministerraad; Besluitvorming in Nederlandse kabinetten' in R.B. Andeweg(ed.), *Ministers en Ministerraad,* (The Hague: SDU), pp.17-41

Andeweg, R. B. (1991) 'The Dutch Prime Minister: Not Just Chairman, Not Yet Chief?', in G. W. Jones (ed.), *West European Prime Ministers* (London: Cass), pp. 116–32.

Andeweg, R. B. (1997a) 'Institutional Reform in Dutch Politics: Elected Prime Minister, Personalized PR, and Popular Veto in Comparative Perspective', *Acta Politica,* vol. 32, Autumn, pp. 227–57.

Andeweg, R. B. (1997b) 'Role Specialisation or Role Switching? Dutch MPs between Electorate and Executive', *Journal of Legislative Studies,* vol. 3, no. 1, pp. 110–17.

Andeweg, R. B. (1999) 'Parties, Pillars and the Politics of Accommodation: Weak or Weakening Linkages? The Case of Dutch Consociationalism', in K. R. Luther and K. Deschouwer (eds), *Party Elites in Divided Societies: Political Parties in Consociational Democracy* (London: Routledge), pp. 108–33.

Andeweg, R. B. (2000) 'From Dutch Disease to Dutch model? Consensus Government in Practice', *Parliamentary Affairs,* vol. 53, pp. 697–709.

Andeweg, R. B. (2001) 'Lijphart versus Lijphart: The Cons of Consensus Democracy in Homogeneous Society', *Acta Politica,* vol. 36, pp. 117–28.

Andeweg, R. B. (2005) 'The Netherlands: The Sanctity of Proportionality', in M. Gallagher and P. Mitchell (eds), *The Politics of Electoral Systems* (Oxford: Oxford University Press), pp. 491–510.

Andeweg, R. B. (2008) 'Coalition Politics in the Netherlands: From Accommodation to Politicization', *Acta Politica,* vol. 43, pp. 254–77.

Andeweg, R. B. (2011) 'Purple Puzzles: The 1994 and 1998 Government Formations in the Netherlands and Coalition Theory' in R. B. Andeweg, L. De Winter and P. Dumont (eds), *Puzzles of Government Formation; Coalition Theory and Deviant Cases,* Abingdon/New York: Routledge, pp. 147–64.

Andeweg, R. B. (2012) 'A Least Likely Case: Parliament and Citizens in the Netherlands', *Journal of Legislative Studies,* vol. 18, no. 3/4, pp. 368–83.

Andeweg, R. B. and W. E. Bakema (1994) 'The Netherlands: Ministers and Cabinet Policy', in M. Laver and K. A. Shepsle (eds), *Cabinet Ministers and Parliamentary Government* (Cambridge University Press), pp. 56–72.

Andeweg, R. B. and E. Cohen De Lara (1999a) 'Foreign Language Sources for the Study of Dutch Politics', in H. Daalder et al. (eds), *Compendium voor Politiek en Samenleving in Nederland* (Alphen aan den Rijn: Samsom), pp. D01001, 1–44.

Andeweg, R. B. and E. Cohen De Lara (1999b) 'Ten Years of Dutch Government and Politics: An English Language Bibliography 1989–1998', *Acta Politica,* vol. 34, Summer/Autumn, pp. 259–78.

Andeweg, R. B. and J. J. A. Thomassen (2005) 'Modes of Political Representation: Toward a New Typology', *Legislative Studies Quarterly,* vol. 30, no. 4, pp. 507–28.

Andeweg, R. B. and J. J. A. Thomassen (2007) *Binnenhof van binnenuit; Tweede Kamerleden over het functioneren van de Nederlandse democratie* (The Hague: ROB).

Andeweg, R. B. and J.J.A. Thomassen (2008) 'Pathways to Party Unity: Sanctions, Loyalty, Homogeneity and Division of Labor in the Dutch Parliament', Paper presented at the Annual Meeting of the American Political Science Association, Boston, Mass.

Andeweg, R. B. and J. J. A. Thomassen (2011) 'Pathways to Party Unity: Sanctions, Loyalty, Homogeneity, and Division of Labor in the Dutch Parliament', *Party Politics,* vol. 17, no. 5, pp. 655–72.

Anker, H. (1998) 'Een Bijzondere Verkiezingscampagne?', in P. Kramer, R. Van Der Maas and L. Ornstein (eds), *Stemmen in Stromenland: De Verkiezingen van 1998 Nader Bekeken* (The Hague: SDU Uitgevers), pp. 114–27.

Arblaster, P. A. (2006) *A History of the Low Countries* (Basingstoke: Palgrave Macmillan).

Auer, A., C. Demmke and R. Polet (1996) *Civil Services in the Europe of Fifteen: Current Situation and Prospects* (Maastricht: European Institute of Public Administration).

Baehr, P. R. (1996) 'Mensenrechten en Ontwikkelingshulp: Nederland en Indonesië', in P. Everts (ed.), *Dilemmas in de Buitenlandse Politiek van Nederland* (Leiden: DSWO), pp. 115–41.

Bakema, W. E. and W. P. Secker (1988) 'Ministerial Expertise and the Dutch Case', *European Journal of Political Research,* vol. 16, pp. 153–70.

Bale, T. and T. Bergman (2006), 'Captives No Longer, But Servants Still? Contract Parliamentarism and the New Minority Governance n Sweden and New Zealand', *Government and Opposition,* vol. 41, pp. 422–49.

Bax, E. H. (1990) *Modernization and Cleavage in Dutch Society* (Aldershot: Avebury).

Baylis, T. A. (1989) *Governing by Committee: Collegial Leadership in Advanced Society* (Albany, NY: State University of New York Press).

Becker, J. (2005) 'Church Membership Investigated (1950–2002)', in E. Sengers (ed), *The Dutch and Their Gods; Secularization and Transformation of Religion in the Netherlands since 1950* (Hilversum: Verloren), pp. 59–71.

Beekelaar G. A. M. and H. De Schepper (1992) 'The First Chamber in the Netherlands, 1815–1848', in H.W. Blom, W.P. Blockmans and H. De Schepper (eds), *Bicameralisme: Tweekamerstelsels Vroeger en Nu* (The Hague: SDU Uitgevers), pp. 278–89.

Bekkers, V.J.J.M., A.J.C. De Moor-Van Vugt, J.M. Bonnes, P. Schoneveld and W.J.M. Voermans (1995) 'The Case of the Netherlands', in S. A. Pappas (ed.), *National Administrative Procedures for the Preparation and Implementation of Community Decisions* (Maastricht: European Institute of Public Administration), pp. 397–440.

Berndsen, R. (1997) 'Afscheid van de Beleidsautonomie? Monetair Beleid na Bretton Woods', in W. Hout and M. Sie Dhian Ho (eds), *Aanpassing onder Druk? Nederland en de Gevolgen van Internationalisering* (Assen: Van Gorcum), pp. 72–83.

Besselink, L. F. M. (2004) *Constitutional Law of the Netherlands: An Introduction with Texts, Cases and Materials* (Nijmegen: Ars Aequi Libri).

Beyers, J., B. Kerremans and P. Bursens (2000) 'European Policy Preparation and Implementation in the Three Benelux Countries', in E. Zeff and E. Pirro (eds), *The European Union and the Member States: Cooperation, Coordination, and Compromise* (Boulder, CO: Lynne Rienner), pp. 59–88.

Blankenburg, E. (2006) 'Dutch Legal Culture: Persisting or Waning?', in J. Chorus P. H. Gerver and E. Hondius (eds), *Introduction to Dutch Law*, 4th edn (Alphen: Kluwer), pp. 13–52.

Blom, J. C. H. (1977) 'The Second World War and Dutch Society: Continuity and Change', in A. C. Duke and C. A. Tamse (eds), *Britain and the Netherlands: Vol. VI: War and Society* (The Hague: Martinus Nijhoff), pp. 228–48.

Blom, J. C. H. (2000) 'Pillarisation in Perspective', *West European Politics,* vol. 23, no. 3, pp. 153–64.

Blom, J. C. H. and E. Lamberts (eds) (2006) *History of the Low Countries* (New York: Berghahn).

Blondel, J. and F. Müller-Rommel (1997) *Cabinets in Western Europe,* 2nd edn (New York: St Martin's Press).

Bodenheimer, S. (1978) 'The Denial of Grandeur: The Dutch Context', in J. H. Leurdijk (ed.), *The Foreign Policy of the Netherlands* (Alphen aan den Rijn: Sijthoff and Noordhof), pp. 235–84.

Boogers, M. (2010) *Lokale Politiek in Nederland: De Logica en Dynamiek van Plaatselijke Politiek,* 2nd edn (The Hague: Lemma).

Boogman, J. C. (1978) *Random 1848: De Politieke Ontwikkeling van Nederland 1840–1858* (Bussum: Unieboek BV).

Bovens, M. and A. Wille (2008) 'Deciphering the Dutch Drop: Ten Explanations for Decreasing Political Trust in the Netherlands', *International Review of Administrative Sciences,* vol. 74, pp. 283–305.

Bovens, M. and A. Wille (2010) 'The Education Gap in Participation and Its Political Consequences', *Acta Politica,* vol. 45, no. 4, pp. 393–422.

Bovens, M. and A. Wille (2012) 'The Education Gap in Participation: A Rejoinder', *Acta Politica,* vol. 47, no. 3, pp. 259–71.

Bovens, M. and K. Yesilkagit (2010) 'The EU as Lawmaker: The Impact of EU Directives on National Regulation in the Netherlands', *Public Administration,* vol. 88, pp. 57–74.

Bovens M., G. J. Brandsma, D. Thesingh and T. Wever (2010) 'Aan het pluche gekleefd? Aard en achtergrond van het aftreden van Nederlandse bewindslieden', *Beleid en Maatschappij,* vol. 37, no. 4, pp. 319–40.

Brants, K., W. Kok and P. Van Praag, Jr (1982) *De Strijd om de Kiezersgunst: Verkiezing-scampagnes in Nederland* (Amsterdam: Uitgeverij Kobra).

Breeman, G. and A. Timmermans (2012) 'Myths and Milestones: The Europeanization of the Legislative Agenda in the Netherlands', in S. Brouard, O. Costa and T. König (eds), *The Europeanization of Domestic Legislatures: The Empirical Implications of the Delors' Myth in Nine Countries* (New York: Springer), pp. 151–72.

Brenninkmeijer, A. F. M. (2006) 'Judicial Organization', in J. Chorus, P. H. Gerver and E. Hondius (eds), *Introduction to Dutch Law,* 4th edn (Alphen aan den Rijn: Kluwer), pp. 53–61.

Broder, D. S. (1972) *The Party's Over: The Failure of Politics in America* (New York: Harper & Row).

Buruma, I. (2006) *Murder in Amsterdam* (New York: Penguin).

Buunk, H. (1999) *De Economie in Nederland* (Groningen: Wolters-Noordhoff).

BZK (Ministry of the Interior and Kingdom Relations) (2011) *Evaluatie Kaderwet Adviescolleges: Derde Staat van Advies 2005–2010* (The Hague: Ministry of the Interior and Kingdom Relations).

Castenmiller, P. and M. van Dam (2010) 'Onderzoek: In Grote Stad Meer Wethouders Van Buiten', *VNG Magazine,* 5 November.

CBS (*Centraal Bureau voor de Statistiek*) (2001) *Tweehonderd jaar statistiek in tijdreeksen, 1800–1999* (Voorburg/Heerlen) pp. 19–26.

CBS (*Centraal Bureau voor de Statistiek*) (2012) *Jaarrapport Integratie 2012* (The Hague/Heerlen).

Center for Global Development (2013) Available at: www.cgdev.org; accessed 17 December 2013.

Cohen, M. J., A. P. M. Coomans and C. Flinterman (1993) 'Rechter en Politiek', in R. B. Andeweg, A. Hoogerwerf and J. J. A. Thomassen (eds), *Politiek in Nederland,* 4th edn (Alphen aan den Rijn: Samsom H. D. Tjeenk Willink), pp. 299–317.

ComScore (2011). 'Nederland wereldwijd nummer 1 in bereik in van Twitter en LinkedIn in maart 1011', 26 April 2011, available at: www.comscore.com.

Correljé, A. (1997) 'Naar Nieuwe Verhoudingen in het Energiebeleid', in W. Hout and M. Sie Dhian Ho (eds), *Aanpassing onder Druk? Nederland en de Gevolgen van Internationalisering* (Assen: Van Gorcum), pp. 165–78.

Council for Public Administration (2004) *Nationale Coordinatie van EU–Beleid: Een Politick en Proactief Proces* (The Hague: ROB).

Cox, R. H. (1993) *The Development of the Dutch Welfare State: From Workers' Insurance to Universal Entitlement* (Pittsburgh, PA: University of Pittsburgh Press).

CPB (2012) Macro–Economische Verkenningen (MRV). Available at: http://www.cpb.nl/ publicatie/macro–economische–verkenning–mev–2012; accessed 28 November 2013.

Cramer, N. (1980) 'De Kroon op het Werk van 1813', in C. A. Tamse (ed.), *De Monarchie in Nederland* (Amsterdam: Elsevier), pp. 9–60.

Crum, B. J. J. (2007) *The EU Constitutional Treaty in the Netherlands* (WRR Webpublications 25, available at: www.wrr.nl).

Curtis, J. E., D. E. Baer and E. G. Grabb (2001) 'Nations of Joiners: Explaining Voluntary Association Membership in Democratic Societies', *American Sociological Review,* vol. 66, pp. 783–805.

Daalder, H. (1966) 'The Netherlands: Opposition in a Segmented Society', in R. A. Dahl (ed.), *Political Oppositions in Western Democracies* (New Haven, CT: Yale University Press), pp. 188–236.

Daalder, H. (1974) *Politisering en Lijdelijkheid in de Nederlandse Politick* (Assen: Van Gorcum).

Daalder, H. (1985) 'De Tweede Wereldoorlog en de binnenlandse politiek', in D. Barnouw,M. de Keizer and G. van der Stroom (eds), *1940–1945: Onverwerkt verleden?* (Utrecht: HES Uitgevers), pp. 27–45.

Daalder, H. (1989) 'Ancient and Modern Pluralism in the Netherlands', The 1989 Erasmus Lectures at Harvard University, Center for European Studies Working Paper Series.

Daalder, H. and R. A. Koole (1988) 'Liberal Parties', in E. Kirchner (ed.), *Liberal Parties in Western Europe* (Cambridge University Press), pp. 155–77.

Daalder, H., R.A. Koole, J.W. Becker and F.M. Van Der Meer (eds) (2002) *Compendium voor Politick en Samenleving in Nederland* (Alphen aan den Rijn: Samsom).

Dankers, J., B. van Bavel, T. Jaspers and J. Peet (eds) (2010) *SER 1950–2010: Zestig Jaar Denkwerk voor Draagvlak* (Amsterdam: Boom).

Daudt, H. (1982) 'Political Parties and Government Coalitions in the Netherlands since 1945', *Netherlands Journal of Sociology,* vol. 18, pp. 1–24.

Davids Committee (2010) *Rapport Commissie van Onderzoek Besluitvorming Irak* (Amsterdam: Boom).

De Groot-Van Leeuwen, L. E. (1992) 'The Equilibrium Elite: Composition and Position of the Dutch Judiciary', *Netherlands Journal of Social Sciences,* vol. 28, pp. 141–54.

De Hart, J. (2005) *Landelijk Vereinigd: Grote Ledenorganisaties over Ontwikkelingen op het Maatschappelijk Middenveld* (The Hague: Sociaal en Cultureel Planbureau).

De Hart, J. (2013) *Zwevende Gelovigen: Oude religie en nieuwe spiritualiteit* (The Hague: Sociaal en Cultureel Planbureau).

De Hond, M. (2012) 'De Tweede Kamerverkiezingen van 2012'. Available at: http://www.maurice.nl/wp-content/uploads/2012/09/De-analyse-van-de-verkiezingsuitslag-van-TK2012.pdf; accessed 24 November 2013.

De Lange, S. and M. Rooduijn (2011) 'Een populistische tijdgeest in Nederland? Een inhoudsanalyse van de verkiezingsprogramma's van politieke partijen', in R. B. Andeweg and J. Thomassen (eds), *Democratie doorgelicht* (Leiden University Press), pp. 319–35.

De Moor-Van Vugt, A. J. C. and B. W. N. De Waard (2006) 'Administrative Law', in J. Chorus, P. H. Gerver and E. Hondius (eds), *Introduction to Dutch Law,* 4th edn (Alphen aan den Rijn: Kluwer), pp. 343–67.

De Rooij, R. (2003) *Nederlandse Gemeenten en Provincies in de Europese Unie* (Deventer: Kluwer).

De Rooy, P. (1997) 'Farewell to Pillarization', *Netherlands Journal of Social Sciences,* vol. 33, pp. 27–42.

De Swaan, A. (1982) 'The Netherlands: Coalitions in a Segmented Polity', in E. C. Browne, and J. Dreijmanis (eds), *Government Coalitions in Western Democracies* (New York: Longman).

De Vrankrijker, A. C. J. (1946) *De Grenzen van Nederland: Overzicht van Wording en Politieke Tendenzen* (Amsterdam: Contact).

De Vries, C. E. (2007a) 'Sleeping Giant: Fact or Fairytale? How European Integration Affects National Elections', *European Union Politics,* vol. 8, pp. 363–85.

De Vries, C. E. (2007b) *European Integration and National Elections: The Impact of EU Issue Voting on National Electoral Politics* (Amsterdam: Vrije Universiteit).

De Vries, M. S. (2004) 'Institutional Fleecing: The Slow Death of Dutch Provinces', *Public Organization Review,* vol. 4, pp. 295–315.

De Vries, M. W. M. (1999) 'Governing With Your Closest Neighbour', PhD dissertation, Catholic University of Nijmegen.

De Winter, L. and Dumont, P. (2008) 'Uncertainty and Complexity in Cabinet Formation', in K. Strøm, W. C. Müller and T. Bergman (eds), *Cabinets and Coalition Bargaining: The Democratic Life Cycle in Western Europe* (Oxford University Press), pp. 123–58.

De Wolff, P. and W. Driehuis (1980) 'A Description of Post War Economic Developments and Economic Policy in the Netherlands', in R. T. Griffiths (ed.), *The Economy and Politics of the Netherlands since 1945* (The Hague: Martinus Nijhoff), pp. 13–60.

Dekker, P. (2000) 'Politieke Participatie', in J. Thomassen, K. Aarts and H. Van Der Kolk (eds), *Politieke Veranderingen in Nederland 1971–1998* (The Hague: SDU Uitgevers), pp. 77–92.

Del Grosso, N. Y. (2000) *Parlement en Europese Integratie* (Deventer: Kluwer).

Delsen, L. (2002) *Exit Polder Model? Socioeconomic Change in the Netherlands* (Westport, CT: Praeger).

Den Ridder, J. (forthcoming*)* 'Schakels of obstakels? Nederlandse politieke partijen en de eensgezindheid, verdeeldheid en representativiteit van partijleden', PhD dissertation, Leiden University.

Denters, B., P. J. Klok and H. Van Der Kolk (2005) 'The Reform of the Political Executive in Dutch Local Government', in R. Berg and N. Rao (eds), *Transforming Political Leadership in Local Government* (Basingstoke: Palgrave Macmillan), pp. 15–28.

Derksen, W. and L. Schaap (2010) *Lokaal Bestuur,* 6th edn (Dordrecht: Convoy).

Donner, J. and J. M. Kan (1956) *De Nederlandse Kiezer: een onderzoek naar zijn gedragingen en opvattingen* (The Hague: Staatsdrukkerij– en Uitgeverijbedrijf).

Dorussen, H. and M. Taylor (2001) 'The Political Context of Issue-Priority Voting: Coalitions and Economic Voting in the Netherlands, 1970–1999', *Electoral Studies,* vol. 20, no. 2, pp. 399–426.

Douma, W. T., K. Pieters, K. Feenstra and R. Koch-Harmanova (2007), *Pilot-Monitor EU Invloed; een onderzoek naar de realiseerbaarheid van een permanente monitor voor het meten van de invloed van Europese regelgeving op in Nederland geldende wet- en regelgeving* (The Hague: T.M.C. Asser Instituut).

Downs, A. (1957) *An Economic Theory of Democracy* (New York: Harper & Row).

Dragstra, L. (2008) *Enige opmerkingen over partijfinanciering* (Nijmegen: Wolf Legal Publishers).

Drees, W. (1965) *De Vorming van het Regeringsbeleid*, Assen: Van Gorcum.

Dutch Electoral Counncil, available at: www.kiesraad.nl.

Dutch Parliamentary Election Study, available at: www.dpes.nl; see also http://easy.dans.knaw.nl.

Dutch Parliamentary Study (2006) (for information contact R. B. Andeweg on andeweg@fsw. leidenuniv.nl).

Dutch Parliamentary Study (2010) (for information contact R. B. Andeweg on andeweg@fsw. leidenuniv.nl).

Duverger, M. (1951) *Les parties politiques*, 2nd edn, revd and updated (Paris: A. Colin).

Duverger, M. (1959) *Political Parties: Their Organization and Activity in the Modern State*, 2nd revd edn in English (London: Methuen).

Duyvendak, J. W., M. Hurenkamp and E. Tonkens (2010) 'Culturalization of Citizenship in the Netherlands' in E. Chebel d'Appolonia and S. Reich (eds), *Managing Ethnic Diversity after 9/11: Integration, Security, and Civil Liberties in Transatlantic Perspective* (New Brunswick, NJ: Rutgers University Press).

Economic Affairs (2001, 2004). Ministry of Economic Affairs, Netherlands Foreign Trade Agency. Available at: www.hollandtrade.com; accessed 2001 and 2004.

Effing, R., J. van Hillegersberg and T. Huiberts (2011) 'Social Media and Political Participation: Are Facebook, Twitter and YouTube Democratizing Our Political Systems?', *Electronic Participation: Lecture Notes in Computer Science,* vol. 6847, pp. 25–35.

Eldersveld, S. J., J. Kooiman and T. Van Der Tak (1981) *Elite Images of Dutch Politics, Accommodation and Conflict* (Ann Arbor, MI: University of Michigan Press).

Elzinga, D. J. and C. Wisse (1988) *De Parlementaire Fracties* (Groningen: Wolters-Noordhoff).

Entzinger, H. B. (1998) 'Immigratie en de Multi-Ethnische Samenleving', in H. Daalder, H. et al. (eds) *Compendium voor Politiek en Samenleving in Nederland* (Alphen aan den Rijn: Samsom/H. D. Tjeenk Willink), pp. B0300, 1–71.

European Commission (2012) *European Economic Forecast, Spring 2012*. Available at: http://ec.europa.eu/economy_finance/publications/european_economy/2012/ee1upd_en.htm; accessed 24 January 2014.

Everts, P. P. (1983) 'Public Opinion, the Churches and Foreign Policy: Studies of Domestic Factors in the Making of Dutch Foreign Policy', Doctoral dissertation, Leyden University.

Everts, P. P. (2008) *De Nederlanders en de Wereld; Publieke Opinies na de Koude Oorlog* (Assen: Van Gorcum).

Expatica (2009) 'The Netherlands: "the most Calvinist nation in the world", 15 July 2009, Avaliable at Expatica.com, Accessed 6 March 2014.

Fiers, S. and A. Krouwel (2005) 'The Low Countries: From "Prime Minister" to "President-Minister"', in T. Poguntke and P. Webb (eds), *The Presidentialization of Politics: A Comparative Study of Modern Democracies* (Oxford University Press), pp. 128–58.

Finance, Ministry of. Available at: http://www.rijksbegroting.n1/2008/home.

Foreign Affairs (2004) Ministry of Foreign Affairs. Available at: www.minbuza.nl; accessed 2004.

Forum (Institute for Multicultural Affairs) (2012) *Factbook: The Position of Muslims in the Netherlands: Facts and Figures* (Utrecht: Forum).

Fuchs, D. and H.-D. Klingemann (1989) 'The Left–Right Schema', in M. Kent Jennings and J. Van Deth, (eds), *Continuities in Political Action* (Berlin: De Gruyter), pp. 203–34.

Geuijen, K., P. 't Hart, S. Princen and K. Yesilkagit (2008) *The New Eurocrats: National Civil Servants in EU Policy-Making* (Amsterdam University Press).

Gijswijt, T. (2011) 'De trans-Atlantische Elite en de Nederlandse buitenlandse politiek sinds 1945', in D. Hellema, M. Segers and J. Rood (eds), *Bezinning op het Buitenland; het Nederlands buitenlands beleid in een onzekere wereld* (The Hague: Clingendael), pp. 31–46.

Gladdish, K. R. (1972) 'Two-Party vs. Multi-Party, the Netherlands and Britain', *Acta Politica*, vol. 7, no. 3, pp. 342–61.

Gladdish, K. R. (1991) *Governing from the Centre* (London: Hurst).

Glastra Van Loon, J. F. (1964) 'Kiezen of Delen', *Nederlands Juristenblad*, pp. 1133–42, 1161–7.

Goodin, R. E. (2001) 'Work and Welfare: Towards a Post-Productivist Welfare Regime', *British Journal of Political Science*, vol. 31, pp. 13–39.

Gosman, J. G. and W. P. Secker (2000) 'De Monarchie', in H. Daalder et al. (eds), *Compendium voor Politiek en Samenleving in Nederland* (Alphen aan den Rijn: Samsom/H. D. Tjeenk Willink), pp. A0400, 1–40.

Goudswaard, K. P. (1990) 'Budgetary Policies in the Netherlands: 1982–1990', in *Finanzarchiv* (Tübingen: J. C. B. Mohr), pp. 271–84.

Green-Pedersen, C. (2001) 'The Puzzle of Dutch Welfare State Retrenchment', *West European Politics*, vol. 24, pp. 135–50.

Green-Pedersen, C. (2002) *The Politics of Justification: Party Competition and Welfare-State Retrenchment in Denmark and the Netherlands from 1982 to 1998* (Amsterdam University Press).

Griffiths, J., A. Bood and H. Weyers (1998) *Euthanasia and Law in the Netherlands* (Amsterdam University Press).

Griffiths, R. T. (1980a) 'The Netherlands Central Planning Bureau' and 'The Netherlands and the European Communities', in R. T. Griffiths (ed.), *The Economy and Politics of the Netherlands since 1945* (The Hague: Martinus Nijhoff), pp. 135–61, 277–303.

Griffiths, R. T. (ed.) (1980b) *The Economy and Politics of the Netherlands since 1945* (The Hague: Martinus Nijhoff).

Hakhverdian, A., W. Van Der Brug and C. De Vries (2012) 'The Emergence of a 'Diploma Democracy'? The Political Education Gap in the Netherlands, 1971–2010, *Acta Politica* vol. 47, no. 3, pp. 229–47.

Harmsen, R. (1999) 'The Europeanization of National Administrations: A Comparative Study of France and the Netherlands', *Governance*, vol. 12, pp. 81–113.

Haverland, M. (2009) 'How Leader States Influence EU Policy-making: Analysing the Expert Strategy', *European Integration online Papers (EIoP)*, vol. 13, art. 25, available at: http//eiop.or/at/eiop/texte/2009-025a.htm.

Heldring, J. L. (1978) 'De Nederlandse Buitenlandse Politiek na 1945', in E. Van Den Beugel, J.C. Boogman, J.L. Heldring, J.H. Leurdijk, R.K. Tezler, and P. Van 't Veer (eds.), *Nederlandse Buitenlandse Politiek: heden en verleden* (Baarn: Anthos).

298 *Bibliography*

Hellema, D. (1995) *Buitenlandse Politiek van Nederland* (Utrecht: Spectrum).
Hellema, D. (2010) *Nederland in de Wereld: de buitenlandse politiek van Nederland,* 4th edn (Houten: Spectrum).
Hellema, D., M. Segers and J. Rood (eds) (2011) *Bezinning op het Buitenland: het Nederlands buitenlands beleid in een onzekere wereld* (The Hague: Clingendael).
Hemerijck, A. and J. Visser (2002) 'Het "Nederlandse Mirakel" Revisited', *Tijdschrift voor Arbeidsvraagstukken,* vol. 18, pp. 291–305.
Hendriks, F. (2001) 'Polder Politics in the Netherlands: The "Viscous State" Revisited', in F. Hendriks and T. Toonen (eds), *Polder Politics: The Reinvention of Consensus Democracy in the Netherlands* (Aldershot: Ashgate), pp. 21–40.
Hendriks, F. (2009) 'Democratic Reform between the Extreme Makeover and the Reinvention of Tradition: The Case of the Netherlands', *Democratization,* vol. 16, pp. 243–68.
Hendriks, F. and A. Michels (2011) 'Democracy Transformed? Reform in Britain and the Netherlands (1990–2010)', *International Journal of Public Administration,* vol. 34, pp. 307–17.
Hendriks, F., J. Van Ostaaijen and M. Boogers (2011) *Legitimiteitsmonitor Democratisch Bestuur* (The Hague: Ministry of the Interior and Kingdom Relations).
Hendriks, F., J. Van Ostaaijen, K. Van Der Krieken and M. Keijzers (2013) *Legitimiteitsmonitor Democratisch Bestuur 2013* (The Hague: Ministry of the Interior and Kingdom Relations).
Hendriks, F. and T. Toonen (eds) (2001) *Polder Politics: The Reinvention of Consensus Democracy in the Netherlands* (Aldershot: Ashgate), pp. 21–40.
Hennis, M. (1997) 'Nieuwe Actoren en Instituties in Het Landbouwbeleid', in W. Hout and M. Sie Dhian Ho (eds), *Aanpassing order Druk? Nederland en de Gevolgen van Internationalisering* (Assen: Van Gorcum), pp. 179–91.
Hillebrand, R. (1992) 'De Antichambre van het Parlement', Doctoral dissertation, Leyden University.
Hirsi Ali, A. (2006) *The Caged Virgin* (New York: Free Press).
Hirsi Ali, A. (2007) *Infidel* (New York: Free Press).
Hofstede, G. (2001) *Culture's Consequences: Comparing Values, Behaviors, Institutions, and Organizations Across Nations* (Thousand Oaks, CA: Sage).
Høgelund, J. (2003) *In Search of Effective Disability Policy: Comparing the Developments and Outcomes of the Dutch and Danish Disability Policies* (Amsterdam University Press).
Holbrooke, R. (1998) *To End a War* (New York: Random House).
Hollandtrade (2012) *Holland Compared: Facts and Figures, Spring 2012,* available at: www.hollandtrade.com.
Hollandtrade (2013) Available at: www.hollandtrade.com, accessed 28 November 2013.
Holzhacker, R. (2002) 'National Parliamentary Scrutiny over EU Issues: Comparing the Goals and Methods of Government and Opposition Parties', *European Union Politics,* vol. 3, pp. 459–79.
Honig, J. W. (1993) *Defense Policy in the North Atlantic Alliance: The Case of the Netherlands* (Westport, CT: Praeger).
Hoogenboom, R. and M. Van Vliet (2000) 'Uitgepolderd? Over het Welvaartscheppende Vermogen van Nederland Anno 2000', *Ministerie van Economische Zaken,* available at: www.minez.nl.
Hoogendijk, P. A. (1971) *Partijpropaganda in Nederland* (Amsterdam: Agon Elsevier).
Houska, J. J. (1985) *Influencing Mass Political Behavior: Elites and Political Subcultures in the Netherlands and Austria* (Berkeley, CA: University of California Press).
Hout, W. and M. Sie Dhian Ho (eds) (1997) *Aanpassing onder Druk? Nederland en de Gevolgen van Internationalisering* (Assen: Van Gorcum).
Howe, P. (2006) 'Political Knowledge and Political Participation in the Netherlands: Comparisons with the Canadian Case, *International Political Science Review*, vol. 27, pp. 137–66.

Hulst, R. and A. Van Montfort. (2007) 'The Netherlands: Cooperation as the Only Viable Strategy', in R. Hulst and A. Van Montfort (eds), *Inter-Municipal Cooperation in Europe* (Dordrecht: Springer), pp. 139–68.

Inglehart, R. (1977) *The Silent Revolution: Changing Values and Political Styles Among Western Publics* (Princeton, NJ: Princeton University Press).

Inglehart, R. and C. Welzel (2005) *Modernization, Cultural Change and Democracy: The Human Development Sequence* (Cambridge University Press).

International Chamber of Commerce (ICC) (2013) *ICC Open Markets Index*, 2nd edn (Paris: ICC).

IOB (Policy and Operations Evaluation Department) (2008) *Primus Inter Pares: een evaluatie van het Nederlandse EU voorzitterschap 2004*, IOB Evaluatie 314. Available at: www.minbuza.nl.

Irwin, G. A. (2006) *Bandwagon Without a Band* (Leiden University).

Irwin, G. A. and J. J. M. Van Holsteyn (1989a) 'Decline of the Structured Model of Electoral Competition', in H. Daalder and G. A. Irwin (eds), *Politics in the Netherlands: How Much Change?* (London: Cass), pp. 21–41.

Irwin, G. A. and J. J. M. Van Holsteyn (1989b) 'Towards a More Open Model of Competition', in H. Daalder and G. A. Irwin (eds), *Politics in the Netherlands: How Much Change?* (London: Cass), pp. 112–38.

Irwin, G. A. and J. J. M. Van Holsteyn (1997) "Where to From Here? Revamping Electoral Politics in the Netherlands", *West European Politics*, vol. 20, no. 2 (April), pp. 93–118.

Irwin, G. A. and J. J. M. Van Holsteyn (1999) 'Parties and Politicians in the Parliamentary Election of 1998', *Acta Politica*, vol. 34, pp. 130–57.

Irwin, G. A. and J. J. M. Van Holsteyn (2002) 'De Kloof tussen Burger en Bestuur', in J. J. M. van Holsteyn and C. Mudde (eds), *Democratie in Verval* (Meppel: Boom).

Irwin, G. A. and J. J. M. Van Holsteyn (2008) 'Scientific Progress, Educated Guesses or Speculation? On Some Old Predictions with Respect to Electoral Behaviour in the Netherlands', *Acta Politica*, vol. 43, nos 2–3, pp. 180–202.

Irwin, G. A. and J. J. M. Van Holsteyn (2011) "Sterft, Gij oude vormen en gecachten? Over kiezers, verkiezingen en kiesstelsel in Nederland" in R. Andeweg and J. Thomassen (eds), *Democratie doorgelicht: Het functioneren van het Nederlandse Democratie.* (Leiden University Press), pp. 335-48.

Irwin, G. A. and J. J. M. Van Holsteyn (2012) 'Strategic Electoral Considerations Under Proportional Representation', *Electoral Studies*, vol. 31, no. 1, pp. 184–91.

Irwin, G. A., C. Van Der Eijk, J. J. M. Van Holsteyn and B. Niemöller (1987) 'Verzuiling, Issues, Kandidaten en Ideologie in de Verkiezingen van 1986', *Acta Politica*, vol. 22, no. 2, pp. 129–80.

Israel, J. I. (1995) *The Dutch Republic: Its Rise, Greatness and Fall, 1477–1806* (Oxford: Clarendon Press).

Jacobs, K. T. E. (2011) *The Power of the People: Direct Democratic and Electoral Reform in Austria, Belgium and the Netherlands*, Doctoral dissertation, Radboud University Nijmegen.

Jones, E. (1999) 'Is "Competitive" Corporatism an Adequate Response to Globalisation? Evidence from the Low Countries', *West European Politics*, vol. 22, pp. 159–81.

Kaarbo, J. (2012) *Coalition Politics and Cabinet Decision Making: A Comparative Analysis of Foreign Policy Choices* (Ann Arbor, MI: University of Michigan Press).

Kaarbo, J. and C. Cantir (2013) 'Role Conflict in Recent Wars: Danish and Dutch Debates over Iraq and Afghanistan', *Cooperation and Conflict*, DOI: 10.1177/0010836713482815.

Kanne, P. (2012) (opersonal communication).

KASKI (Radboud University Nijmegen), available at: www.ru.nl/kaski.

Katz, R. S. and P. Mair (1995) 'Changing Models of Party Organization: The Emergence of the Cartel Party', *Party Politics*, vol. 1, no. 1, pp. 5–28.

Katzenstein, P. J. (1985) *Small States in World Markets: Industrial Policy in Europe* (Ithaca, NY: Cornell University Press).

Keman, H. (1994) 'The Netherlands', in H. D. Klingemann, R. I. Hofferbert and I. Budge (eds), *Parties, Policies and Democracy* (Boulder, CO: Westview Press), pp. 206–21.

Keman, H. (ed.) (2008) 'Dutch Politics', *Acta Politica,* vol. 43, Special Issue, 2–3, July.

Keman, H. and P. Pennings (2011). 'Oude en nieuwe conflictdimensies in de Nederlandse politiek na 1989: Een vergelijkende analyse'. in R. Andeweg and J. Thomassen (eds), *Democratie doorgelicht. Het functioneren van de Nederlandse democratie* (Leiden University Press), pp. 247-66.

Kennedy, J. C. (1995) *Nieuw Babylon in aanbouw: Nederland in de jaren zestig* (Amsterdam/ Meppel: Boom).

Keuning, H. K. (1965) *Het Nederlandse Volk in zijn Woongebied* (Den Haag: H. P. Leopolds Uitgeversmij NV).

Kickert, W. (2003) 'Beneath Consensual Corporatism: Traditions of Governance in the Netherlands', *Public Administration,* vol. 81, pp. 119-40

Kickert, W. (2012) 'State Responses to the Fiscal Crisis in Britain, Germany and the Netherlands', *Public Management Review,* 14: 299–309

Kiesraad (2007) *Statistische Gegevens: Tweede Kamerverkiezingen 22 November 2006* (The Hague: Kiesraad).

King, A. (1969) 'Political Parties in Western Democracies', *Polity,* vol. 2, pp. 111–41.

King, A. (2001) *Does the United Kingdom Still Have A Constitution?* (London: Sweet & Maxwell).

Kleinnijenhuis, J. and J. A. De Ridder (2007) 'De Nieuwskaravaan', in K. Aarts, H. Van Der Kolk and M. Rosema (eds), *Een Verdeeld Electoraat: De Tweede Kamerverkiezingen van 2006* (Utrecht: Spectrum), pp. 120–38.

Kleinnijenhuis, J., O. Scholten, W. Van Atteveldt, A. Van Hoof, A. Krouwel, D. Oegema, J. A. de Ridder, N. Ruigrok and J. Takens (2007) *Nederland Vijfstromenland: De rol van de media en stemwijzers bij de verkiezingen van 2006* (Amsterdam: Uitgeverij Bert Bakker).

Klingemann, H.-D. (1979) 'Measuring Ideological Conceptualizations', in S.H. Barnes, SM. Kaase, K.R. Allerbeck, B.G. Farah, F. Heunks, R. Inglehart, M.K. Jennings, H.D. Klingemann, A. Marsh and L. Rosenmayr, *Political Action* (Beverly Hills, CA: Sage Publications), pp. 215–54.

Knapen, B., G. Arts, Y. Kleistra, M. Klem and M. Rem (2011) *Attached to the World: On the Anchoring and Strategy of Dutch Foreign Policy* (Amsterdam University Press).

Kohl, L. (1986) 'The Oosterschelde Barrier: Man Against the Sea', *National Geographic Magazine,* vol. 170, pp. 526–37.

Kooiman, J., P. Yntsema and L. Lintsen (1988) 'The Netherlands', in S. A. Pappas (ed.), *National Administrative Procedures for the Preparation and Implementation of Community Decisions* (Maastricht: European Institute of Public Administration), pp. 573–636.

Koole, R. (1992) *De opkomst van de moderne kaderparttj: Veranderende partijorganisatie in Nederland 1960–1990* (Utrecht: Het Spectrum).

Koole, R. (1994) 'The Vulnerability of the Modern Cadre Party in the Netherlands', in R. S. Katz and P. Mair (eds), *How Parties Organize: Change and Adaptation in Party Organizations in Western Democracies* (London: Sage), pp. 278–303.

Koole, R. A. (2011) 'Partijfinanciën in Nederland: ontwikkelingen en regelgeving', in R. B. Andeweg and J. Thomassen (eds), *Democratie doorgelicht* (Leiden University Press), pp. 221–37.

Koole, R. A. (2012) *Party Primaries for Leadership Selection: The Dutch Case.* Paper presented at the ECPR Workshop on 'Party Primaries in Europe: Consequences and Challenges' held at the ECPR Joint Sessions, University of Antwerp, 10–15 April.

Koole, R. A. and H. Daalder (2002) 'Dutch Consociationalism and Corporatism: A Case of Institutional Persistence', in *Acta Politica,* vol. 37, Special Issue, pp. 23–43.

Koole, R. A. and M. Leijenaar (1988) 'The Netherlands: The Predominance of Regionalism', in M. Gallagher and M. Marsh (eds), *Candidate Selection in Comparative Perspective: The Secret Garden of Politics* (London: Sage), pp. 617–731.

Koole, R. A. and H. Van De Velde (1992) 'The Netherlands', in R. S. Katz and P. Mair (eds) *How Parties Organize* (London: Sage), pp. 617–731.

Koopmans, T. (2003) *Courts and Political Institutions: A Comparative View* (Cambridge University Press).

Kossmann, E. H. (1978) *The Low Countries 1780–1940* (Oxford: Clarendon Press).

Kossmann-Putto, J. A. and E. H. Kossmann (1994) *The Low Countries: History of the Northern and Southern Netherlands* (Rekkem: Stichting Ons Erfdeel).

Kriesi, H., E. Grande, R. Lachat, M. Dolezal, S. Bornschier and T. Frey (2008) *West European Politics in the Age of Globalization* (Cambridge University Press).

Krouwel, A. (1996) 'Partijverandering in Nederland: De Teloorgang van de Traditionele Politieke Partij?', in *Jaarboek 1995* (Groningen: Documentatiecentrum Nederlandse Politieke Partijen), pp. 168–91.

Krouwel, A. and A. P. M. Lucardie (2008) 'Waiting in the Wings: New Parties in the Netherlands', *Acta Politica,* vol. 43, pp. 278–307.

Kruyt, J. P. (1950) *Verzuiling* (Zaandijk: Heijnis).

Langenberg, H. and B. Nauta (2007) 'Werkgelegenheid in de periode 1968–2006: crisis begin jaren '80 vormde keerpunt', *Sociaaleconomische trends,* Centraal Bureau voor de Statistiek, 4th quarter.

Laqueur, W. (1981) 'Hollanditis: A New Stage in European Neutralism', *Commentary,* vol. 72, no. 2, 19–26 August.

Lechner, F. J. (2008) *The Netherlands: Globalization and National Identity* (London: Routledge).

Leijenaar, M. and K. Niemöller (1997) 'The Netherlands', in P. Norris (ed.), *Passages to Power: Legislative Recruitment in Advanced Democracies* (Cambridge University Press), pp. 114–36.

Lijphart, A. (1966) *The Trauma of Decolonization* (New Haven, CT: Yale University Press).

Lijphart, A. (1968) 'Typologies of Democratic Systems', *Comparative Political Studies,* vol. 1, pp. 3–44.

Lijphart, A. (1971) 'Verzuiling', in A. Hoogerwerf (ed.), *Verkenningen in de politiek* (Alphen aan de Rijn: Samsom).

Lijphart, A. (1974) 'The Netherlands: Continuity and Change in Voting Behaviour', in R. Rose (ed.) *Electoral Behaviour: A Comparative Handbook* (New York: Free Press).

Lijphart, A. (1975) *The Politics of Accommodation: Pluralism and Democracy in the Netherlands,* 2nd edn (Berkeley, CA: University of California Press; 1st edn 1968).

Lijphart, A. (1977) *Democracy in Plural Societies: A Comparative Exploration* (New Haven, CT: Yale University Press).

Lijphart, A. (1989) 'From the Politics of Accommodation to Adversarial Politics in the Netherlands: A Reassessment', in H. Daalder and G. A. Irwin (eds), *Politics in the Netherlands: How Much Change?* (London: Cass), pp. 139–53.

Lijphart, A. (1992) *Verzuiling, Pacificatie en Kentering,* 9th edn (Haarlem: Becht).

Lijphart, A. (2012) *Patterns of Democracy: Government Forms and Performance in Thirty-Six Countries,* 2nd edn (New Haven, CT: Yale University Press).

Lipschits, I. (1969) *Links en Rechts in de Politiek* (Meppel: J. A. Boom en Zoon).

Louwerse, T. (2011) 'Political Parties and the Democratic Mandate: Comparing Collective Mandate Fulfilment in the United Kingdom and the Netherlands', Doctoral dissertation, Leiden University.

Lubbers, R. (1997) 'In Seeking a "Third Way", the Dutch Model is Worth a Look', *International Herald Tribune,* 16 September, available at: www.iht.com.

Lubbers, R. F. M. and C. Lemckert (1980) 'The Influence of Natural Gas on the Dutch Economy', in R. T. Griffiths (ed.), *The Economy and Politics of the Netherlands since 1945* (The Hague: Martinus Nijhoff), pp. 87–114.

Lucardie, A. P. M. (2003) 'Partijen in de Penarie: Hoe de Pijlers van Ons Politiek Bestel in Financiëlenood Geraken', in J. M. Reijntjes and H. C. G. Spoormans (eds), *Zijn Politici te Koop? Over de Financiering van Politieke Partijen* (Deventer: Kluwer), pp. 15–27.

Lucardie, A. P. M. (2008) 'Twee in dertien uit: electoraal succes en falen van nieuwe partijen in 2006', *Jaarboek 2006* (Groningen: Documentatiecentrum Nederlandse Politieke Partijen), pp. 154-74.

Lucardie, A. P. M. and G. Voerman (2007) 'Op Weg Naar de Verkiezingen: Partijprogrammas en de Selectie van Kandidaten', in *Een verdeeld electoraat: De Tweede Kamerverkiezingen van 2006* (Utrecht: Spectrum), pp. 74–96.

Lucardie, A. P. M. and G. Voerman (2011) 'Democratie binnen partijen', in R. B. Andeweg and J. Thomassen (eds), *Democratie doorgelicht* (Leiden University Press), pp. 185–201.

Lucardie, A. P. M., M. Bredewold, G. Voerman and N. Van De Walle (2008) 'Kroniek 2006: Overzicht van de partijpolitieke gebeurtenissen van het jaar 2006', *Jaarboek 2006* (Groningen: Documentatiecentrum Nederlandse Politieke Partijen), pp. 15–105.

Lucardie, A. P. M., G. Voerman and J. K. Van Zonneveld (2010) *Partijfinanciering in Europa: Een vergelijkend onderzoek naar regelingen voor overheidssubsidies en giften voor politieke partijen* (Groningen: Documentatiecentrum Nederlandse Politieke Partijen).

Luther, K. R. (1999) 'A Framework for the Comparative Analysis of Political Parties and Party Systems in Consociational Democracy', in K. R. Luther and K. Deschouwer (eds), *Party Elites in Divided Societies: Political Parties in Consociational Democracy* (London: Routledge), pp. 3–19.

Luther, K. R. and K. Deschouwer (1999) 'Prudent Leadership to Successful Adaptation? Pillar Parties and Consociational Democracy Thirty Years On', in K. R. Luther and K. Deschouwer (eds), *Party Elites in Divided Societies: Political Parties in Consociational Democracy* (London: Routledge), pp. 243–63.

Luyten, J. W. and Middendorp, C. P. (1990) 'Links, Rechts en Politieke Strijdpunten', *Sociale Wetenschappen,* pp. 113–39.

Mair, P. (1994) 'The Correlates of Consensus Democracy and the Puzzle of Dutch Politics', *West European Politics,* vol. 17, no. 4, pp. 97–123.

Mair, P. (2008) 'Electoral Volatility and the Dutch Party System: A Comparative Perspective', *Acta Politica,* vol. 43, pp. 234–53.

Mair, P. (2011) 'Is Governing Becoming More Contentious?' in M. Rosema, B. Denters and K. Aarts (eds), *How Democracy Works; Political Representation and Policy Congruence in Modern Societies* (Amsterdam: Pallas), pp. 39–52.

Mair, P. and C. Mudde (1998) 'The Party Family and its Study', *Annual Review of Political Science,* vol. 1, pp. 211-29.

Mair, P. and I. Van Biezen (2001) 'Party Membership in Twenty European Democracies, 1980–2000', *Party Politics,* vol. 7, no. 1, pp. 5–21.

Malcontent, P. (2011) 'De Toekomst van de Nederlandse Ontwikkelingssamenwerking', in D. Hellema, M. Segers and J. Rood (eds), *Bezinning op het Buitenland; het Nederlands buitenlands beleid in een onzekere wereld* (The Hague: Clingendael), pp. 173–92.

Mallinson, W. (2010) *From Neutrality to Commitment; Dutch Foreign Policy, NATO and European Integration* (London: I.B.Tauris).

Masselink, M. and P. Van Den Noord (2009) 'The Global Financial Crisis and Its Effects on the Netherlands', *Ecfin Country Focus,* vol. 6, issue 10, available at http://ec.europa.eu/economy_finance/publications/publication16339_en.pdf.

Mastenbroek, E. (2007) 'The Politics of Compliance: Explaining the Transposition of EC Directives in the Netherlands', Doctoral dissertation, Leiden University.

Mastenbroek, E. and S. Princen (2010) 'Time for EU Matters: the Europeanization of Dutch Central Government', *Public Administration,* vol. 88, pp. 154–69.

Middendorp, C. P. (1991) *Ideology in Dutch Politics* (Assen: Van Gorcum).

Milward, A. S. (2000) *The European Rescue of the Nation-State* (London: Routledge).

Ministry of Economic Affairs (2008) *National Reform Programme for the Netherlands (2008–2010),* available at: http://www.rijksoverheid.nl/documenten-en-publicaties/rapporten/2009/05/07/national-reform-programme-for-the-netherlands-2008-2010-in-the-context-of-the-lisbon-strategy.html.

Ministry of the Interior (2011), *Evaluatie Kaderwet Adviescolleges: Derde Staat van Advies 2005-2010*, (The Hague: Ministerie van Binnenlandse Zaken en Koninkrijksrelaties).

Mitchell, P. and B. Nyblade (2008) 'Government Formation and Cabinet Type', in K. Strøm, W. C. Müller and T. Bergman (eds), *Cabinets and Coalition Bargaining: The Democratic Life Cycle in Europe* (Oxford University Press), pp. 201–35.

Mudde, C. and J. Van Holsteyn (2000) 'The Netherlands: Explaining the Limited Success of the Extreme Right', in P. Hainsworth (ed.), *The Politics of the Extreme Right* (London: Pinter), pp. 144–71.

Müller, W. C. and K. Strøm (2000) 'Conclusion: Coalition Governance in Western Europe', in W. C. Müller, and K. Strøm (eds), *Coalition Governments in Western Europe* (Oxford University Press), pp. 559–92.

Müller, W. C. and K. Strøm (2008) 'Coalition Agreements and Cabinet Governance', in K. Strøm, W. C. Müller and T. Bergman (eds), *Cabinets and Coalition Bargaining: The Democratic Life Cycle in Western Europe* (Oxford University Press), pp. 159–200.

Nijeboer, A. (2005) 'The Dutch Referendum', *European Constitutional Law Review*, vol. 1, pp. 393–405.

Nomden, K. (1999) 'The Intermediate Level of Government in the Netherlands: The Surviving Provinces', in T. Larsson, K. Nomden and F. Petiteville (eds), *The Intermediate Level of Government in European States: Complexity Versus Democracy* (Maastricht: European Institute of Public Administration), pp. 245–63.

Norton, P. (2002) 'Introduction', in P. Norton (ed.), *Parliaments and Citizens in Western Europe* (London: Cass).

OECD (2006) *Society at a Glance: OECD Social Indicators* (Paris: OECD).

OECD (2008) *Economic Survey of the Netherlands 2008*, available at: www.oecd.org.

OECD (2012) *Economic Survey of the Netherlands 2012*, available at: www.oecd.org.

OECD (2013) OECD Factbook Statistics, available at: http://www.oecd-ilibrary.org/economics/data/oecd-factbook-statistics_factbook-data-en.

OECD (2014) OECDiLibrary 'Employment rate of older workers', available at: http://www.oecd-ilibrary.org/employment/employment-rate-of-older-workers_20752342-table6.

Oldersma, J. (1997) 'The Corporatist Channel and Civil Society in the Netherlands', in Van Deth, J. W. (ed.) *Private Groups and Public Life* (London: Routledge), pp. 144–62.

Oldersma, J. (1999) 'Adviescolleges', in H. Daalder et al. (eds), *Compendium voor Politiek en Samenleving* (Alphen aan den Rijn: Samsom), pp. C1100, 1–33.

Onwuteaka-Philipsen, B. N., A. Brinkman-Stoppelenburg, C. Penning, G. J. F. De Jong-Krul and J. J. M. van Delden (2012) 'Trends in End-of-Life Practices Before and After the Enactment of the Euthanasia Law in the Netherlands from 1990 to 2010: A Repeated Cross-Sectional Survey', *The Lancet,* vol. 380, pp. 908–15.

Otjes, S. (2011) 'The Fortuyn Effect Revisited: How Did the LPF Affect the Dutch Parliamentary Party System?', *Acta Politica*, vol. 46, pp. 400–24.

Otjes, S. (2012) 'Imitating the Newcomer', Doctoral dissertation, Leiden University.

Panebianco, A. (1988) *Political Parties: Organization and Power* (Cambridge University Press).

Pellikaan, H. and J. W. De Keijser (1998) 'Kamerleden in de Politieke Ruimte', in M. Bovens, H. Pellikaan and M. J. Trappenburg (eds), *Nieuwe Tegenstellingen in de Nederlandse Politiek* (Amsterdam: Boom), pp. 165–86.

Pellikaan, H., S. L. de Lange and T. Van Der Meer (2007) 'Fortuyn's Legacy: Party System Change in the Netherlands', *Comparative European Politics*, vol. 5, pp. 282–302.

Pellikaan, H., T. Van Der Meer and S. De Lange (2003) 'The Road from a Depoliticized to a Centrifugal Democracy', *Acta Politica,* vol. 38, no. 1, pp. 23–50.

Pennings, P. (1991) *Verzuiling en Ontzuiling: De Lokale Verschillen* (Kampen: Kok).

Pennings, P. and H. Keman (2003) 'The Dutch Parliamentary Elections in 2002 and 2003: The Rise and Decline of the Fortuyn Movement', *Acta Politica,* vol. 38, pp. 51–68.

Pennings, P. and H. Keman (2008) 'The Changing Landscape of Dutch Politics since the 1970s: A Comparative Exploration', *Acta Politica,* vol. 43, pp. 154–79.

Peters, K. (2007) *Het Opgeblazen Bestuur: Een Kritische Kijk op de Provincie* (Amsterdam: Boom).

Pollmann, J. (2011) *Catholic Identity and the Revolt of the Netherlands, 1520–1635* (Oxford University Press).

Polsby, N. W. (1975) 'Legislatures', in F. I. Greenstein, and N. W. Polsby (eds), *Handbook of Political Science* (Reading, MA: Addison-Wesley), pp. 277–96.

Prak, M. and J. L. Van Zanden (2013) *Nederland en het Poldermodel; Sociaal-Economische Geschiedenis van Nederland, 1000–2000* (Amsterdam: Bert Bakker).

Progress Report (2007) *2007 Progress Report on the Dutch National Reform Programme for 2005–2008: In the Context of the Lisbon Strategy.* Available at: http://ec.europe.eu/growthandjobs/pdf/ nrp2007/NL_nrp_en.pdf.

Putnam, R. D. (2000) *Bowling Alone; The Collapse and Revival of American Community* (New York: Simon & Schuster).

Putnam, R. D., S. J. Pharr and R. J. Dalton (2000) 'What's Troubling the Trilateral Democracies?', in S. J. Pharr and R. D. Putnam (eds) *Disaffected Democracies* (Princeton University Press), pp. 3–27.

Raadschelders, J. C. N. (1994) 'Understanding the Development of Local Government: Theory and Evidence from the Dutch Case', *Administration and Society,* vol. 25, pp. 410–43.

Raunio, T. and S. Hix (2000) 'Backbenchers Learn to Fight Back: European Integration and Parliamentary Government', *West European Politics,* vol. 23, pp. 142–68.

Relbanks (2013) Available at: www.relbanks.com; accessed 17 December 2013.

Reyn, S. (2009) *Atlantis Lost: The American Experience with De Gaulle, 1958–1969* (Amsterdam University Press).

Riker, W. (1982) 'The Two-Party System and Duverger's Law: An Essay on the History of Political Science', *American Political Science Review,* vol. 76, pp. 753–66.

Robinson, A. D. (1961) *Dutch Organized Agriculture in International Politics, 1945–1960* (The Hague: Martinus Nijhoff).

Rochon, T. R. (1999) *The Netherlands: Negotiating Sovereignty in an Interdependent World* (Boulder, CO: Westview Press).

Roes, T. (2008) *Facts and Figures of the Netherlands; Social and Cultural Trends* (The Hague: SCP).

Rose, R. and I. McAllister (1986) *Voters Begin to Choose. From Closed-Class to Open Elections in Britain* (London: Sage).

Rosema, M. (2004) *The Sincere Vote,* Doctoral dissertation, Leiden University.

Rosema, M. (2006) 'Partisanship, Candidates and Prospective Voting', *Electoral Studies,* vol. 25, no. 3, pp. 467–88.

Salverda, W. (2005) 'The Dutch Model: Magic in a Flat Landscape?', in U. Becker and H. Schwartz (eds), *Economic 'Miracles'* (Amsterdam University Press).

Sartori, G. (1976) *Parties and Party Systems* (Cambridge University Press).

Schaap, L. (2009) 'De Burgemeester: Netherlands' Mayoral Leadership in Consensual Democracy and Collegial Policy-Making', in H. Reynaart, K. Steyvers, P. Delwit and J. B. Pilet (eds), *Local Political Leadership in Europe* (Bruges: Nomos/Vanden Broele), pp. 149–69

Schama, S. (1977) *Patriots and Liberators: Revolution in the Netherlands, 1780–1813* (New York: Knopf).

Schama, S. (1987) *The Embarrassment of Riches: An Interpretation of Dutch Culture in the Golden Age* (New York: Knopf).

Scheepers, P., J. Lammers and J. Peters (1994) 'Religion and Class Voting in the Netherlands', *Netherlands Journal of Social Sciences,* vol. 30, pp. 5–24.

Scheffer, P. (1988) *Een Tevreden Natie: Nederland en het Wederkerend geloof in de Europese Status Quo* (Amsterdam: Bakker).

Schöffer, I. (1973) *A Short History of the Netherlands* (Amsterdam: Allert de Lange).
Schudson, M. (1998) *The Good Citizen: A History of American Civil Life* (New York: The Free Press).
SCP (Sociaal en Cultureel Planbureau) (2000) *Sociaal en Cultureel Rapport 2000, Nederland in Europa* (The Hague).
SCP (Sociaal en Cultureel Planbureau) (2001) *The Netherlands in a European Perspective* (The Hague).
Secker, W. (1991) *Ministers in Beeld; de sociale en functionele herkomst van de Nederlandse ministers (1848–1990)* (Leiden: DSWO Press).
Secker, W. (1994) 'The Social Background and Recruitment of Dutch Ministers since 1848 in a Comparative Perspective', *Netherlands Journal of Social Sciences,* vol. 30, pp. 128–47.
Secker, W. (2000) 'Representatives of the Dutch People: The Smooth Transformation of the Parliamentary Elite in a Consociational Democracy, 1849–1998', in H. Best and M. Cotta (eds), *Parliamentary Representatives in Europe, 1848–2000* (Oxford University Press), pp. 270–309.
Secker, W. P. (1991) *Ministers in Beeld: De Sociale en Functionele Herkomst van de Nederlandse Ministers (1848–1990)* (Leiden: DSWO).
Second Chamber (2013) available at: www.houseofrepresentatives.nl/impact-eu-netherlands; accessed 6 August 2013.
Segers, M. (2013) *Reis naar het Continent: Nederland en de Europese Integratie, 1950 tot Heden* (Amsterdam: Bert Bakker).
Sengers, E. (ed.) (2005) *The Dutch and Their Gods: Secularization and Transformation of Religion in the Netherlands since 1950* (Hilversum: Verloren).
SER (Sociaal-Economische Raad) (2002) *Working on Occupational Disability: Policy Proposal* (The Hague).
SER (Sociaal-Economische Raad) (2010) *De Kracht van Overleg: Uitleg over de Nederlandse Overlegeconomie* (The Hague).
Siaroff, A. (1999) 'Corporatism in 24 Industrial Democracies: Meaning and Measurement', *European Journal of Political Research,* vol. 36, pp. 175–205.
Slaughter, A. M. (2004) *A New World Order* (Princeton University Press).
Sniderman, P. M. and L. Hagendoorn (2007) *When Ways of Life Collide; Multiculturalism and Its Discontents in the Netherlands* (Princeton University Press).
Soetendorp, R. B. (1989) 'The Netherlands and Israel: From a Special to a Normal Relationship', *Internationale Spectator,* vol. 43, pp. 697–700.
Soetendorp, R. B. and R. B. Andeweg (2001) 'Dual Loyalties: The Boundary Role of the Dutch Permanent Representation to the EU', in H. Kassim, A. Menon, B. G. Peters and V. Wright (eds), *The National Co-ordination of EU Policy: The European Level* (Oxford University Press), pp. 211–28.
Soetendorp, R. B. and K. Hanf (1998) 'The Netherlands: Growing Doubts of a Loyal Member', in K. Hanf and R. B. Soetendorp (eds) *Adapting to European Integration: Small States and the European Union* (London: Longman), pp. 36–51.
State Budget (2008) *Miljoenennota 2008* (The Hague: SDU Uitgevers), available at: http://www.regering.nl/Het_kabinet/Begroting_2008/Miljoenennota_2008.
State Budget (2009) *Miljoenennota 2009* (The Hague: SDU Uitgevers), available at: http://www.rijksbegroting.nl/2009/voorbereiding/miljoenennota.
State Budget (2010) *Miljoenennota 2010* (The Hague: SDU Uitgevers), available at: http://www.rijksbegroting.nl/2010/voorbereiding/miljoenennota.
Statistics Netherlands (various dates) available at: http://statline.cbs.nl/statweb.
Steen, T. and F. Van Der Meer (2011) 'Public Service Bargains in Dutch Top Civil Service', *Public Policy and Administration,* vol. 26, pp. 209–32.
Steunenberg, B. (1992) 'Coalition Theories: Empirical Evidence for Dutch Municipalities', *European Journal of Political Research,* vol. 22, pp. 245–78.

Steunenberg, B. (1997) 'Courts, Cabinets, and Coalition Parties: The Politics of Euthanasia in a Parliamentary Setting', *British Journal of Political Science*, vol.27, pp.551-71.

Stuurman, S. (1983) *Verzuiling, Kapitalisme en Patriarchaat* (Nijmegen: SUN).

Suvarierol, S. and C. Van Den Berg (2008) 'Bridge Builders or Bridgeheads in Brussels? The World of Seconded National Experts', in K. Geuijen, P. 't Hart, S. Princen and K. Yesilkagit (eds), *The New Eurocrats: National Civil Servants in EU Policy-Making* (Amsterdam University Press), pp. 103–27.

Swank, O. H. and R. Eisinga (1999) 'Economic Outcomes and Voting Behaviour in a Multi-Party System: An Application to the Netherlands', *Public Choice*, vol. 101, pp. 195–213.

't Hart, P. and A. Wille (2006) 'Ministers and Top Officials in the Dutch Core Executive: Living Together, Growing Apart?', *Public Administration*, vol. 84, pp. 121–46.

Taagepera, R. and M. S. Shugart (1989) *Seats and Votes: The Effects and Determinants of Electoral Systems* (New Haven, CT: Yale University Press).

Tan, A. C. (1998) 'Party Transformation and Party Membership Decline: The Case of the Netherlands', *Jaarboek 1997* (Groningen: Documentatiecentrum Nederlandse Politieke Partijen), pp. 221–37.

Ten Napel, H. M. (1997) 'The Development of Dutch Christian Democracy', in E. Lamberts (ed.), *Christian Democracy in the European Union 1945–1995* (Leuven University Press), pp. 51–64.

Thomassen, J. (1976) 'Party Identification as a Cross-National Concept: Its Meaning in the Netherlands', in I. Budge, I. Crewe, and D. Farlie (eds), *Party Identification and Beyond* (London: Wiley), pp. 63–79.

Thomassen, J. J. A. (1999) 'Political Communication between Political Elites and Mass Publics: The Role of Belief Systems' in W. Miller, R. Pierce, J. Thomassen, R. Herrera, S. Holmberg, P. Esaiasson and B. Wessels., *Policy Representation in Western Democracies* (Oxford University Press), pp. 33-58.

Thomassen, J. J. A. (2000) 'Politieke Veranderingen en het Functioneren van de Parlementaire Democratie in Nederland', in J. Thomassen, K. Aarts and H. Van Der Kolk (eds), *Politieke Veranderingen in Nederland 1971–1998* (The Hague: SDU Uitgevers), pp. 203–17.

Thomassen, J. J. A. (2007) *Citizens and the Legitimacy of the European Union* (WRR Web-publications 19: www.wrr.nl).

Thomassen, J. and J. Van Deth (1989) 'How New Is Dutch Politics?', in H. Daalder and G. A. Irwin (eds), *Politics in the Netherlands: How Much Change?* (London: Cass), pp. 61–78.

Thomassen J. J. A. and R. B. Andeweg (2004) 'Beyond Collective Representation: Individual Members of Parliament and Interest Representation in the Netherlands', *Journal of Legislative Studies*, vol. 10(4), pp. 47–69.

Thomassen, J. J. A., M. P. C. M. Van Schendelen, M. L. Zielonka-Goei and H. Den Haan (1992) *Dutch Members of Parliament 1990: Codebook* (Leiden University: Drukkerij van de Faculteit der Sociale Wetenschappen).

Thurlings, J. M. G. (1978) *De Wankele Zuil* (Deventer: Van Loghum Slaterus).

Timmermans, A. (1998) 'Policy Conflicts, Agreements and Coalition Governance', *Acta Politica*, vol. 33, pp. 409–32.

Timmermans, A. (2003) *High Politics in the Low Countries: An Empirical Study of Coalition Agreements in Belgium and the Netherlands* (Aldershot: Ashgate).

Timmermans, A. and R. B. Andeweg (2000) 'The Netherlands: Still the Politics of Accommodation?', in W. C. Müller and K. Strøm (eds), *Coalition Governments in Western Europe* (Oxford University Press), pp. 356–98.

Timmermans, A. and R. B. Andeweg (2003) 'The Netherlands: Rules and Mores in Delegation and Accountability', in K. Strøm, W. C. Müller, and T. Bergman (eds), *Delegation and Accountability in Parliamentary Democracies* (Oxford University Press), pp. 498–522.

Toirkens, S. J. (1988) *Schijn en Werkelijkheid van het Bezuinigingsbeleid 1975–1986* (Deventer: Kluwer).

Toonen, T. A. J. (1987) 'The Netherlands: A Decentralized Unitary State in a Welfare Society', *West European Politics*, vol. 10, pp. 108–29.

Toonen, T.A.J. (1990) 'The Unitary State as a System of Co-Governance: The Case of The Netherlands', *Public Administration*, vol. 68, pp. 281-97.

Toonen, T. A. J. (1992) 'Dutch Provinces and the Struggle for the Meso', in L. J. Sharpe (ed.) *Between Locality and Centre: The Rise of the Meso in Europe* (London: Sage).

Toonen, T. A. J. (1996) 'On the Administrative Condition of Politics: Administrative Transformation in the Netherlands', *West European Politics,* vol. 19, pp. 609–32.

Toonen, T. A. J. (2000) 'Governing a Consensus Democracy: The Interplay of Pillarization and Administration', *West European Politics,* vol. 23, no. 3, pp. 165–78.

Trappenburg, M. and C. Mudde (2000) 'Rommelen in de Marge: Nederlandse Politieke Partijen over de Toelating van Nieuwkomers', in M. Bovens, H. Pellikaan, and M. Trappenburg (eds) *Nieuwe Tegenstellingen in de Nederlandse Politiek*, 2nd edn (Meppel: Boom), pp. 98–121.

Trappenburg, M. and J. Van Holsteyn (2001) 'Too Good to Be True? Law and Public Opinion on Euthanasia in the Netherlands', Paper presented at the 2001 Joint Annual Meeting of the Law and Society Association and the Research Committee on Sociology of Law, Budapest.

Tromp, B. (1985) 'Het Verval van Politieke Partijen', *Het Parool,* 20 December.

Tros, F. H. (2003) 'Werkgevers- en Werknemersorganisaties in Nederland', in H. Daalder et al. (eds) *Compendium voor Politiek en Samenleving in Nederland* (Alphen aan den Rijn: Samsom), pp. B1200, 1–54.

Uleri, P. V (1996) 'Introduction', M. Gallagher and P. V. Uleri (eds), *The Referendum Experience in Europe* (London: Macmillan), pp. 1–19.

Van Biezen, I. , P. Mair and Th. Poguntke (2012) 'Going, going, ... gone? The Decline of Party Membership in Contemporary Europe', *European Journal of Political Research*, vol. 51, pp. 24-56.

Van Deemen, A. M. A. (1990) 'Theories of Center Parties and Cabinet Formations with an Application to the Dutch Parliamentary System', *Acta Politica*, vol. 25, pp. 187–208.

Van Den Berg, E. and J. De Hart (2008) *Maatschappelijke Organisaties in Beeld: Grote Ledenorganisaties Over Actuele Ontwikkelingen op het Maatschappelijk Middenveld* (The Hague: SCP).

Van Den Berg, J. T. J., D. J. Elzinga and J. J. Vis (1992) *Parlement en Politiek* (The Hague: SDU Uitgevers).

Van Den Bos, J. M. M. (1991) 'Dutch EC Policy Making', PhD dissertation, University of Utrecht.

Van Den Braak, B. (1998) *De Eerste Kamer: Geschiedenis, Samenstelling en Betekenis 1815–1995* (The Hague: SDU Uitgevers).

Van Den Broek, E. M. (2003) 'The Media as a Source of Subsidy', MA thesis, Leiden University.

Van Der Beugel, E. H. (1995) 'Nederland in de naoorlogse westelijke samenwerking' *Internationale Spectator* vol.49, pp. 126-32

Van Der Beugel, E. H. (1995) 'Nederland in de Naoorlogse Westelijke Samenwerking', *Internationale Spectator,* vol. 49, pp. 126–32.

Van Der Brug, W. (1998) 'The Informed Electorate: Political Perceptions and Party Behaviour', *Acta Politica,* vol. 33, pp. 20–55.

Van Der Brug, W. (2000) 'Politieke Problemen, Prioriteiten en Partijkeuze', in J. Thomassen, K. Aarts and H. Van Der Kolk (eds), *Politieke veranderingen in Nederland 1971–1998* (The Hague: SDU Uitgevers), pp. 187–202.

Van Der Brug, W. (2003) 'How the LPF Fuelled Discontent: Empirical Tests of Explanations of LPF Support', *Acta Politica,* vol. 38, pp. 89–106.

Van Der Brug, W. (2004) 'Voting for the LPF: Some Clarifications', *Acta Politica,* vol. 39, pp. 84–91.

Van Der Doelen, R. C. J. and J. H. De Jong (1990) 'Energy Policy', in M. Wolters and P. Coffrey (eds), *The Netherlands and EC Membership Evaluated* (London: Pinter), pp. 62–9.

Van Der Eijk, C. and M. N. Franklin (2004) 'Potential for Contestation on European Matters at National Elections in Europe', in G. Marks and M. Steenbergen (eds), *European Integration and Political Conflict* (Cambridge University Press).

Van Der Eijk, C. and B. Niemöller (1983) *Electoral Change in the Netherlands: Empirical Results and Methods of Measurement.* University of Amsterdam.

Van Der Eijk, C. and B. Niemöller (1987) 'Electoral Alignments in the Netherlands', *Electoral Studies,* vol. 6, pp. 17–39.

Van Der Harst, J. (2011) 'Nederland in de ban van Euroscepsis?', in D. Hellema, M. Segers and J. Rood (eds), *Bezinning op het Buitenland; het Nederlands buitenlands beleid in een onzekere wereld* (The Hague: Clingendael), pp. 77–92.

Van Der Kolk, H. (2000) 'Aarzelende, Zwevende en Wisselende Kiezers', in J. Thomassen, K. Aarts and H. Van der Kolk (eds), *Politieke Veranderingen in Nederland, 1971–1998* (The Hague: SDU Uitgevers), pp. 93–106.

Van Der Kolk, H. (2007) 'Electoral System Change in the Netherlands: The Road from PR to PR', *Representation,* vol. 43, pp. 271–87.

Van Der Kolk, H. and J. Thomassen (eds) (2006) 'The Dutch Electoral System on Trial', *Acta Politica,* vol. 41, Special Issue, pp. 2–3.

Van Der Meer, F. M. and G. S. A. Dijkstra (2000) 'The Development and Current Features of the Dutch Civil Service System', in A. J. G. Bekke and F. M. Van Der Meer (eds), *Civil Service Systems in Western Europe* (Cheltenham: Elgar), pp.148–88.

Van Der Meer, F. M. and G. S. A. Dijkstra (2011) 'The Dutch Civil Service System', in F. M. Van Der Meer (ed) *Civil Service Systems in Western Europe,* 2nd edn (Cheltenham: Elgar), pp. 148–88.

Van Der Meer, F. M. and J. C. N. Raadschelders (1999) 'The Senior Civil Service in the Netherlands: A Quest for Unity', in E. C. Page and V. Wright (eds), *Bureaucratic Elites in Western European States* (Oxford University Press), pp. 205–28.

Van Der Meer, F. M. and J. C. N. Raadschelders (2007) 'The Changing Role of the Senior Civil Service in Dutch National Government', in E. C. Page and V. Wright (eds), *From the Active to the Enabling State: The Changing Role of Top Officials in European Nations* (Basingstoke: Palgrave Macmillan), pp. 99–120.

Van Der Meer, F. M. and L. J. Roborgh (1993) *Ambtenaren in Nederland: Omvang, Bureaucratisering en Representativiteit van het Ambtelijk Apparaat* (Alphen aan den Rijn: Samsom/H. D. Tjeenk Willink).

Van Der Meer, F. and T. J. Toonen (2005) 'Competency Management and Civil Service Professionalism in Dutch Central Government', *Public Administration,* vol. 83, pp. 839–52.

Van Der Meer, M., J. Visser, T. Wilthagen, and P.F. Van Der Heijden (2003) *Weg van het Overleg? Twintig Jaar na Wassenaar: Nieuwe verhoudingen in het Nederlandse model* (Amsterdam University Press).

Van Der Schyff, G. (2010) 'Constitutional Review by the Judiciary in the Netherlands: A Bridge Too Far?', *German Law Journal,* vol. 11, pp. 275–90.

Van Der Veen, R. and W. Trommel (1999) 'Managed Liberalization of the Dutch Welfare State: A Review and Analysis of the Reform of the Dutch Social Security System', *Governance,* vol. 12, pp. 289–310.

Van Der Zwan, A. (2004) 'How the LPF Fuelled Discontent: A Comment', *Acta Politica,* vol. 39, pp. 79–83.

Van Doorn, J. A. A. (1985) 'Tolerantie als Tactiek', *Intermediar,* vol. 20, September, pp. 29–33.

Van Egmond, M., N. D. De Graaf and C. Van Der Eijk (1998) 'Electoral Participation in the Netherlands: Individual and Contextual Influence', *European Journal of Political Research,* vol. 34, pp. 281–300.

Van Geffen, S. (2001) *The Court Rules: Modelling and Testing Supreme Court Influence on Policy* (Assen: Van Gorcum).

Van Holsteyn, J. J. M. (2013) 'The Dutch parliamentary elections of September 2012', *Electoral Studies*, forthcoming, available at ahttp://ac.els-cdn.com/S0261379413001431/1-s2.0-S0261379413001431-main.pdf?_tid=2e090d8c-55e0-11e3-a8a1-00000aab0f26&acd nat=1385390888_867287d465f9ddf674ef074990180c09 t.

Van Holsteyn, J. J. M. and R. B. Andeweg (2008) 'Niemand is Groter dan de Partij: Over de Personalisering van de Nederlandse Electorate Politiek', in G. Voerman (ed.), *Jaarboek Documentatiecentrum Nederlandse Politieke Partijen 2006* (Groningen: Documentatiecentrum Nederlandse Politieke Partijen), pp. 105–34.

Van Holsteyn, J. J. M. and R. B. Andeweg (2010) 'Demoted Leaders and Exiled Candidates: Disentangling Party and Person in the Voter's Mind', *Electoral Studies,* vol. 29, pp. 628–35.

Van Holsteyn, J. J. and J. M. Den Ridder (2005) 'Een reus in de polder? Nederlandse keizers en het electorale belang van Europese integratie', in H. Vollard and B. Boer, *Euroscepsis in Nederland* (Utrecht: Uitgeverij Lemma BV), pp. 23–44.

Van Holsteyn, J. J. M. and J. M. Den Ridder (2008) 'Verandering in continuïteit', *Bestuurskunde,* vol. 3, pp. 39–46.

Van Holsteyn, J. J. and G. A. Irwin (2003) 'Never a Dull Moment: Pim Fortuyn and the Dutch Election of 2002', *West European Politics,* vol. 26, no. 2, April, pp. 41–66.

Van Holsteyn, J. J. M. and G. A. Irwin (2013) 'Effecten van peilingen op kiezers: schets van een onderzoeksprogramma', *Beleid en Maatschappij,* vol. 40, no. 2, pp. 180–4.

Van Holsteyn, J. J. M. and M. Trappenburg (1998) 'Citizens' Opinions on New Forms of Euthanasia: A Report from the Netherlands', *Patient Education and Counseling,* vol. 35, no. 1, pp. 63–73.

Van Holsteyn, J. J. M., G. A. Irwin and J. M. Den Ridder (2003) 'In the Eye of the Beholder: The Perception of the List Pim Fortuyn and the Parliamentary Elections of May 2002', *Acta Politica,* vol. 38, pp. 69–88.

Van Houwelingen, P., J. De Hart and P. Dekker (2011) 'Maatschappelijke en politieke participatie en betrokkenheid.', in R. Bijl, J. Boelhouser, M. Cloïn and E. Plommer (eds), *De Sociale Staat van Nederland 2011* (The Hague: Sociaal en Cultureel Planbureau), pp. 185–210.

Van Keulen, M. (2006) *Going Europe or Going Dutch: How the Dutch Government Shapes European Union Policy* (Amsterdam University Press).

Van Koppen, P. J. (1992) 'Judicial Policy-Making in the Netherlands: The Case by Case Method', *West European Politics,* vol. 15, pp. 80–92.

Van Koppen, P. J. and J. Ten Kate (2003) *De Hoge Raad in Persoon: Benoemingen in de Hoge Raad der Nederlanden 1838–2003* (Deventer: Kluwer).

Van Mourik, B. (2012) *Parlementaire Controle op Europese Besluitvorming* (Nijmegen: Wolf Legal Publishers).

Van Praag, P. (1993) 'Hoe Uniek Is de Nederlandse Consensusdemocratie?', in U. Becker (ed.), *Nederlandse Politiek in Historisch en Vergelijkend Perspectief* (Amsterdam: Het Spinhuis), pp. 151–78.

Van Praag, P. (1994) 'Conflict and Cohesion in the Dutch Labour Party', in D. S. Bell and E. Shaw (eds), *Conflict and Cohesion in Western European Social Democratic Parties* (New York: Pinter), pp. 133–50.

Van Praag, P. (2003) 'The Winners and Losers in a Turbulent Political Year', *Acta Politica,* vol. 38, pp. 5–22.

Van Praag, P. (2007) 'De Verkiezingscampagne: Professioneler en Feller', in K. Aarts, H. Van Der Kolk and M. Rosema (eds), *Een Verdeeld Electoraat: De Tweede Kamerverkiezingen van 2006* (Utrecht: Spectrum), pp. 97–119.

Van Praag, P. (2008) 'Rune versus Verdonk: Was Dat nu Echt het Probleem van de VVD?', in *Jaarboek 2006* (Groningen: Documentatiecentrum Nederlandse Politieke Partijen), pp. 135–53.

Van Praag, P. and K. Brants (1999) 'The 1998 Campaign: An Interaction Approach', *Acta Politica,* vol. 34, pp. 179–99.

Van Praag, P. and K. Brants (2007) 'Professioneler, Harder en Persoonlijker: Verandering in de Campaignevoering na 1966 en 2002', Paper for the Fourth Annual Conference of the Netherlands Institute of Government, Tilburg, 8 November.

Van Raalte, E. (1959) *The Parliament of the Kingdom of the Netherlands* (London: Hansard Society).

Van Rijt-Veltman, W. V. W. (2010) *De Verenigde Krachten van het MKB* (Zoetermeer: EIM).

Van Roozendaal, P. (1993) 'Cabinets in the Netherlands (1918–1990): The Importance of "Dominant" and "Central" Parties', *European Journal of Political Research,* vol. 23, pp. 35–54.

Van Rossem, M. (2012) *Nederland volgens Maarten van Rossem* (Amsterdam: Nieuw Amsterdam Uitgevers).

Van Santen, R. A. (2009) 'De digitale verkiezingsfolder voorbij? Partijwebsites in de verkiezingscampagne van 2006', in *Jaarboek 2007* (Groningen: Documentatiecentrum Nederlandse Politieke Partijen), pp. 151–75.

Van Schagen, J. (1997) 'The Principle of Continuity and the Efficiency of the Legislative Process', *Journal of Legislative Studies,* vol. 3, no. 4, pp. 115–25.

Van Schendelen, M. P. C. M. (1987) 'The Netherlands: From Low to High Politicisation', in M. P. C. M. van Schendelen and R. J. Jackson (eds), *The Politicisation of Business in Western Europe* (London: Croom Helm).

Van Staden, A. (1978) 'The Role of the Netherlands in the Atlantic Alliance', in J. H. Leurdijk (ed.), *The Foreign Policy of the Netherlands* (Alphen aan den Rijn: Sijthoff & Noordhof), pp. 137–65.

Van Staden, A. (2011) 'Nederlands Veiligheidsbeleid en het Atlantisch primaat. Over bekneld ambities en slijtende grondslagen' in D. Hellema, M. Segers and J. Rood (eds), *Bezinning op het Buitenland: het Nederlands buitenlands beleid in een onzekere wereld* (The Hague: Clingendael), pp. 9–30.

Van Stipdonk, V. (2006) 'Lokaal Bestuur Telt 66 Coalities', *VNG Magazine,* 8 December.

Van Thiel, S. (2004) 'Quangos in Dutch Government', in C. Pollitt and C. Talbot (eds), *Unbundled Government: A Critical Analysis of the Global Trend to Agencies, Quasi Autonomous Bodies and Contractualization* (London: Taylor & Francis), pp. 167–83.

Van Thiel, S. (2006) 'Styles of Reform: Differences in Quango Creation between Policy Sectors in the Netherlands', *Journal of Public Policy,* vol. 26, pp. 115–39.

Van Thiel, S. (2011) 'Zelfstandige Bestuursorganen en de Grenzen van de Ministeriële Verantwoordelijkheid', in R. B. Andeweg and J. Thomassen (eds), *Democratie Doorgelicht: Het Functioneren van de Nederlandse Democratie* (Leiden University Press), pp. 457–76.

Van Thiel, S. (2012) 'Party Patronage in the Netherlands: Sharing Appointments to Maintain Consensus', in P. Kopecky, P. Mair and M. Spirova (eds), *Party Patronage and Party Government in European Democracies* (Oxford: Oxford University Press), pp. 250–71.

Van Thijn, E. (1967) 'Van Partijen naar Stembusaccoorden', in E. Jurgens, D.Th. Kuiper, B. Van Der Lek, E. Van Thijn, H.J. Viersen, and E. Visser., *Open Brief: Partijvernieuwing* (Amsterdam: Arbeiderspers).

Van Thijn, E. (1998) *De Sorry-Democratie: Recente Politieke Affaires en de Ministeriele Verantwoordelijkheid* (Amsterdam: Van Gennep).

Van Thijn, E. (2000) 'De Multiculturele Samenleving: Convergentie of Divergentie', in M. Bovens, H. Pellikaan, and M. Trappenburg (eds) *Nieuwe Tegenstellingen in de Nederlandse Politiek,* 2nd edn (Meppel: Boom), pp. 82–97.

Van Tuijl, M. (2011) 'Success and Failure on the Populist Right: The Case of Wilders and Verdonk', MA thesis, Department of Political Science, University of Leiden.

Van Valkenburg, S. (1943) 'Land and People', in B. Landheer (ed.), *The Netherlands* (Berkeley, CA: University of California Press).

Van Vonno, C. (2012) 'Role Switching in the Dutch Parliament; Reinvigorating Role Theory?', *Journal of Legislative Studies,* vol. 18, no. 2, pp. 119–36.

Van Waarden, F. (2002) 'Dutch Consociationalism and Corporatism: A Case of Institutional Persistence', in *Acta Politica*, vol. 37, Special Issue, pp. 44–67.

Van Wijnen, P. (2000) 'Candidates and Voting Behavior', *Acta Politica*, vol. 35, pp. 430–50.

Van Wijnen, P. (2001) *Policy Voting in Advanced Industrial Democracies: The Case of the Netherlands 1971–1998* (University of Twente).

Verbeek, B. and A. Van Der Vleuten (2008) 'The Domestication of the Foreign Policy of The Netherlands (1989–2007): The Paradoxical Result of Europeanization and Internationalization', *Acta Politica*, vol. 43, pp. 357–77.

Vis, B., K. Van Kersbergen and U. Becker (2008) 'The Politics of Welfare State Reform in the Netherlands: Explaining a Never-Ending Puzzle', *Acta Politica*, vol. 43, pp. 333–56.

Visscher, G. (1994) *Parlementaire Invloed op Wetgeving* (The Hague: SDU Uitgevers).

Visscher, G. (1998) 'De Staten-Generaal', in H. Daalder et al. (eds), *Compendium voor Politiek en Samenleving in Nederland* (Alphen aan den Rijn: Samsom), pp. A0600, 1–105.

Visser, J. and A. Hemerijck (1997) *'A Dutch Miracle': Job Growth, Welfare Reform and Corporatism in the Netherlands* (Amsterdam University Press).

Vlekke, B. H. M. (1943) 'The Dutch Before 1581', in B. Landheer (ed.) *The Netherlands* (Berkeley, CA: University of California Press).

Voerman, G. (1995) 'The Netherlands: Losing Colours, Turning Green', in D. Richardson and C. Rootes (eds), *The Green Challenge* (London: Routledge), pp. 109–27.

Voerman, G. and A. P. M. Lucardie (2012) 'The Netherlands', *European Journal of Political Research, Political Data Yearbook,* vol. 51 pp. 215–20, available at: www.politicaldatayearbook.com.

Voerman, G. and W. Van Schuur (2011) 'De Nederlandse Politieke Partijen en hun leden (1945–2010)', in R. B. Andeweg and J. Thomassen (eds), *Democratie doorgelicht* (Leiden University Press), pp. 203–20.

Vollaard, H. and N. Van Willigen (2011) 'Binnenlandse Steun voor Buitenlands Beleid', in D. Hellema, M. Segers and J. Rood (eds), *Bezinning op het Buitenland: het Nederlands buitenlands beleid in een onzekere wereld* (The Hague: Clingendael), pp. 193–216.

Voorhoeve, J. J. C. (1979) *Peace, Profits and Principles: A Study of Dutch Foreign Policy* (The Hague: Nijhoff).

Vossen, K. (2010) 'Populism in the Netherlands after Fortuyn: Rita Verdonk and Geert Wilders Compared, *Perspectives on European Politics and Society*, vol. 11, no. 1, pp. 22-38.

Walter, A. S. and W. Van Der Brug (2013) 'When the Gloves Come Off: Inter-Party Variation in Negative Campaigning in Dutch Elections, 1981–2010', *Acta Politica*, vol. 48, pp. 367–88.

Walter, A. S. and P. Van Praag (2012) 'Een gemiste kans? De rol van YouTube in de verkiezingscampagne van 2010', *Res Publica*, vol. 4, pp. 443–63.

Waterborg J., K. Lucas and G. J. Lindeboom (2012) 'Tensions between Meritocracy and Democracy? A Reply to the Diploma Democracy Thesis', *Acta Politica*, vol. 47, no. 3, 248–58.

Wetenschappelijke Raad voor het Regeringsbeleid (Scientific Council for Government Policy) (2007b) *Identificatie met Nederland* (Amsterdam University Press).

Wintle, M. (2000) 'Pillarisation, Consociation and Vertical Pluralism in the Netherlands Revisited: A European View', *West European Politics*, vol. 23 no. 3, pp. 139–52.

Woldendorp, J. (2005) *The Polder Model: From Disease to Miracle?* (Amsterdam: Thela Thesis).

Woldendorp, J. (2008) 'English Language Sources for the Study of Dutch Politics , 19982008', *Acta Politica*, vol. 43, pp. 381–428.

Woldendorp, J. (2011) 'Corporatism in Small North-West European Countries, 1970–2006: Business as Usual, Decline, or a New Phenomenon?', Working Paper 30 (2011–01) (Amsterdam: Department of Political Science, VU University).

Woldendorp, J. J. (1995) 'Neo-Corporatism as a Strategy for Conflict Regulation in the Netherlands, 1970–1990', *Acta Politica*, vol. 30, pp. 121–51.

Woldendorp, J. and L. Delsen (2008) 'Dutch Corporatism: Does It Still Work? Policy Formation and Macroeconomic Performance, 1980–2005', *Acta Politica,* vol. 43, pp. 308–32.

Woldendorp, J. and J. E. Keman (2007) 'The Polder Model Reviewed: Dutch Corporatism 1965–2000', *Economic and Industrial Democracy,* vol. 28, no. 3, pp. 317–47.

Wolinetz, S. B. (1977) 'The Dutch Labour Party: A Social-Democratic Party in Transition', in W. E. Paterson and A. H. Thomas (eds), *Social-Democratic Parties in Western Europe* (London: Croom Helm), pp. 342–88.

Wolinetz, S. B. (1988) 'The Netherlands', in S. B. Wolinetz (ed.), *Parties and Party Systems in Liberal Democracies: Continuity amid Change* (London: Routledge), pp. 130–58.

Wolinetz, S. B. (1996) 'Internal Politics and Rates of Change in the Partij van de Arbeid, 1957–1994', in *Jaarboek 1995* (Groningen: Documentatiecentrum Nederlandse Politieke Partijen), pp. 113–26.

Wolinetz, S. B. (1999) 'The Consociational Party System', in K. R. Luther and K. Deschouwer (eds), *Party Elites in Divided Societies: Political Parties in Consociational Democracy* (London: Routledge), pp. 224–42.

Wolters, M. (1984) 'Interspace Politics', PhD dissertation, Leyden University.

Wolters, M. (1990) 'Political and Legal Effects', in M. Wolters and P. Coffey (eds), *The Netherlands and EC Membership Evaluated* (London: Pinter), pp. 62–9.

Ziemann, K. (2009) 'Elite Support for Constitutional Reform in the Netherlands', *Acta Politica*, vol. 44, pp. 314–36.

Index

Printed and bound in Great Britain by
CPI Group (UK) Ltd, Croydon, CR0 4YY